STORY THUS FAR

◎ Asahi is living a normal, sheltered life when she suddenly gets pulled into a pond and is transported to a strange new world. She gets sacrificed to a water dragon god, and he takes her voice from her. Because of her connection to the water dragon god's mysterious powers, Asahi is elevated to the position of priestess in her village. She is unable to find a way to return home, and time passes. As Asahi and the water dragon god spend time together, their relationship begins to change.

◎ A man named Kogahiko starts a war against the village because he wants to obtain Asahi's power. The water dragon god sees that Asahi is miserable that a war has been started over her, so he returns her voice and stops the war. He asks Asahi to marry him, but she says the two of them don't have special feelings for one another. In response, the water dragon god appears in human guise and tells her he will live with her in the human world.

◎ A priestess of Naga informs the emperor of Asahi's and the water dragon god's existence, and the emperor orders Asahi to lend him her power. When Kogahiko tries to kidnap Asahi again, the water dragon god and Asahi's friends rescue her. Tsukihiko, whose mother was in the same situation as Asahi before, attempts to trade his life for Asahi's freedom.

◎ Asahi decides to live with the emperor of Naga, and he asks for her hand in marriage. Jealousy blooms in the water dragon god's heart for the first time. In order to protect Asahi, he sends her back to her own world, just as she'd wanted for so long. Asahi is finally reunited with her family, but she can't seem to forget the water dragon god and the friends she's left behind. She's so troubled that she returns to the other world during a ceremony to call rain. Asahi is overjoyed to be reunited with the water dragon god, but she barely has a moment with him before she gets snatched away into a deep darkness!

The Water Dragon's Bride

8

CONTENTS

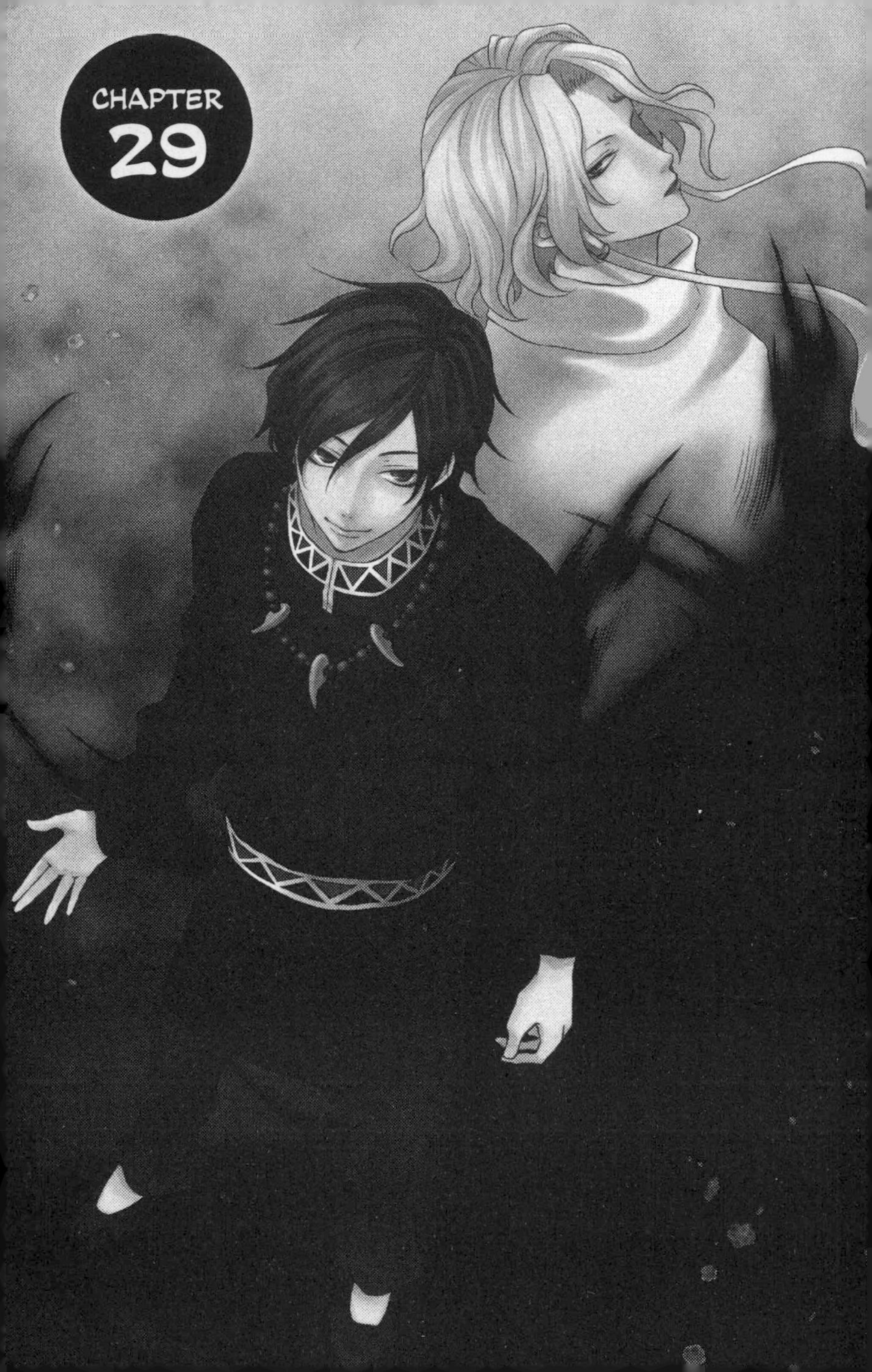
CHAPTER
29

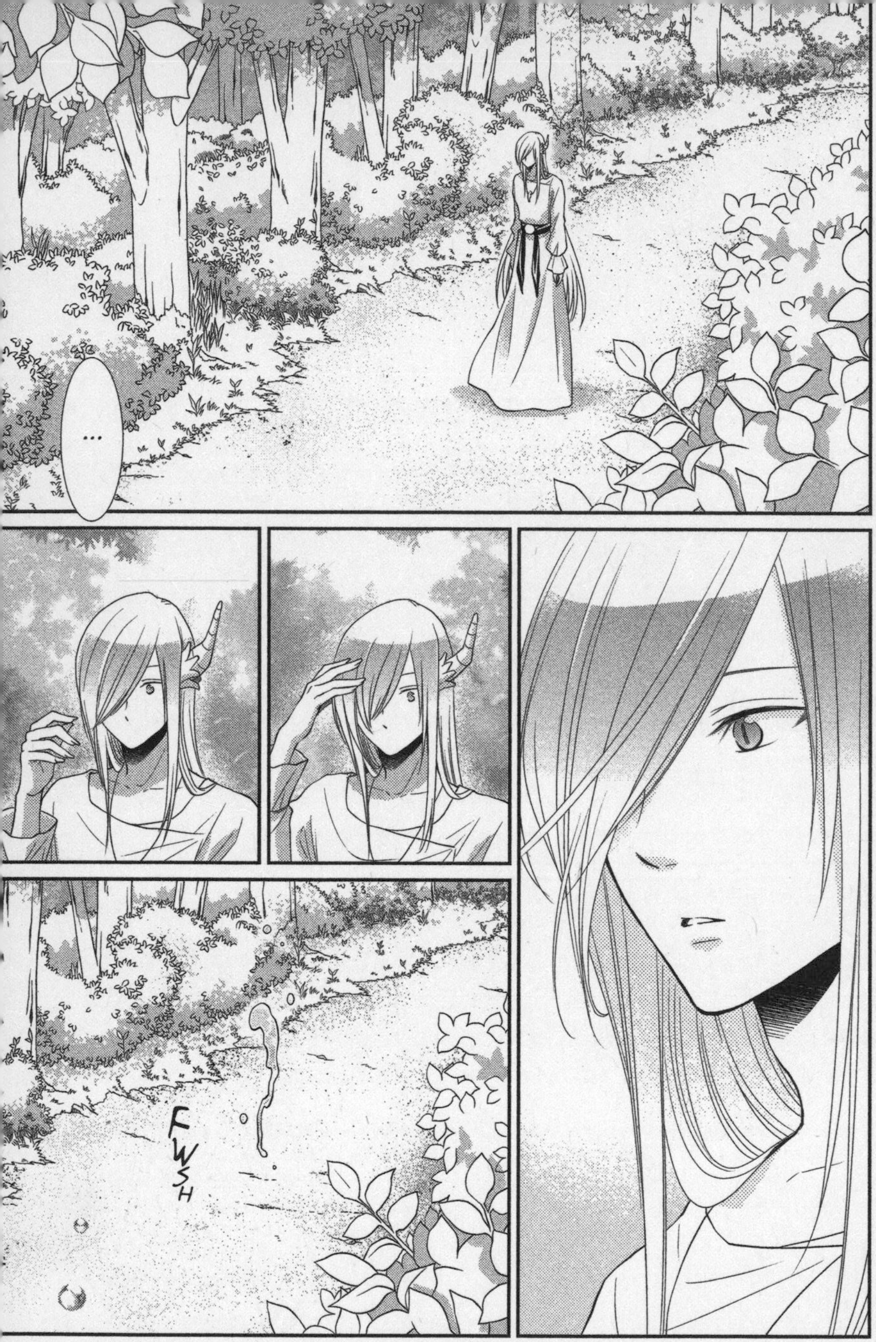
...
FWSH

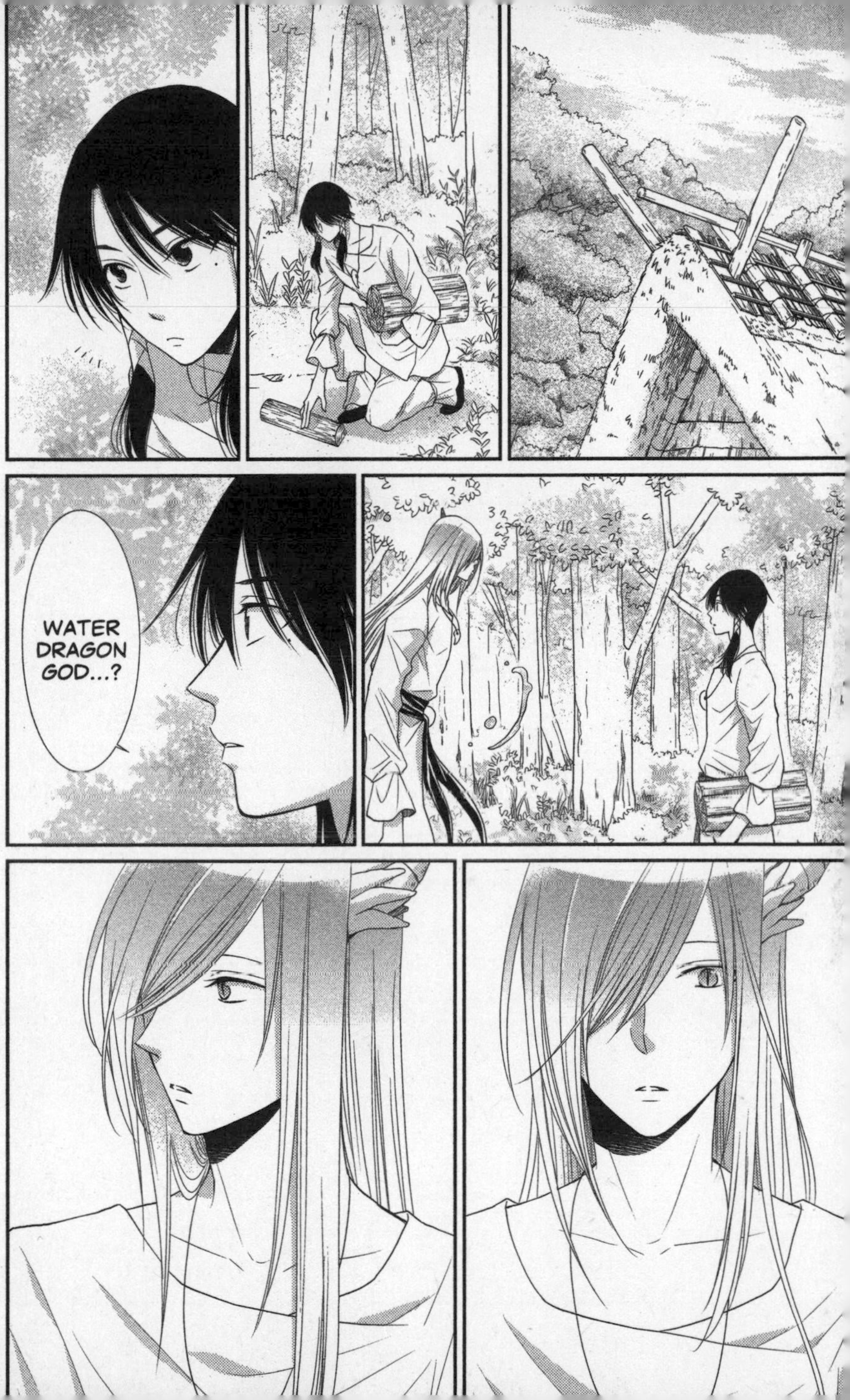
WATER DRAGON GOD...?

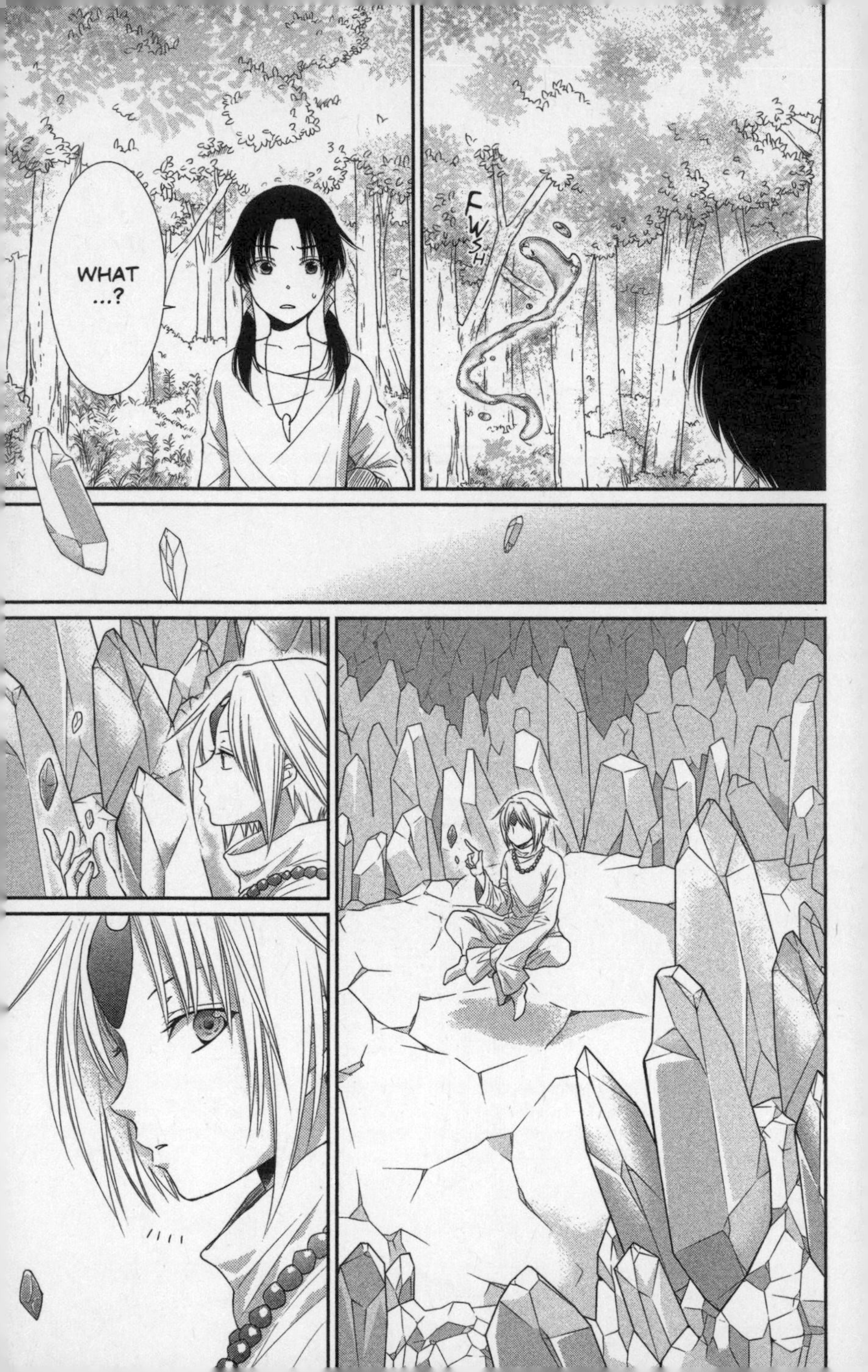
FWSH
WHAT ...?

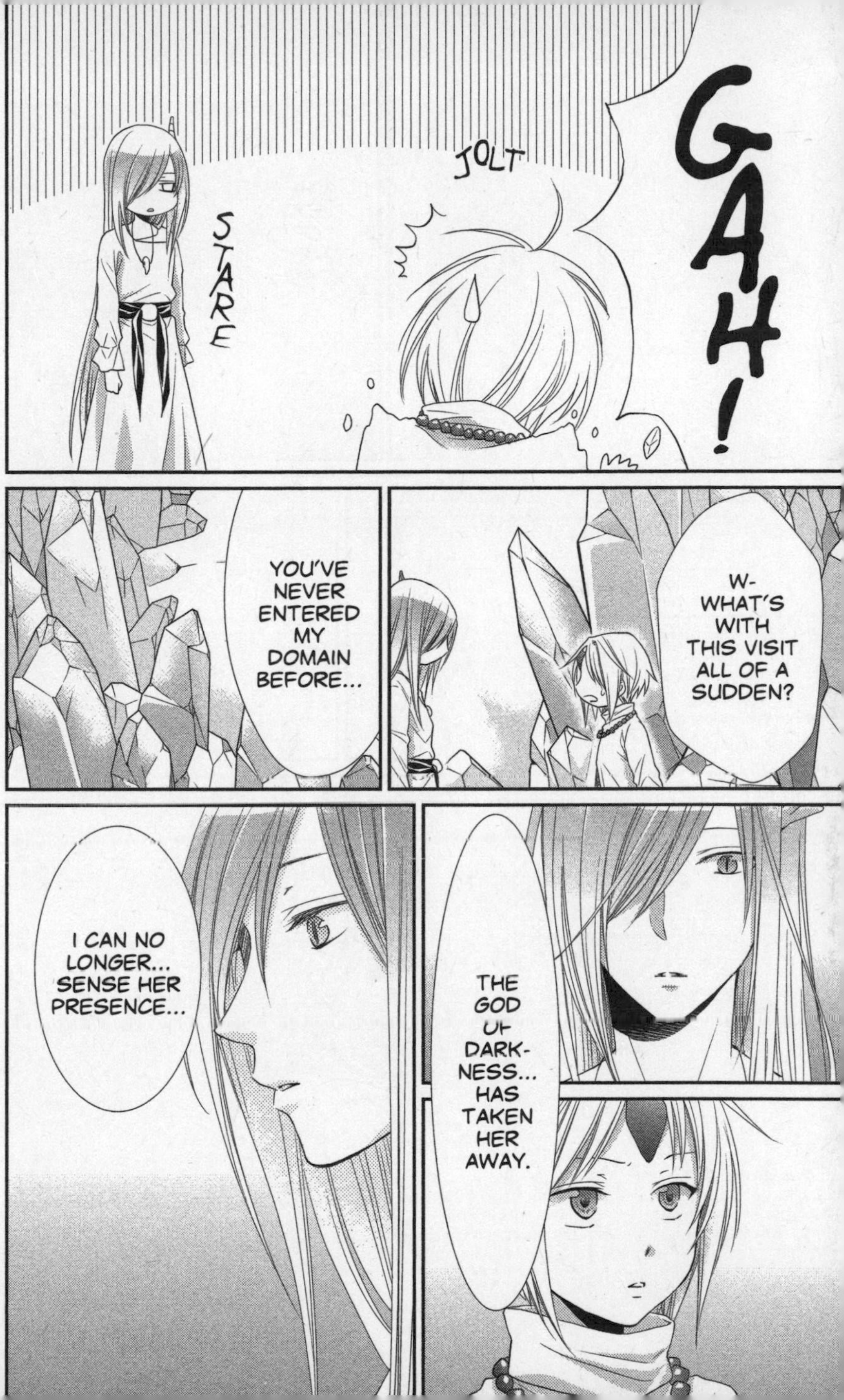
GAH!
JOLT
STARE
W-WHAT'S WITH THIS VISIT ALL OF A SUDDEN?
YOU'VE NEVER ENTERED MY DOMAIN BEFORE...
THE GOD OF DARKNESS... HAS TAKEN HER AWAY.
I CAN NO LONGER... SENSE HER PRESENCE...

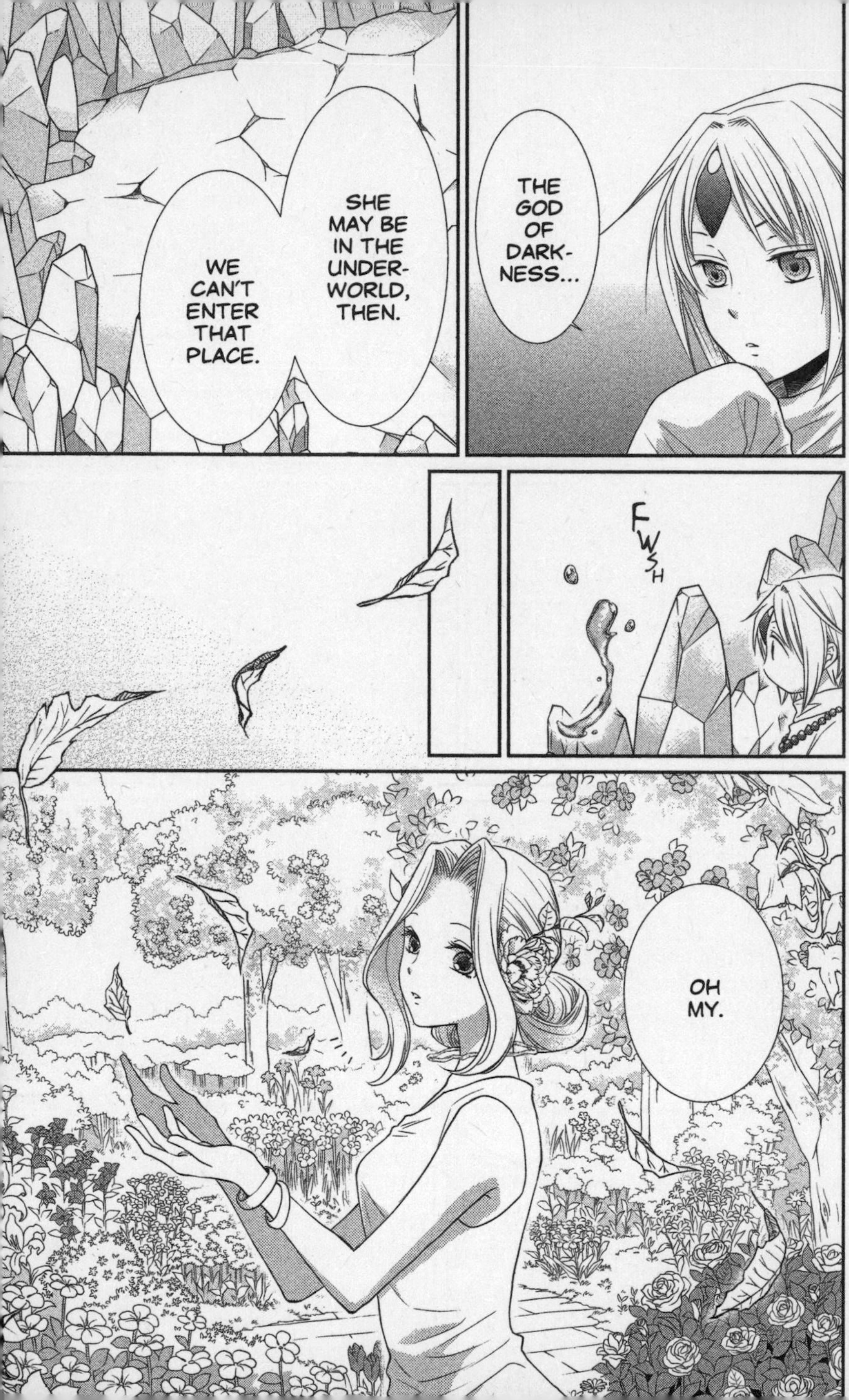
THE GOD OF DARK-NESS...
SHE MAY BE IN THE UNDER-WORLD, THEN.
WE CAN'T ENTER THAT PLACE.
FWSH
OH MY.

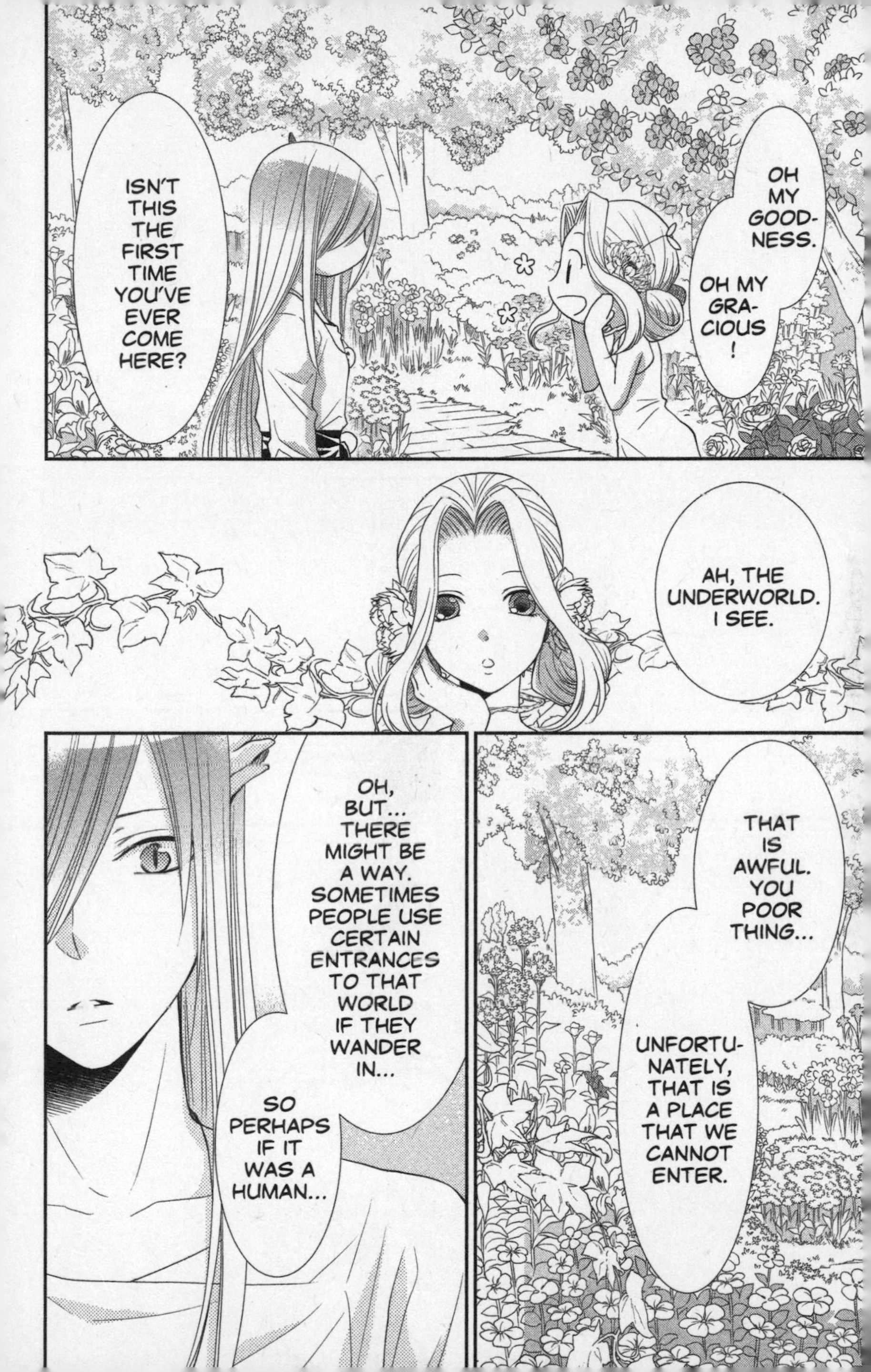
OH MY GOODNESS.
OH MY GRACIOUS!
ISN'T THIS THE FIRST TIME YOU'VE EVER COME HERE?
AH, THE UNDERWORLD. I SEE.
THAT IS AWFUL. YOU POOR THING...
UNFORTUNATELY, THAT IS A PLACE THAT WE CANNOT ENTER.
OH, BUT... THERE MIGHT BE A WAY. SOMETIMES PEOPLE USE CERTAIN ENTRANCES TO THAT WORLD IF THEY WANDER IN...
SO PERHAPS IF IT WAS A HUMAN...

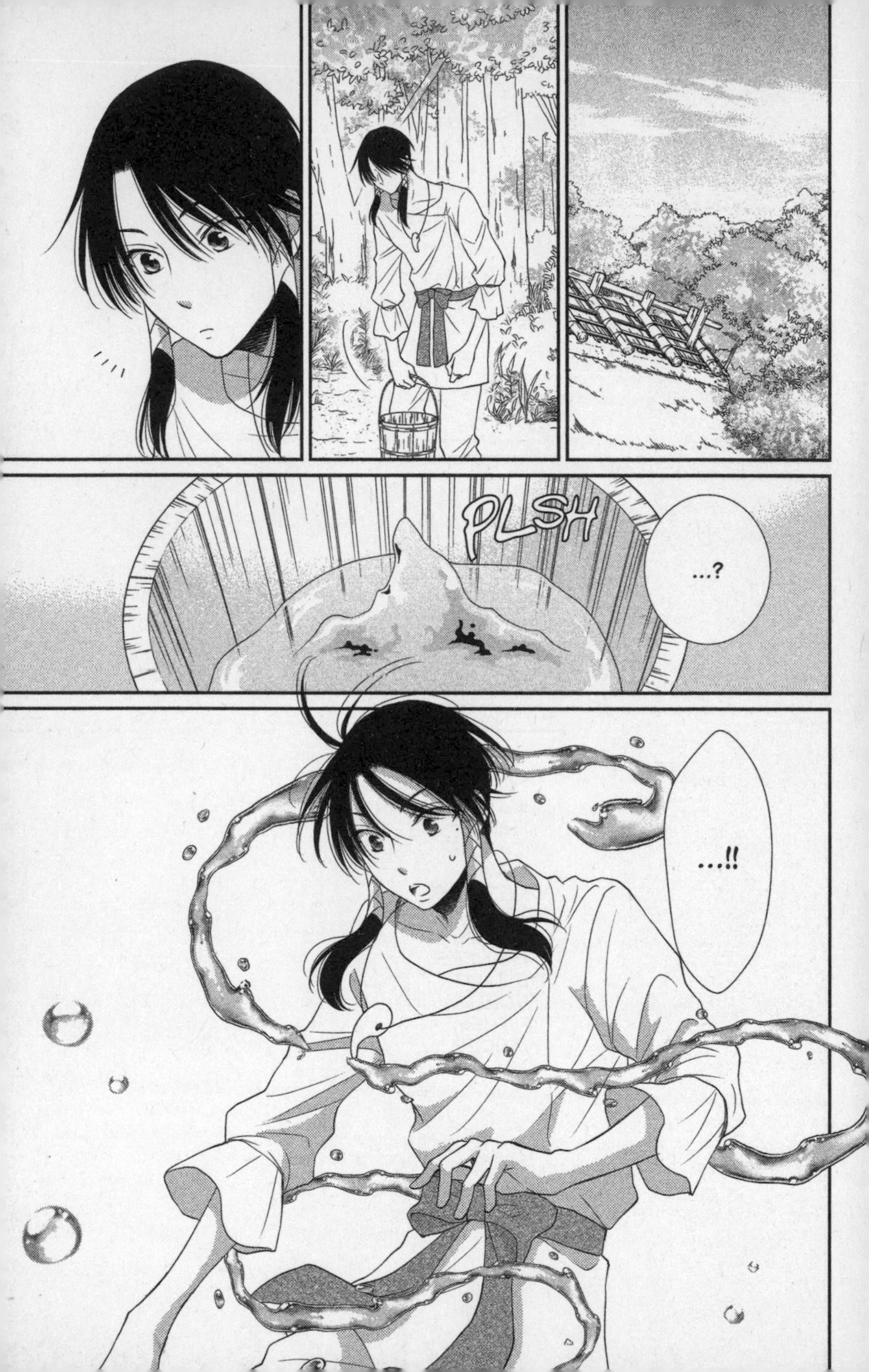
PLSH
...?
...!!

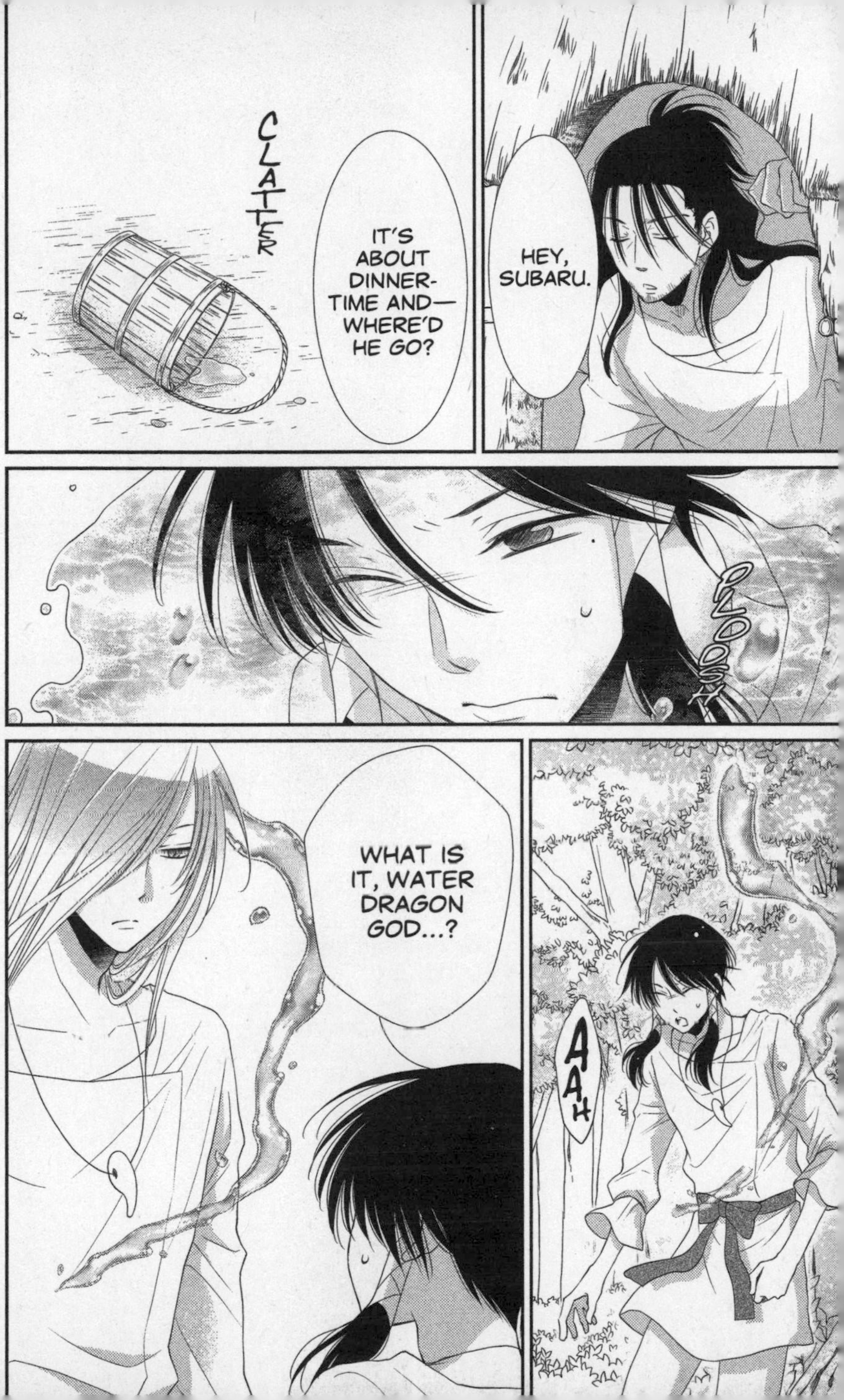
HEY, SUBARU.
IT'S ABOUT DINNER-TIME AND—WHERE'D HE GO?
CLATTER
PLOOSH
AAH
WHAT IS IT, WATER DRAGON GOD...?

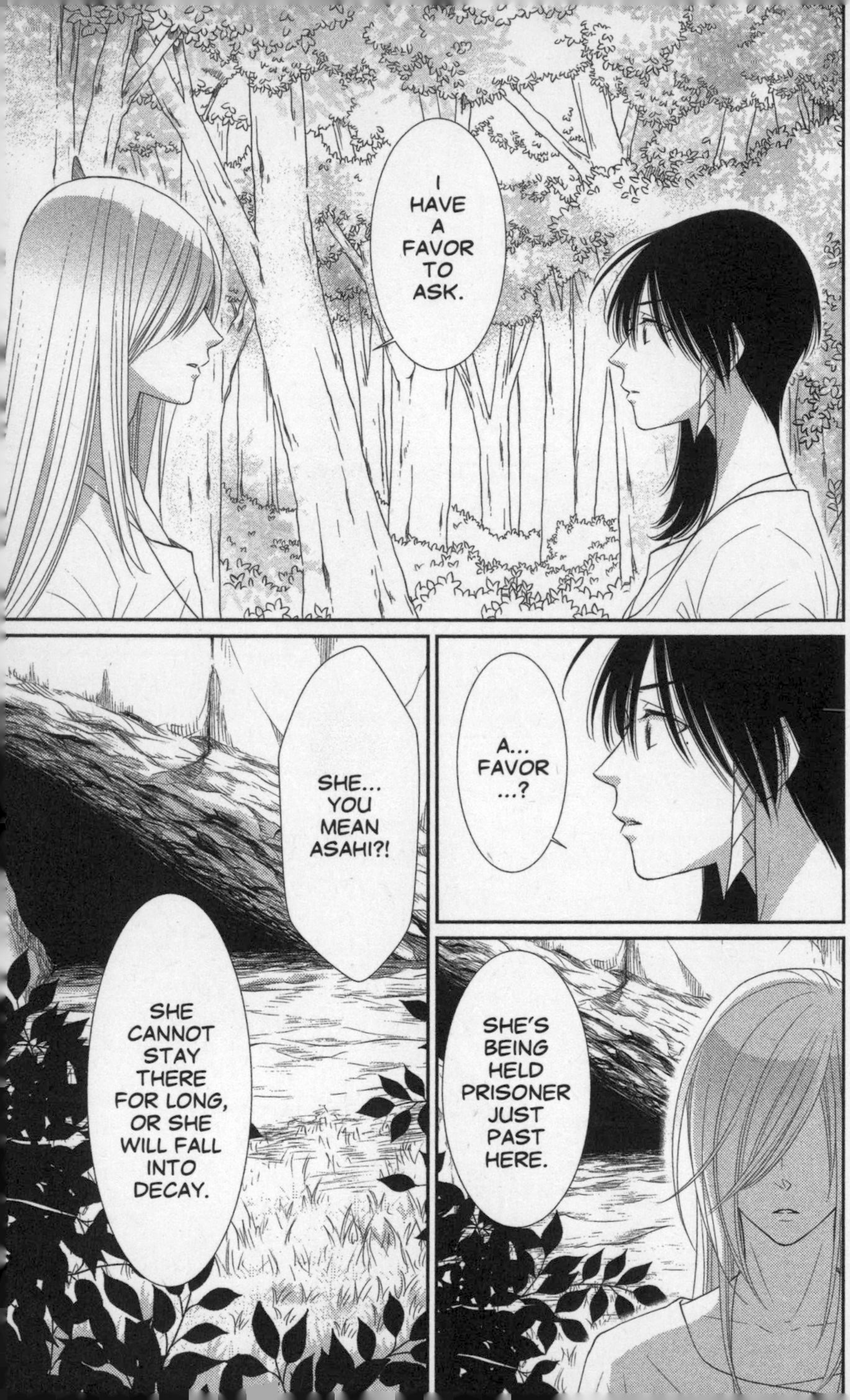
I HAVE A FAVOR TO ASK.
A... FAVOR ...?
SHE'S BEING HELD PRISONER JUST PAST HERE.
SHE... YOU MEAN ASAHI?!
SHE CANNOT STAY THERE FOR LONG, OR SHE WILL FALL INTO DECAY.

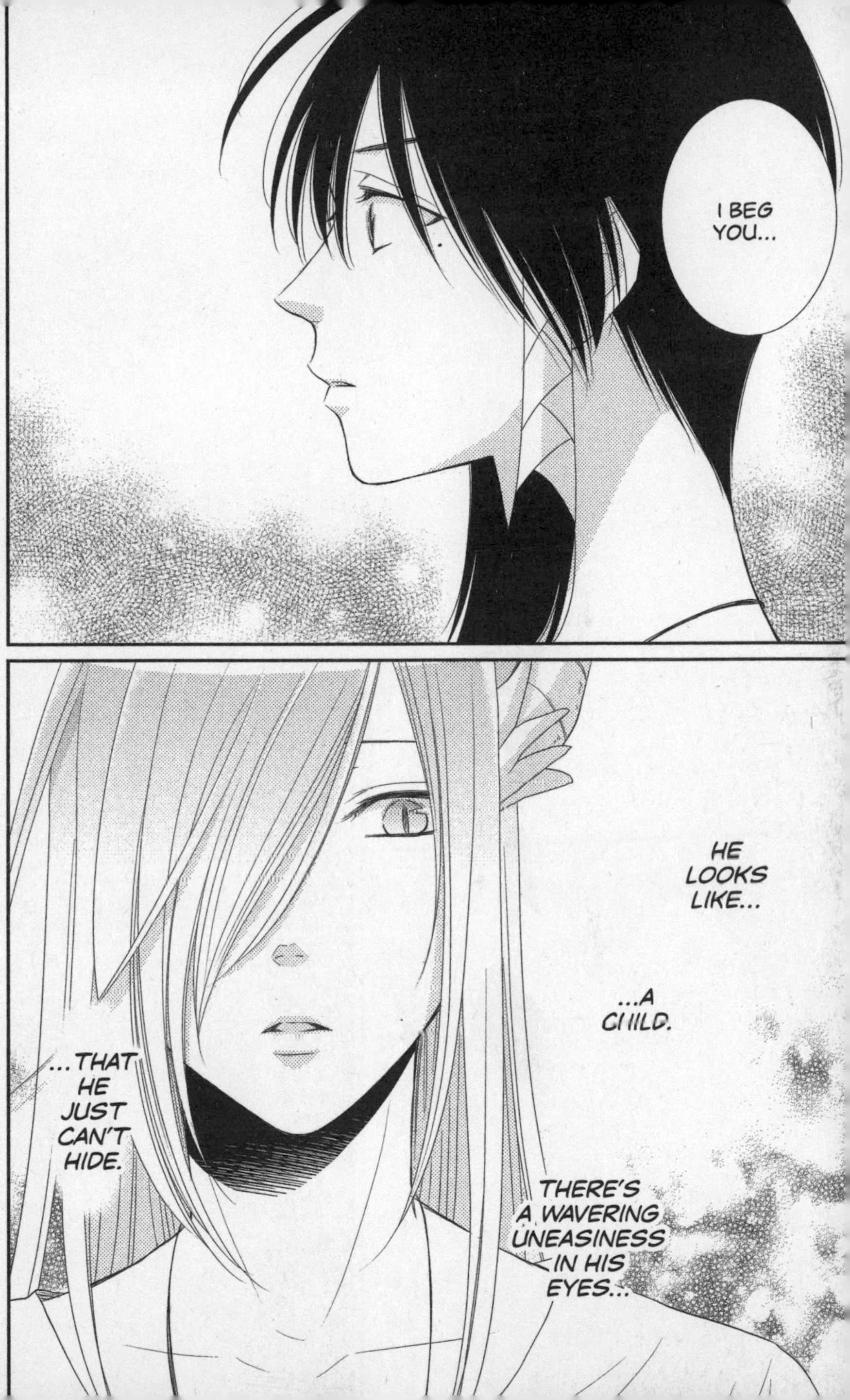
I BEG YOU...
HE LOOKS LIKE...
...A CHILD.
THERE'S A WAVERING UNEASINESS IN HIS EYES...
...THAT HE JUST CAN'T HIDE.

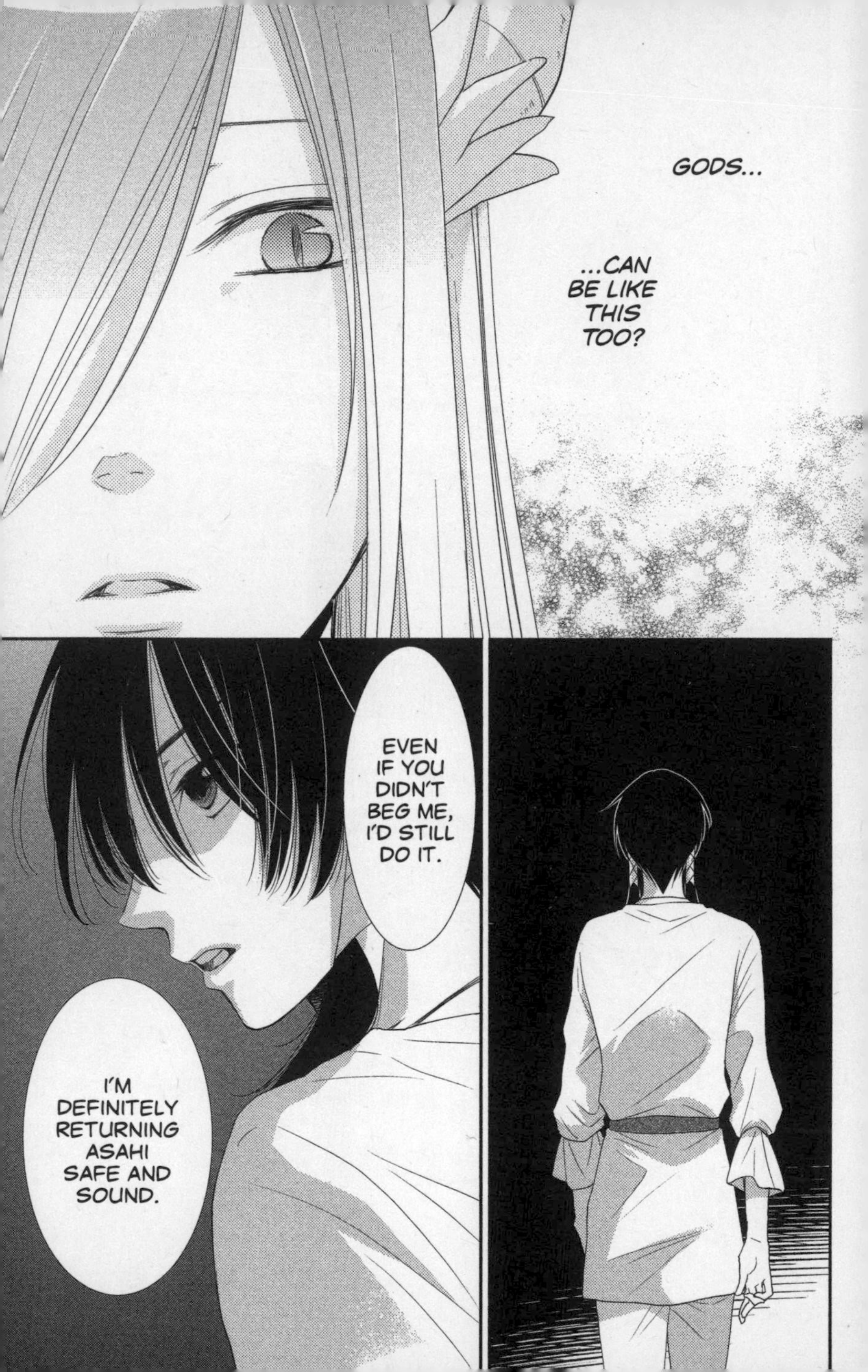
GODS...
...CAN BE LIKE THIS TOO?
EVEN IF YOU DIDN'T BEG ME, I'D STILL DO IT.
I'M DEFINITELY RETURNING ASAHI SAFE AND SOUND.

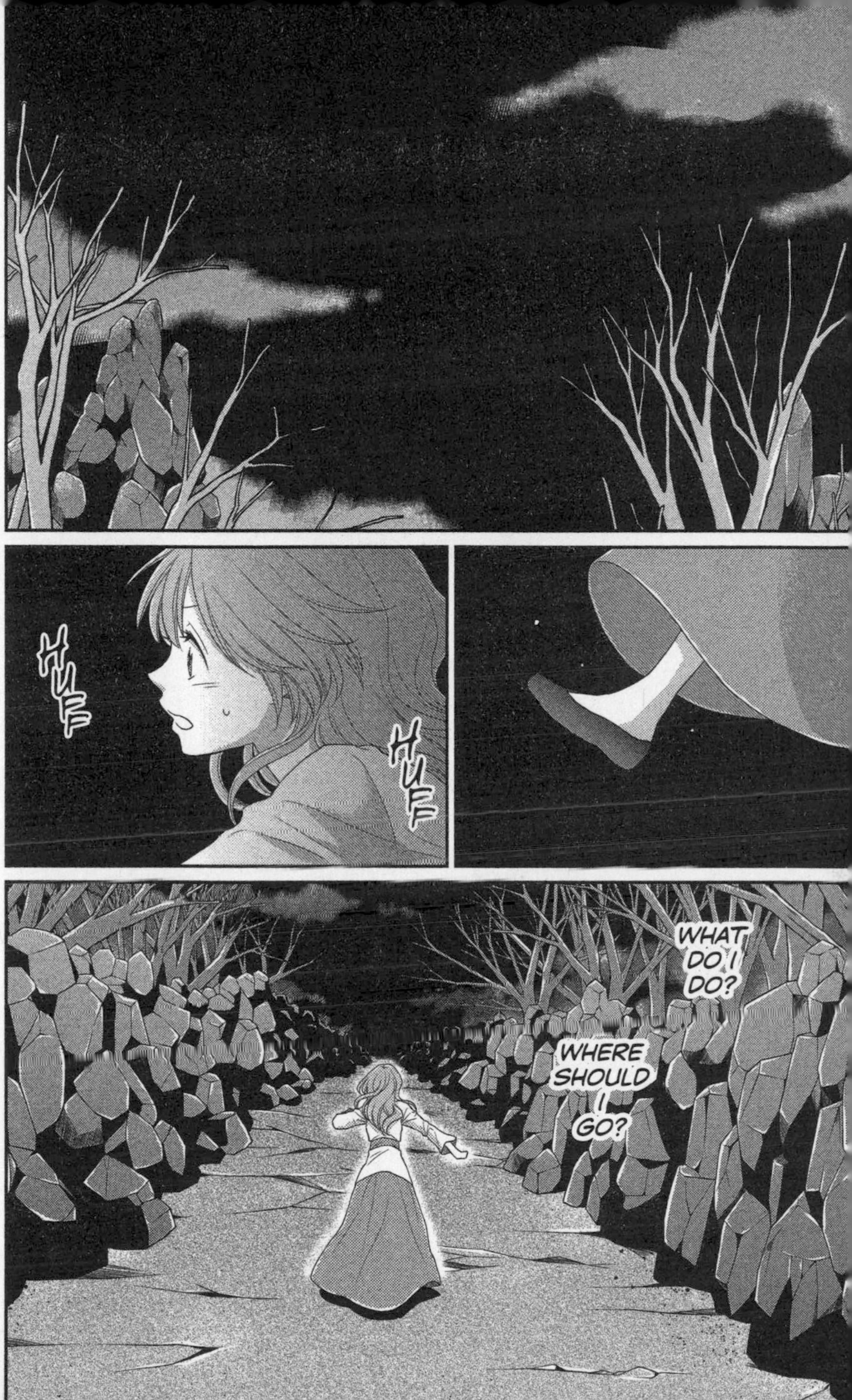
HUFF
HUFF
WHAT DO I DO?
WHERE SHOULD I GO?

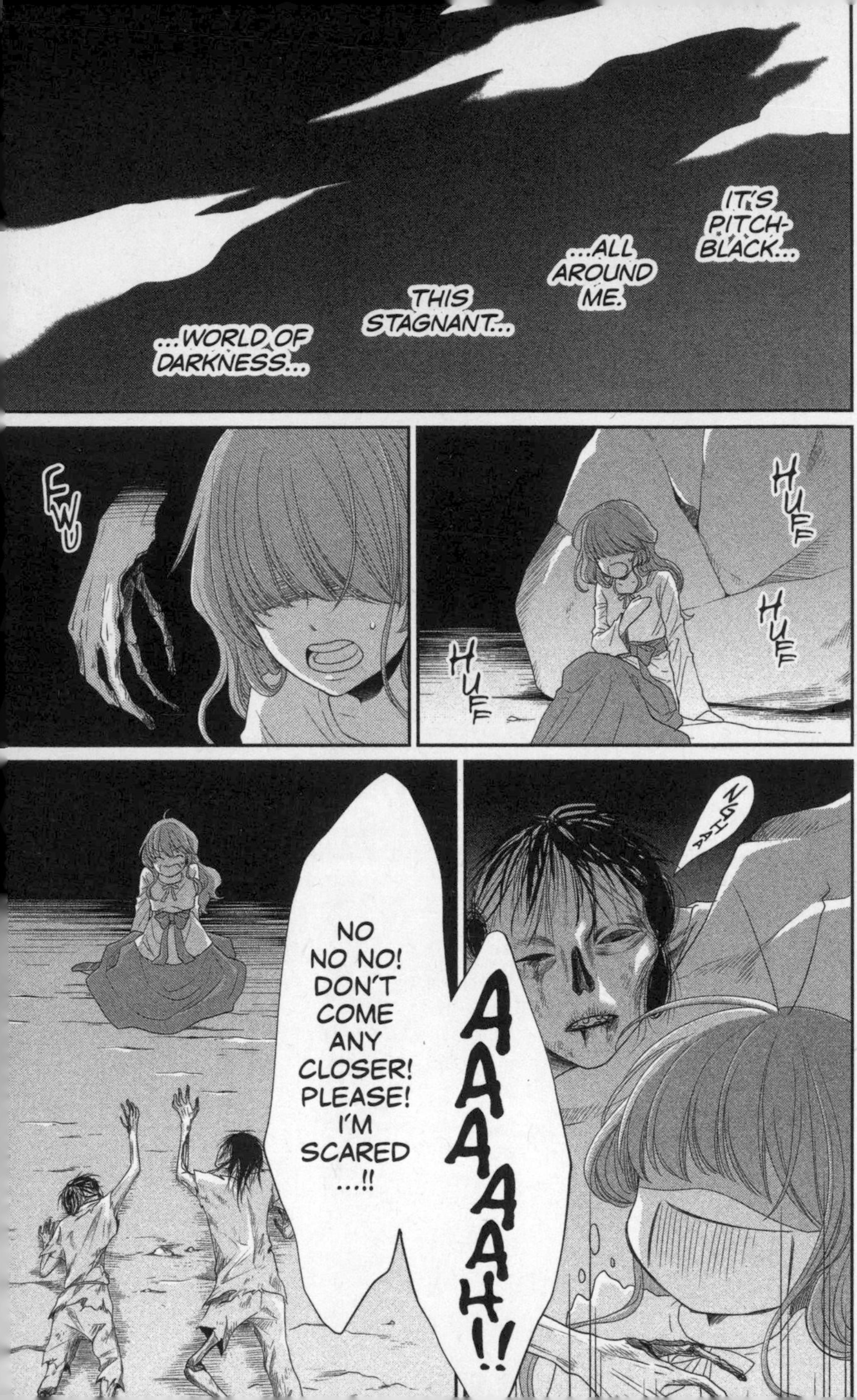
IT'S PITCH-BLACK...
...ALL AROUND ME.
THIS STAGNANT...
...WORLD OF DARKNESS...
HUFF
HUFF
HUFF
FWU
NGHAA
AAAAAH!!
NO NO NO! DON'T COME ANY CLOSER! PLEASE! I'M SCARED ...!!

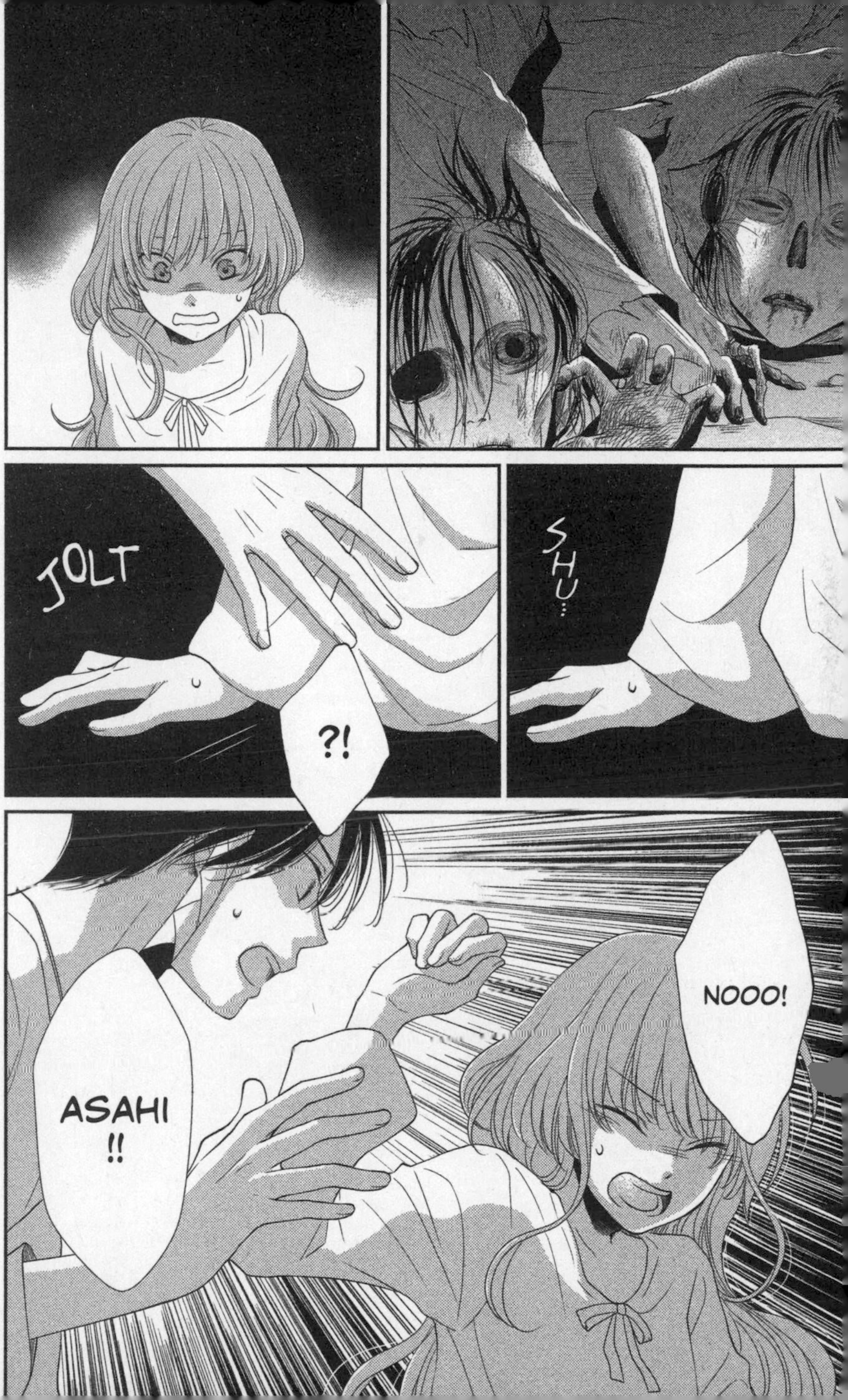
SHU...
JOLT
?!
NOOO!
ASAHI !!

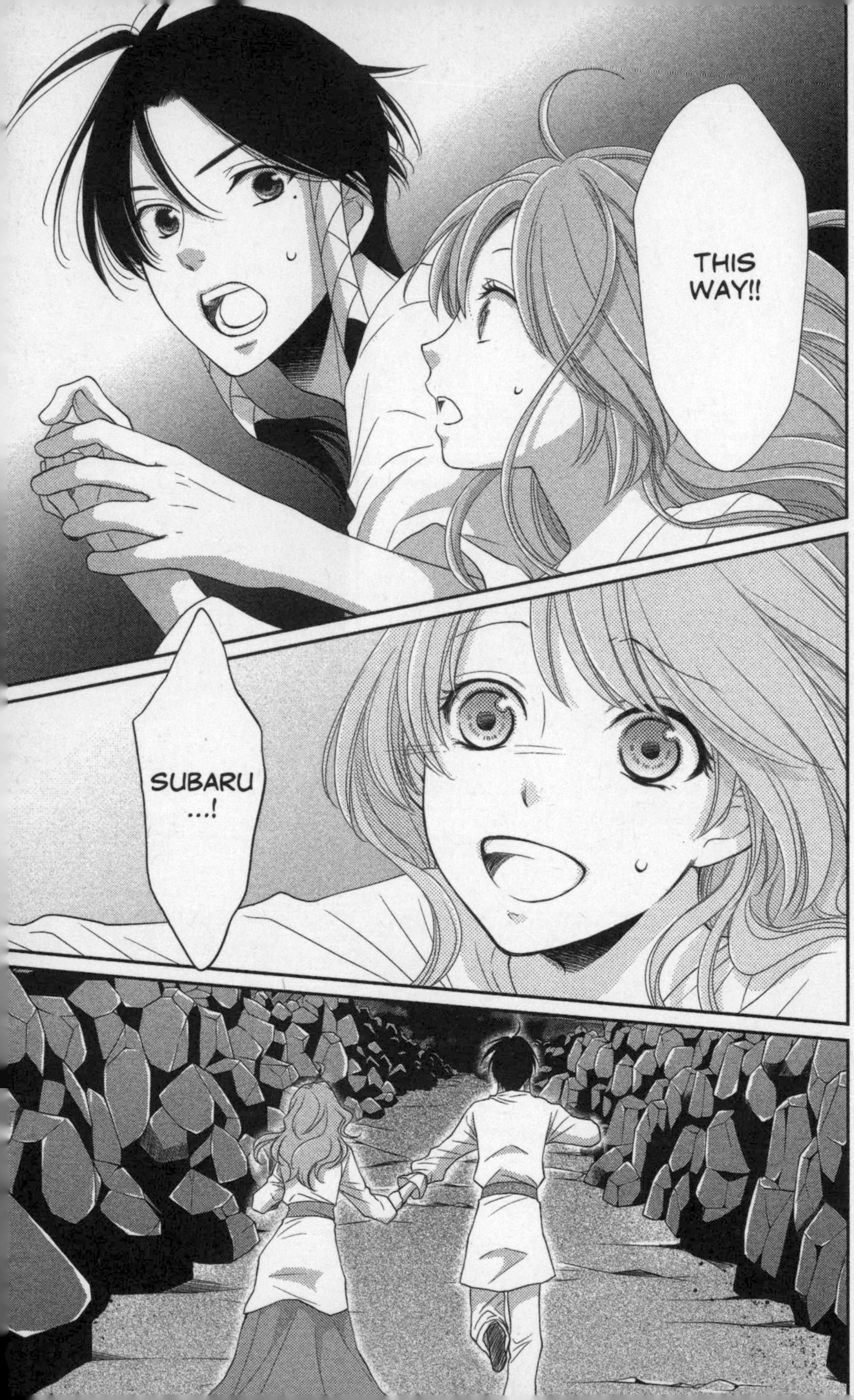
THIS WAY!!
SUBARU ...!

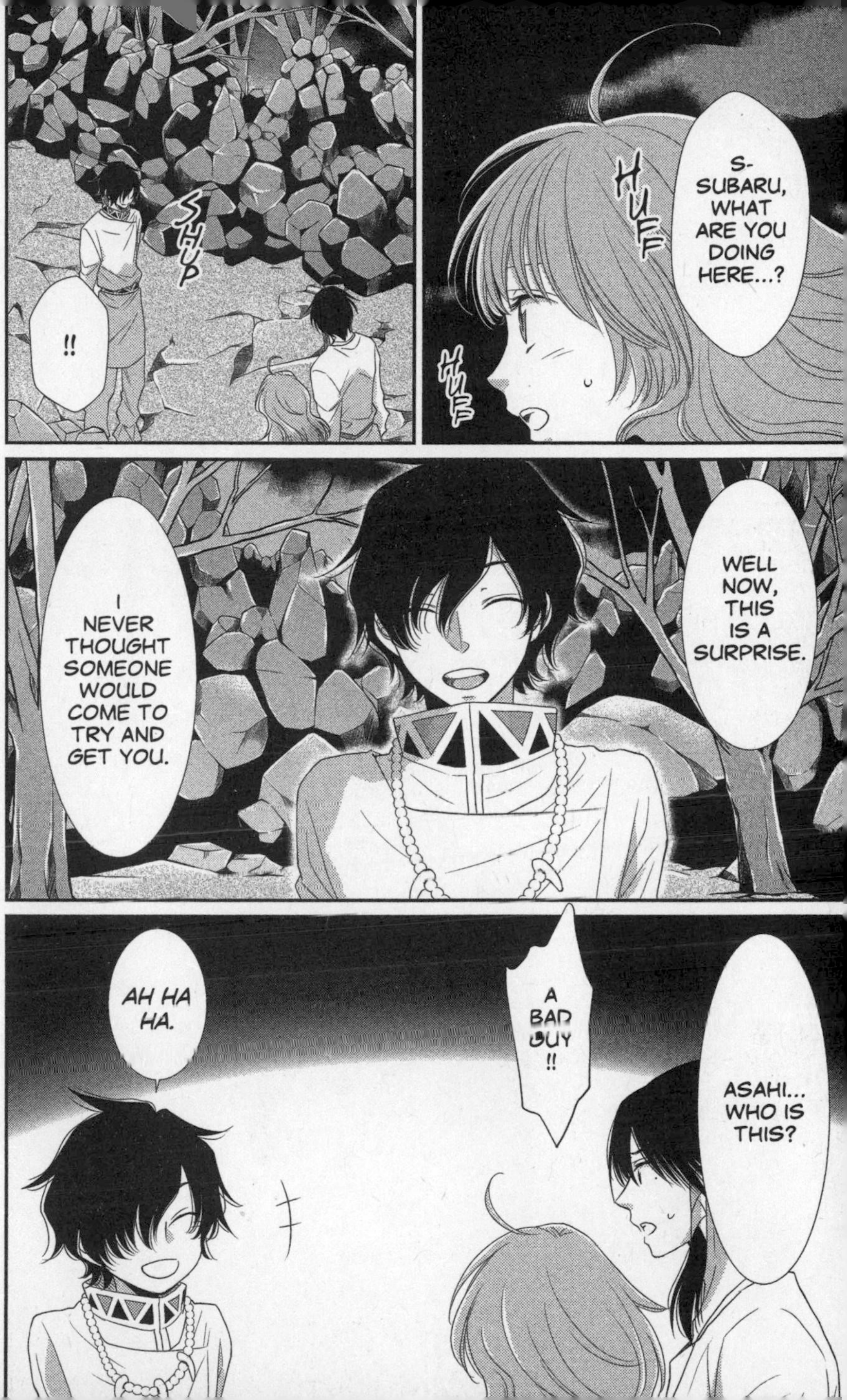
HUFF
S-SUBARU, WHAT ARE YOU DOING HERE...?
HUFF
SHUP
!!
WELL NOW, THIS IS A SURPRISE.
I NEVER THOUGHT SOMEONE WOULD COME TO TRY AND GET YOU.
ASAHI... WHO IS THIS?
A BAD GUY !!
AH HA HA.

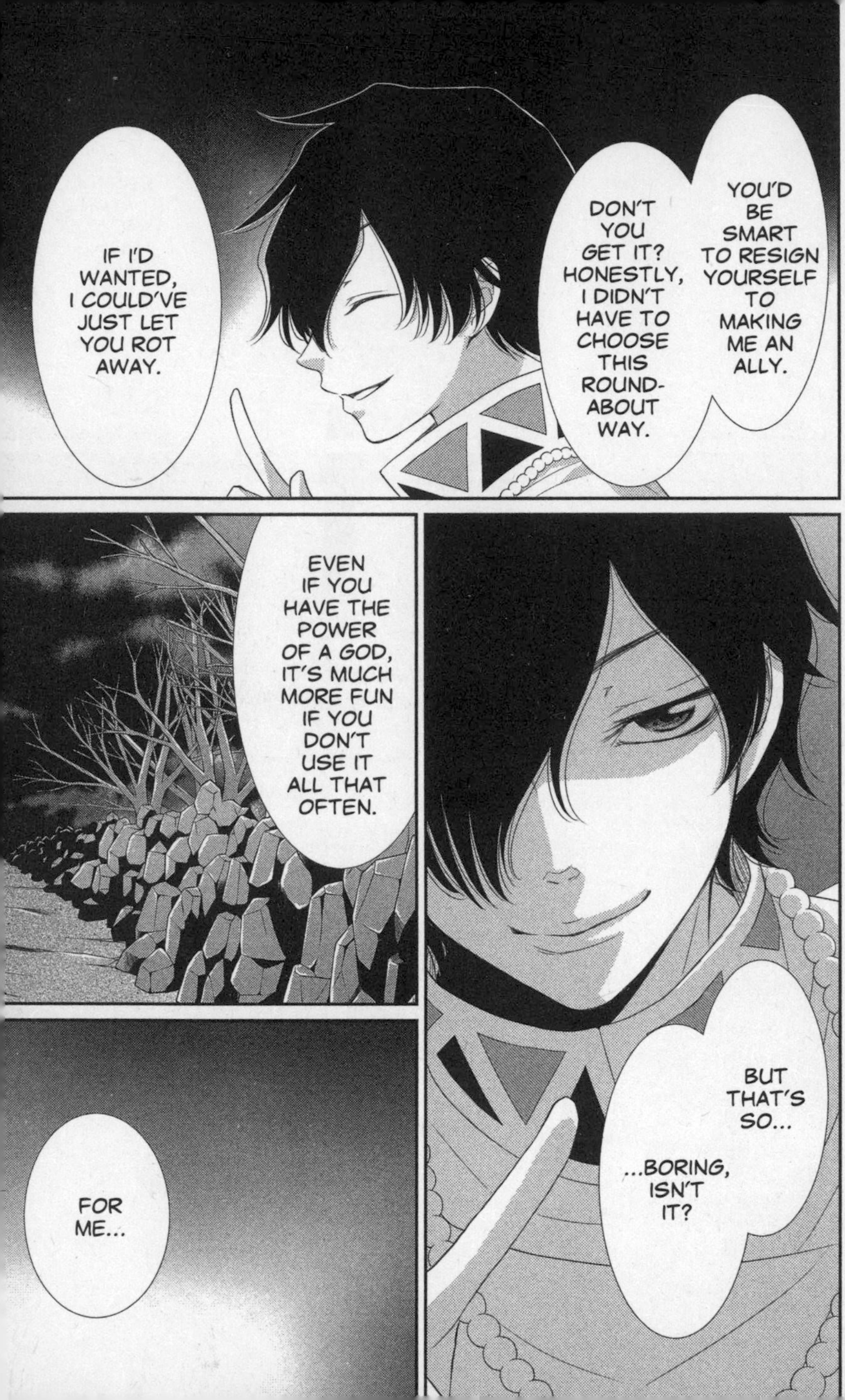
YOU'D BE SMART TO RESIGN YOURSELF TO MAKING ME AN ALLY.
DON'T YOU GET IT? HONESTLY, I DIDN'T HAVE TO CHOOSE THIS ROUND-ABOUT WAY.
IF I'D WANTED, I COULD'VE JUST LET YOU ROT AWAY.
BUT THAT'S SO...
...BORING, ISN'T IT?
EVEN IF YOU HAVE THE POWER OF A GOD, IT'S MUCH MORE FUN IF YOU DON'T USE IT ALL THAT OFTEN.
FOR ME...

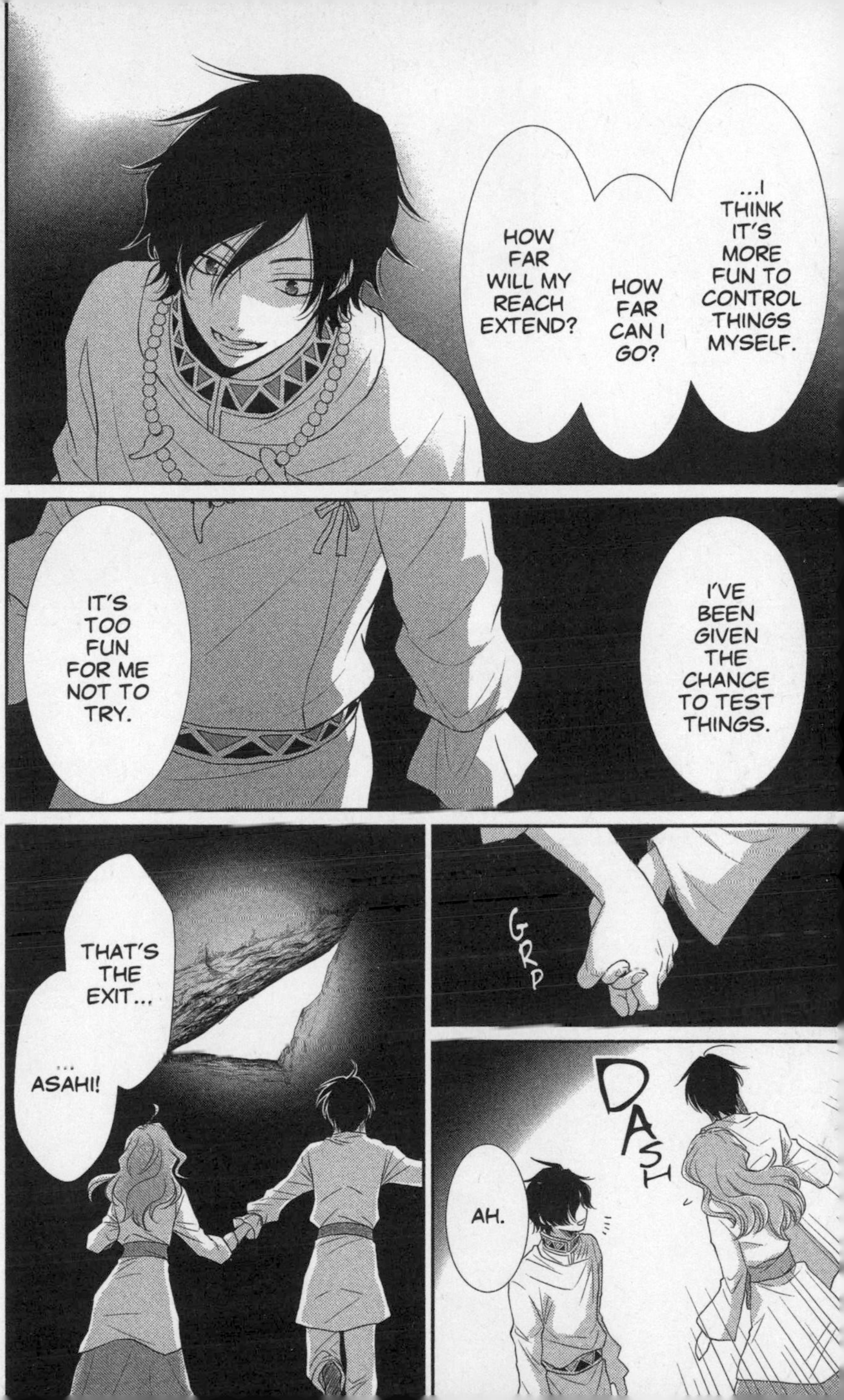
...I THINK IT'S MORE FUN TO CONTROL THINGS MYSELF.
HOW FAR CAN I GO?
HOW FAR WILL MY REACH EXTEND?
I'VE BEEN GIVEN THE CHANCE TO TEST THINGS.
IT'S TOO FUN FOR ME NOT TO TRY.
GRP
DASH
AH.
THAT'S THE EXIT...
... ASAHI!

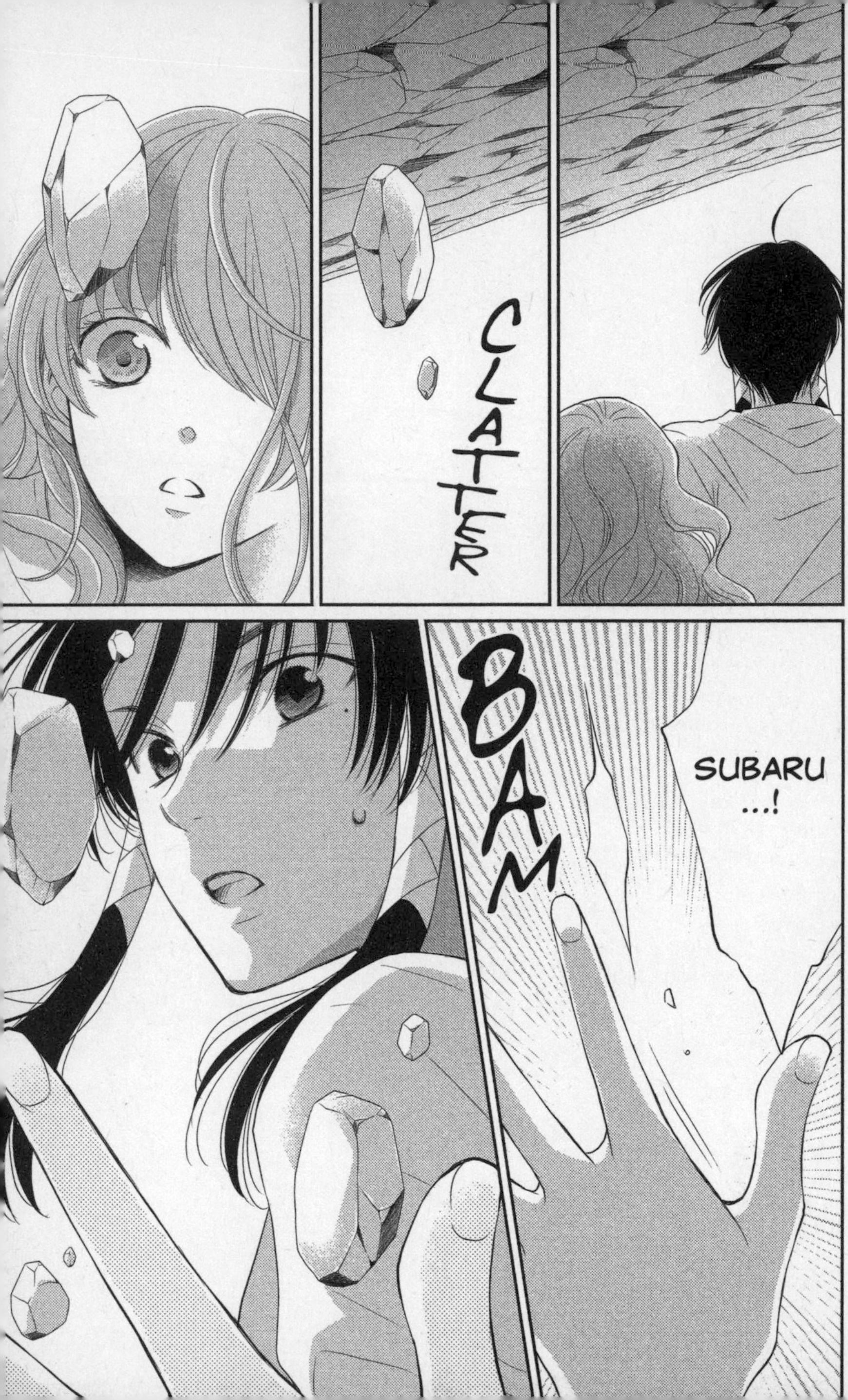
CLATTER
SUBARU ...!
BAM

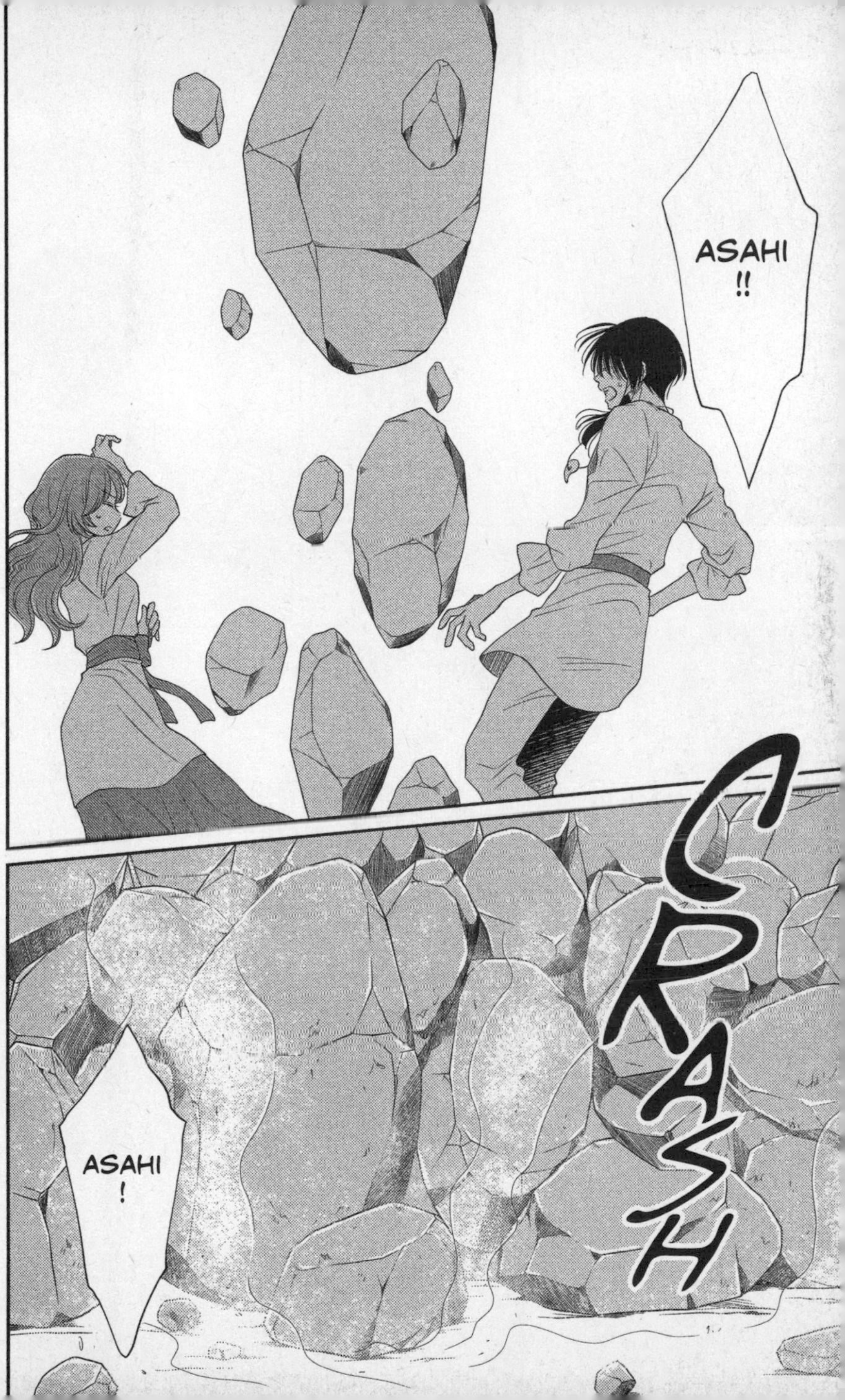
ASAHI !!
CRASH
ASAHI !

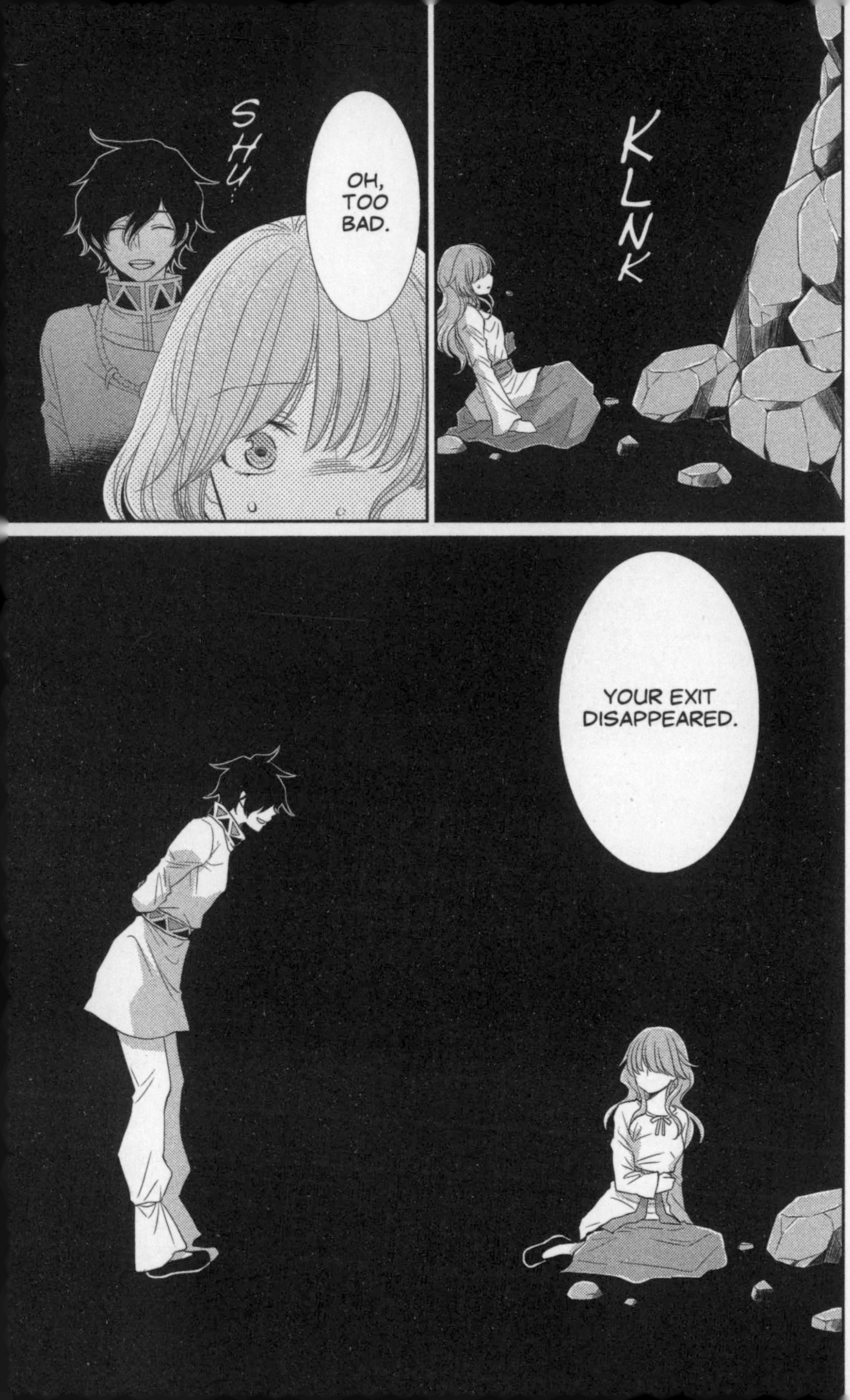
KLNK
SHU...
OH, TOO BAD.
YOUR EXIT DISAPPEARED.

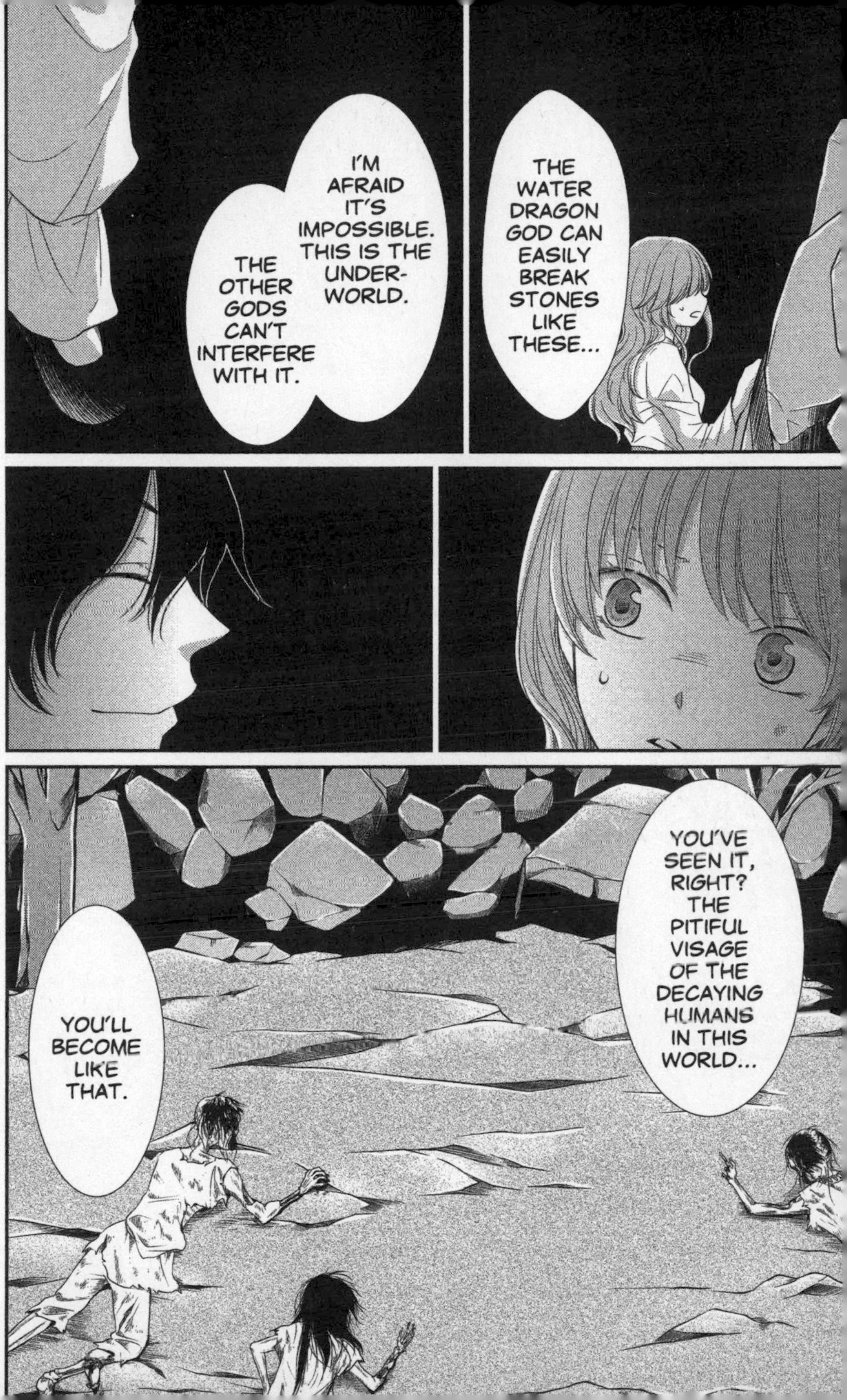
THE WATER DRAGON GOD CAN EASILY BREAK STONES LIKE THESE...
I'M AFRAID IT'S IMPOSSIBLE. THIS IS THE UNDER-WORLD.
THE OTHER GODS CAN'T INTERFERE WITH IT.
YOU'VE SEEN IT, RIGHT? THE PITIFUL VISAGE OF THE DECAYING HUMANS IN THIS WORLD...
YOU'LL BECOME LIKE THAT.

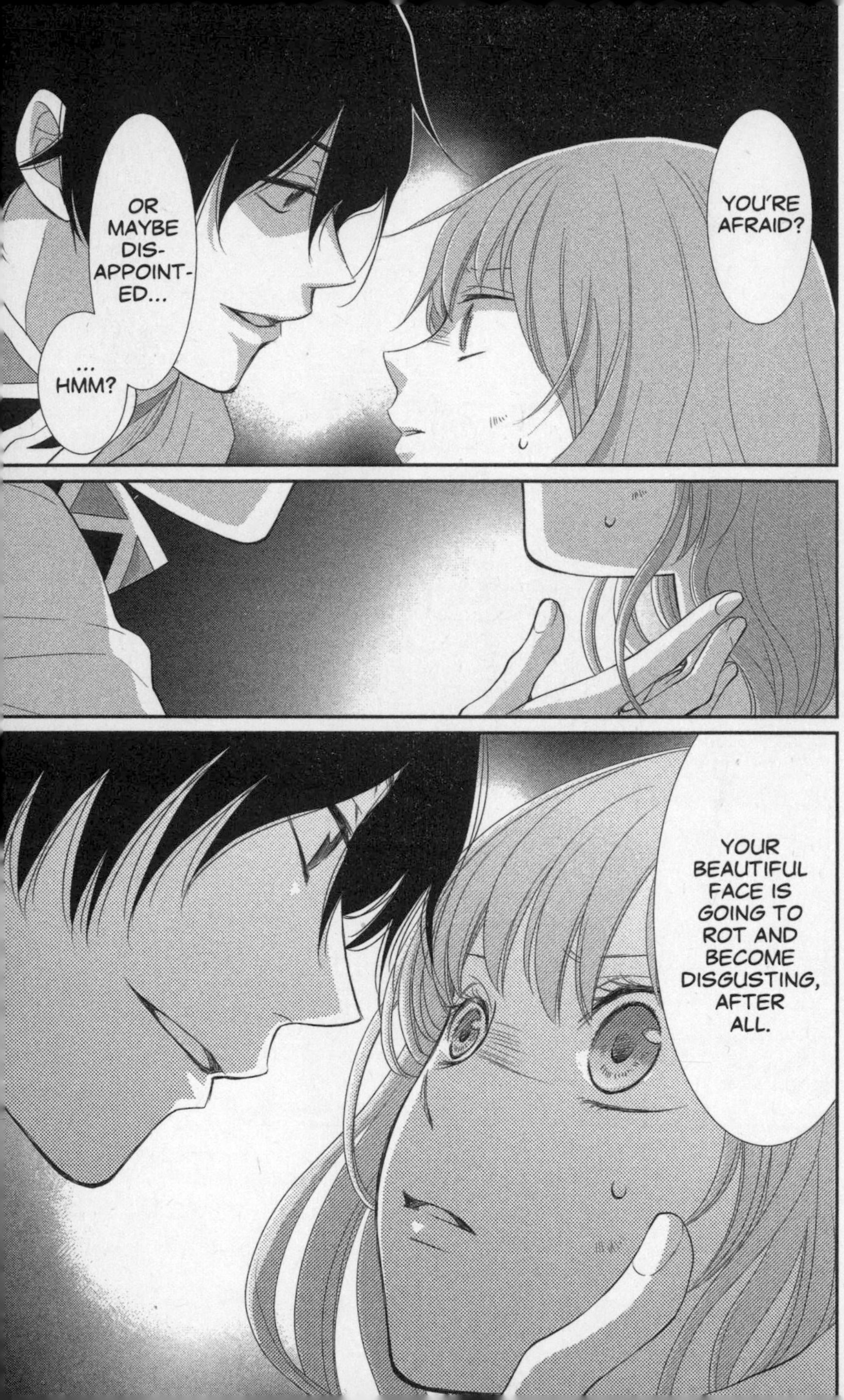
YOU'RE AFRAID?
OR MAYBE DISAPPOINTED...
...HMM?
YOUR BEAUTIFUL FACE IS GOING TO ROT AND BECOME DISGUSTING, AFTER ALL.

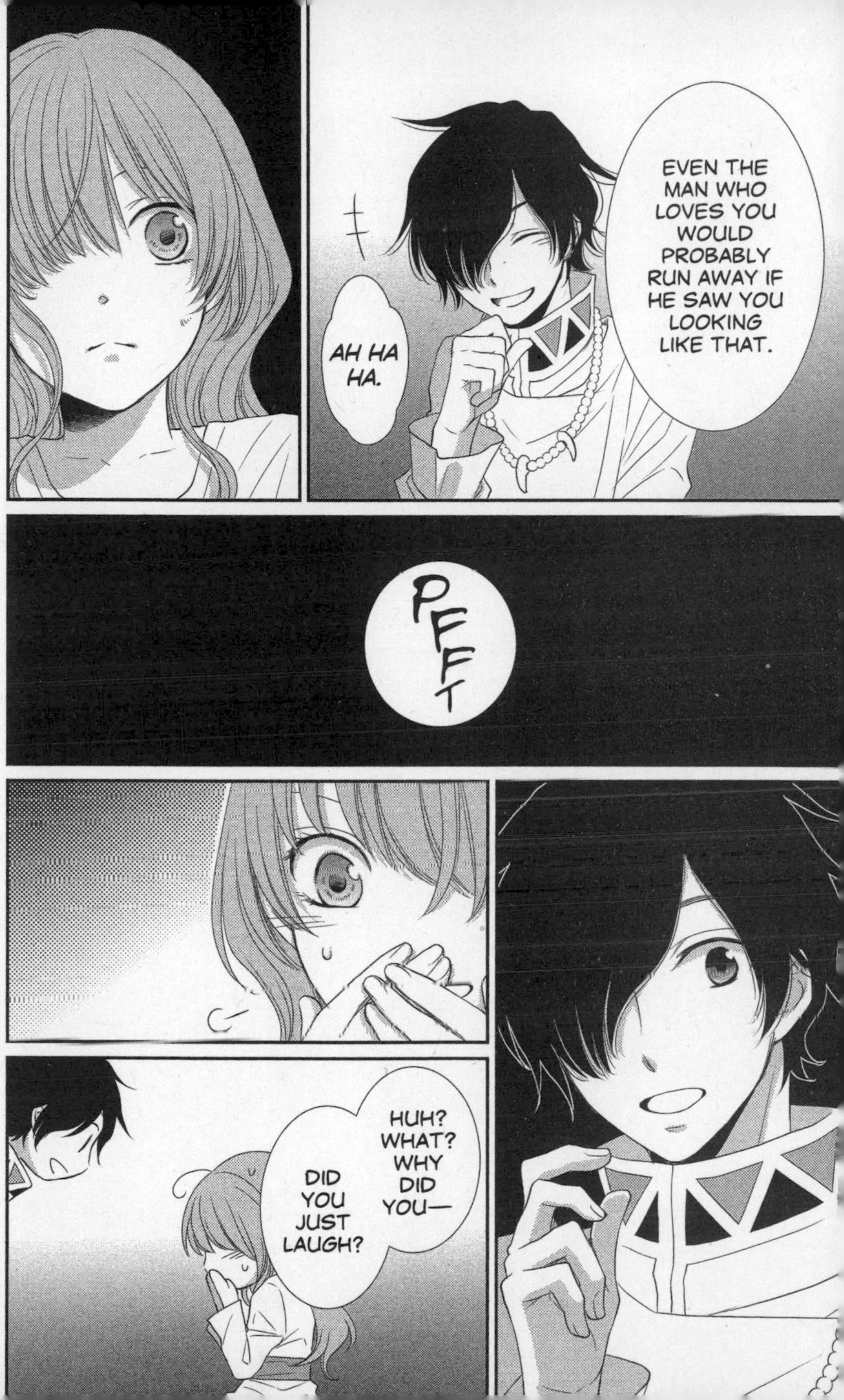
EVEN THE MAN WHO LOVES YOU WOULD PROBABLY RUN AWAY IF HE SAW YOU LOOKING LIKE THAT.
AH HA HA.
PFFT
HUH? WHAT? WHY DID YOU—
DID YOU JUST LAUGH?

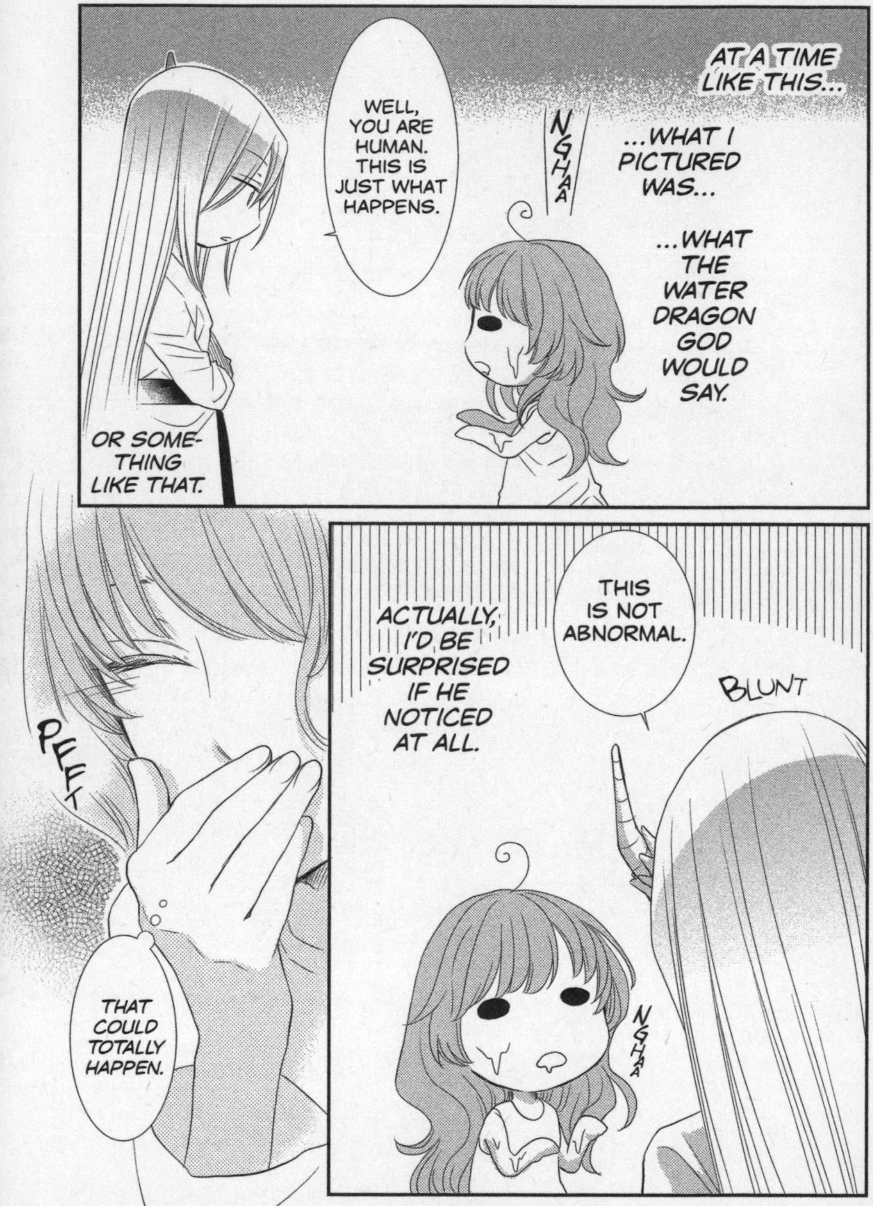
AT A TIME LIKE THIS...
...WHAT I PICTURED WAS...
...WHAT THE WATER DRAGON GOD WOULD SAY.
NGHAA
WELL, YOU ARE HUMAN. THIS IS JUST WHAT HAPPENS.
OR SOME-THING LIKE THAT.
BLUNT
THIS IS NOT ABNORMAL.
NGHAA
ACTUALLY, I'D BE SURPRISED IF HE NOTICED AT ALL.
PFFT
THAT COULD TOTALLY HAPPEN.

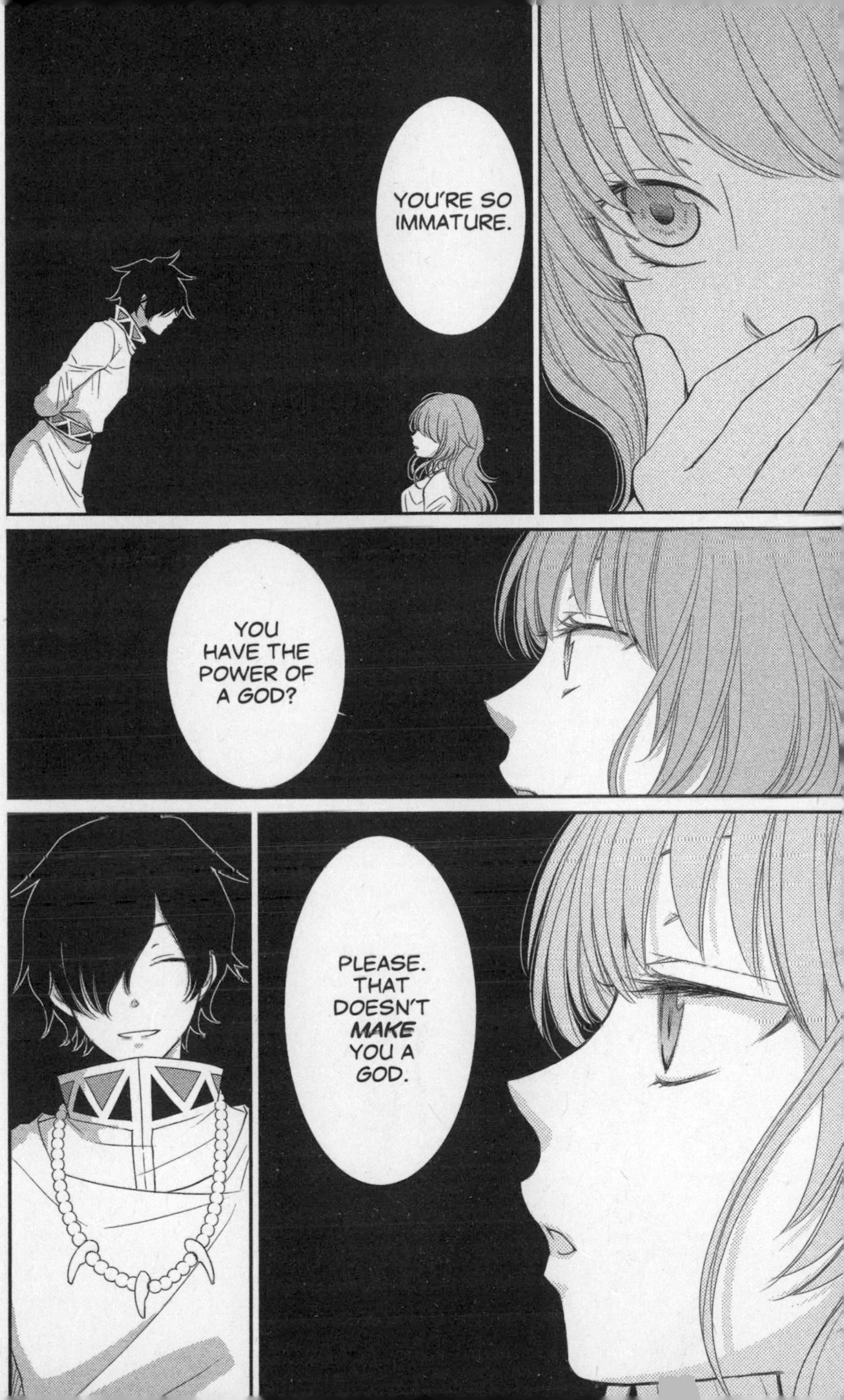
YOU'RE SO IMMATURE.
YOU HAVE THE POWER OF A GOD?
PLEASE. THAT DOESN'T *MAKE* YOU A GOD.

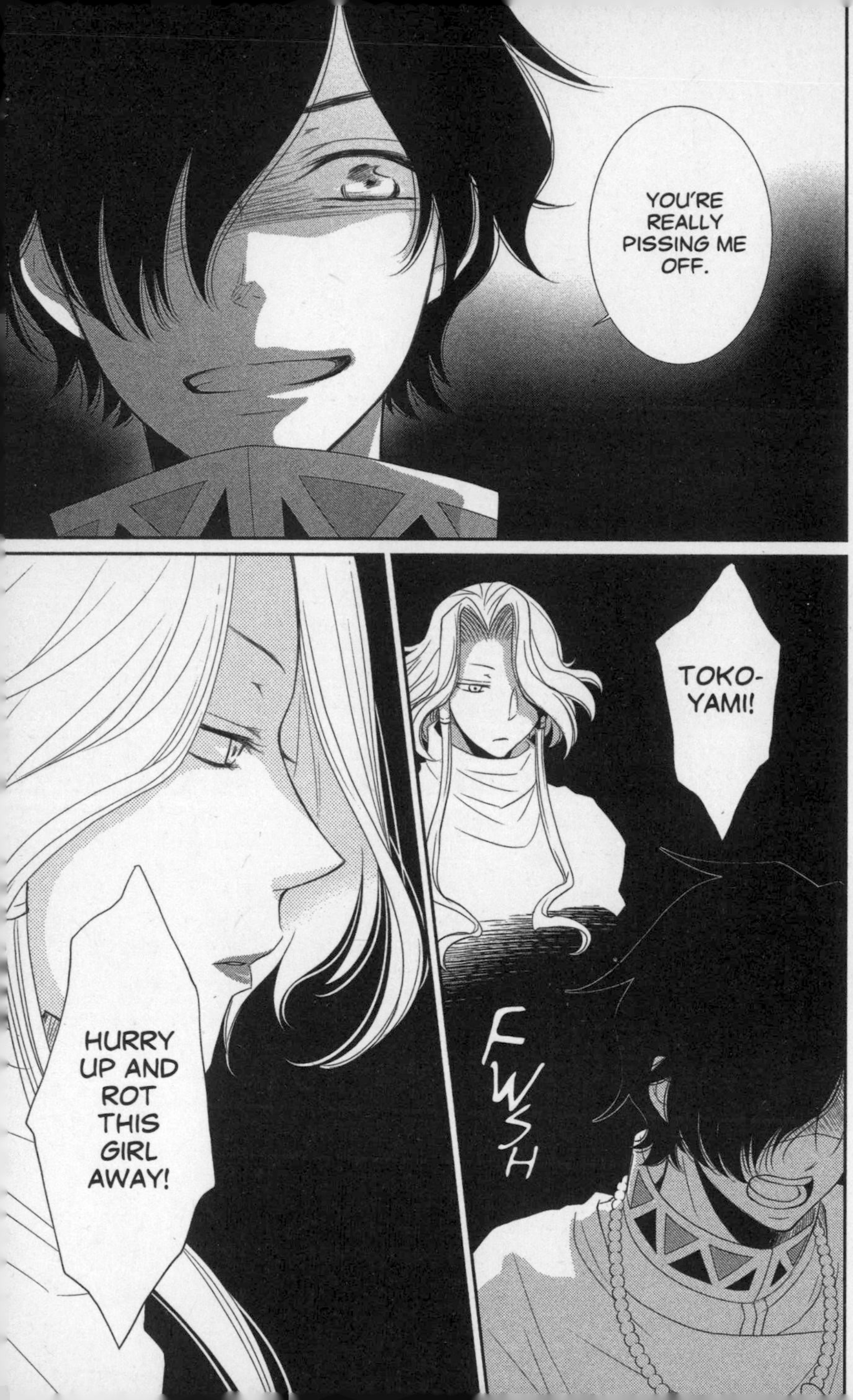
YOU'RE REALLY PISSING ME OFF.
TOKO-YAMI!
FWSH
HURRY UP AND ROT THIS GIRL AWAY!

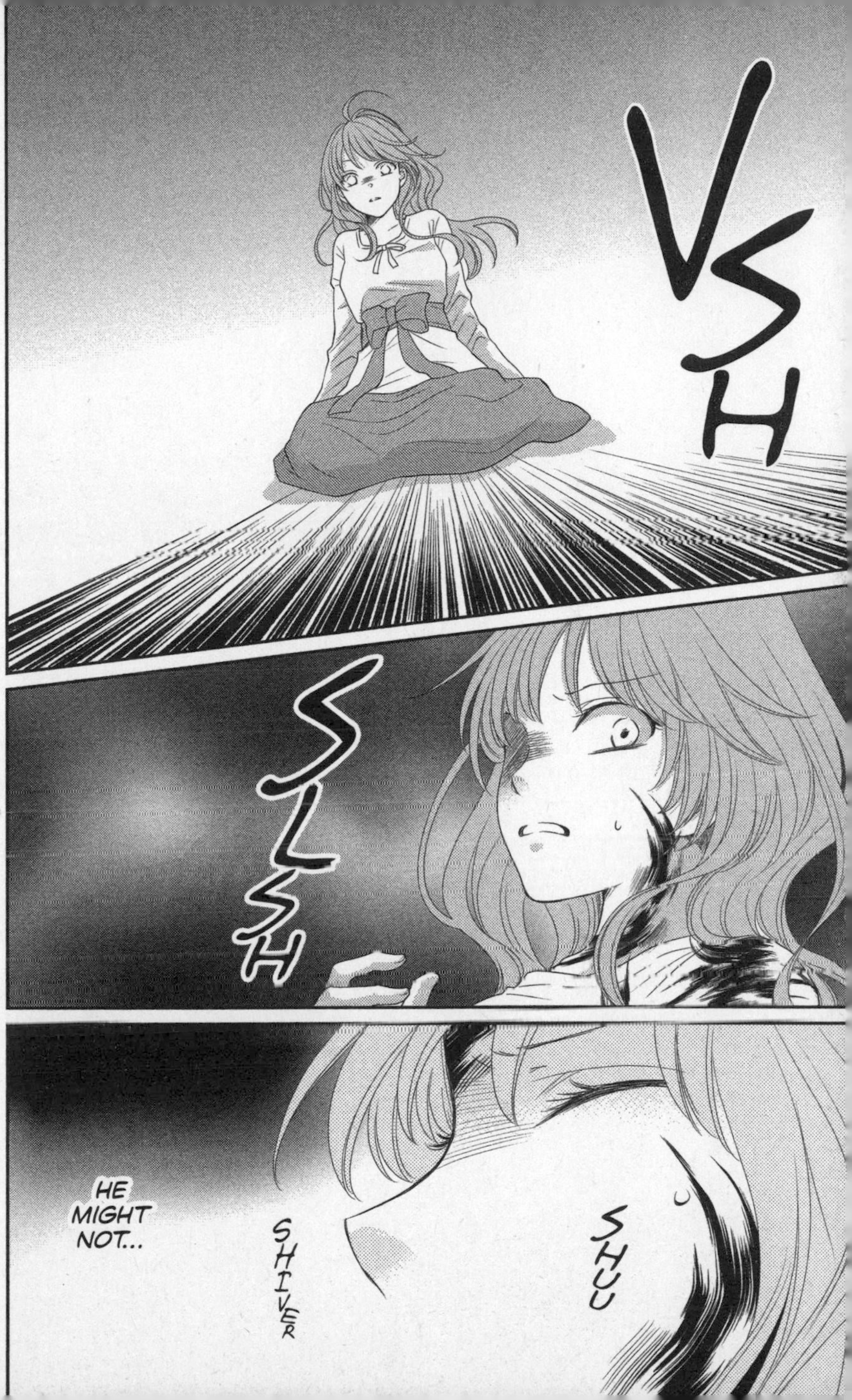
VSH
SLSH
SHUU
SHIVER
HE MIGHT NOT...

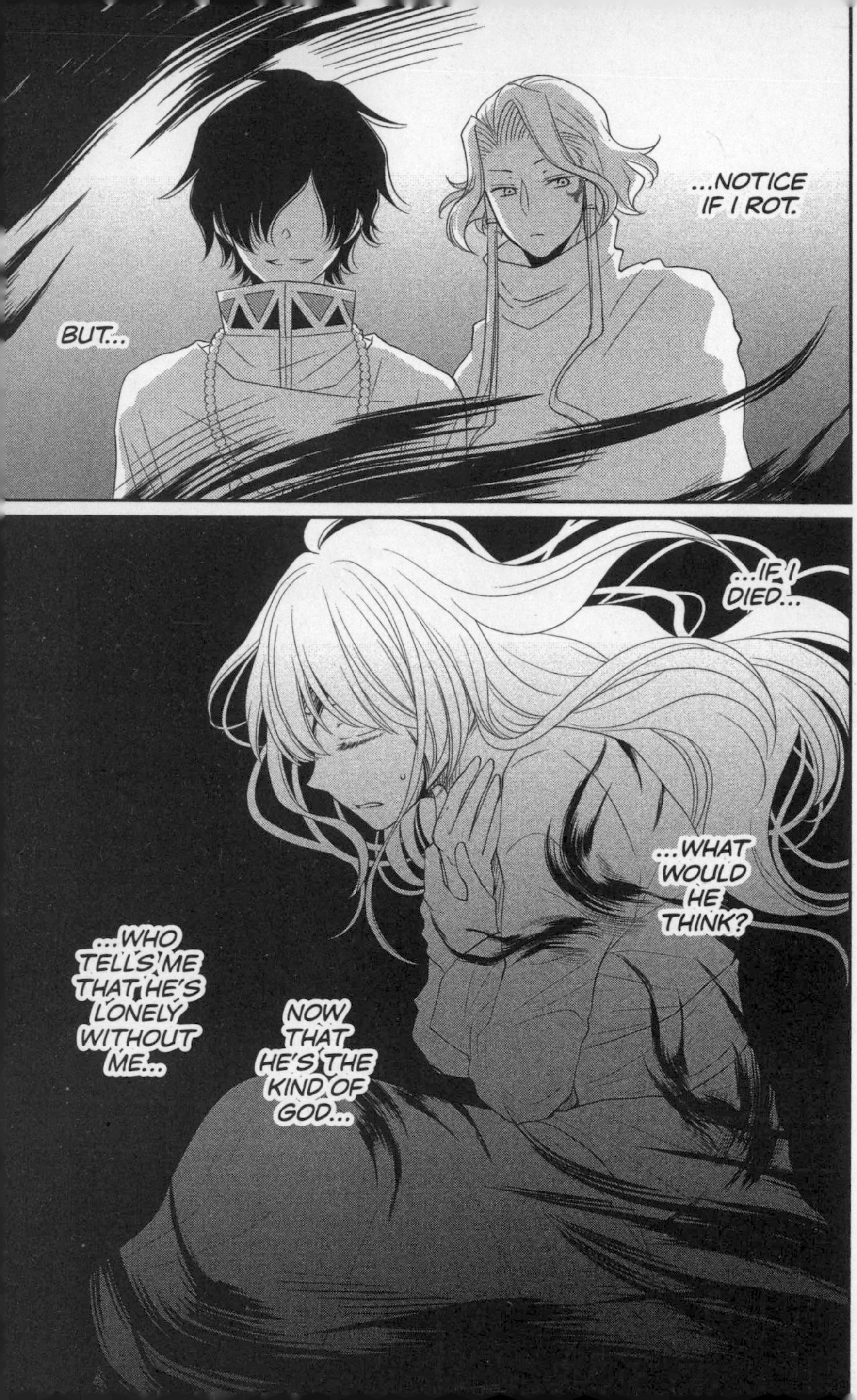
...NOTICE IF I ROT.
BUT...
...IF I DIED...
...WHAT WOULD HE THINK?
NOW THAT HE'S THE KIND OF GOD...
...WHO TELLS ME THAT HE'S LONELY WITHOUT ME...

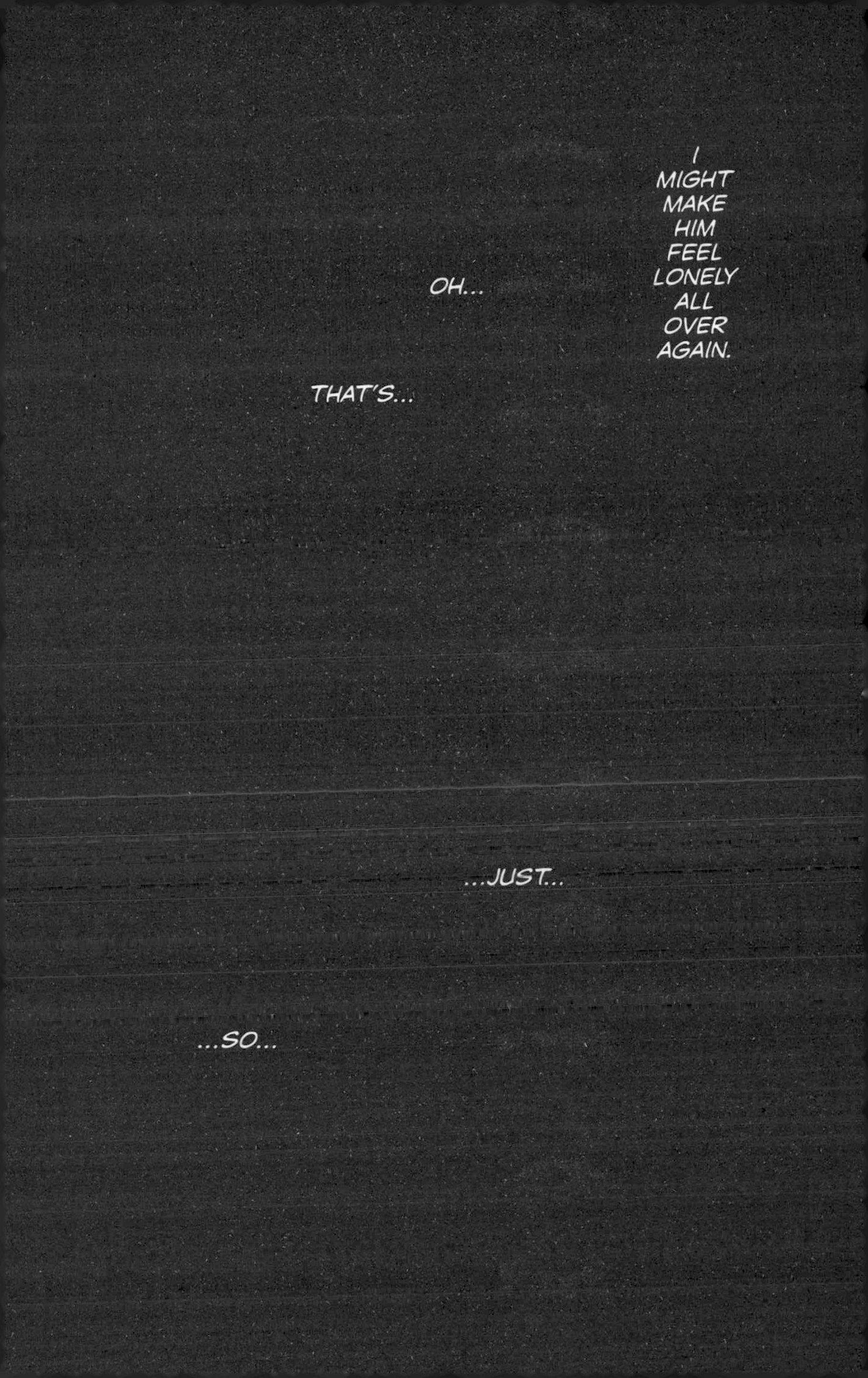
I MIGHT MAKE HIM FEEL LONELY ALL OVER AGAIN.
OH...
THAT'S...
...JUST...
...SO...

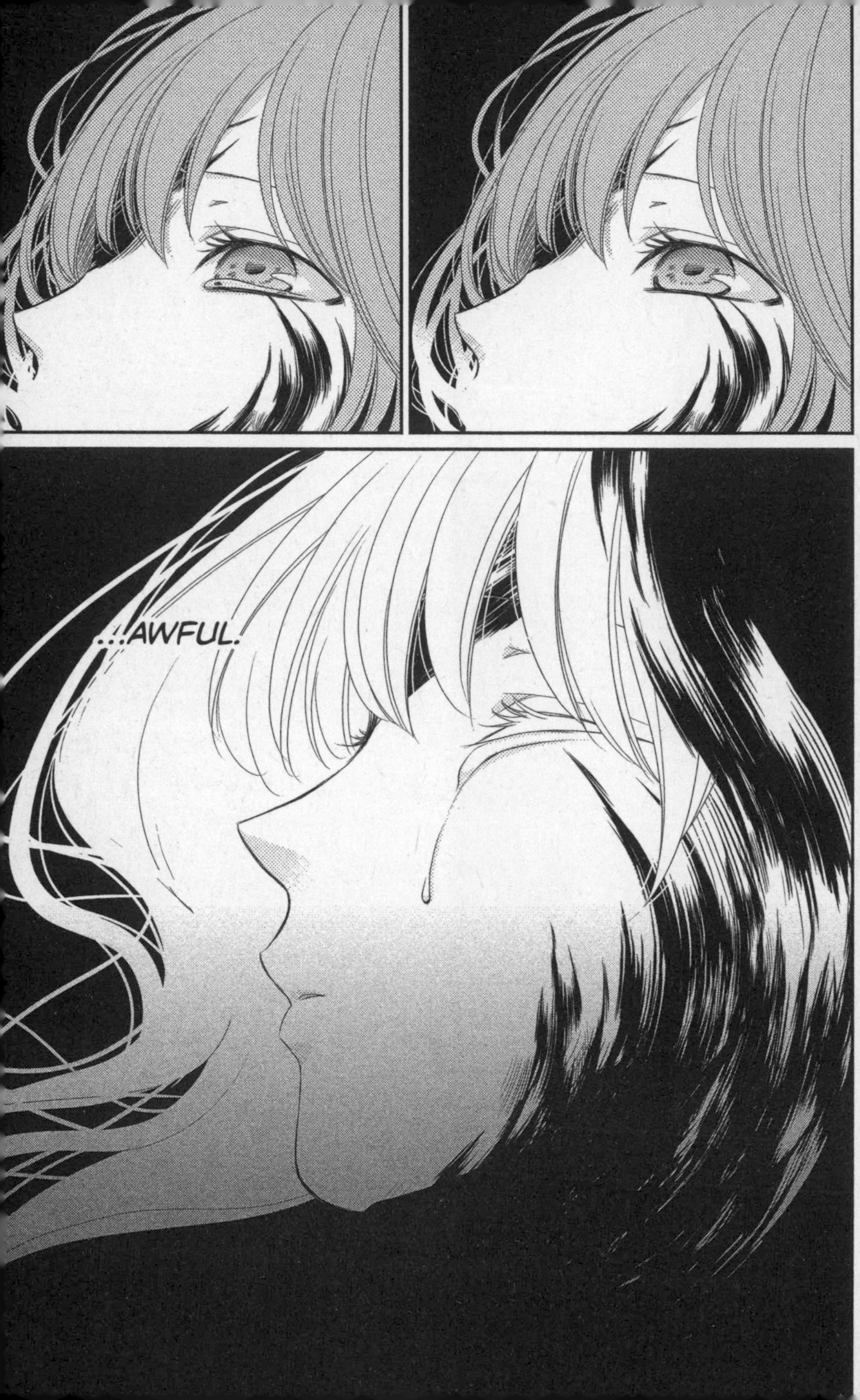
...AWFUL.

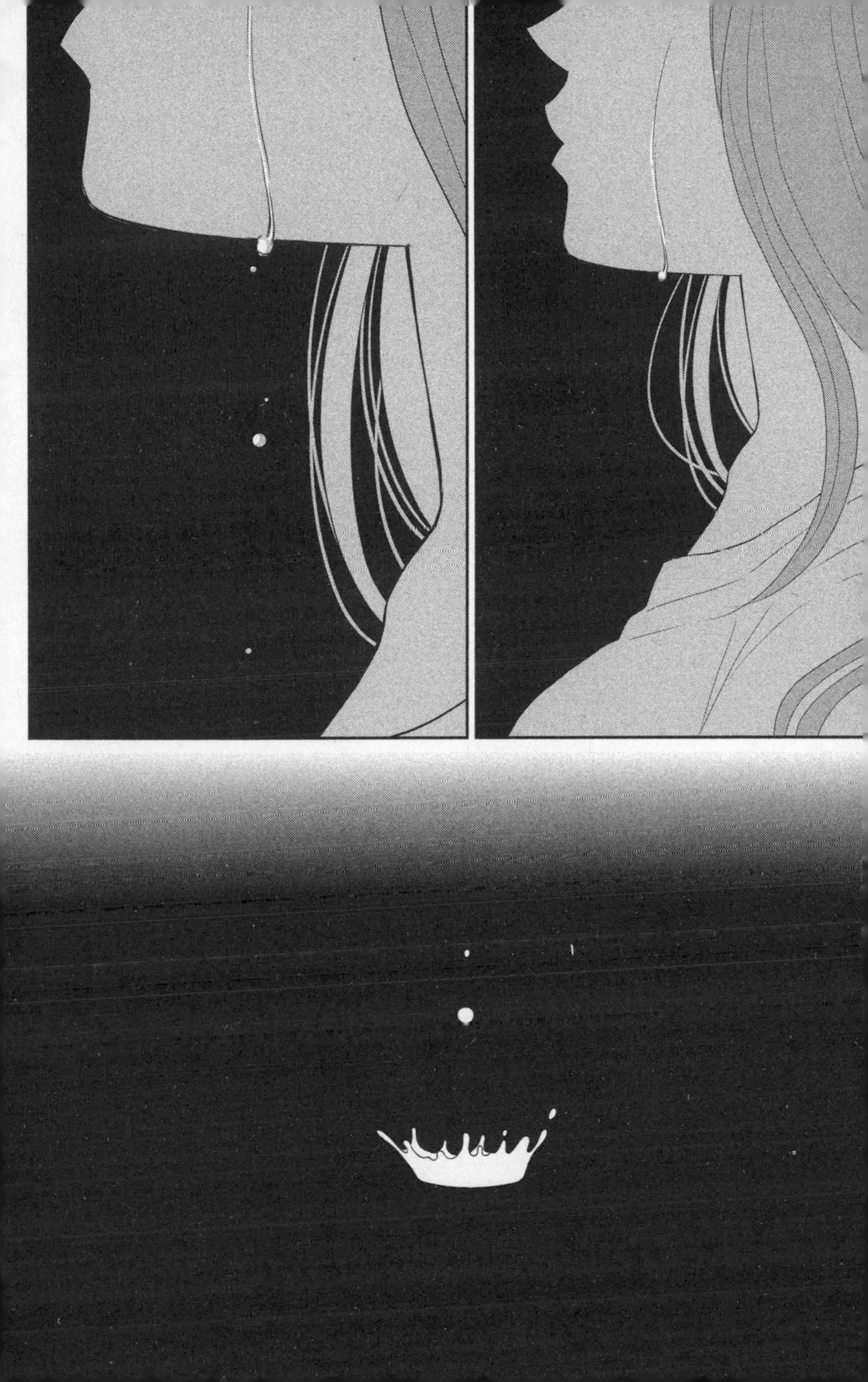

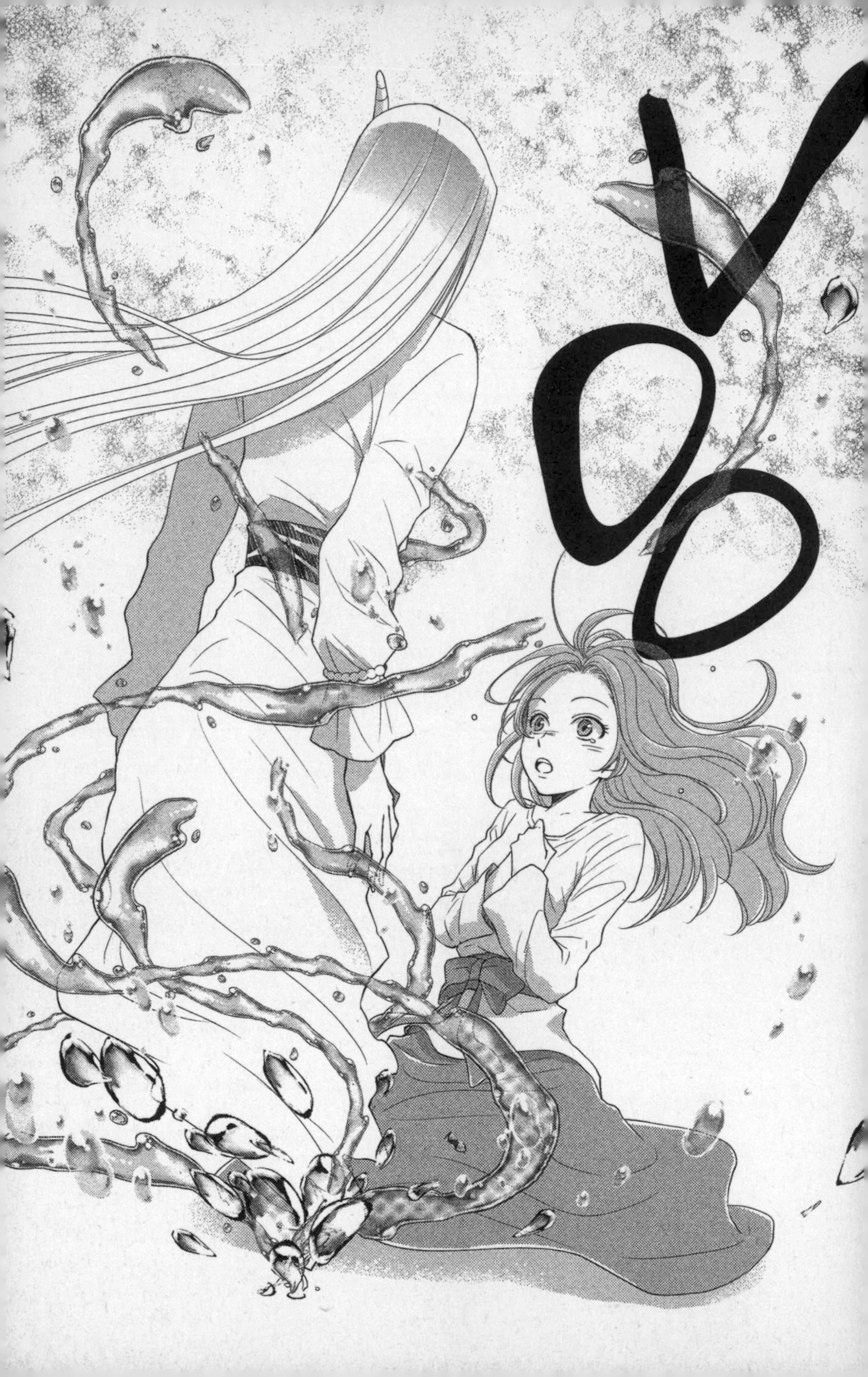
VOO

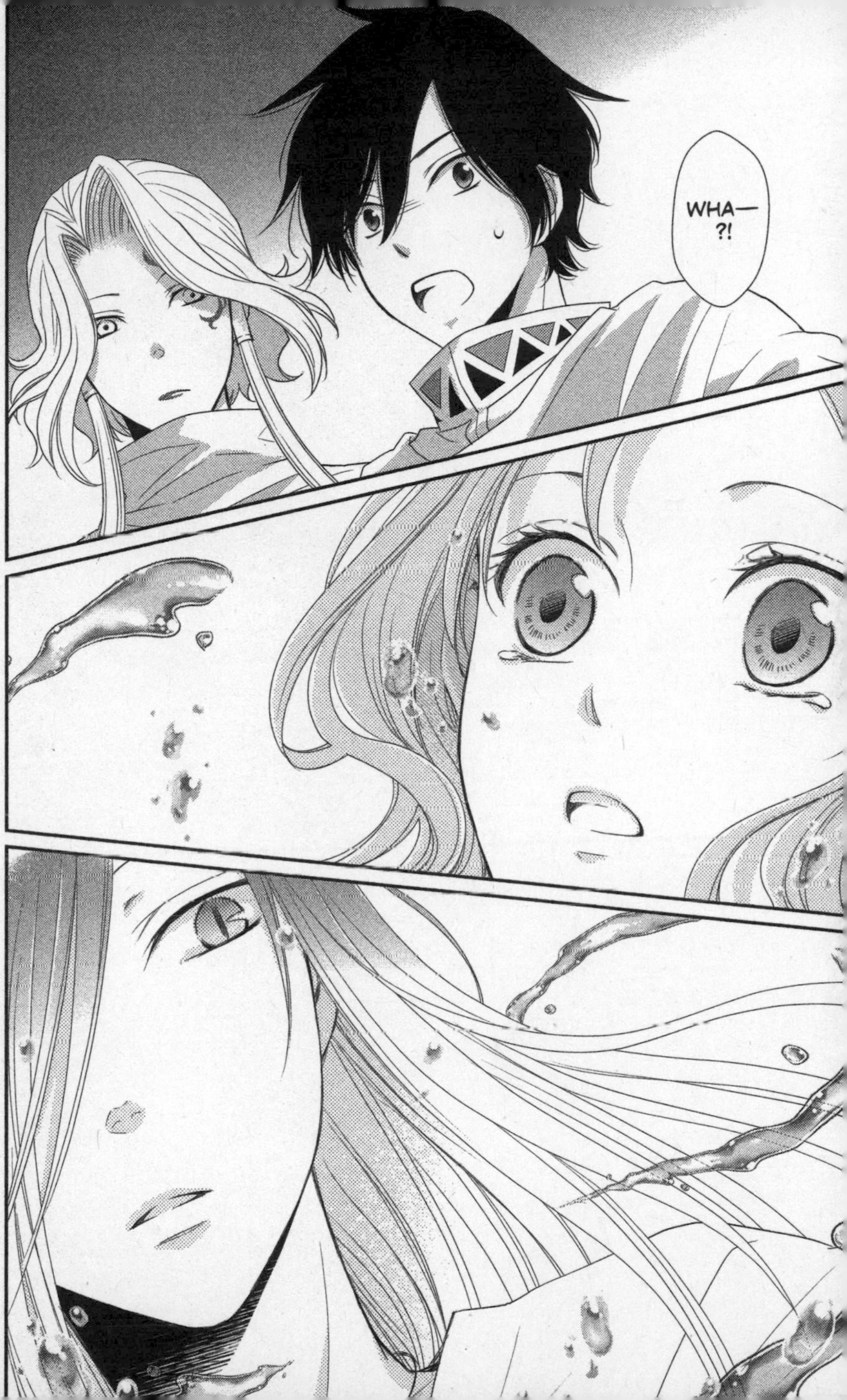
WHA—
?!

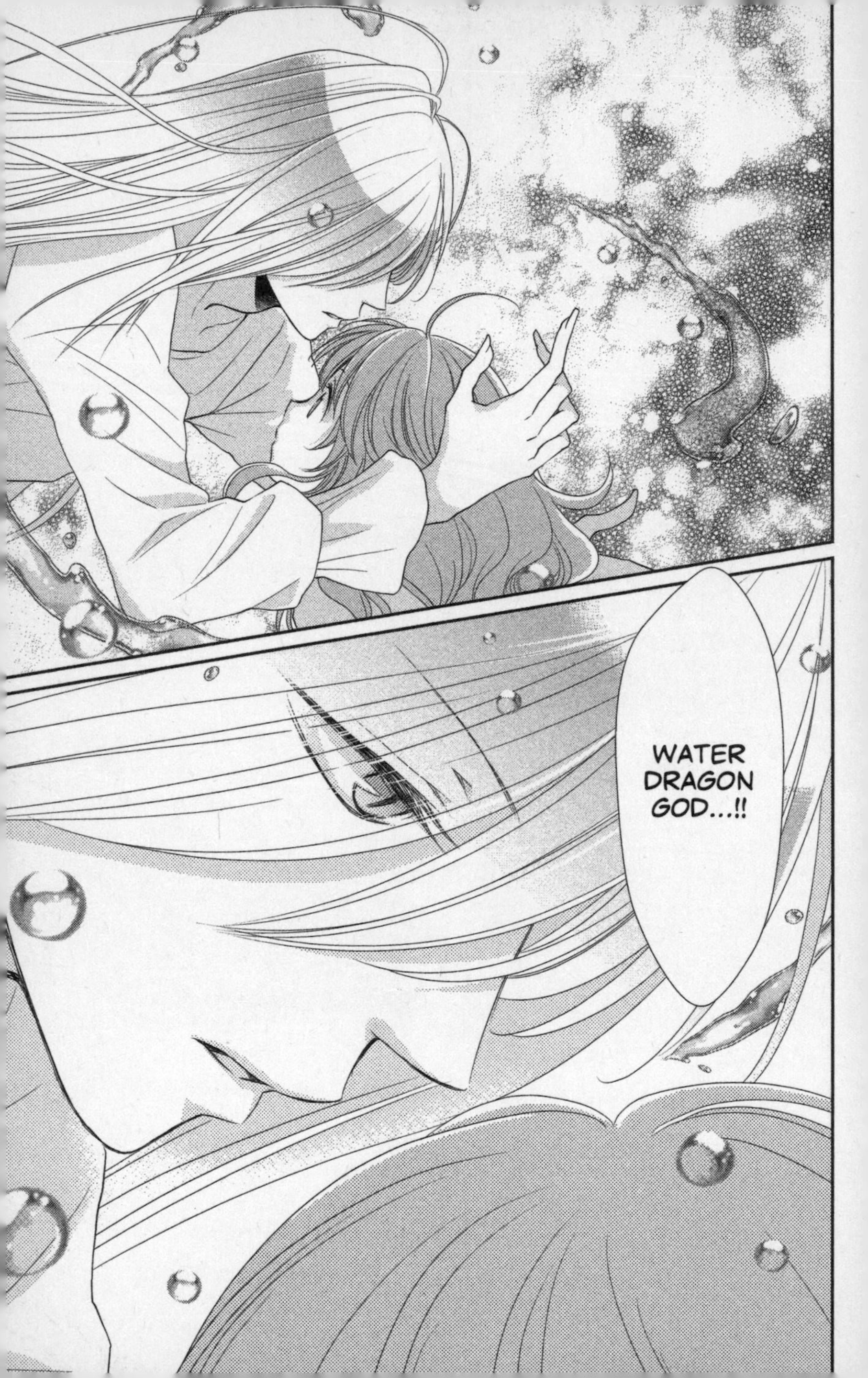
WATER DRAGON GOD...!!

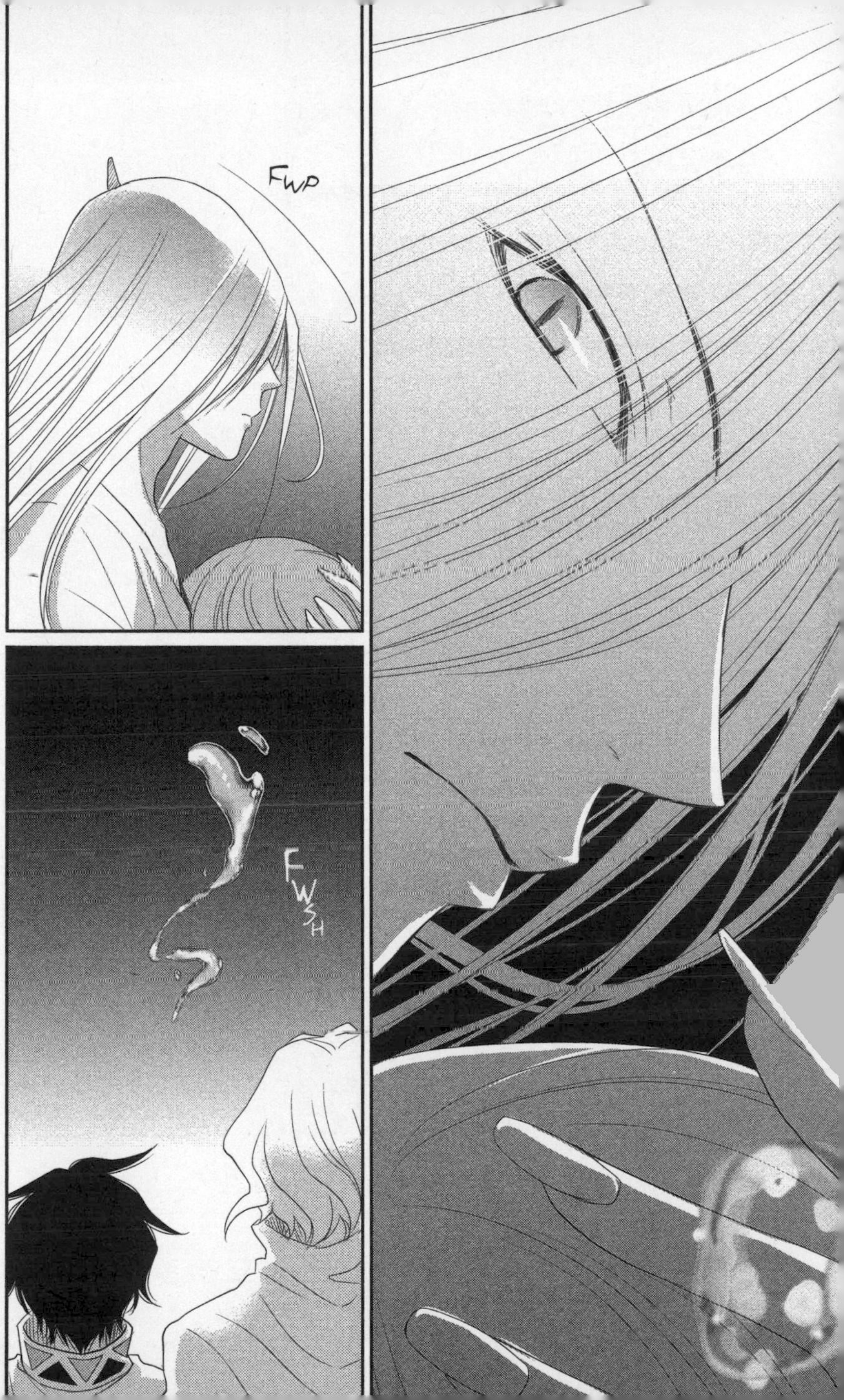
FWP
FWSH

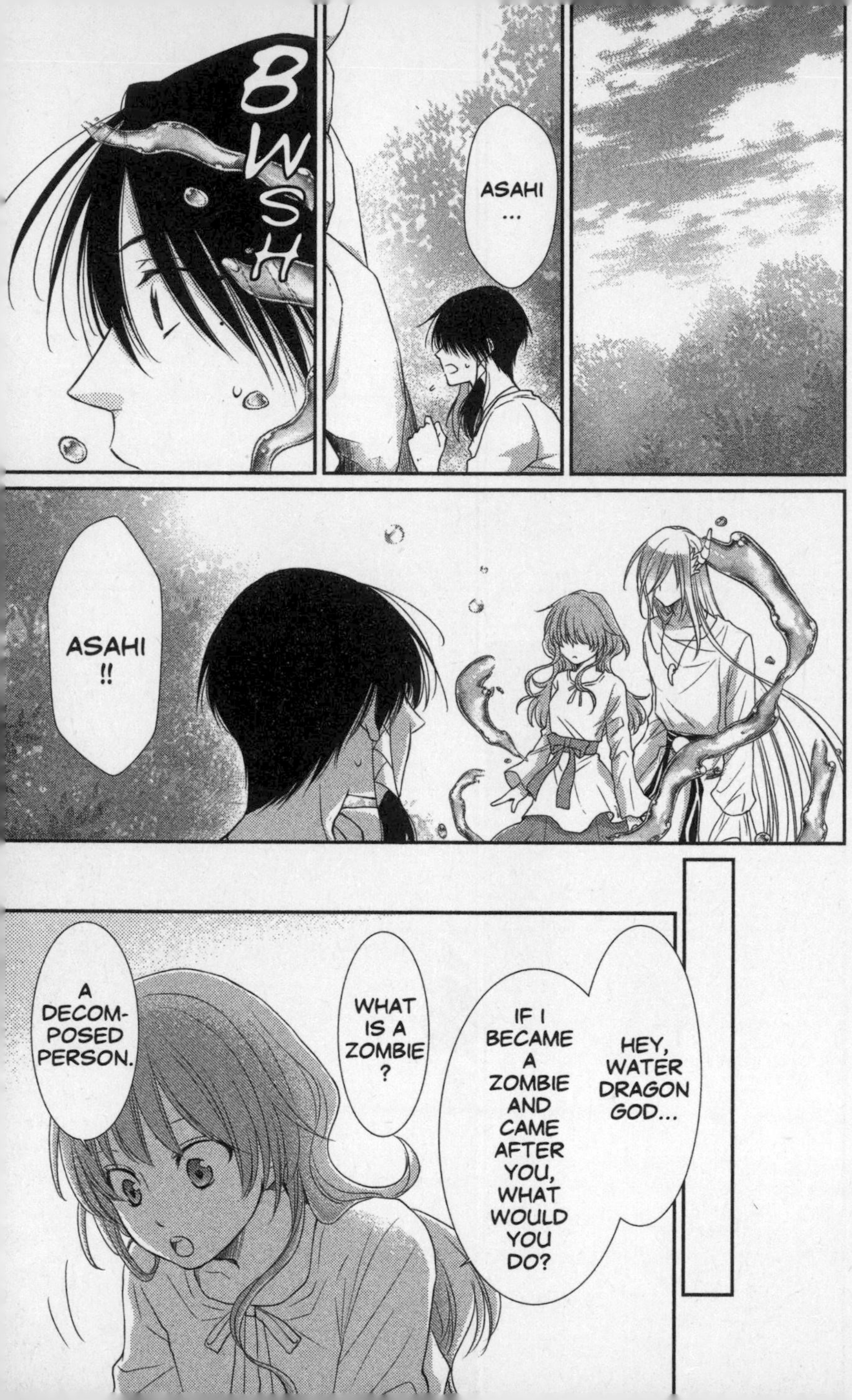
ASAHI ...
BWSH
ASAHI !!
HEY, WATER DRAGON GOD...
IF I BECAME A ZOMBIE AND CAME AFTER YOU, WHAT WOULD YOU DO?
WHAT IS A ZOMBIE?
A DECOMPOSED PERSON.

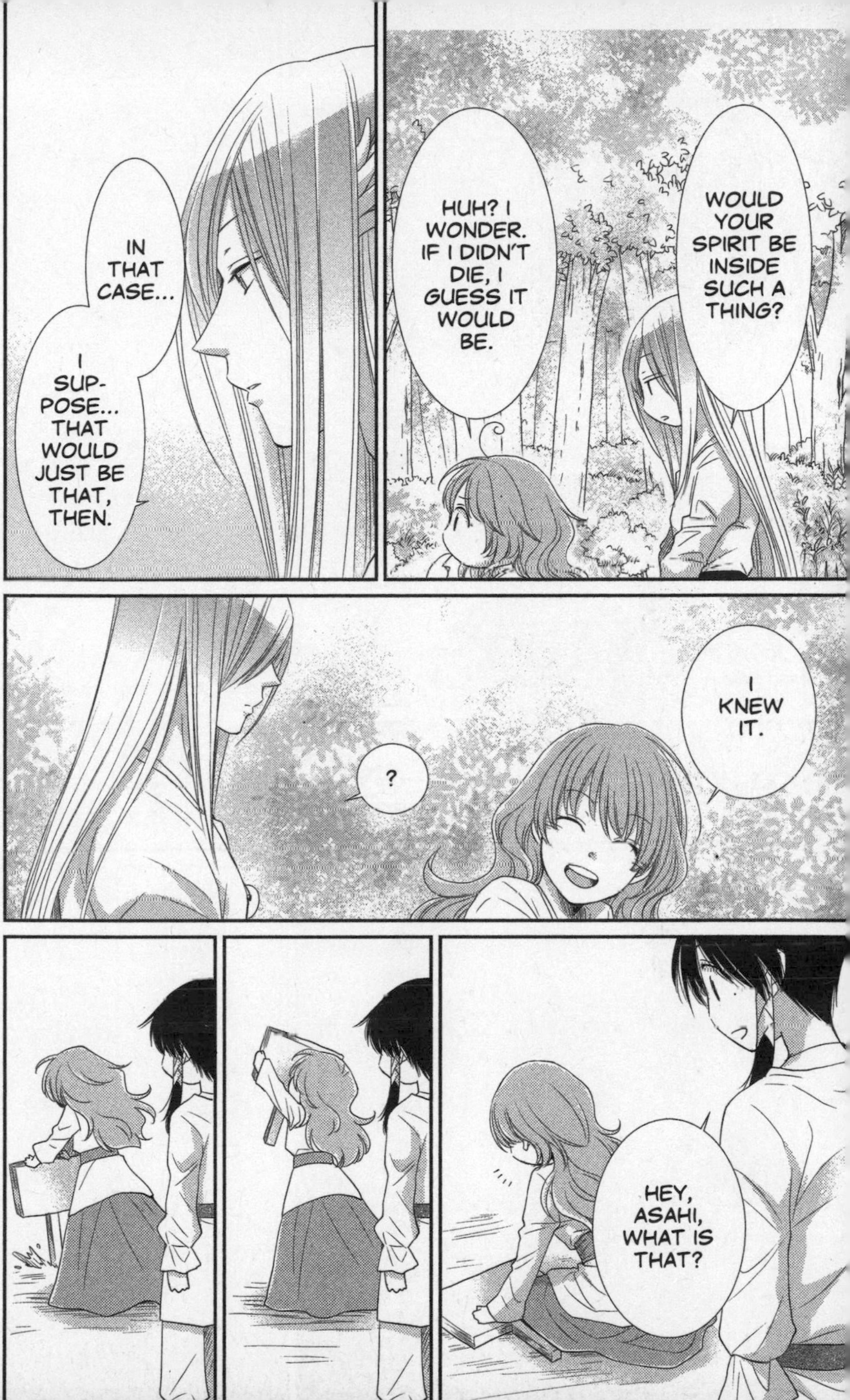
WOULD YOUR SPIRIT BE INSIDE SUCH A THING?
HUH? I WONDER. IF I DIDN'T DIE, I GUESS IT WOULD BE.
IN THAT CASE...
I SUP-POSE... THAT WOULD JUST BE THAT, THEN.
I KNEW IT.
?
HEY, ASAHI, WHAT IS THAT?

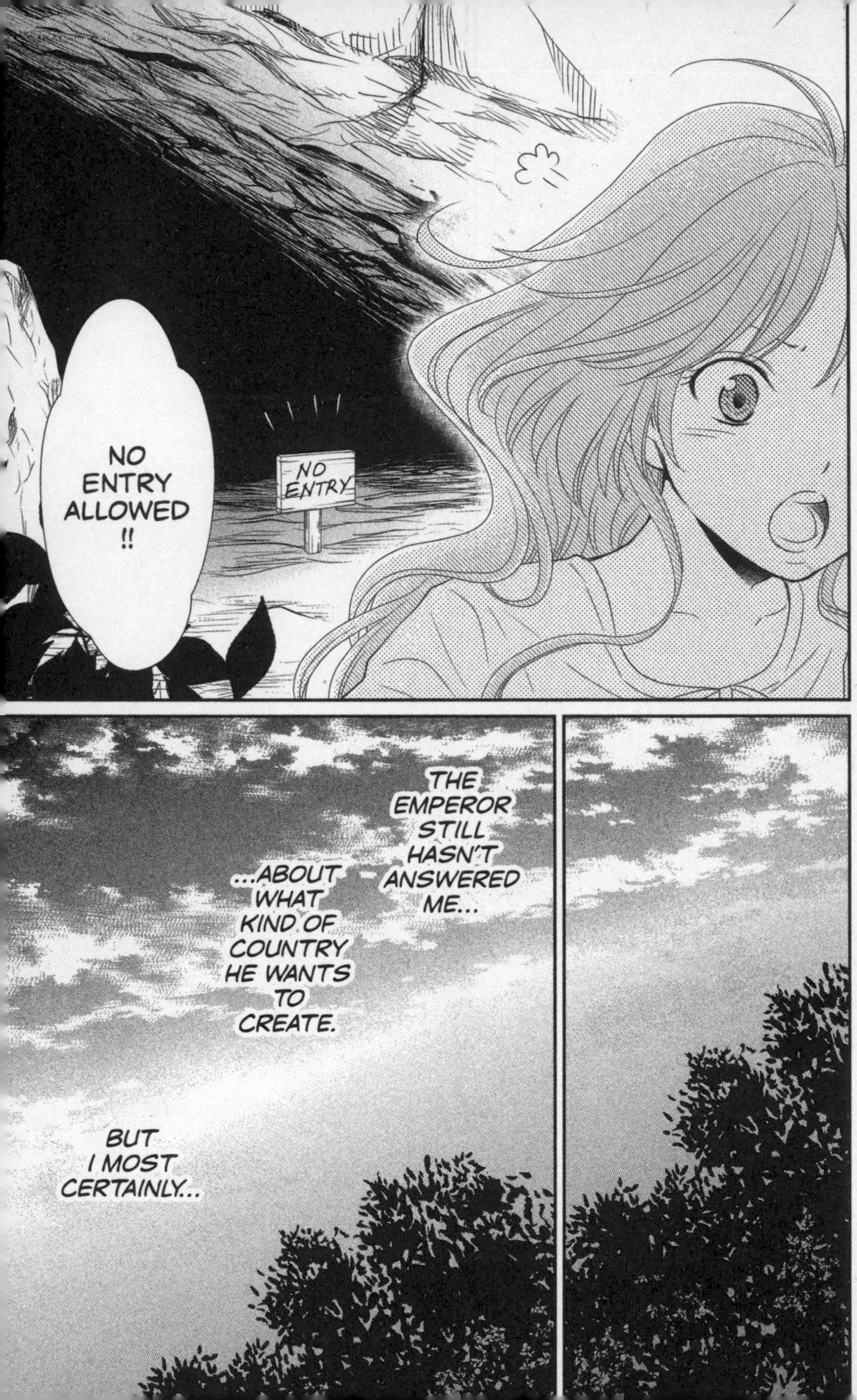
NO ENTRY ALLOWED !!
NO ENTRY
THE EMPEROR STILL HASN'T ANSWERED ME...
...ABOUT WHAT KIND OF COUNTRY HE WANTS TO CREATE.
BUT I MOST CERTAINLY...

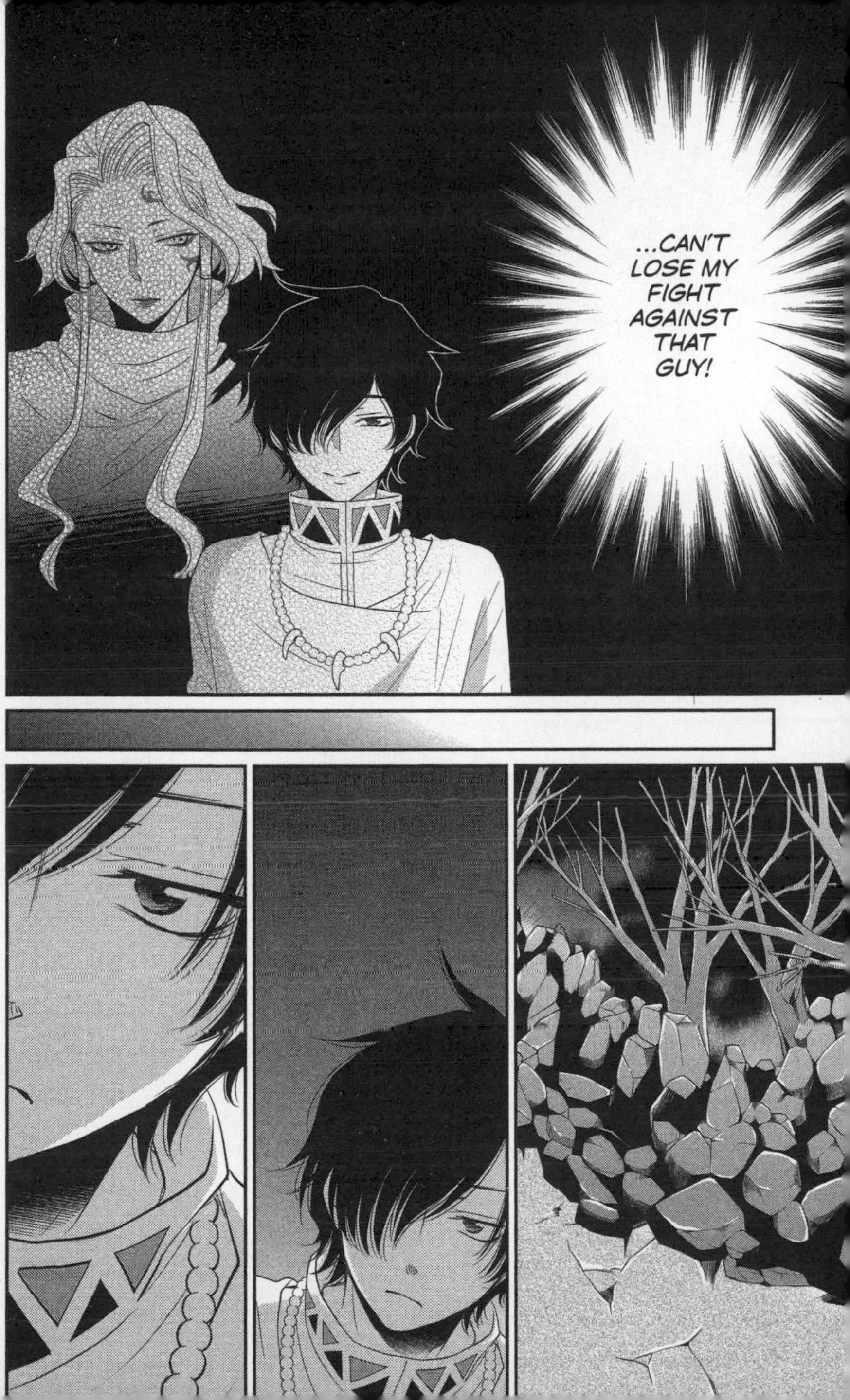
...CAN'T LOSE MY FIGHT AGAINST THAT GUY!

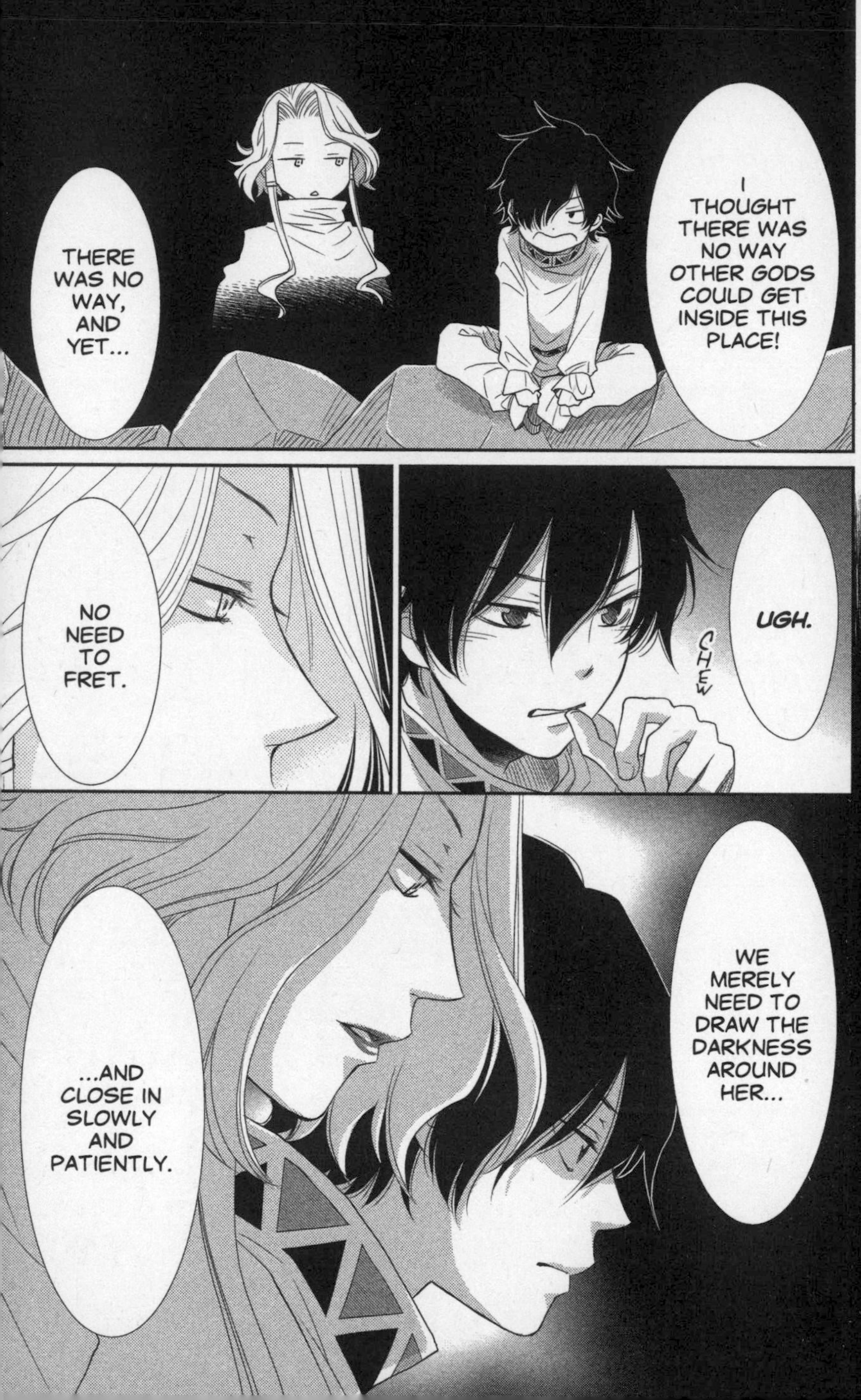
I THOUGHT THERE WAS NO WAY OTHER GODS COULD GET INSIDE THIS PLACE!
THERE WAS NO WAY, AND YET...
UGH.
CHEW
NO NEED TO FRET.
WE MERELY NEED TO DRAW THE DARKNESS AROUND HER...
...AND CLOSE IN SLOWLY AND PATIENTLY.

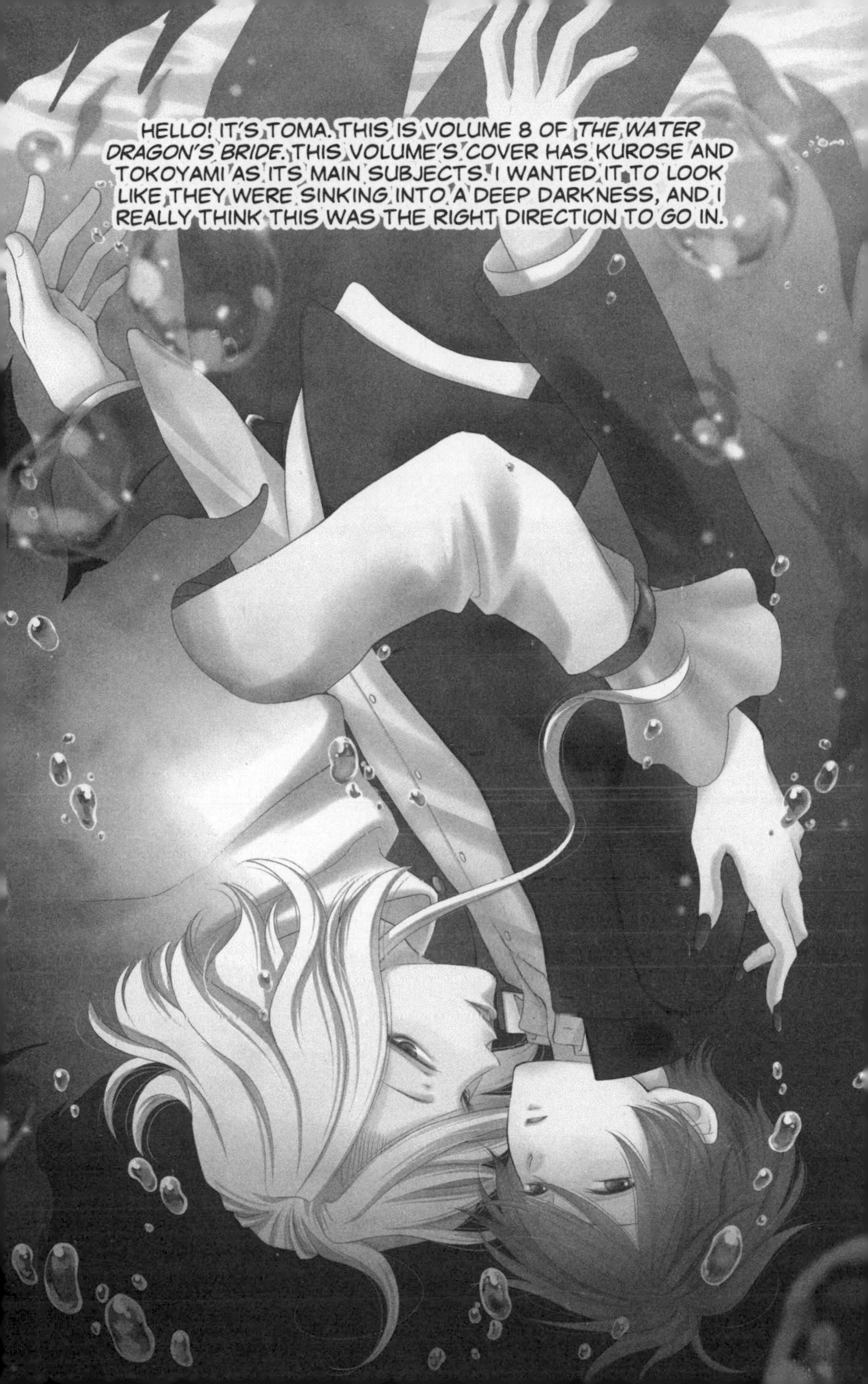
HELLO! IT'S TOMA. THIS IS VOLUME 8 OF THE WATER DRAGON'S BRIDE. THIS VOLUME'S COVER HAS KUROSE AND TOKOYAMI AS ITS MAIN SUBJECTS. I WANTED IT TO LOOK LIKE THEY WERE SINKING INTO A DEEP DARKNESS, AND I REALLY THINK THIS WAS THE RIGHT DIRECTION TO GO IN.

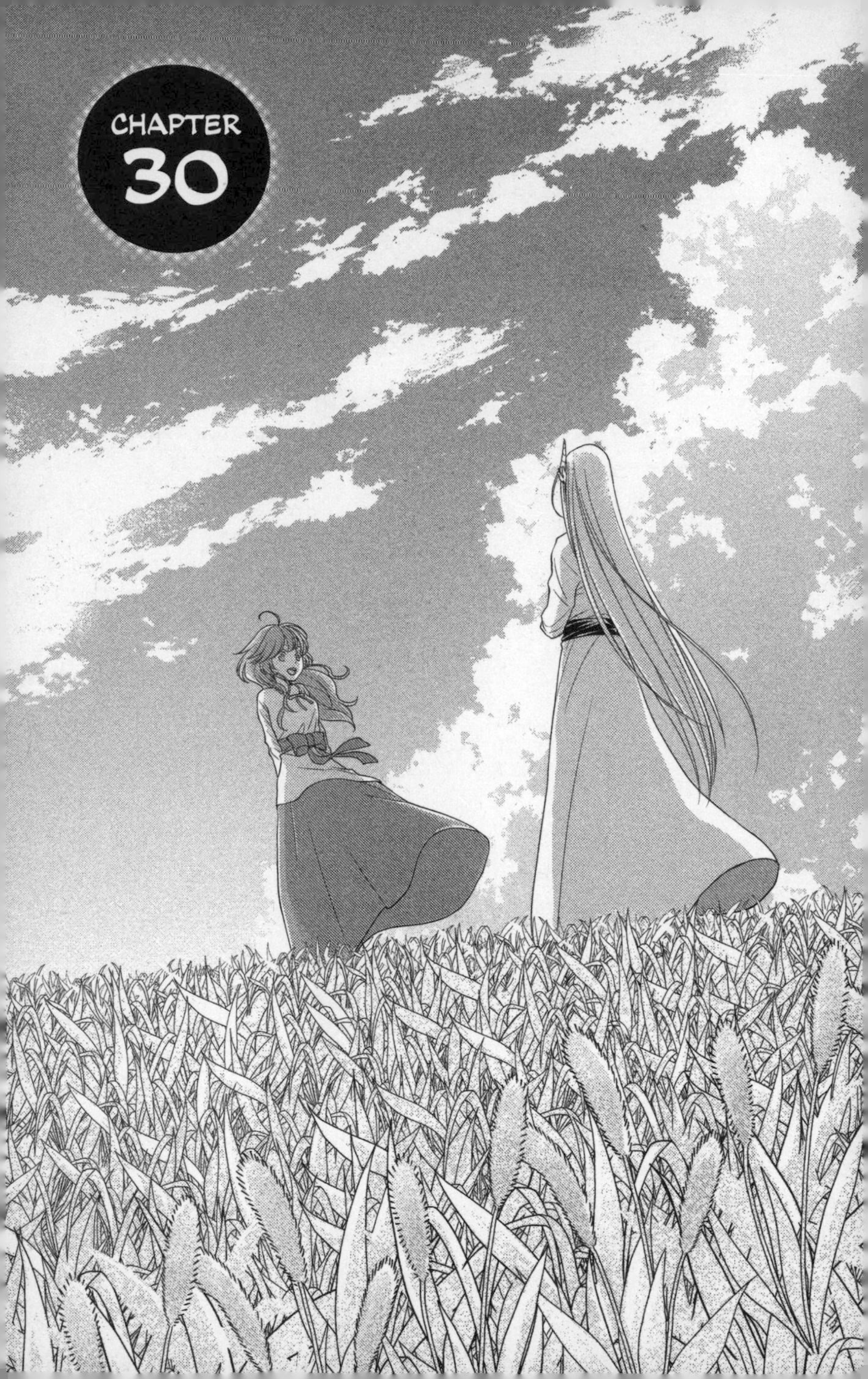
CHAPTER
30

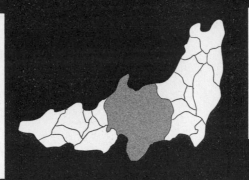

THIS CONTINENT HAS 20 COUNTRIES IN IT.
THE LARGEST IS THE COUNTRY OF NAGA, AND THE OTHER COUNTRIES ARE OF VARIOUS SIZES.
THE NEIGHBORING COUNTRIES CONSTANTLY WAGE WAR ON NAGA IN AN ATTEMPT TO EXPAND THEIR TERRITORY.
IT IS SAID THAT THEY WERE NOT DOING THIS DURING THE REIGN OF THE FATHER OF THE CURRENT EMPEROR OF NAGA...
...AND THAT IS WHY THINGS WERE SO PEACE-FUL THEN.
THAT GAVE THE COUNTRIES AROUND NAGA MORE TIME TO GROW IN POWER.

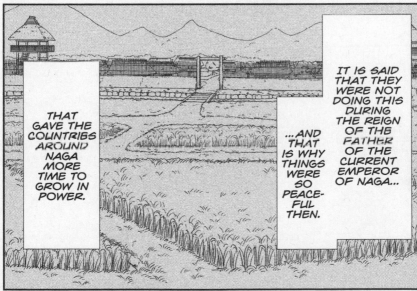

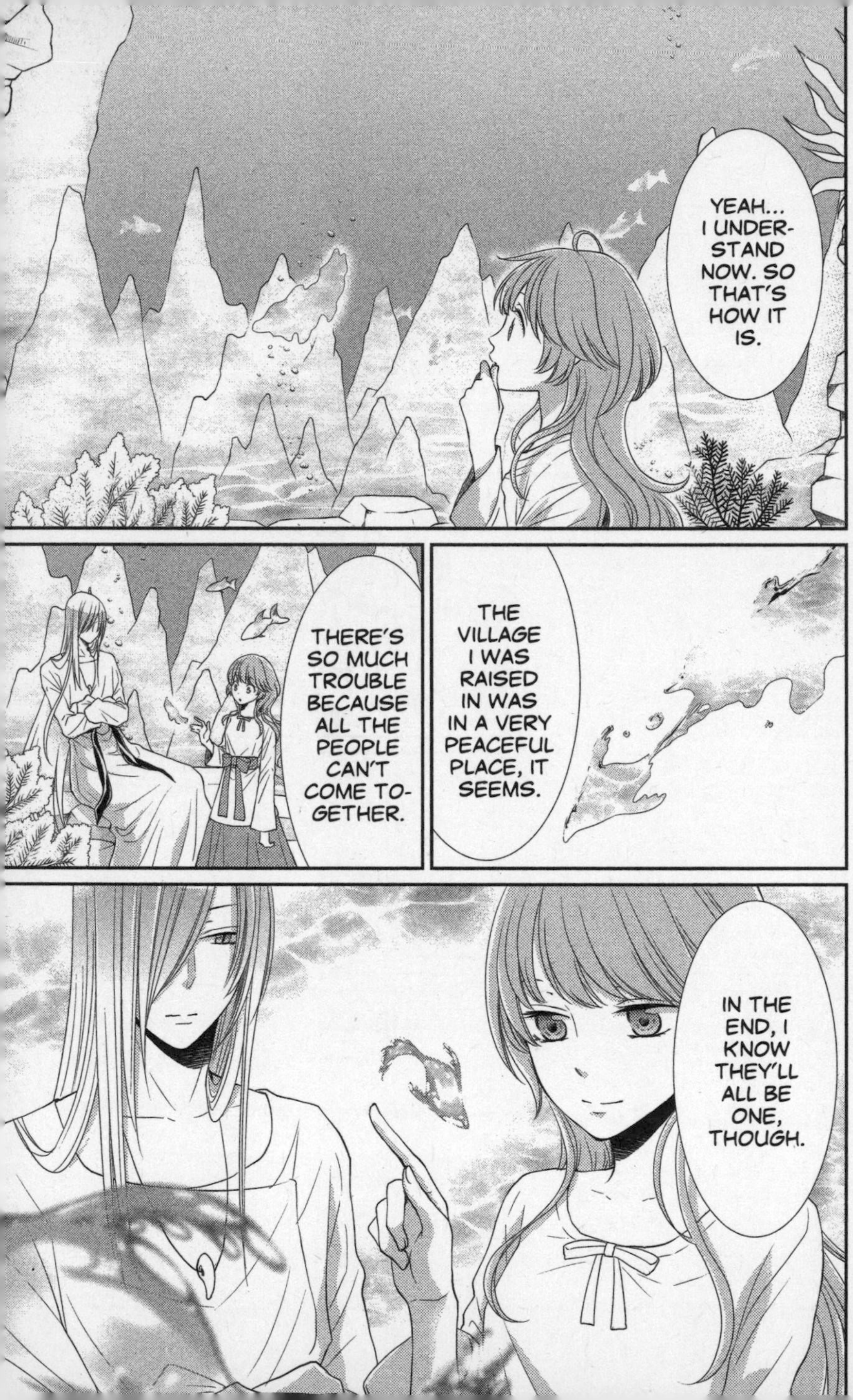
YEAH... I UNDERSTAND NOW. SO THAT'S HOW IT IS.
THE VILLAGE I WAS RAISED IN WAS IN A VERY PEACEFUL PLACE, IT SEEMS.
THERE'S SO MUCH TROUBLE BECAUSE ALL THE PEOPLE CAN'T COME TOGETHER.
IN THE END, I KNOW THEY'LL ALL BE ONE, THOUGH.

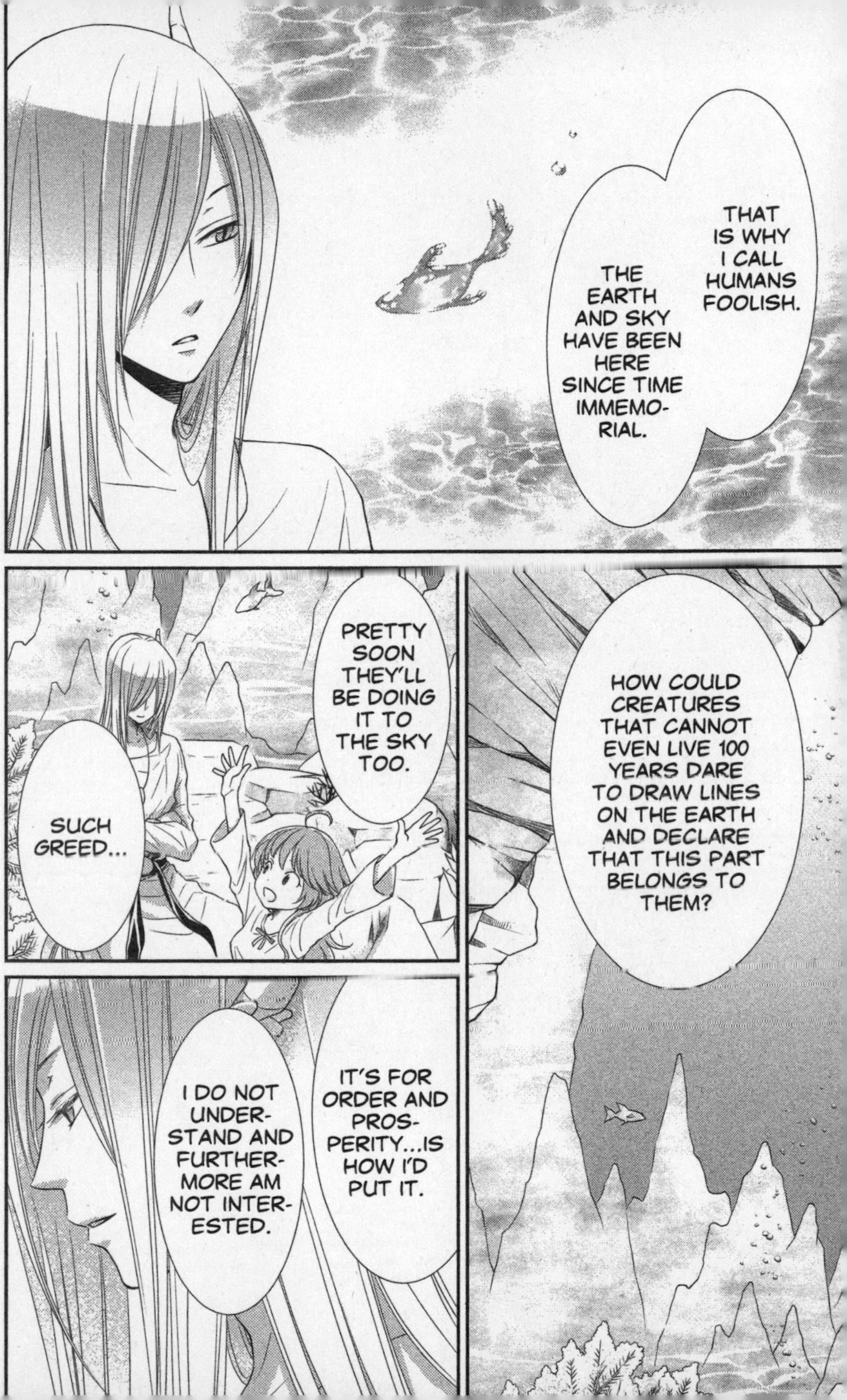
THAT IS WHY I CALL HUMANS FOOLISH.
THE EARTH AND SKY HAVE BEEN HERE SINCE TIME IMMEMORIAL.
HOW COULD CREATURES THAT CANNOT EVEN LIVE 100 YEARS DARE TO DRAW LINES ON THE EARTH AND DECLARE THAT THIS PART BELONGS TO THEM?
PRETTY SOON THEY'LL BE DOING IT TO THE SKY TOO.
SUCH GREED...
IT'S FOR ORDER AND PROSPERITY...IS HOW I'D PUT IT.
I DO NOT UNDERSTAND AND FURTHERMORE AM NOT INTERESTED.

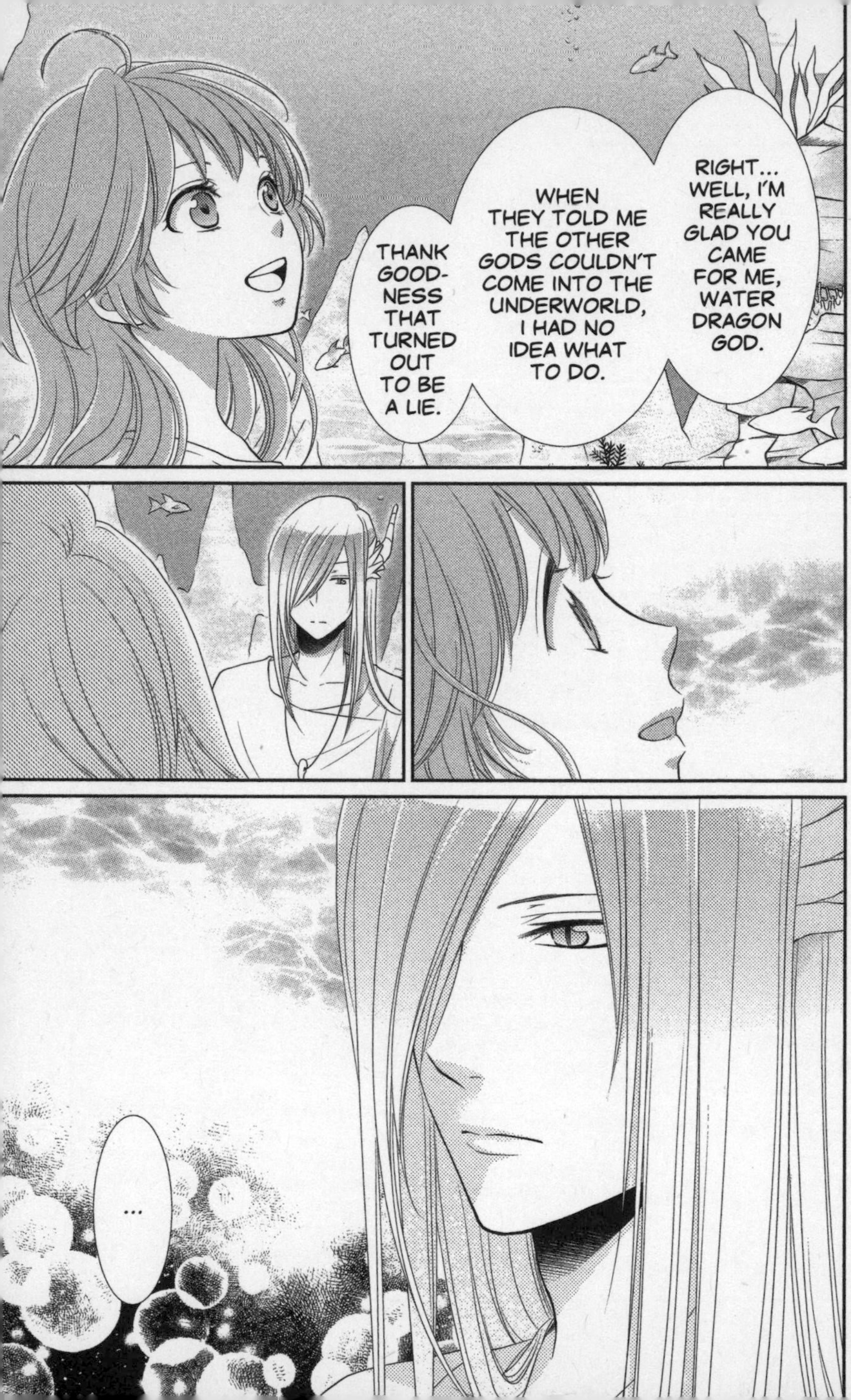
RIGHT... WELL, I'M REALLY GLAD YOU CAME FOR ME, WATER DRAGON GOD.
WHEN THEY TOLD ME THE OTHER GODS COULDN'T COME INTO THE UNDERWORLD, I HAD NO IDEA WHAT TO DO.
THANK GOOD-NESS THAT TURNED OUT TO BE A LIE.
...

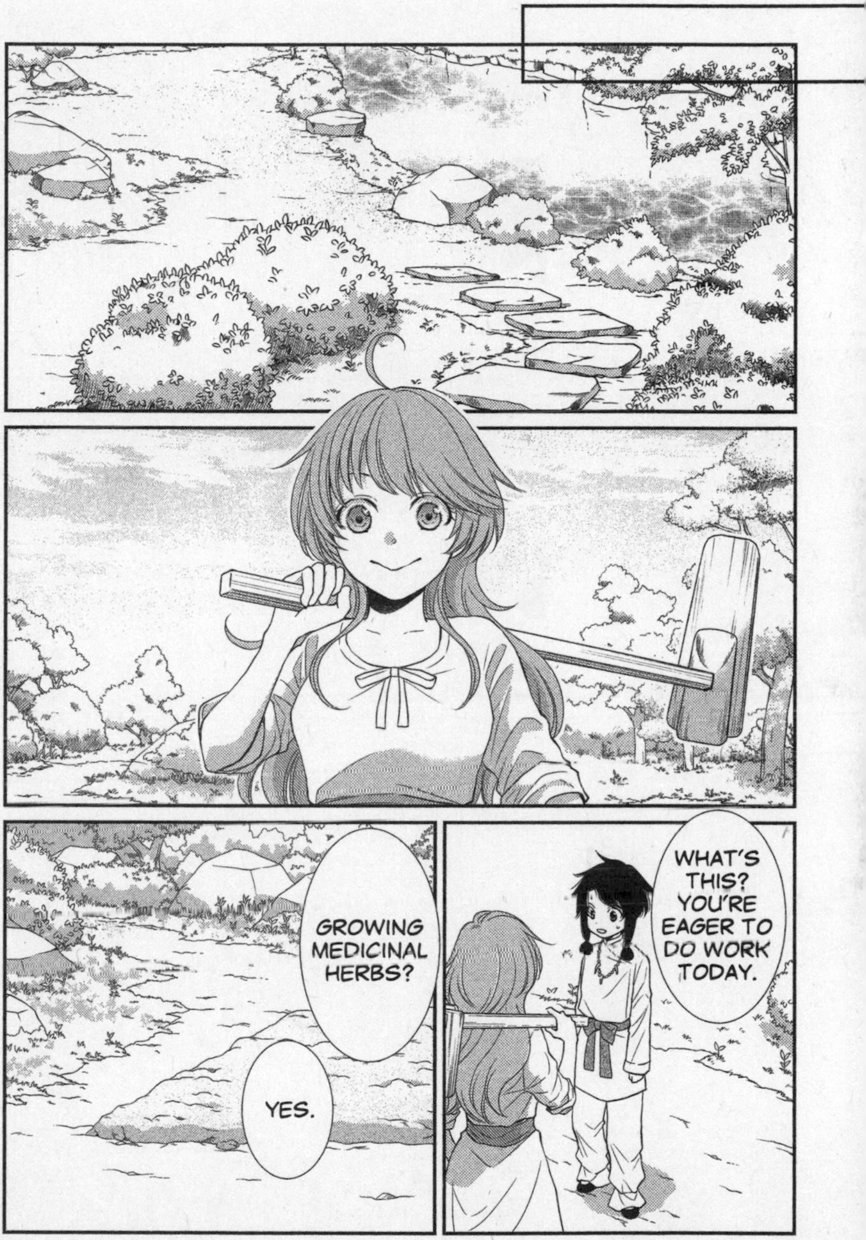
WHAT'S THIS? YOU'RE EAGER TO DO WORK TODAY.
GROWING MEDICINAL HERBS?
YES.

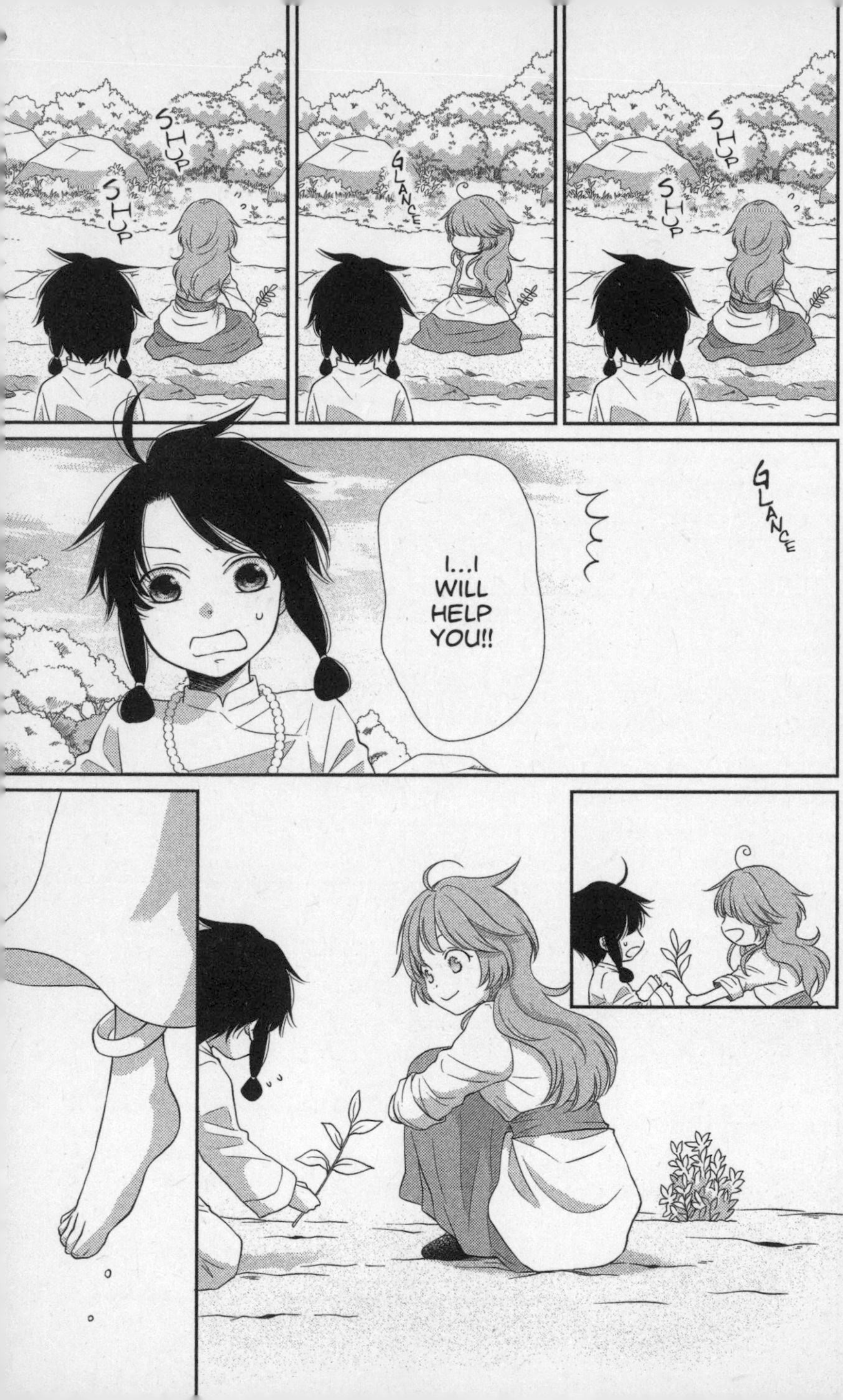
SHUP
SHUP
GLANCE
SHUP
SHUP
GLANCE
I...I WILL HELP YOU!!

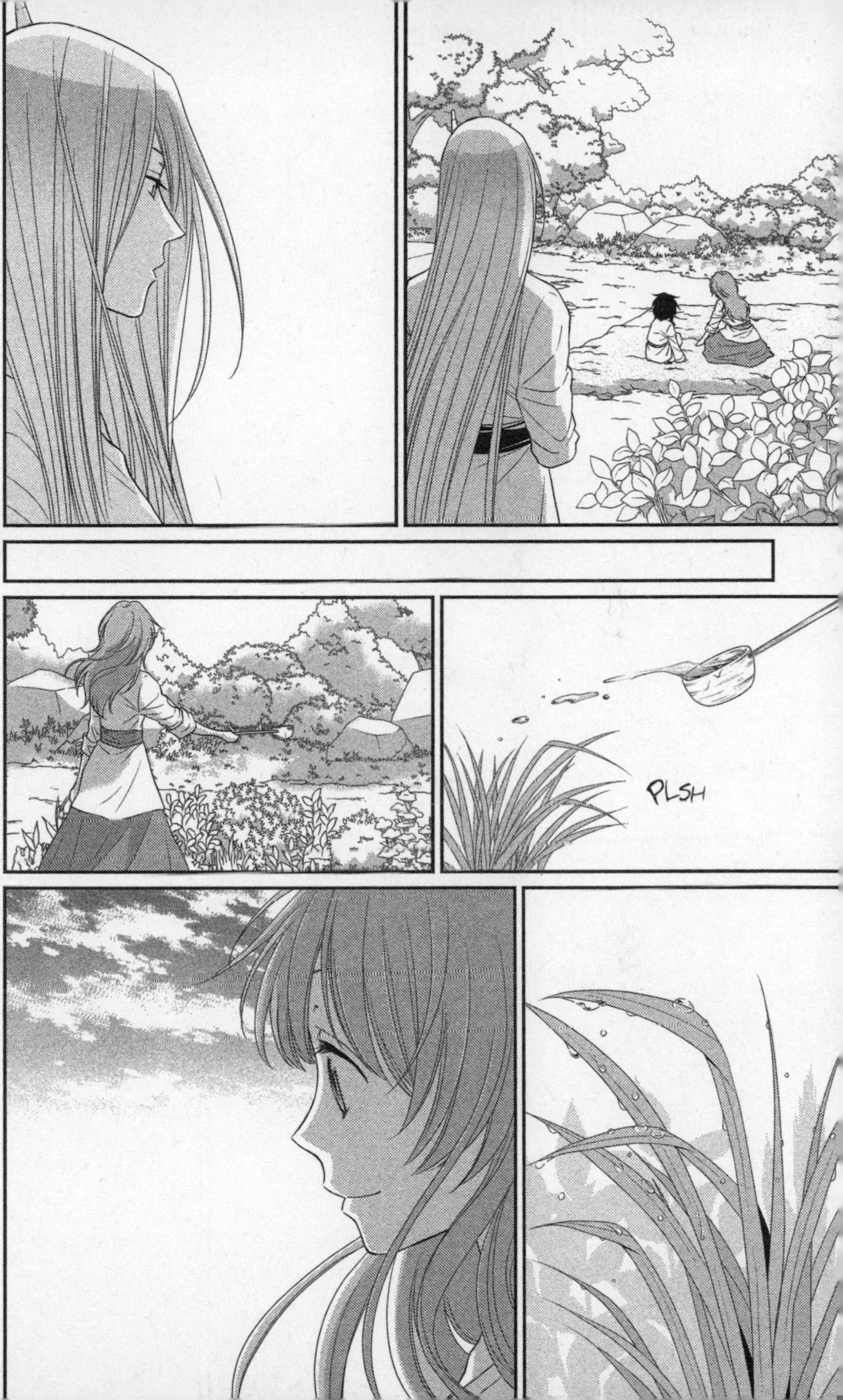
PLSH

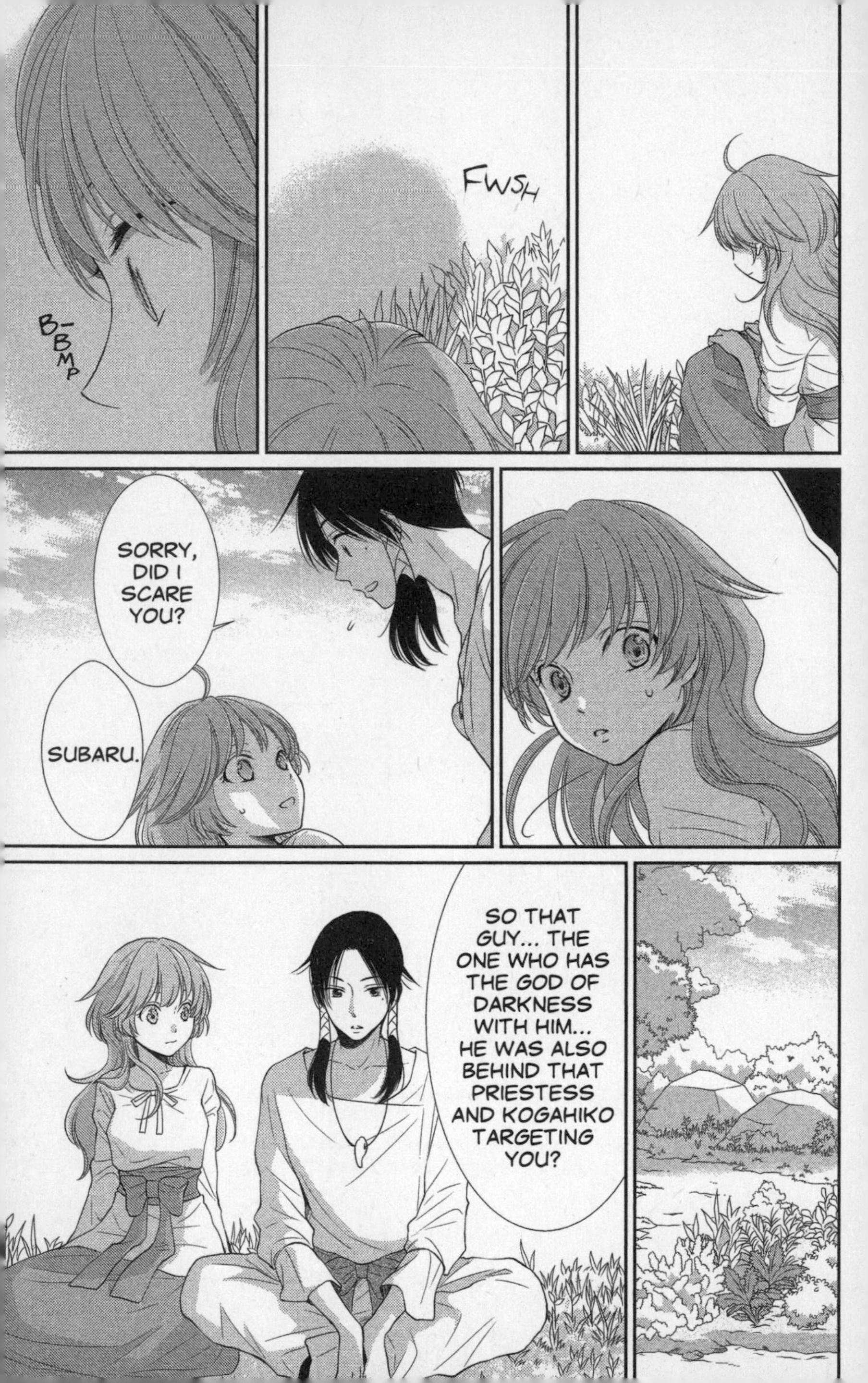
FWSH
B-BMP
SORRY, DID I SCARE YOU?
SUBARU.
SO THAT GUY... THE ONE WHO HAS THE GOD OF DARKNESS WITH HIM... HE WAS ALSO BEHIND THAT PRIESTESS AND KOGAHIKO TARGETING YOU?

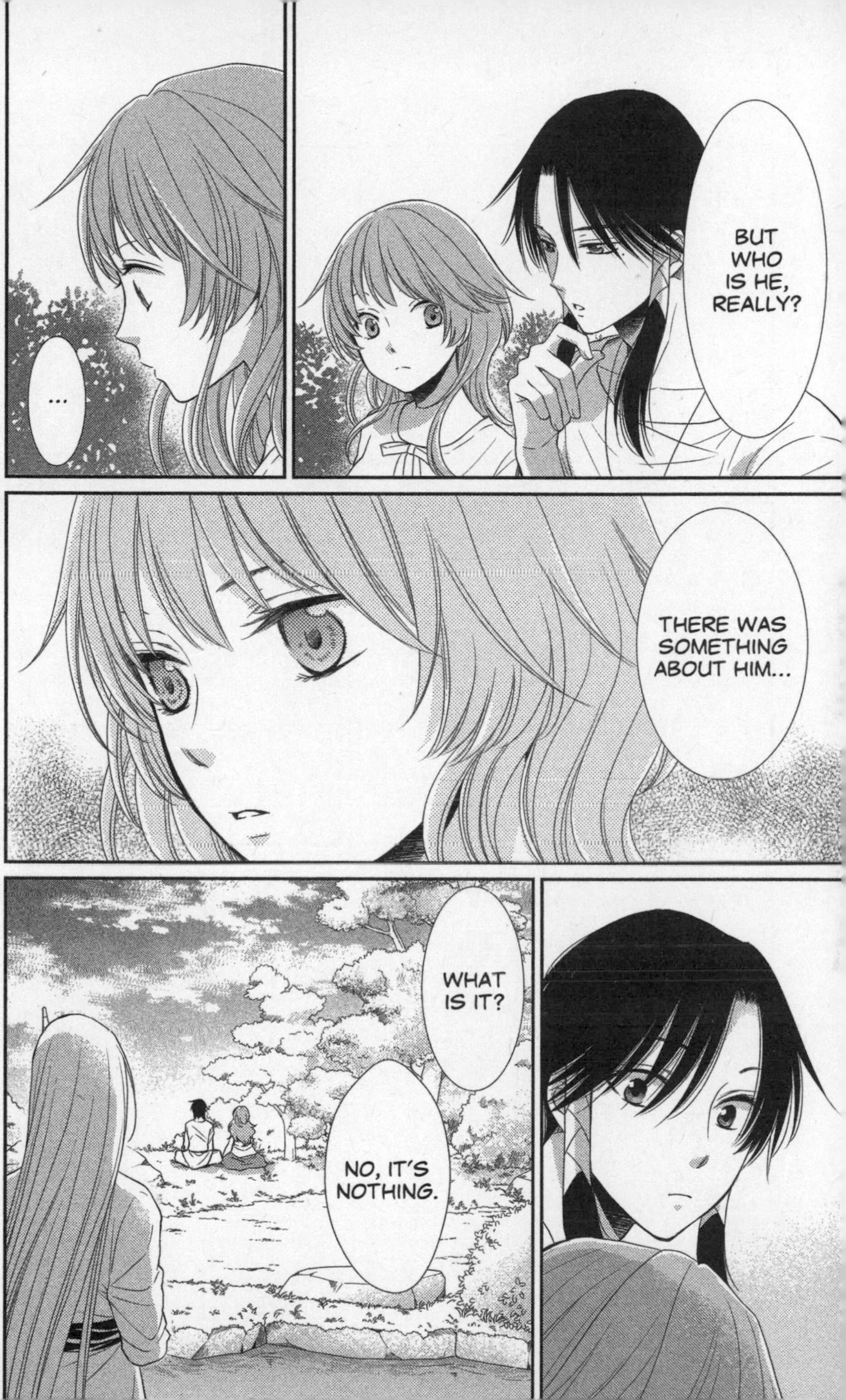
BUT WHO IS HE, REALLY?
...
THERE WAS SOMETHING ABOUT HIM...
WHAT IS IT?
NO, IT'S NOTHING.

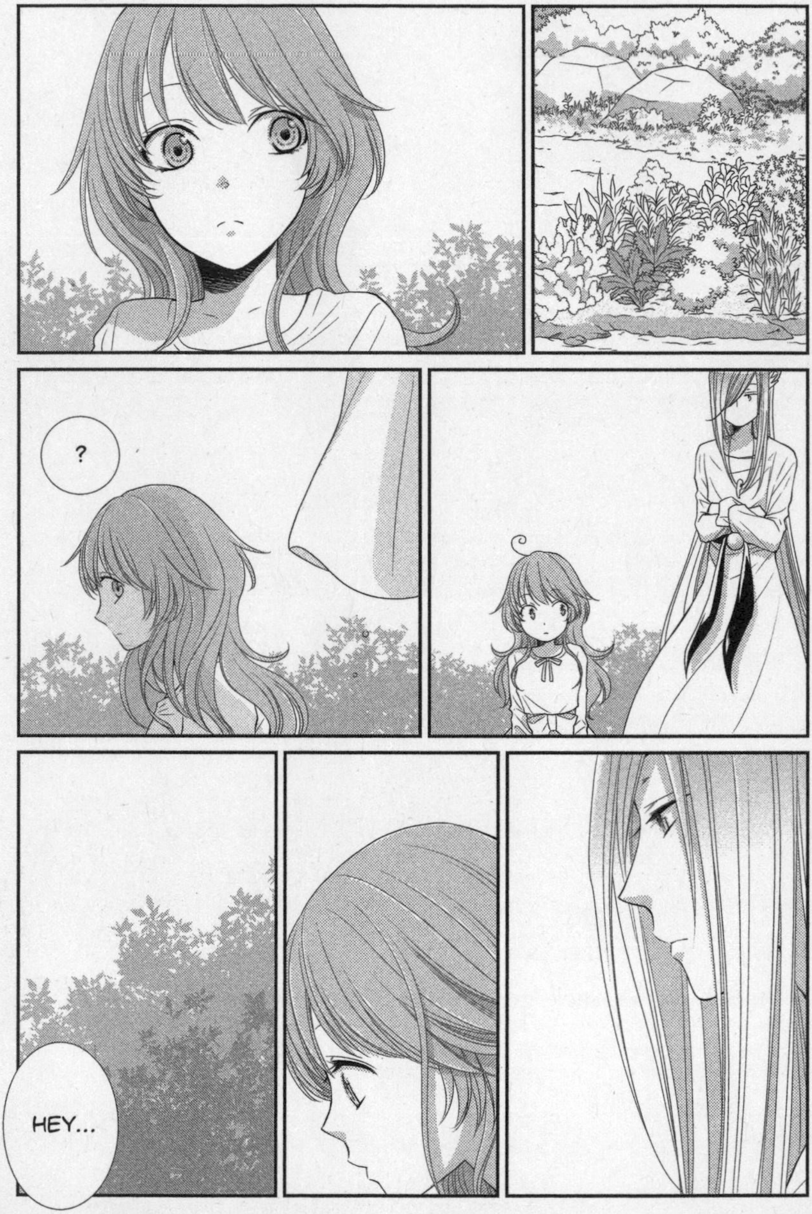
?
HEY...

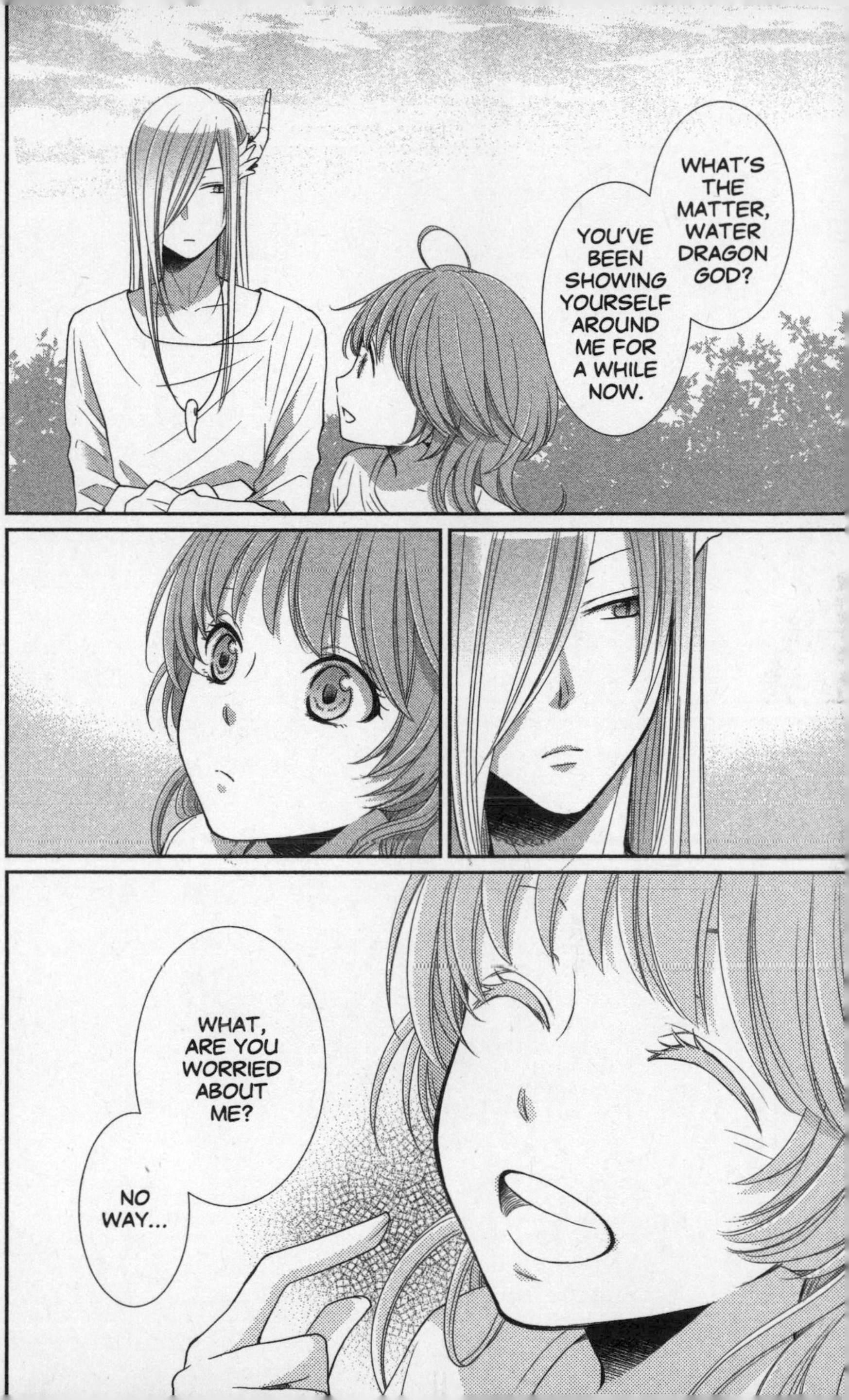
WHAT'S THE MATTER, WATER DRAGON GOD?
YOU'VE BEEN SHOWING YOURSELF AROUND ME FOR A WHILE NOW.
WHAT, ARE YOU WORRIED ABOUT ME?
NO WAY...

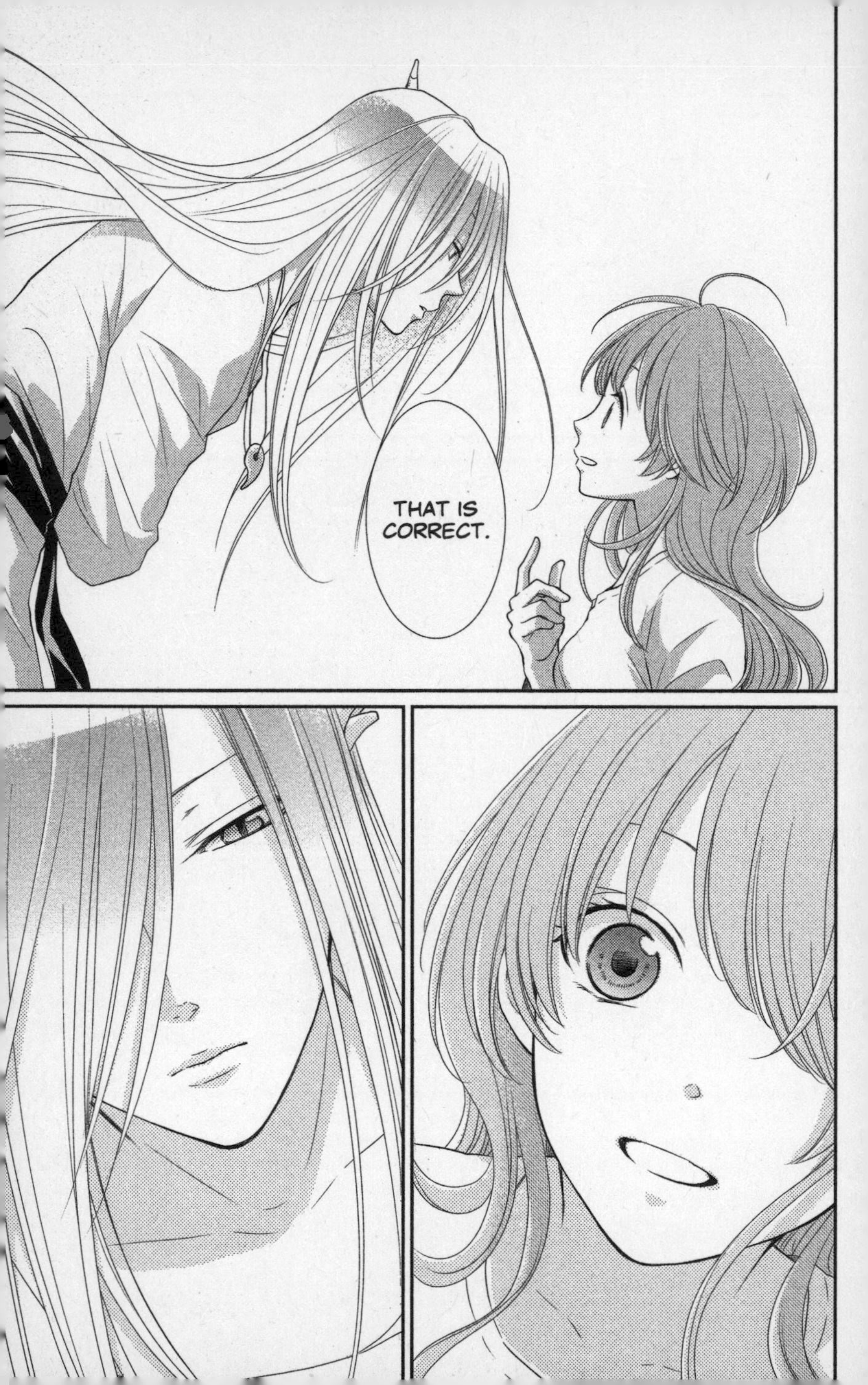
THAT IS CORRECT.

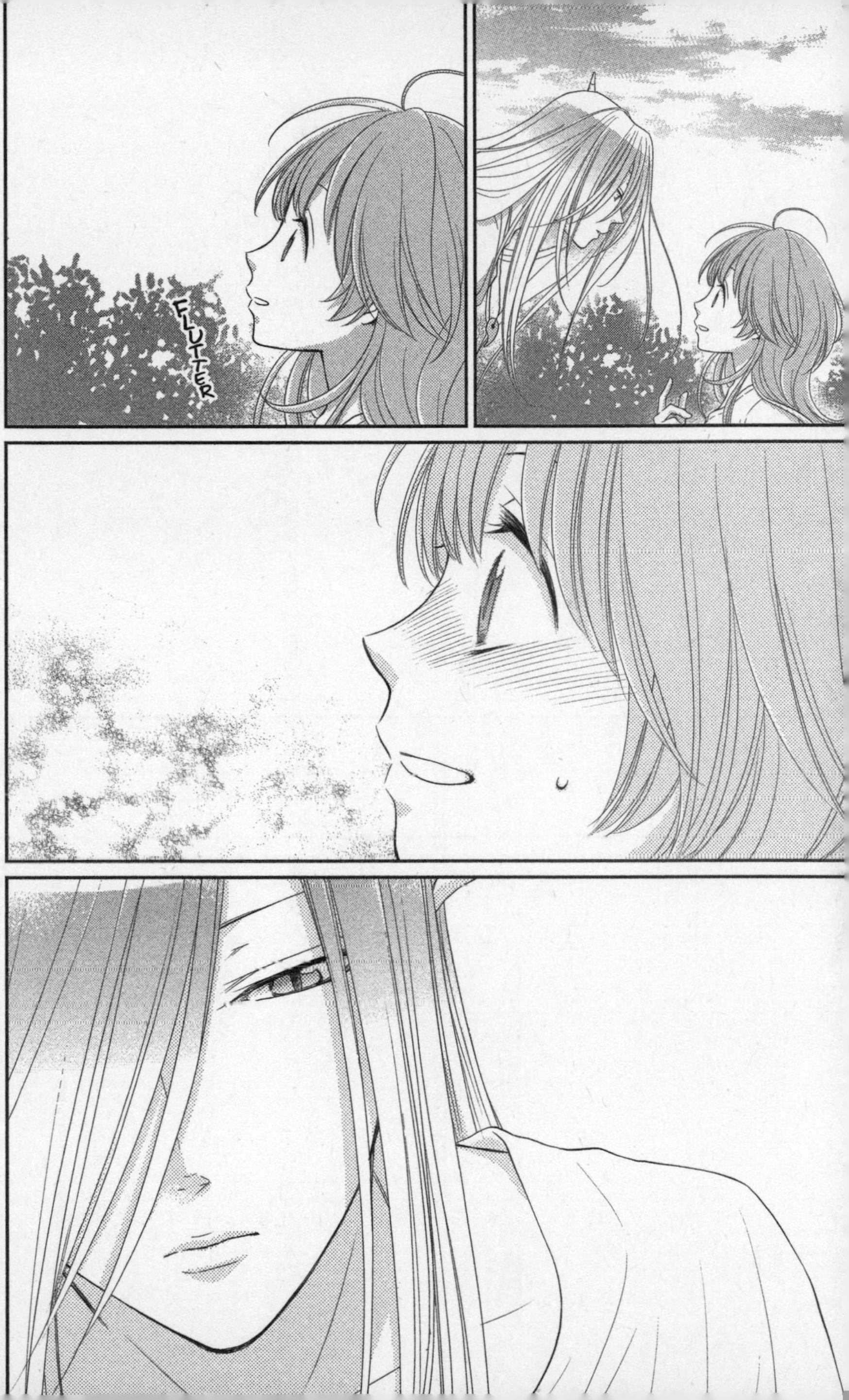
FLUTTER

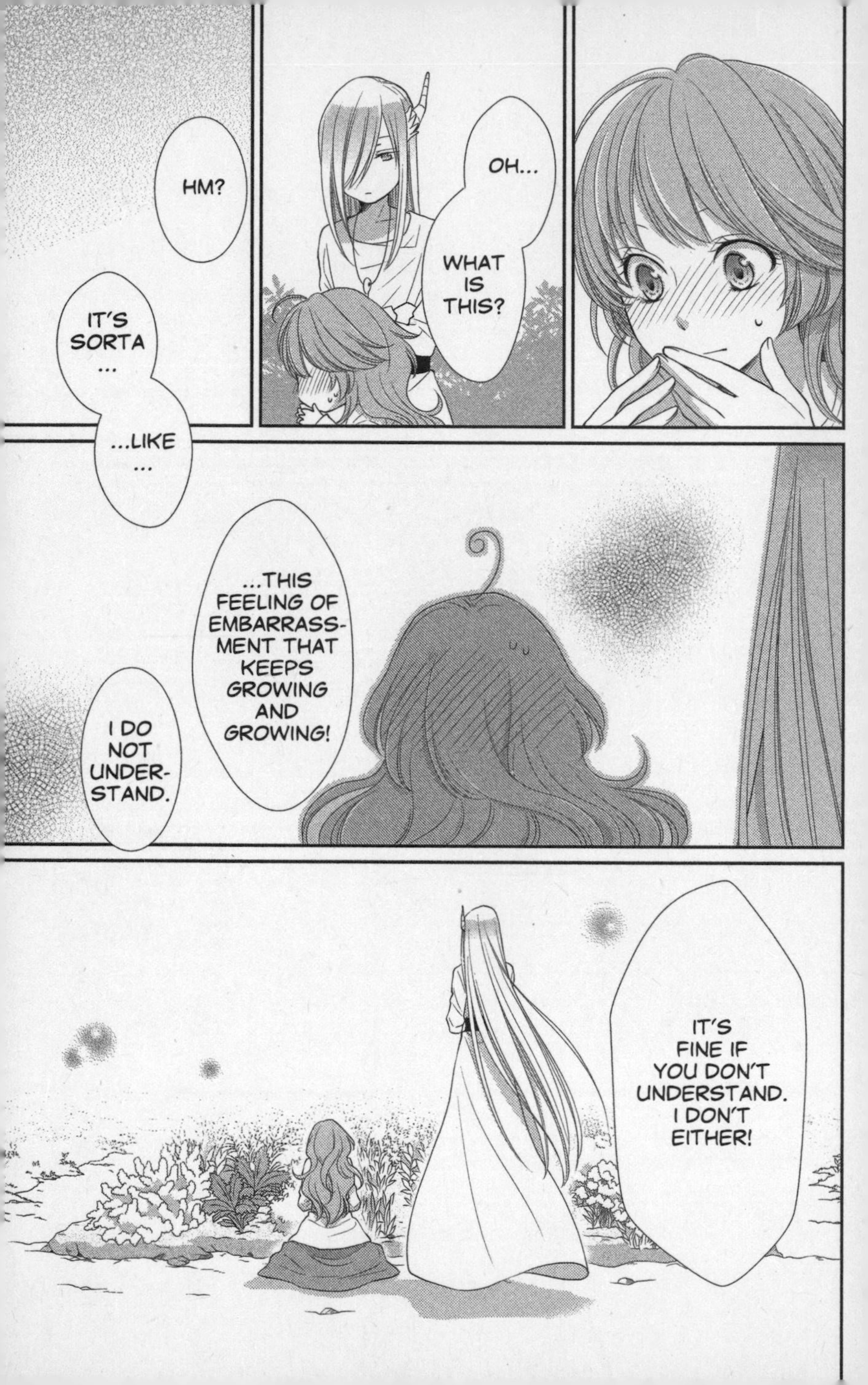
OH... WHAT IS THIS?
HM?
IT'S SORTA ...
...LIKE ...
...THIS FEELING OF EMBARRASSMENT THAT KEEPS GROWING AND GROWING!
I DO NOT UNDERSTAND.
IT'S FINE IF YOU DON'T UNDERSTAND. I DON'T EITHER!

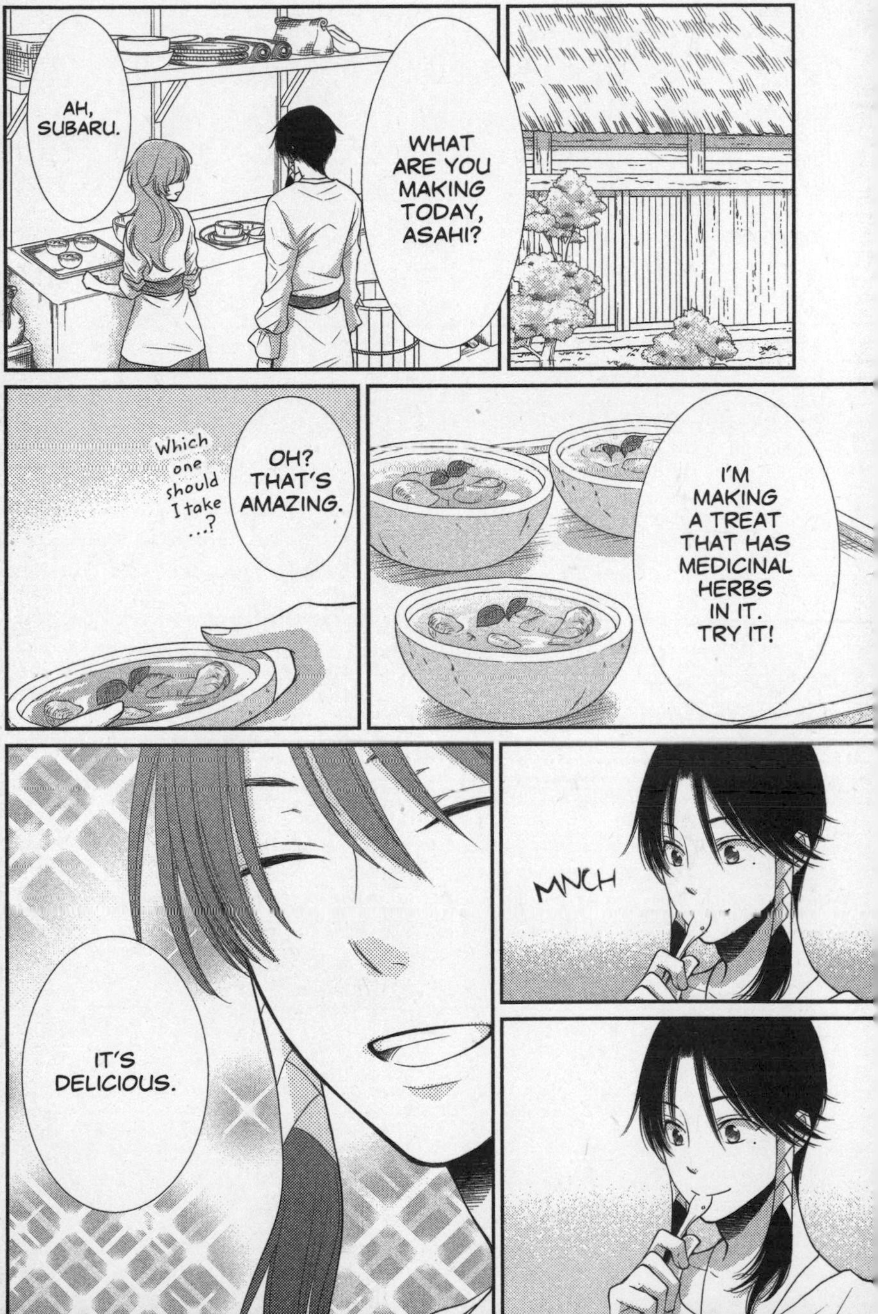
WHAT ARE YOU MAKING TODAY, ASAHI?
AH, SUBARU.
I'M MAKING A TREAT THAT HAS MEDICINAL HERBS IN IT. TRY IT!
OH? THAT'S AMAZING.
Which one should I take ...?
MNCH
IT'S DELICIOUS.

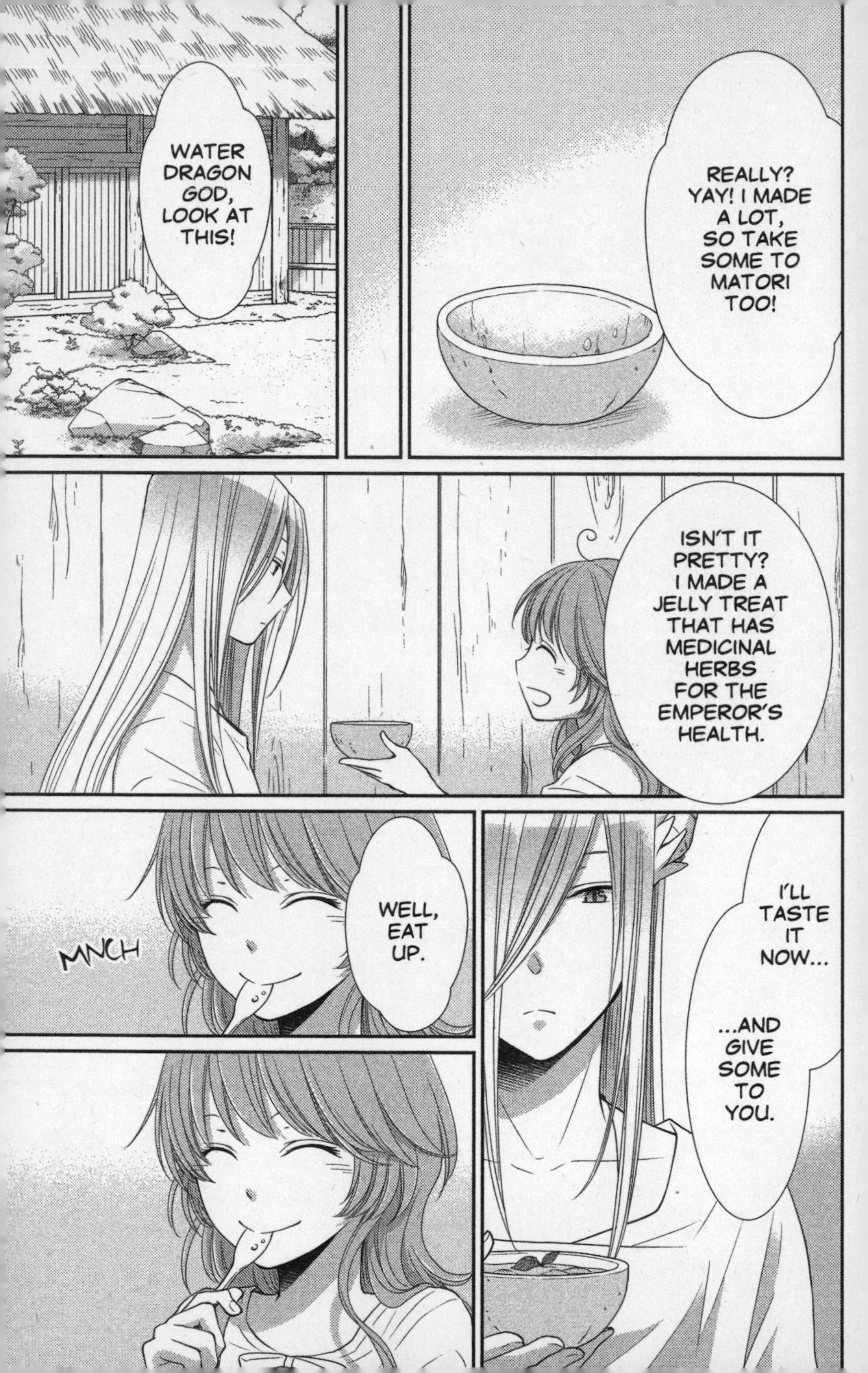
REALLY? YAY! I MADE A LOT, SO TAKE SOME TO MATORI TOO!
WATER DRAGON GOD, LOOK AT THIS!
ISN'T IT PRETTY? I MADE A JELLY TREAT THAT HAS MEDICINAL HERBS FOR THE EMPEROR'S HEALTH.
I'LL TASTE IT NOW...
...AND GIVE SOME TO YOU.
WELL, EAT UP.
MNCH

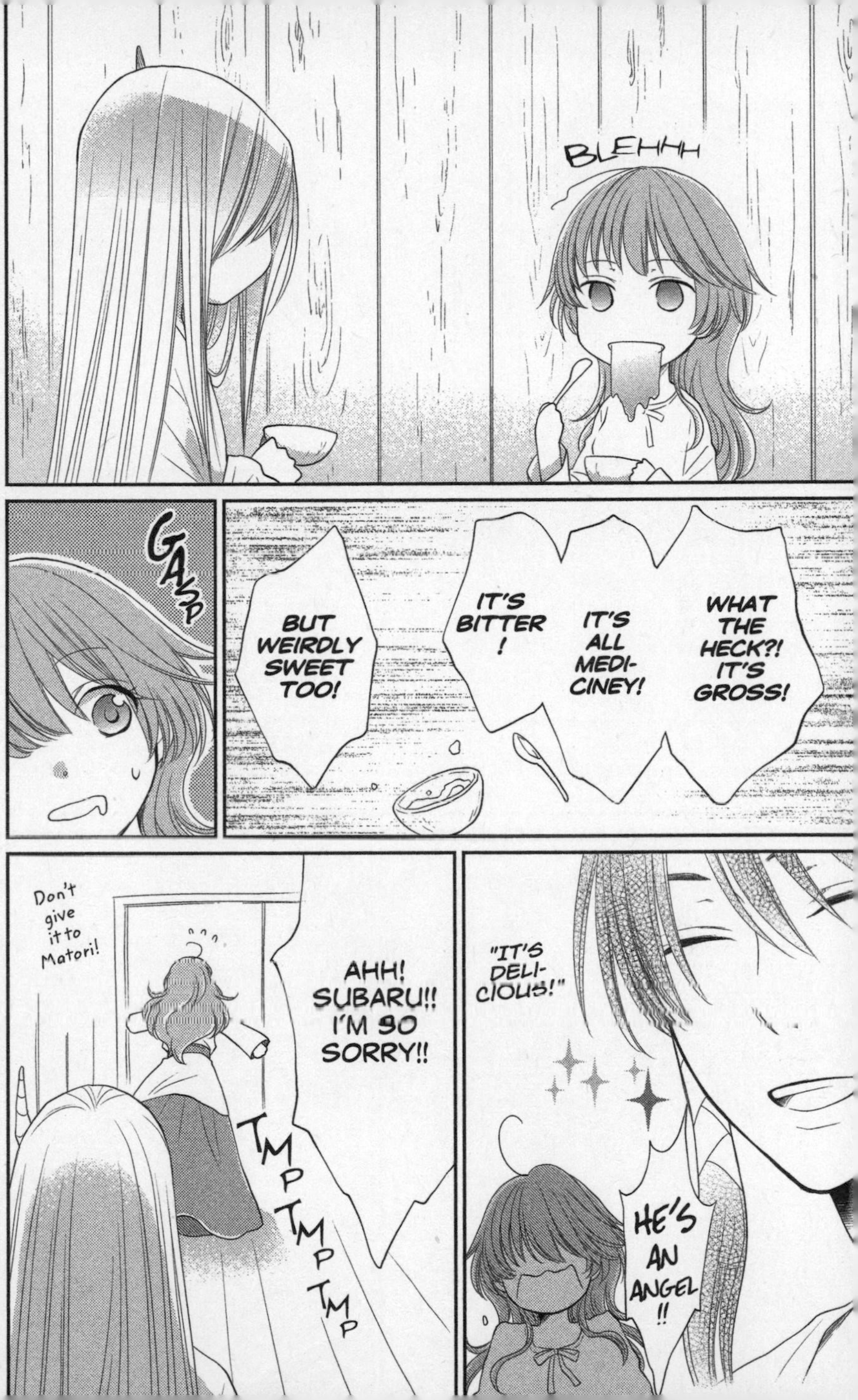
BLEHHH
WHAT THE HECK?! IT'S GROSS!
IT'S ALL MEDI-CINEY!
IT'S BITTER!
BUT WEIRDLY SWEET TOO!
GASP
"IT'S DELI-CIOUS!"
HE'S AN ANGEL!!
Don't give it to Matori!
AHH! SUBARU!! I'M SO SORRY!!
TMP TMP TMP TMP

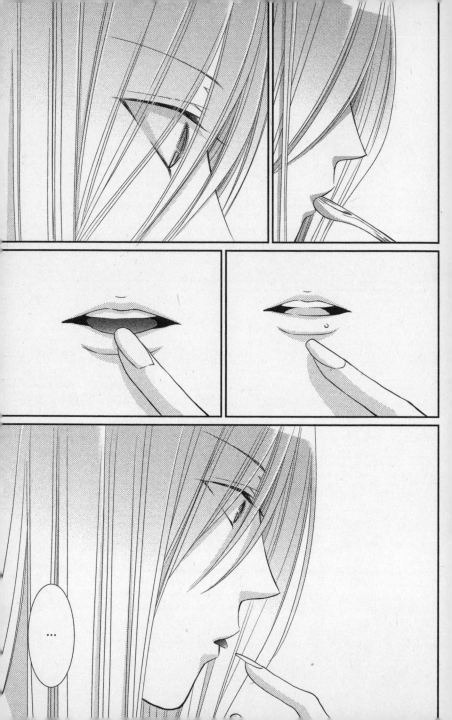

...

ASAHI...

I WOULD LIKE TO PRESENT YOU WITH SERVANTS AND A TEMPLE AS BEFITS YOUR STATUS AS OUR WATER PRIESTESS. DO YOU HAVE ANY PREFERENCES?

SERVANTS ...?!

HOW MANY WILL YOU NEED? A HUNDRED? A THOUSAND?

A THOU —?

I DON'T NEED ANYTHING LIKE THAT, YOUR MAJESTY.

HOW-EVER...

...

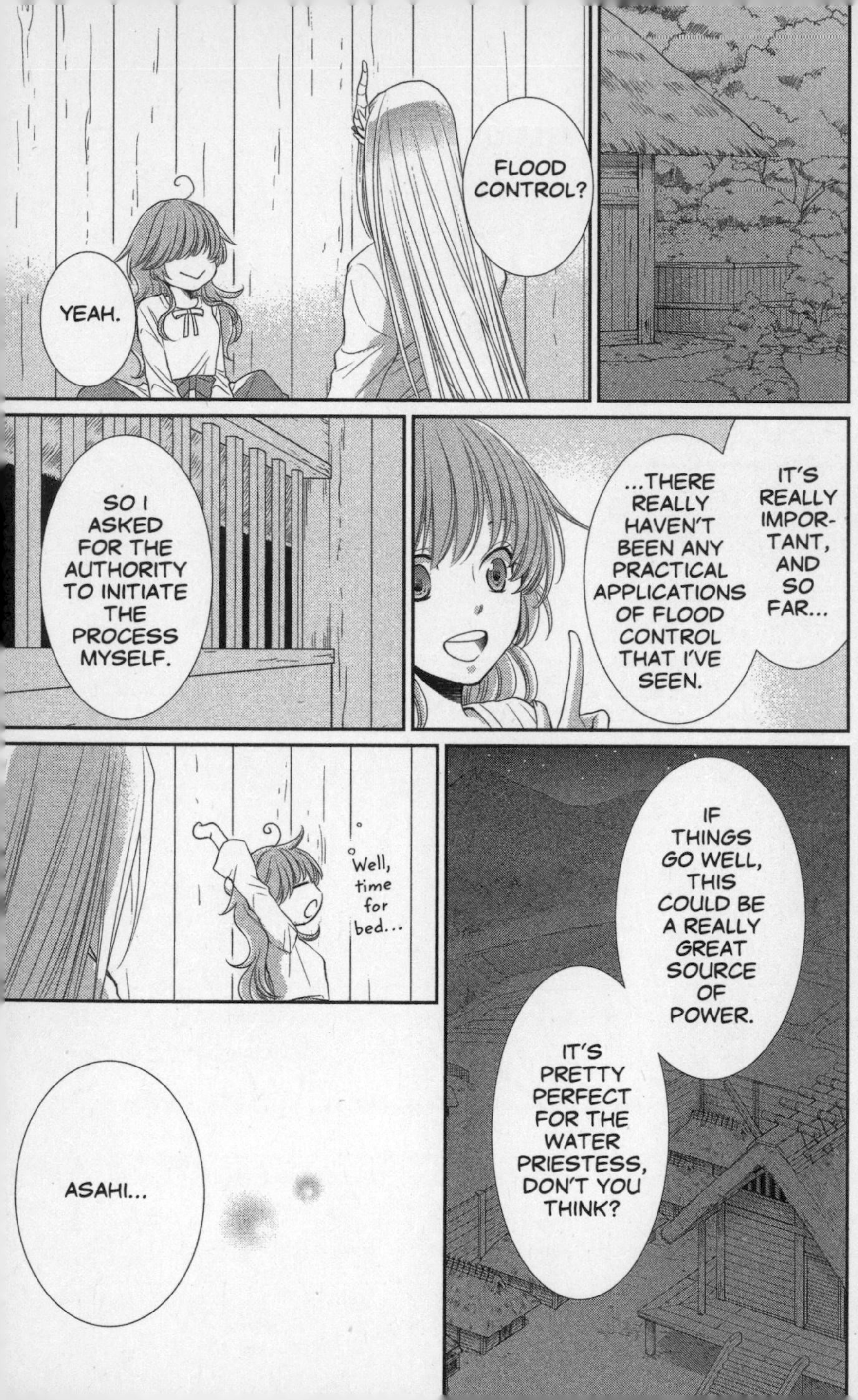
FLOOD CONTROL?
YEAH.
IT'S REALLY IMPORTANT, AND SO FAR...
...THERE REALLY HAVEN'T BEEN ANY PRACTICAL APPLICATIONS OF FLOOD CONTROL THAT I'VE SEEN.
SO I ASKED FOR THE AUTHORITY TO INITIATE THE PROCESS MYSELF.
IF THINGS GO WELL, THIS COULD BE A REALLY GREAT SOURCE OF POWER.
IT'S PRETTY PERFECT FOR THE WATER PRIESTESS, DON'T YOU THINK?
Well, time for bed...
ASAHI...

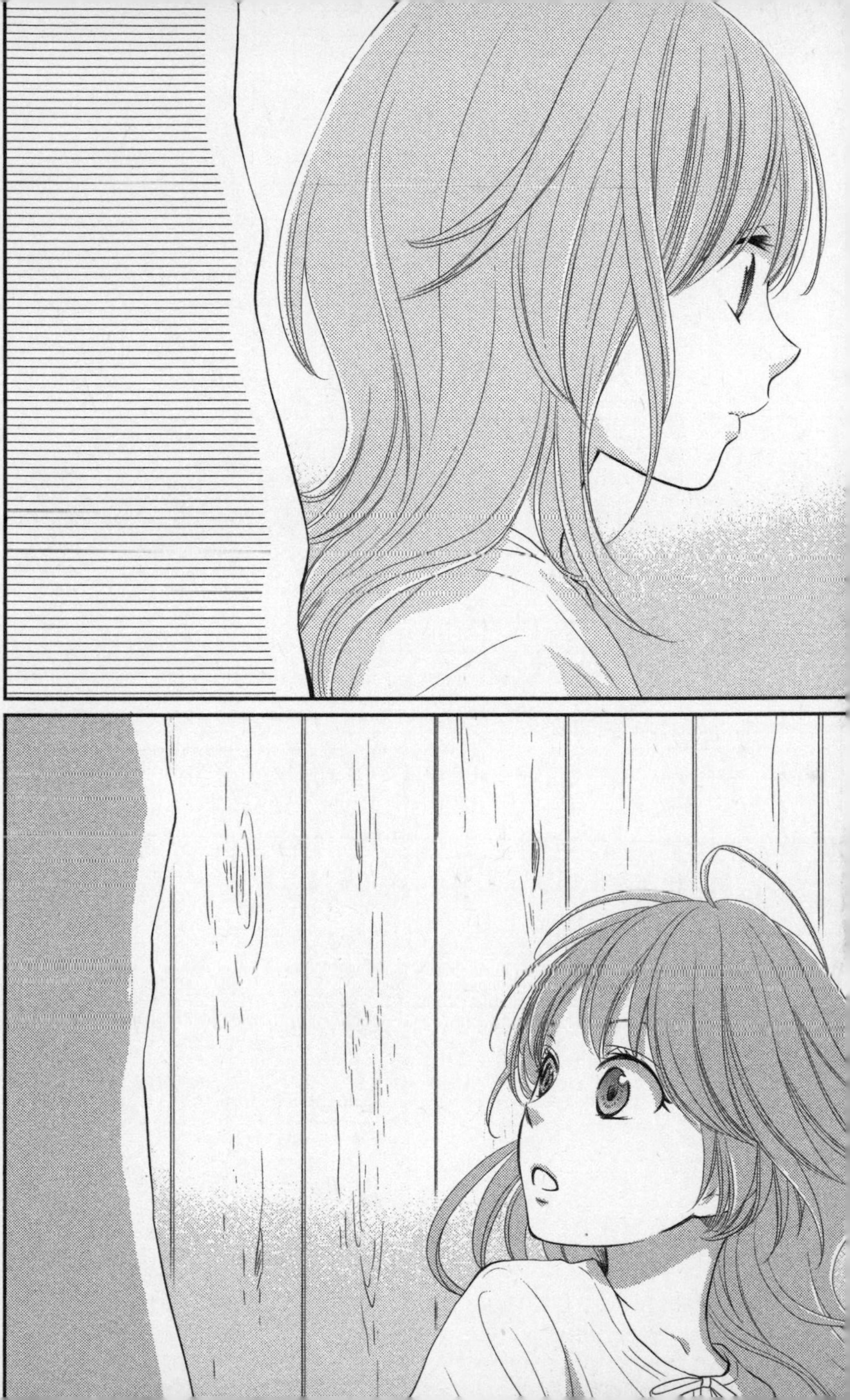

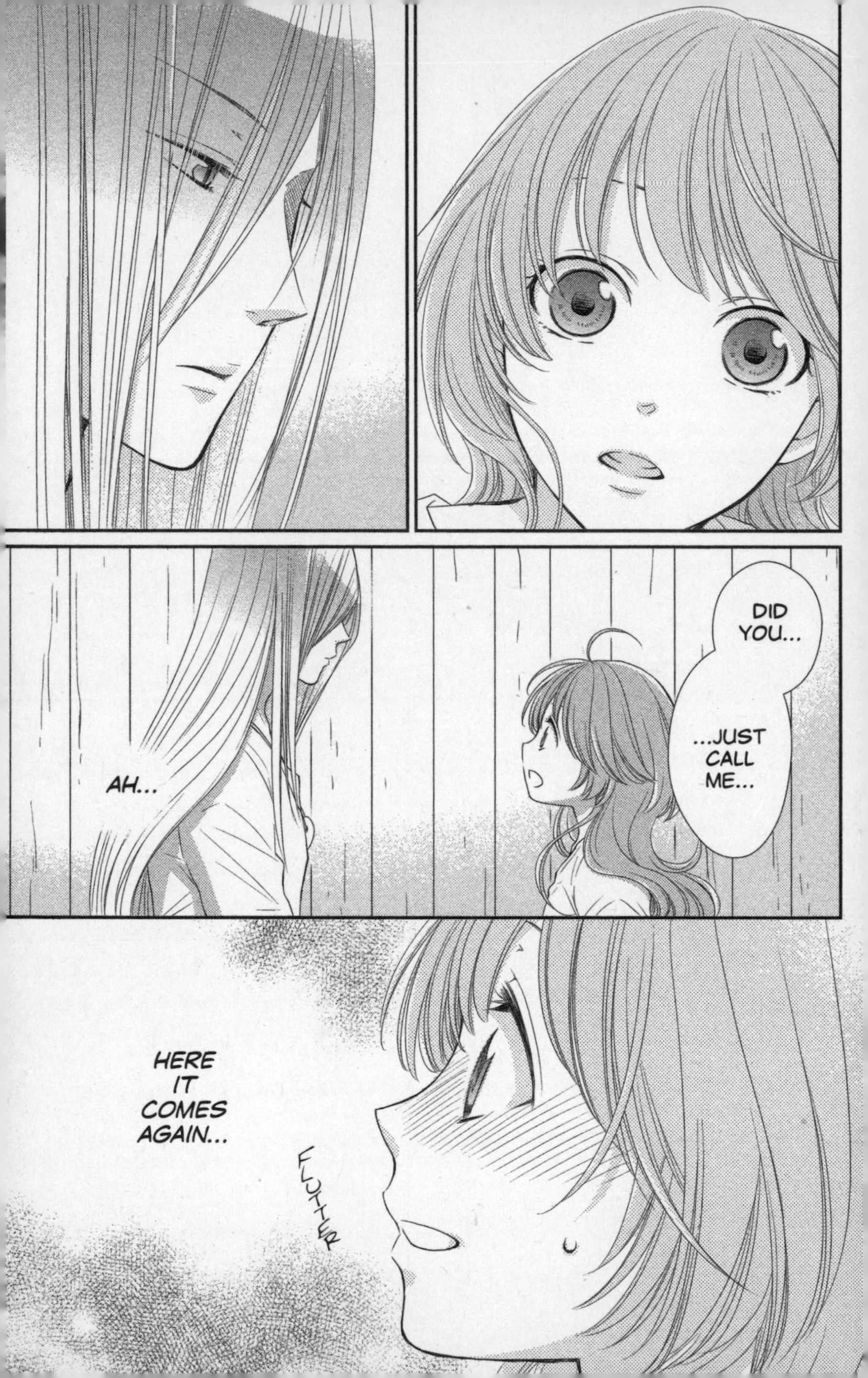
DID YOU...
...JUST CALL ME...
AH...
FLUTTER
HERE IT COMES AGAIN...

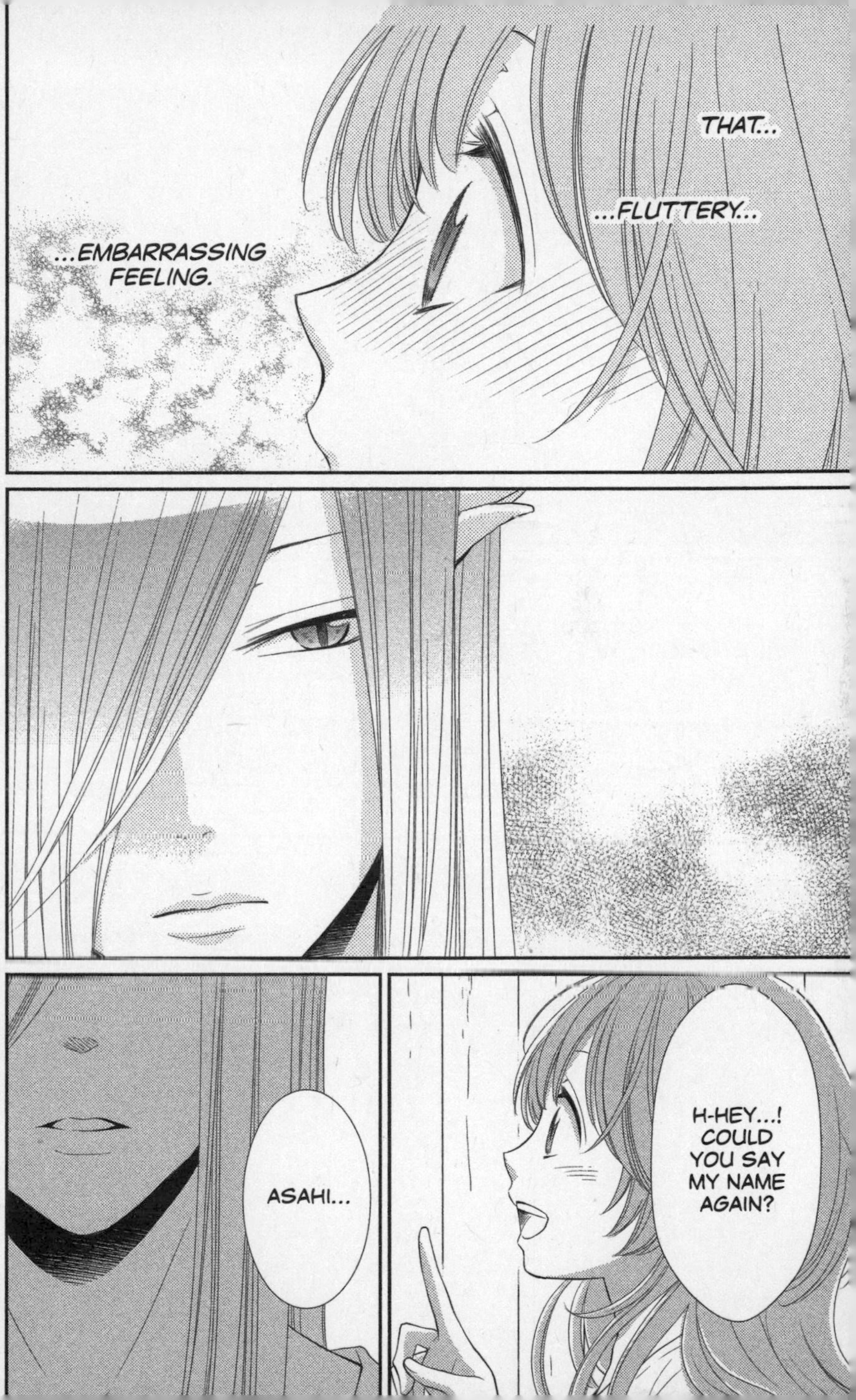
THAT...
...FLUTTERY...
...EMBARRASSING FEELING.
H-HEY...! COULD YOU SAY MY NAME AGAIN?
ASAHI...

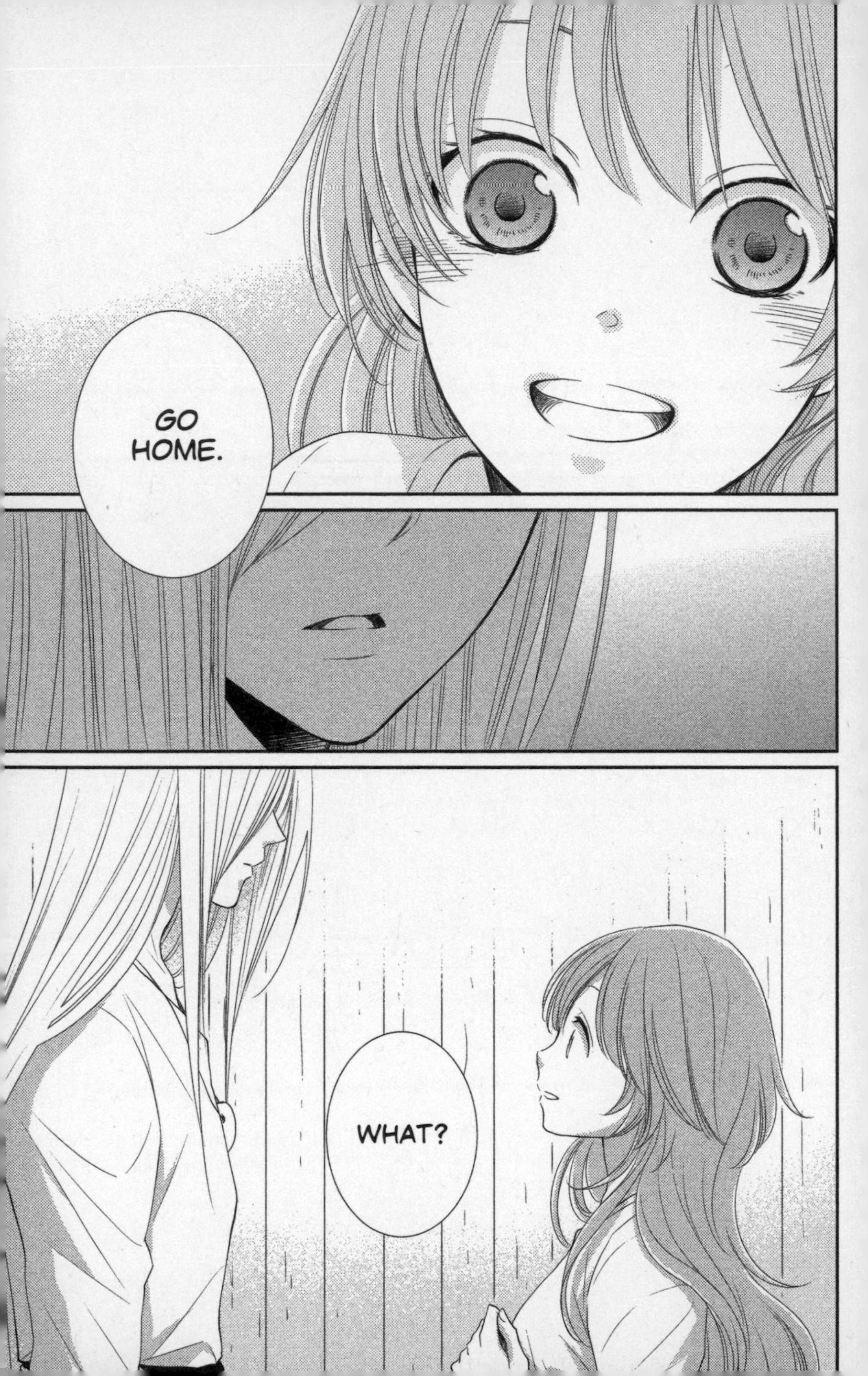
GO HOME.
WHAT?

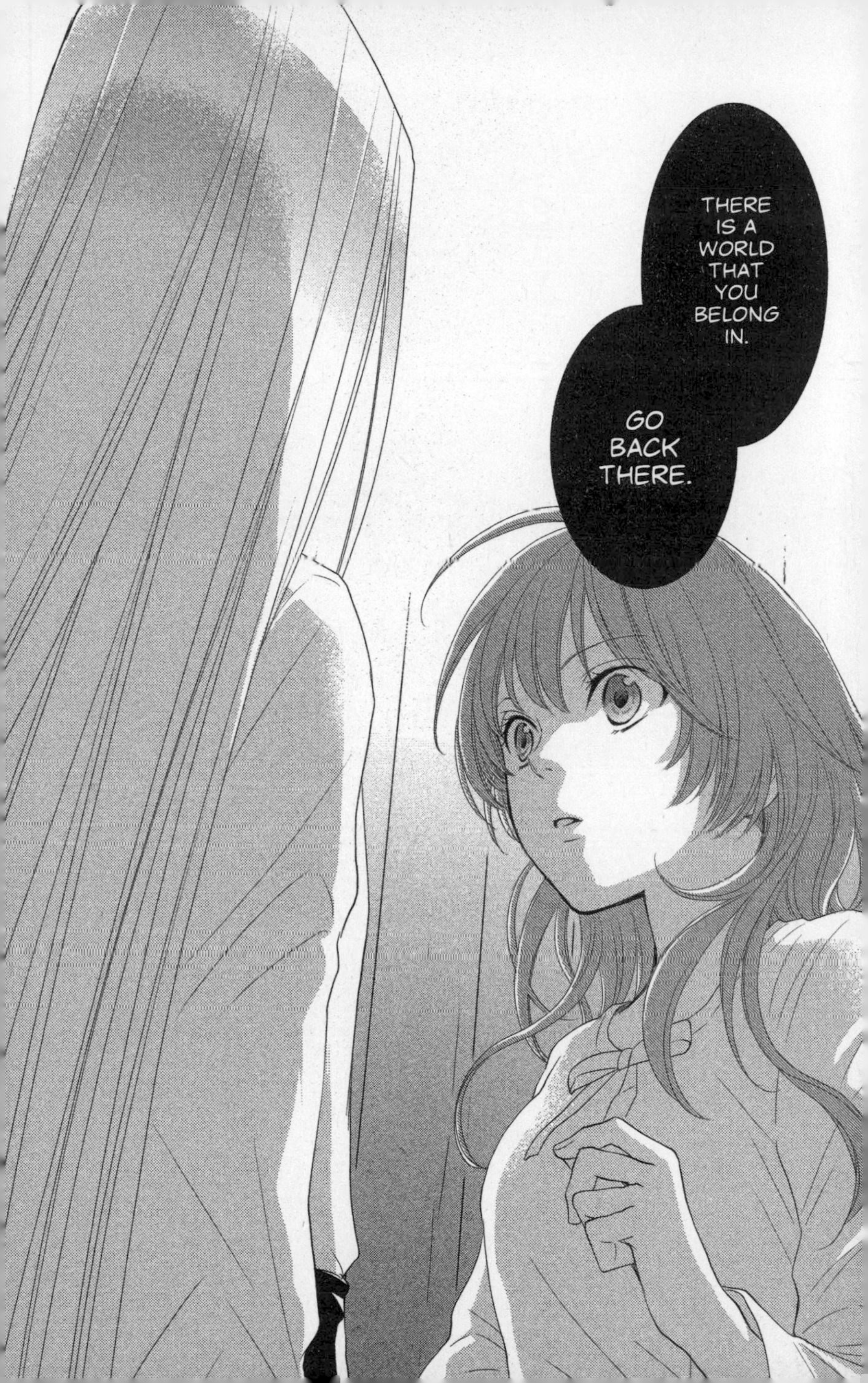
THERE IS A WORLD THAT YOU BELONG IN.
GO BACK THERE.

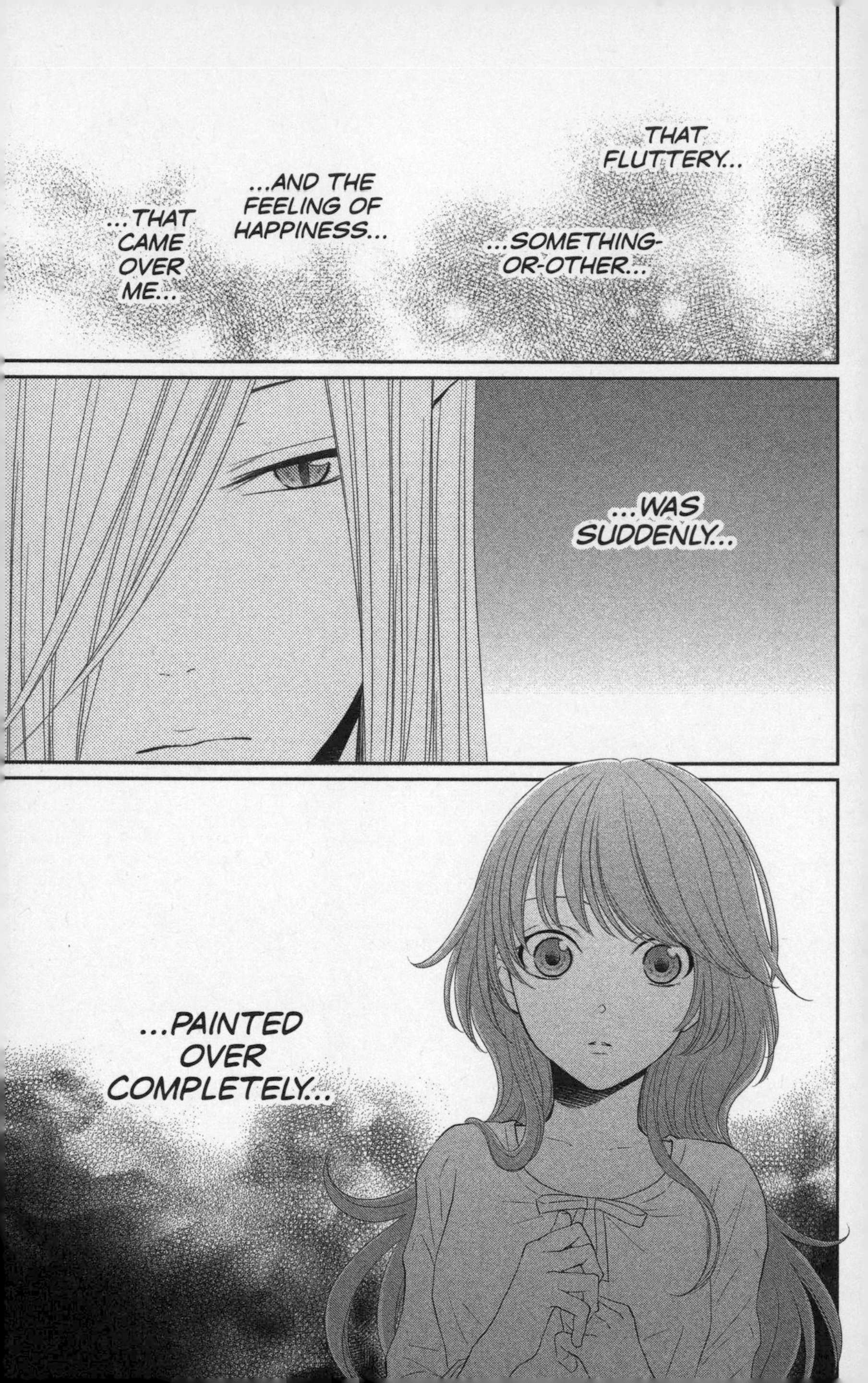
THAT FLUTTERY...
...SOMETHING-OR-OTHER...
...AND THE FEELING OF HAPPINESS...
...THAT CAME OVER ME...
...WAS SUDDENLY...
...PAINTED OVER COMPLETELY...

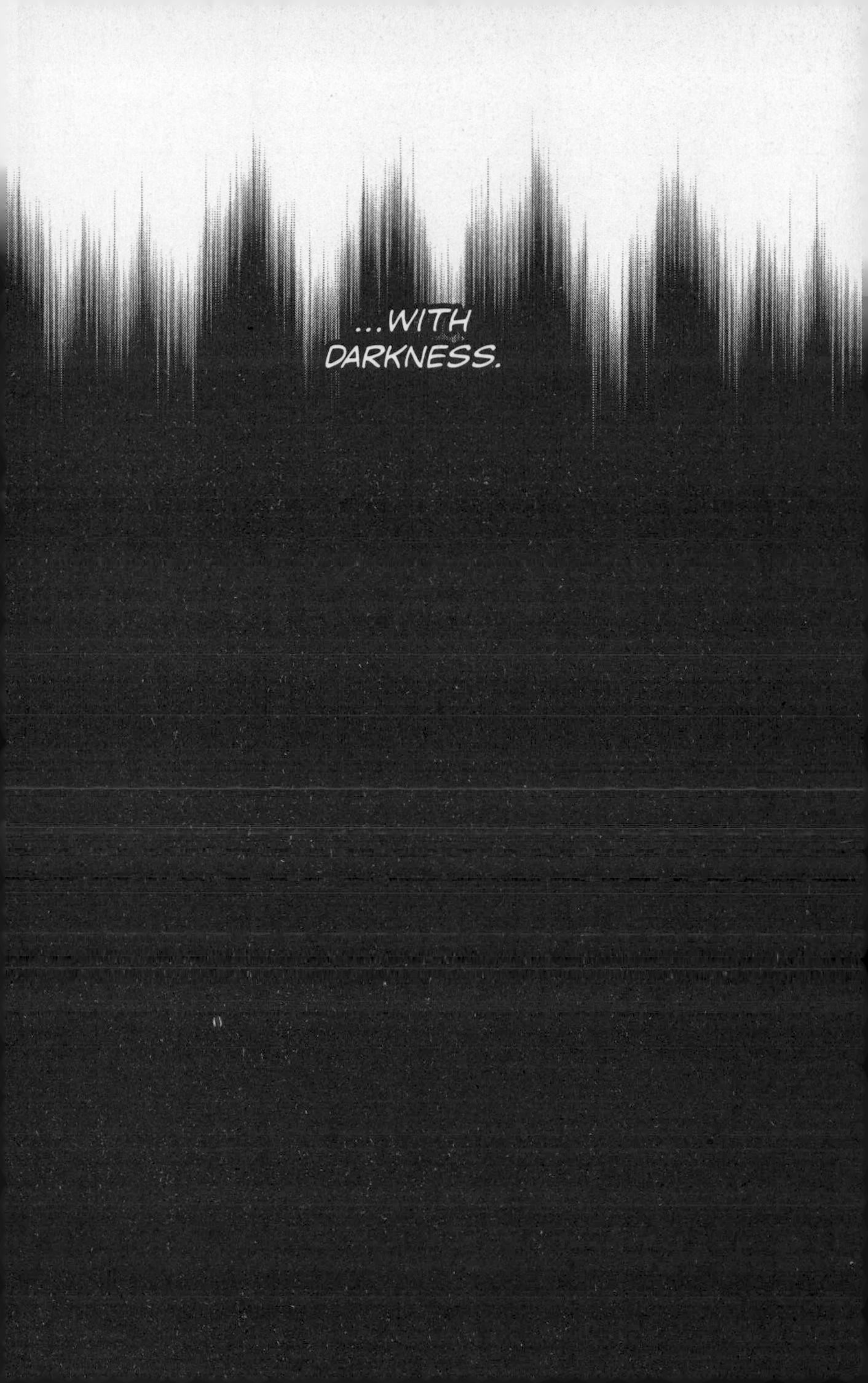
...WITH DARKNESS.

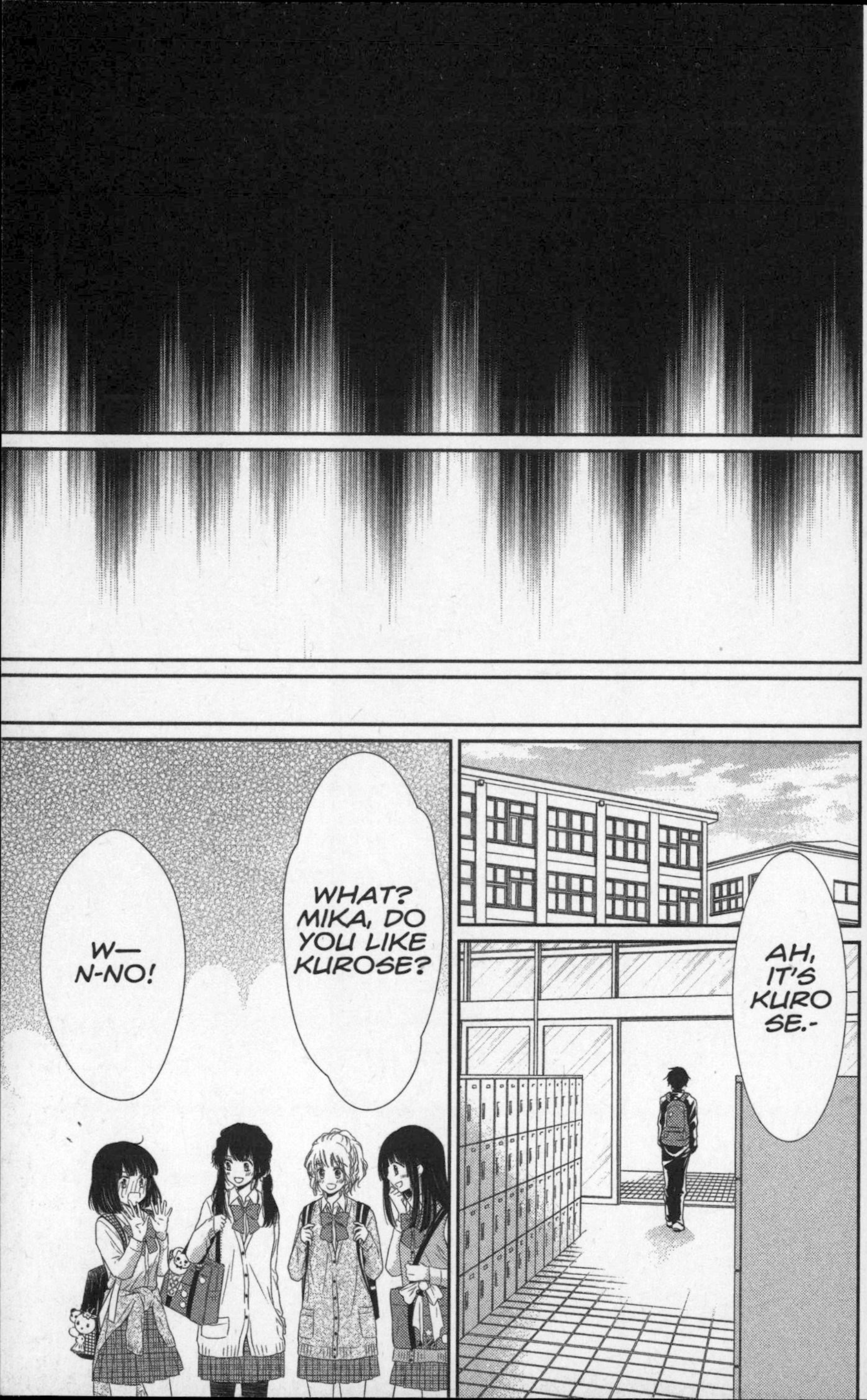
AH, IT'S KURO SE.-
WHAT? MIKA, DO YOU LIKE KUROSE?
W— N-NO!

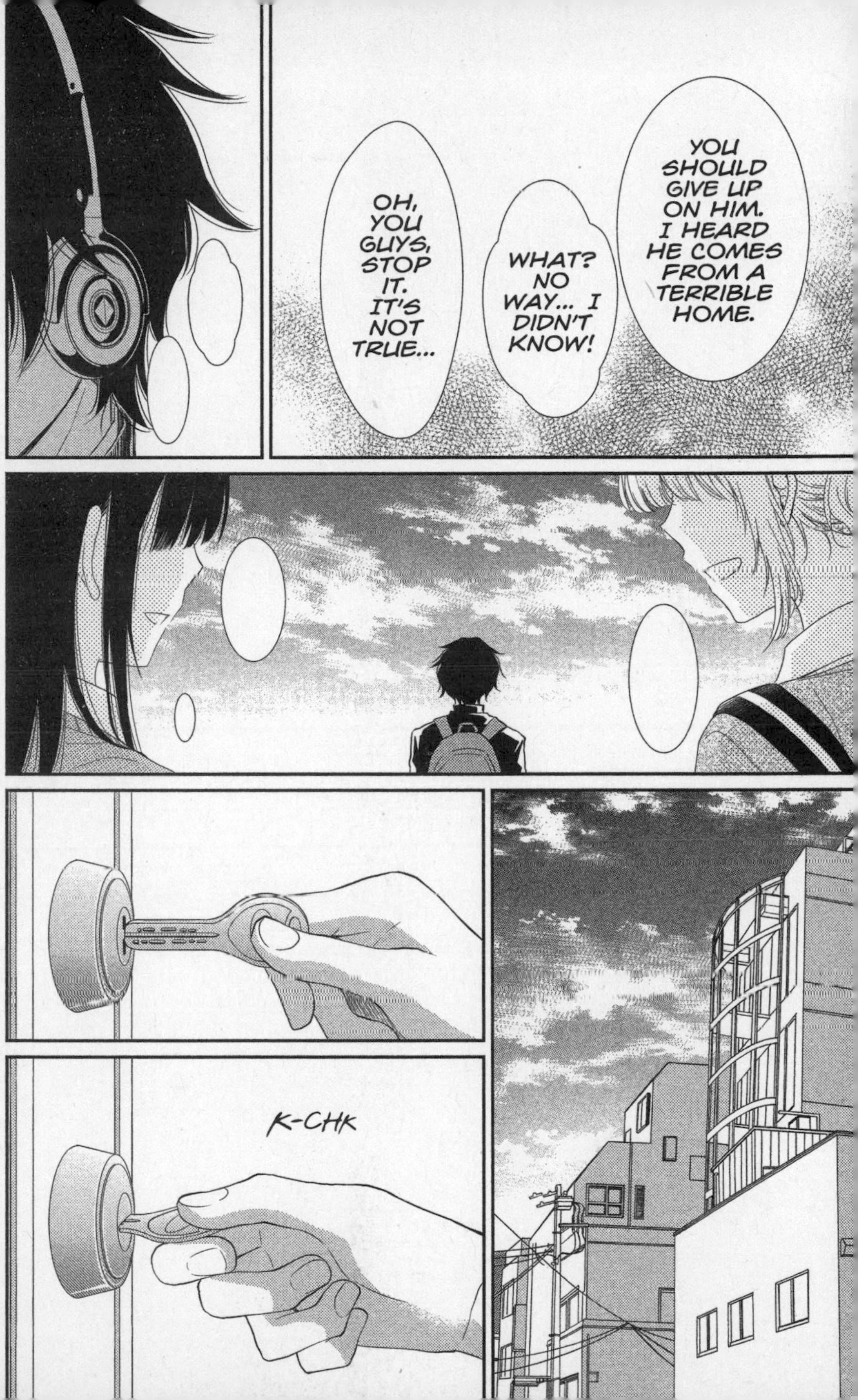
YOU SHOULD GIVE UP ON HIM. I HEARD HE COMES FROM A TERRIBLE HOME.
WHAT? NO WAY... I DIDN'T KNOW!
OH, YOU GUYS, STOP IT. IT'S NOT TRUE...
K-CHK

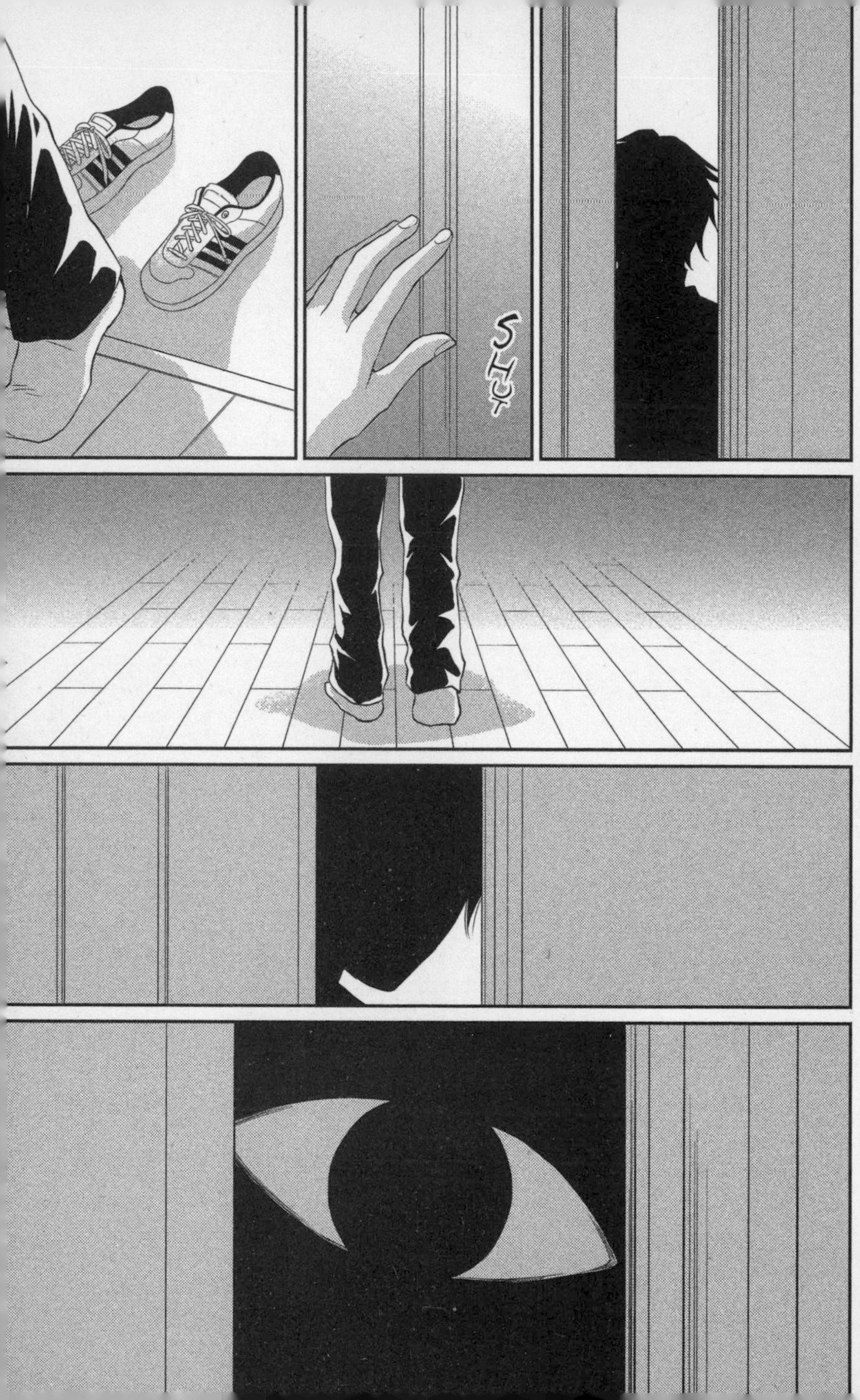
SHUT

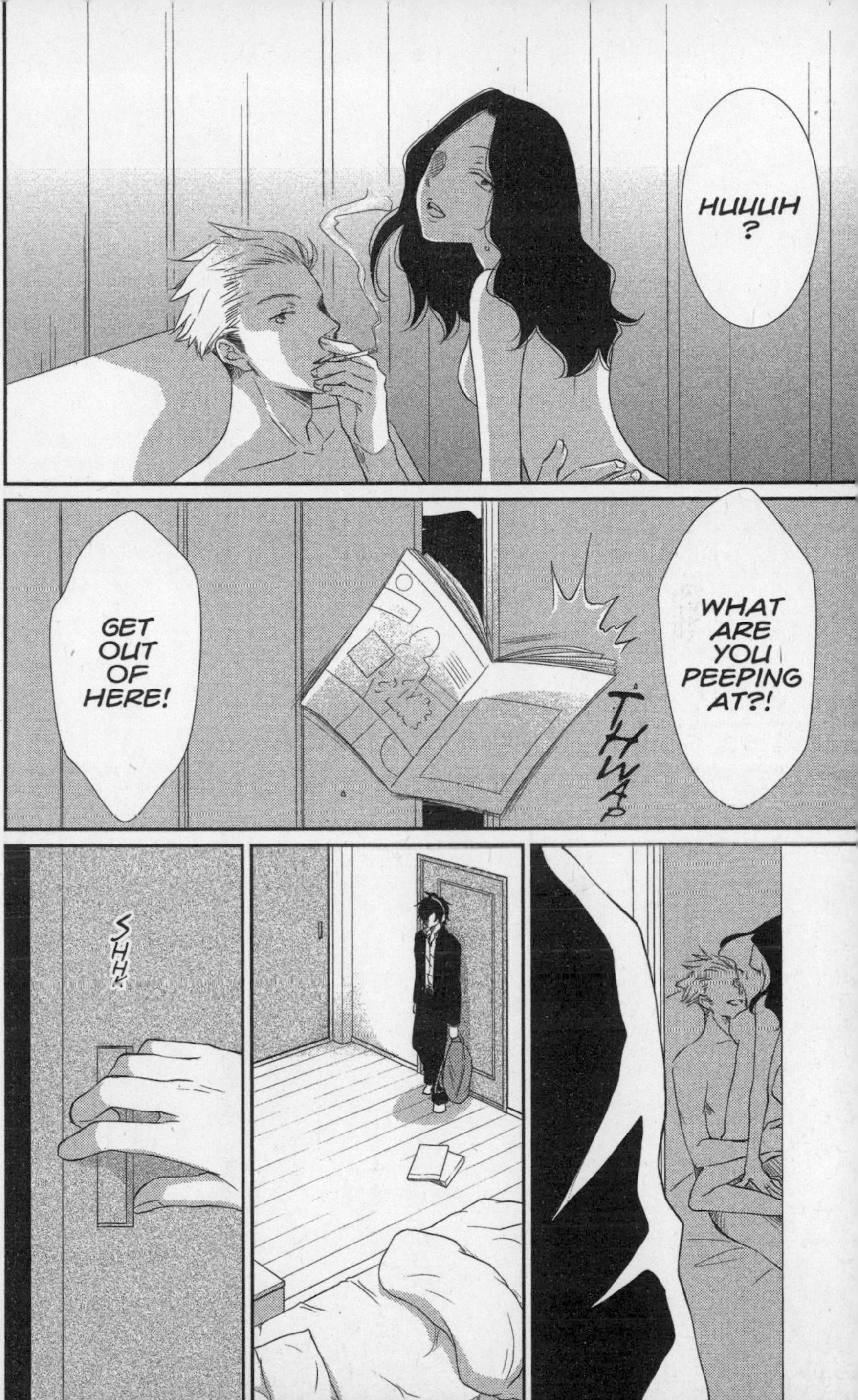
HUUUH?
WHAT ARE YOU PEEPING AT?!
THWAP
GET OUT OF HERE!
SHH

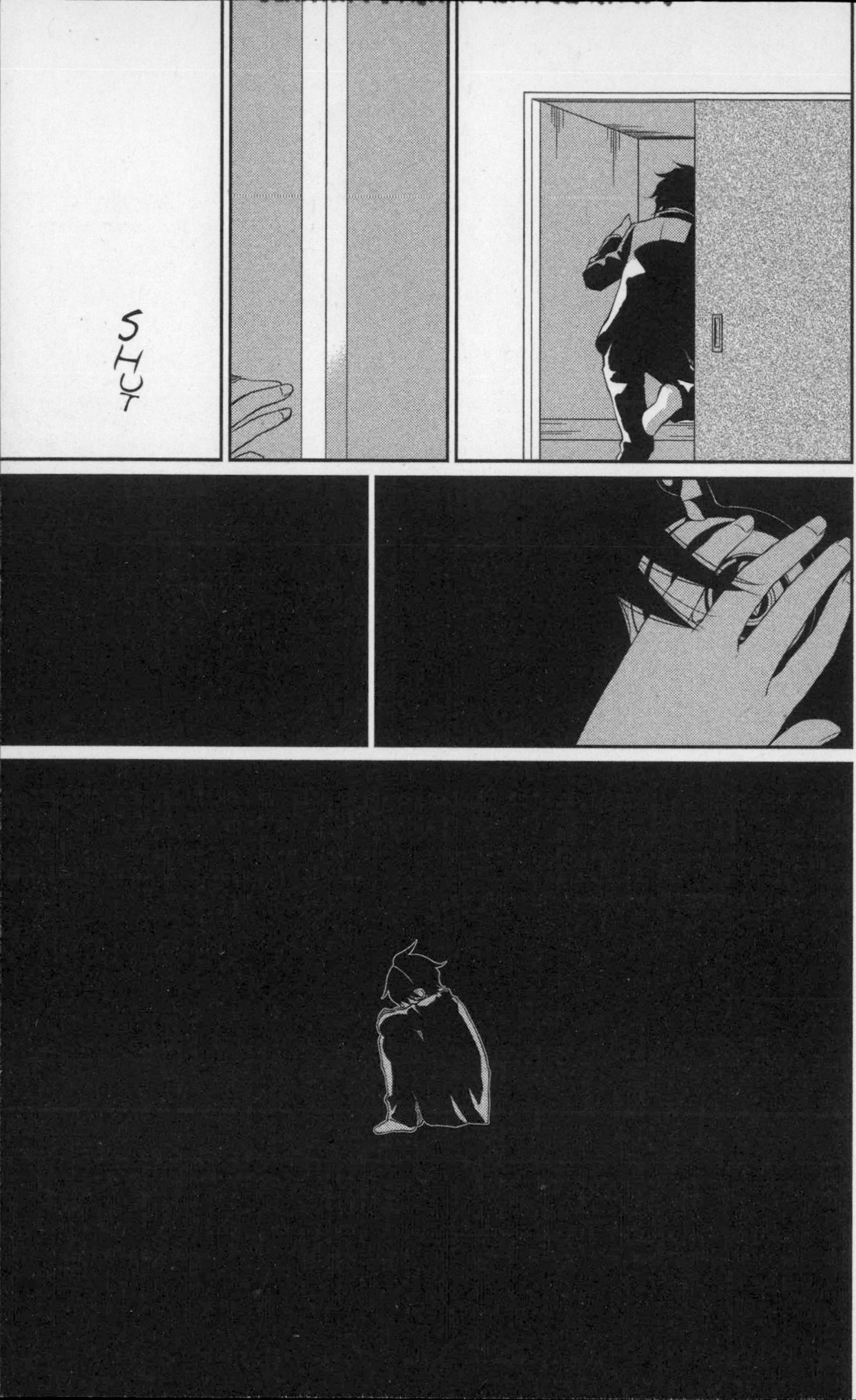
SHUT

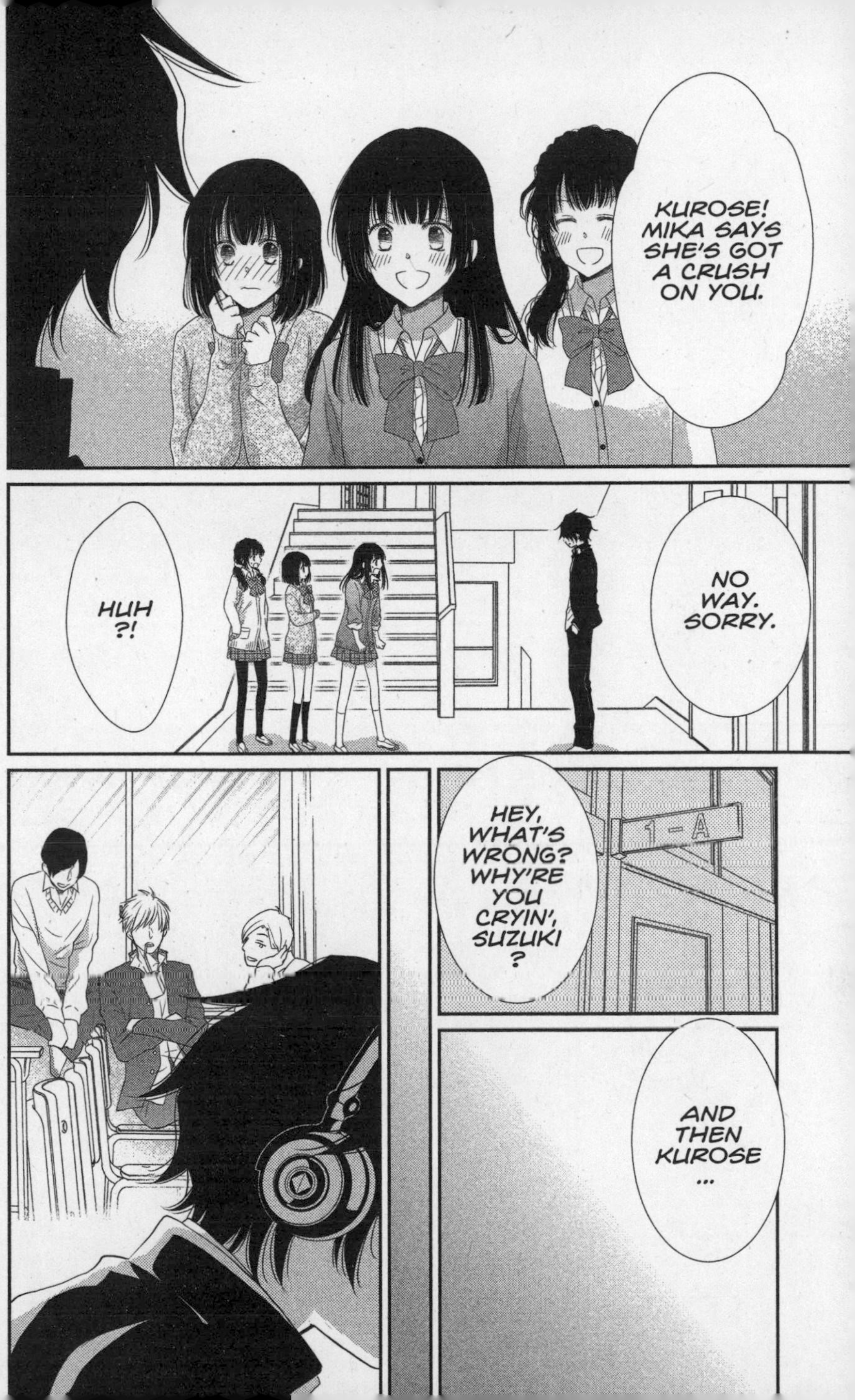
KUROSE! MIKA SAYS SHE'S GOT A CRUSH ON YOU.
NO WAY. SORRY.
HUH?!
1-A
HEY, WHAT'S WRONG? WHY'RE YOU CRYIN', SUZUKI?
AND THEN KUROSE...

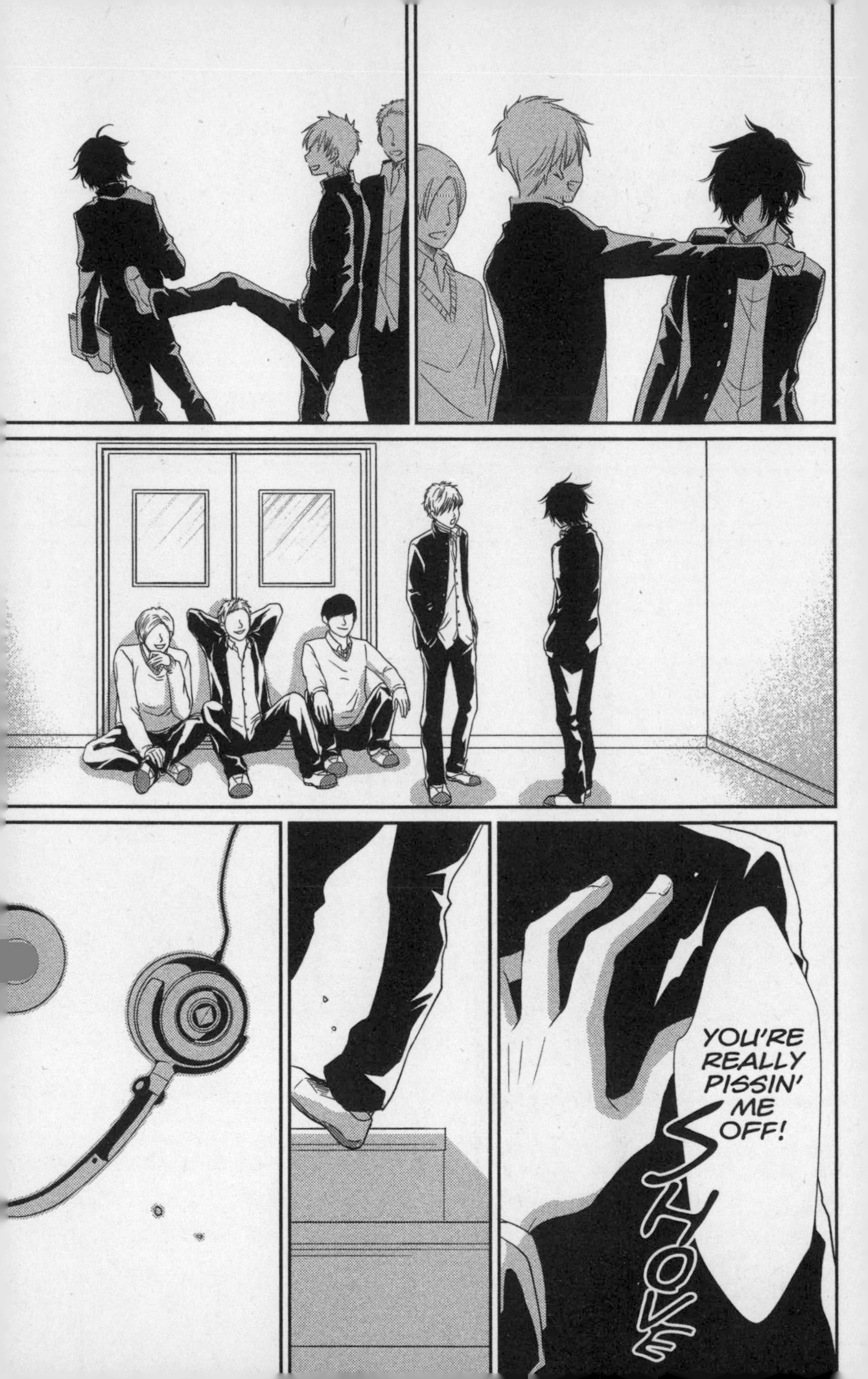
YOU'RE REALLY PISSIN' ME OFF!
SHOVE

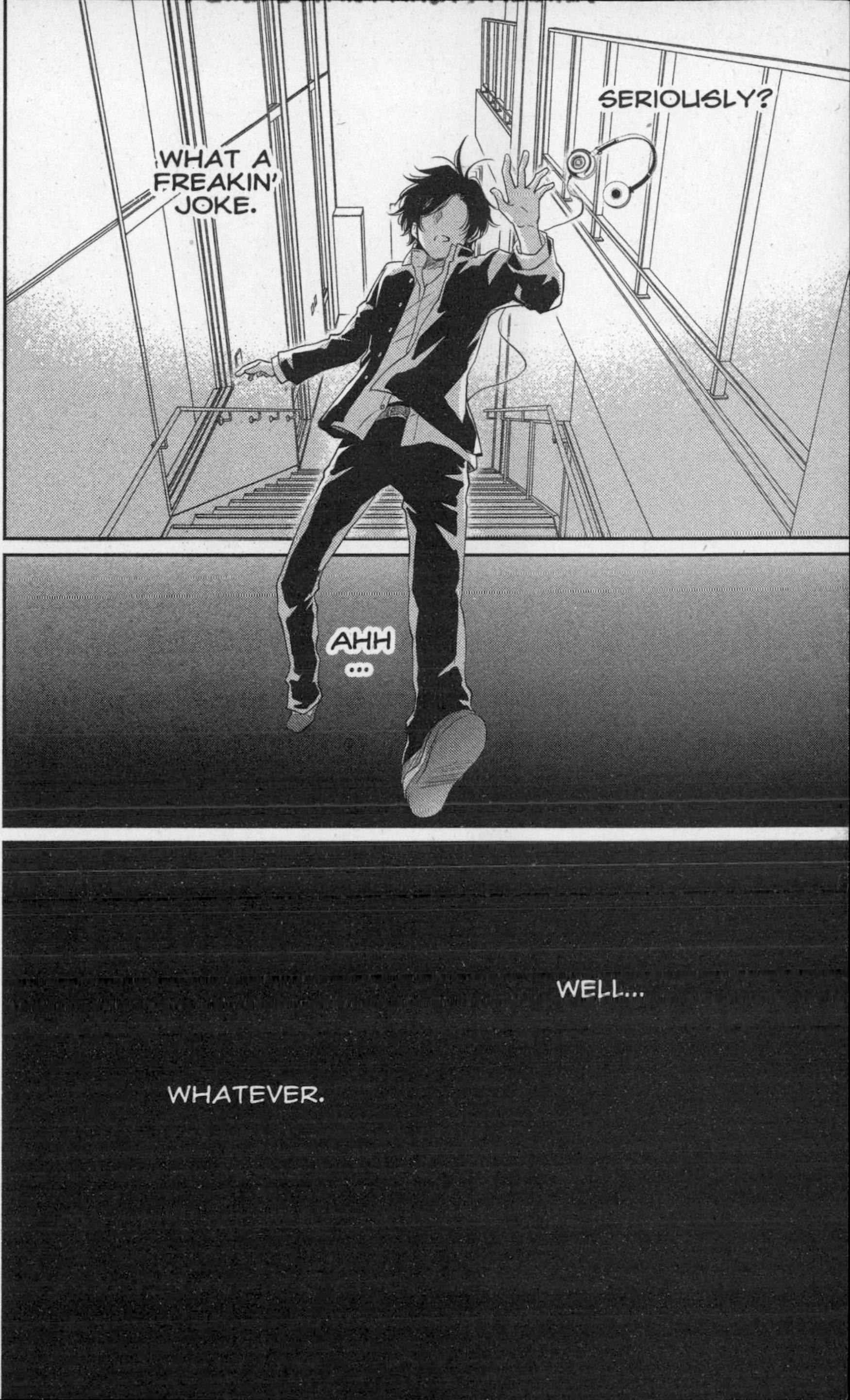
SERIOUSLY?
WHAT A FREAKIN' JOKE.
AHH ...
WELL...
WHATEVER.

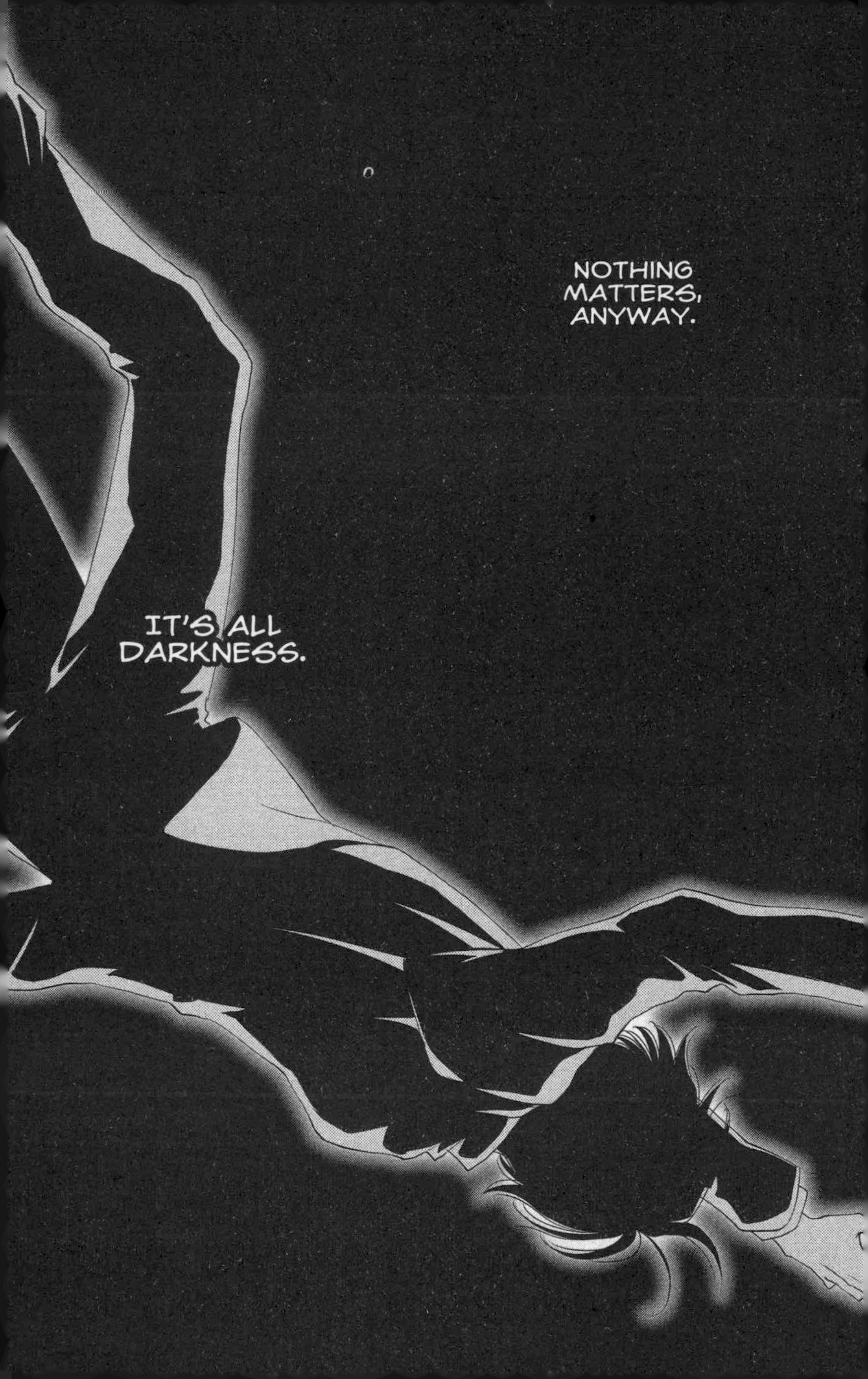
NOTHING MATTERS, ANYWAY.
IT'S ALL DARKNESS.

...?

WAIT,
WHAT?

DID
I...
DIE?

IT'S
PITCH-
BLACK.

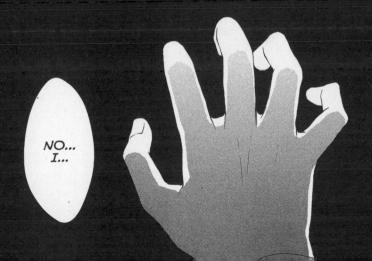

NO...
I...

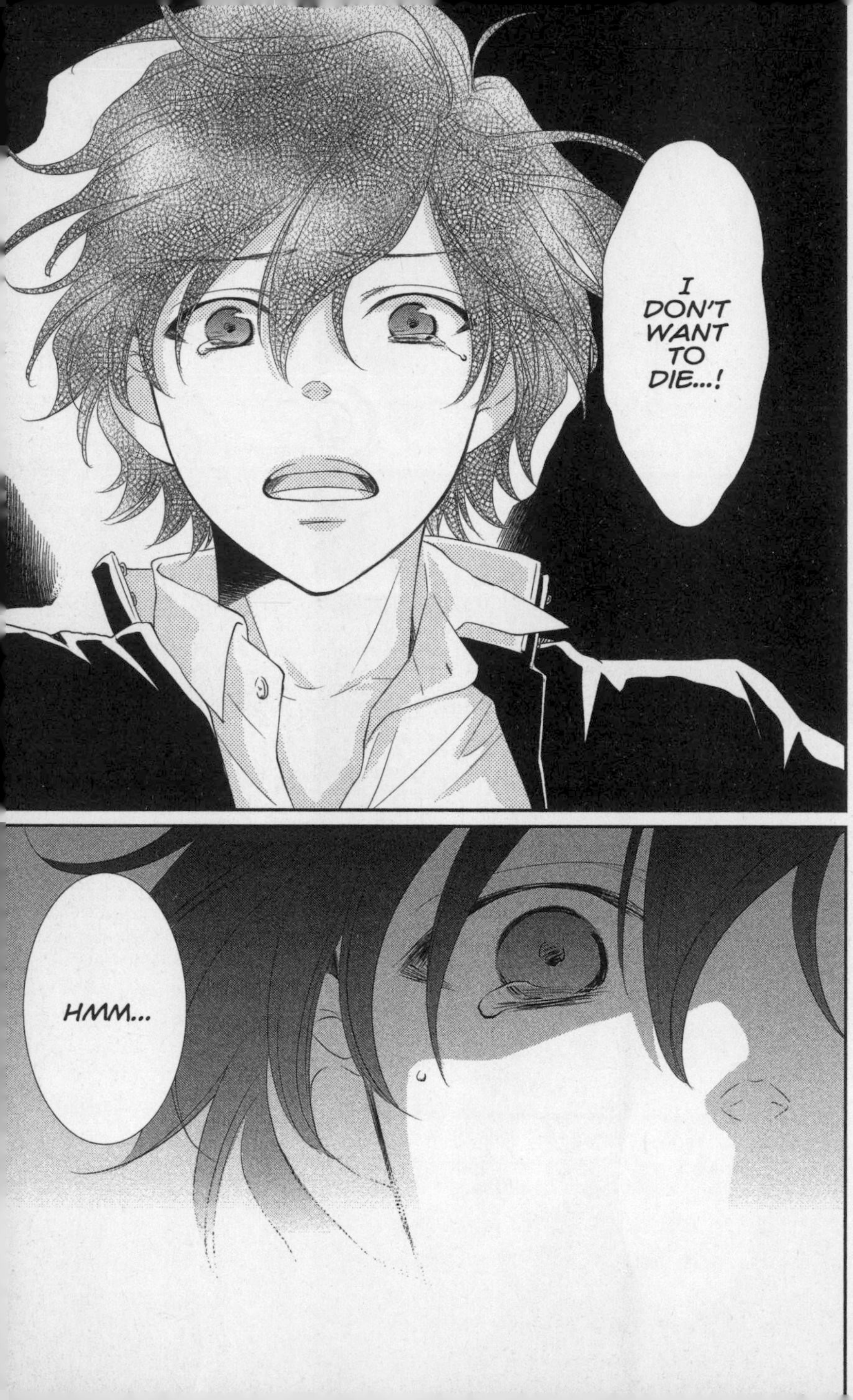
I DON'T WANT TO DIE...!
HMM...

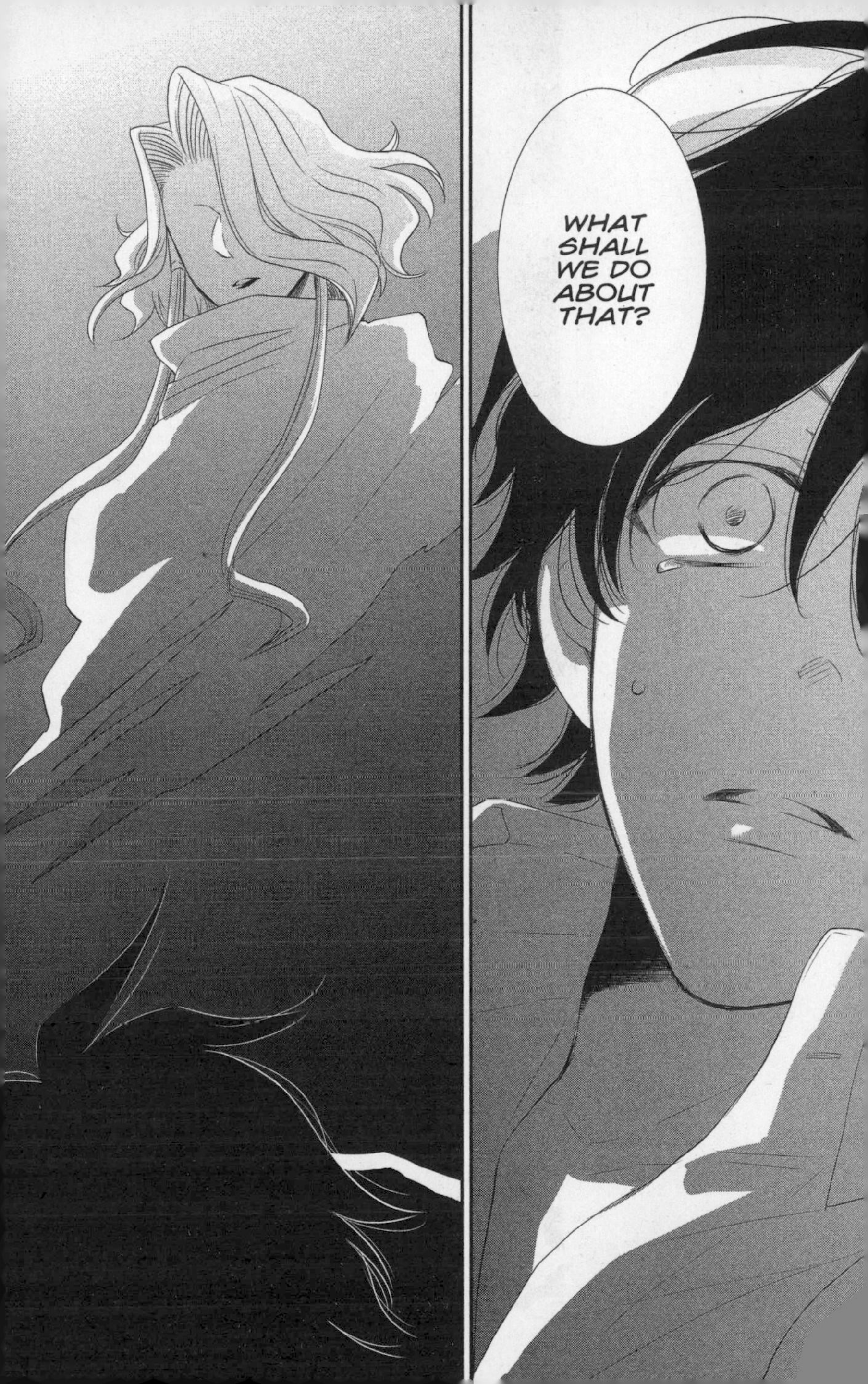
WHAT SHALL WE DO ABOUT THAT?

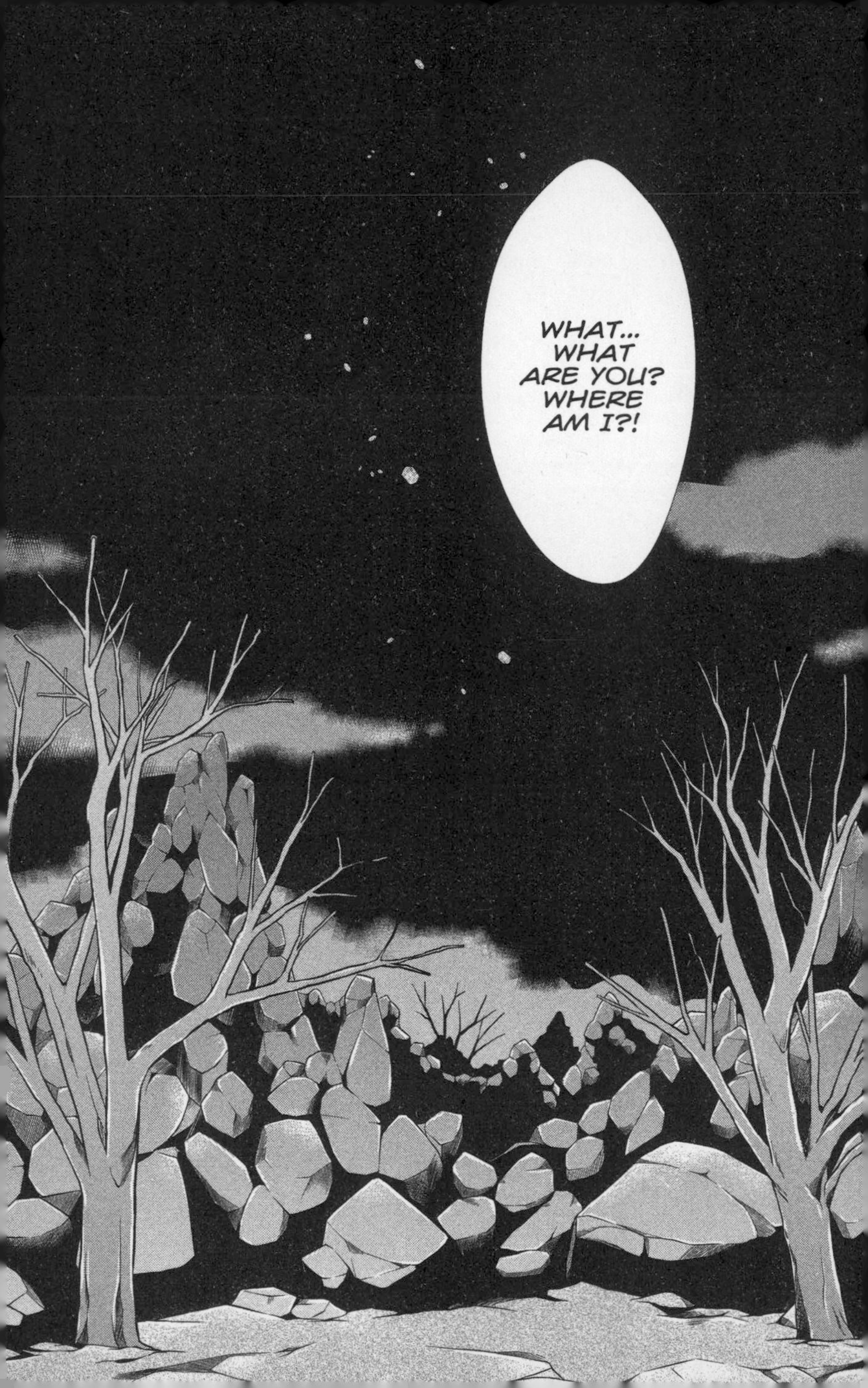
WHAT... WHAT ARE YOU? WHERE AM I?!

It was just a joke in the Chill Zone section, but I really hadn't thought of a name for Kurose. I couldn't think of a name that fit him, so I kept putting it off until it just became a habit to write "XX" on the sketches for my storyboards... Maybe it's a little too simple, but Kurose just fits Kurose, and I'm pretty happy about that.

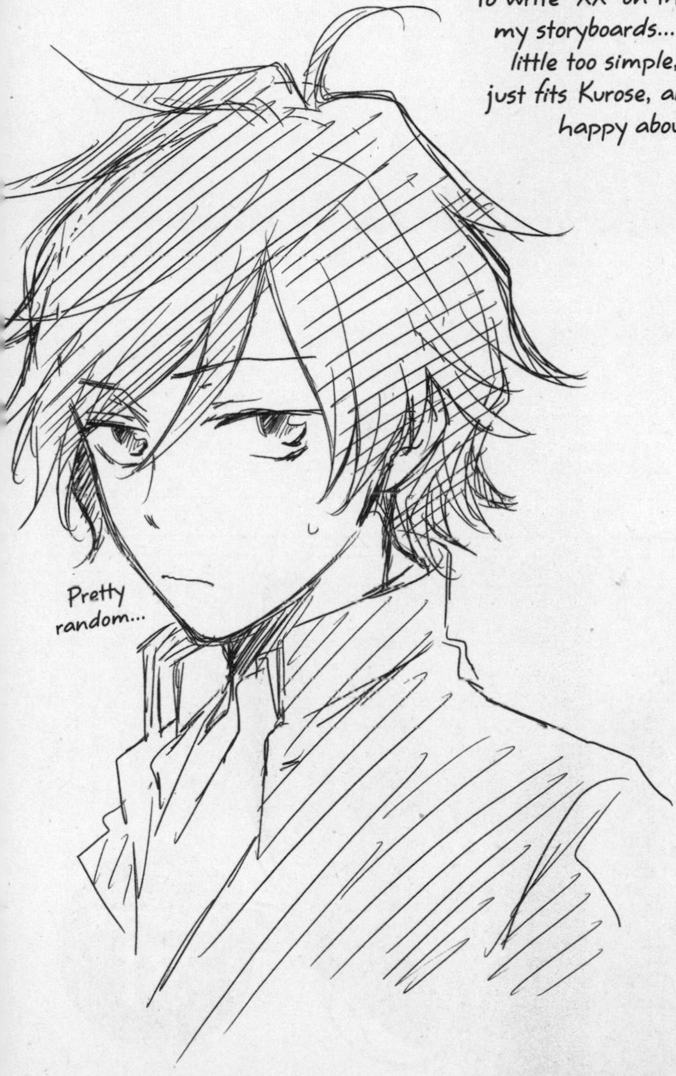
Pretty random...

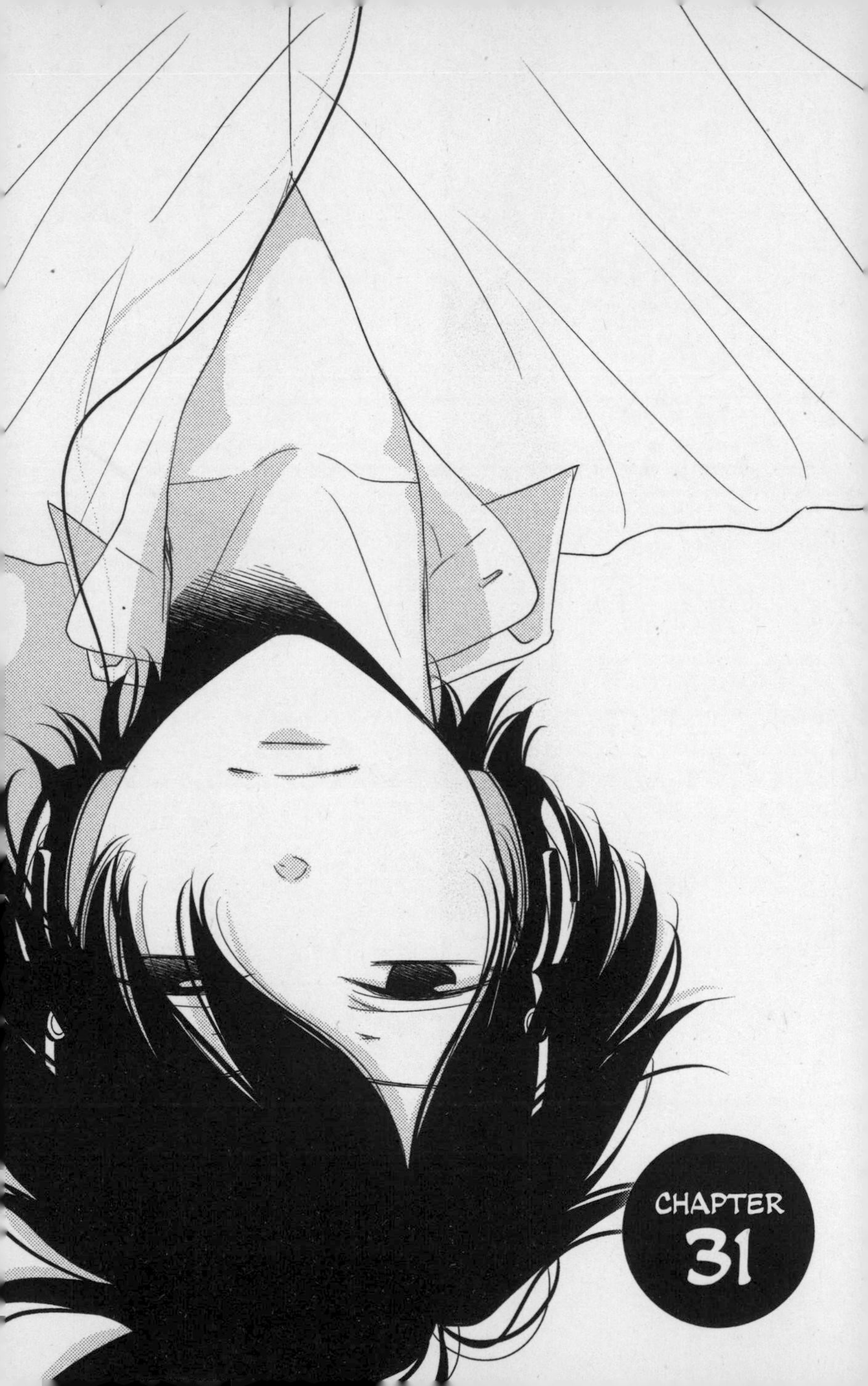
CHAPTER
31

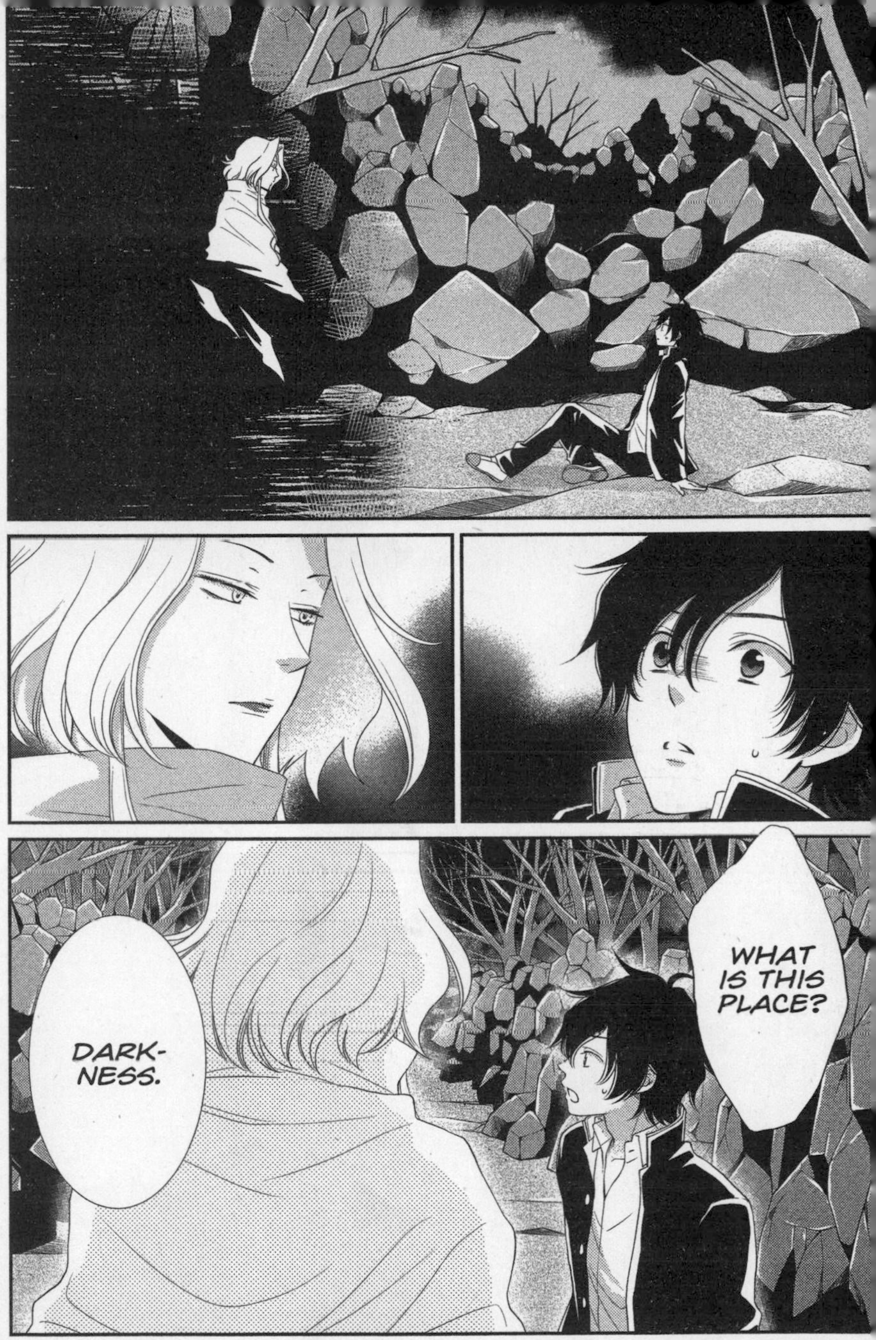
WHAT IS THIS PLACE?
DARK-NESS.

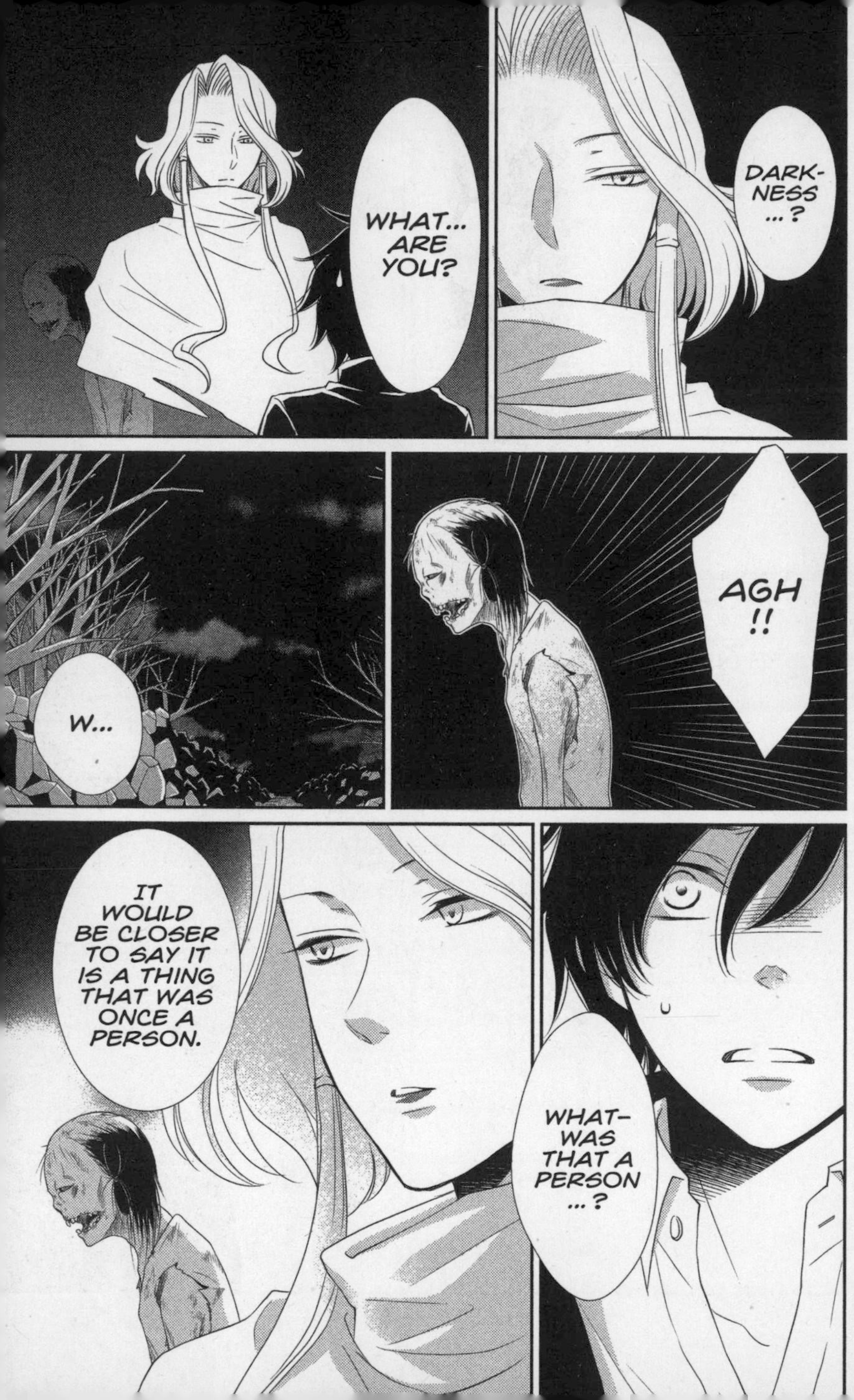
DARK-
NESS
...?
WHAT...
ARE
YOU?
AGH
!!
W...
WHAT-
WAS
THAT A
PERSON
...?
IT
WOULD
BE CLOSER
TO SAY IT
IS A THING
THAT WAS
ONCE A
PERSON.

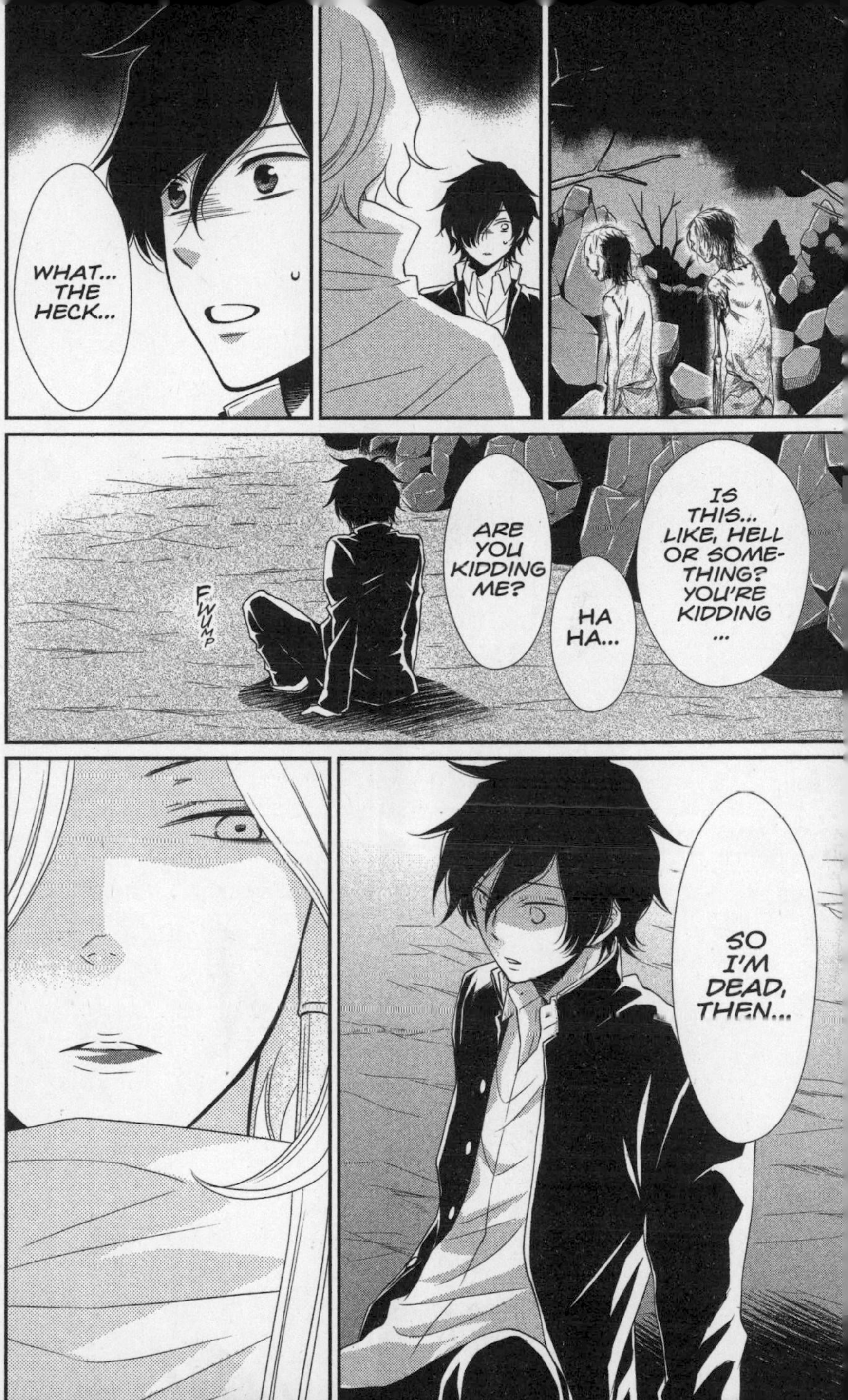
WHAT... THE HECK...
IS THIS... LIKE, HELL OR SOME-THING? YOU'RE KIDDING ...
HA HA...
ARE YOU KIDDING ME?
FWUMP
SO I'M DEAD, THEN...

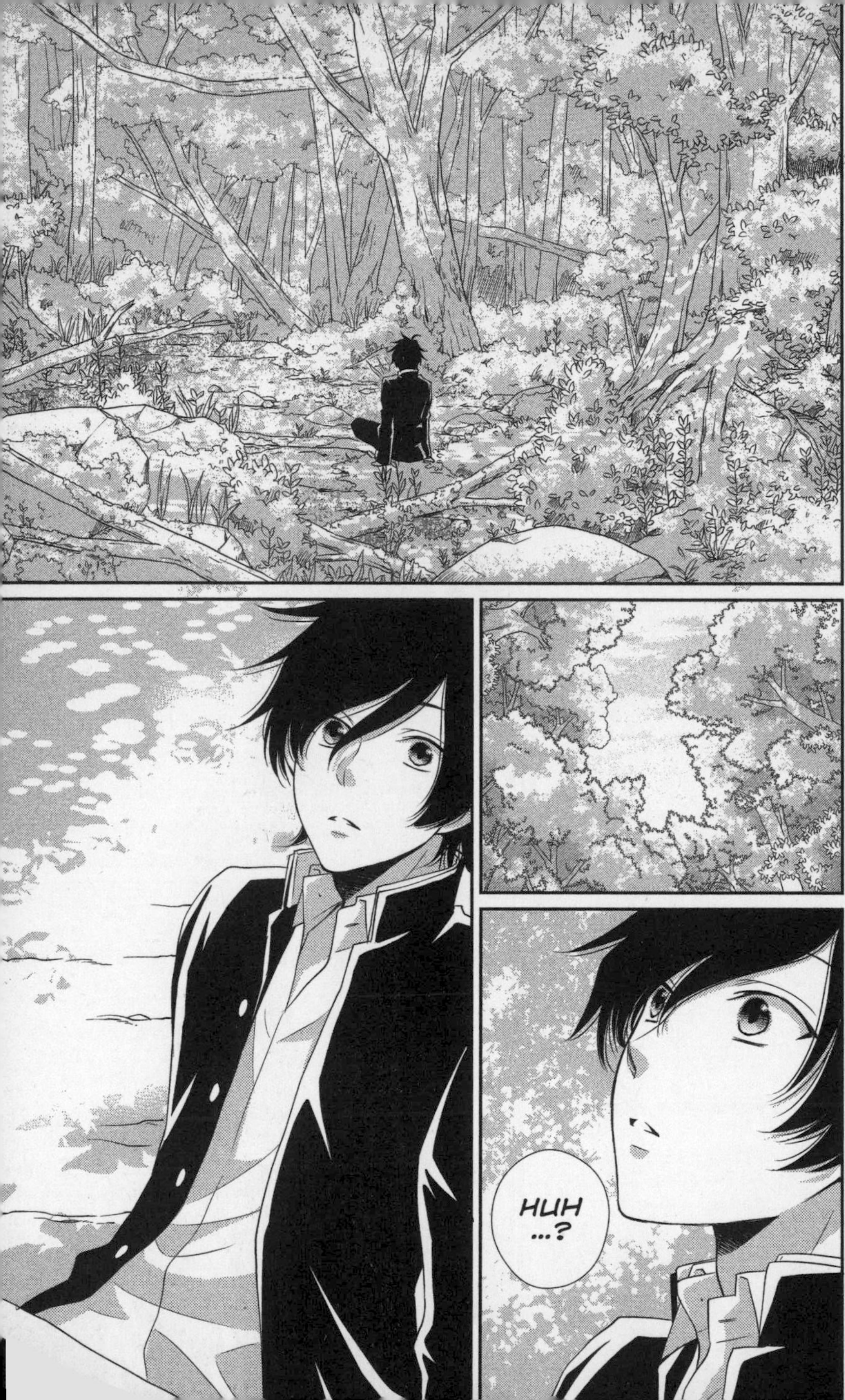
HUH
...?

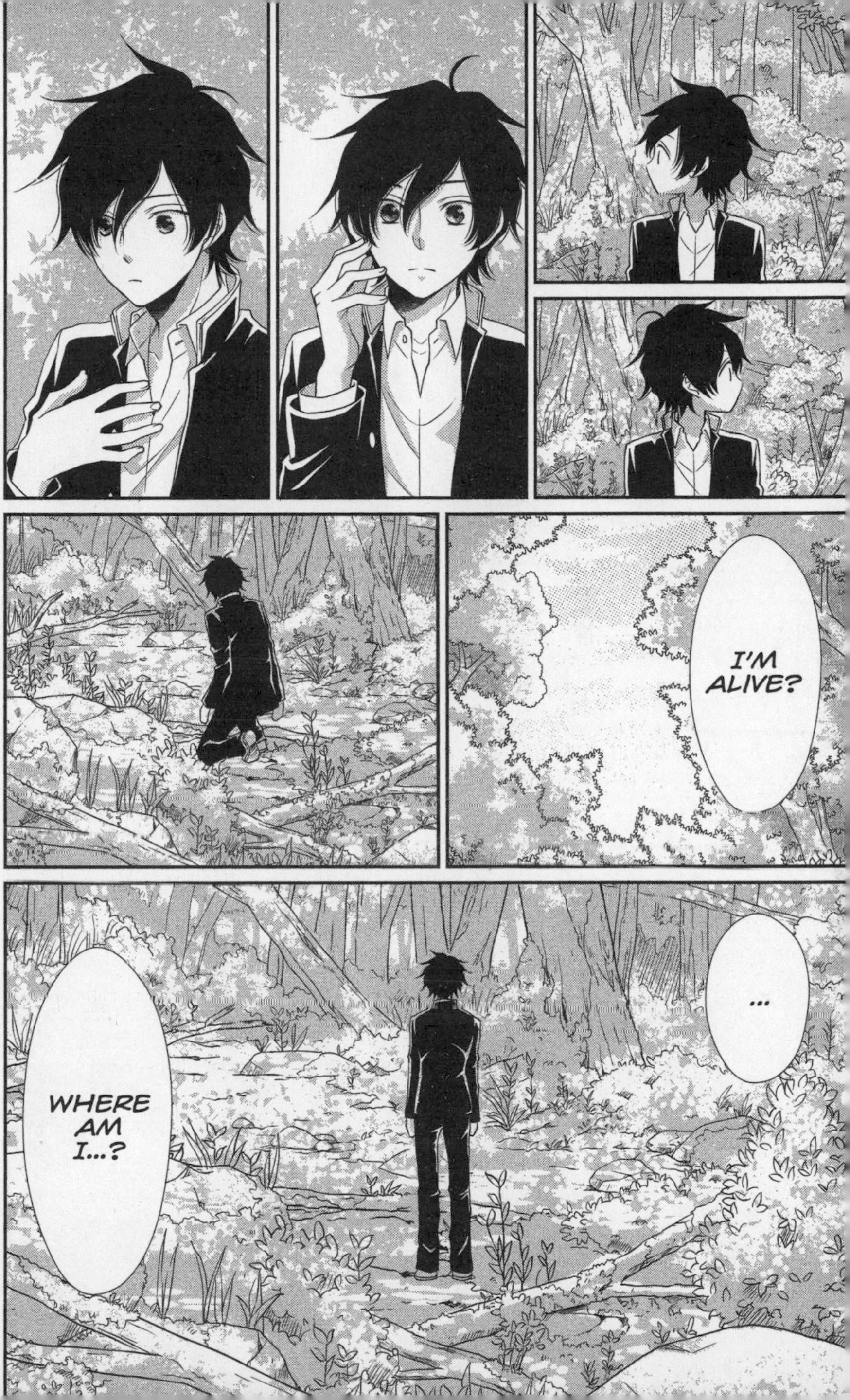
I'M ALIVE?
...
WHERE AM I...?

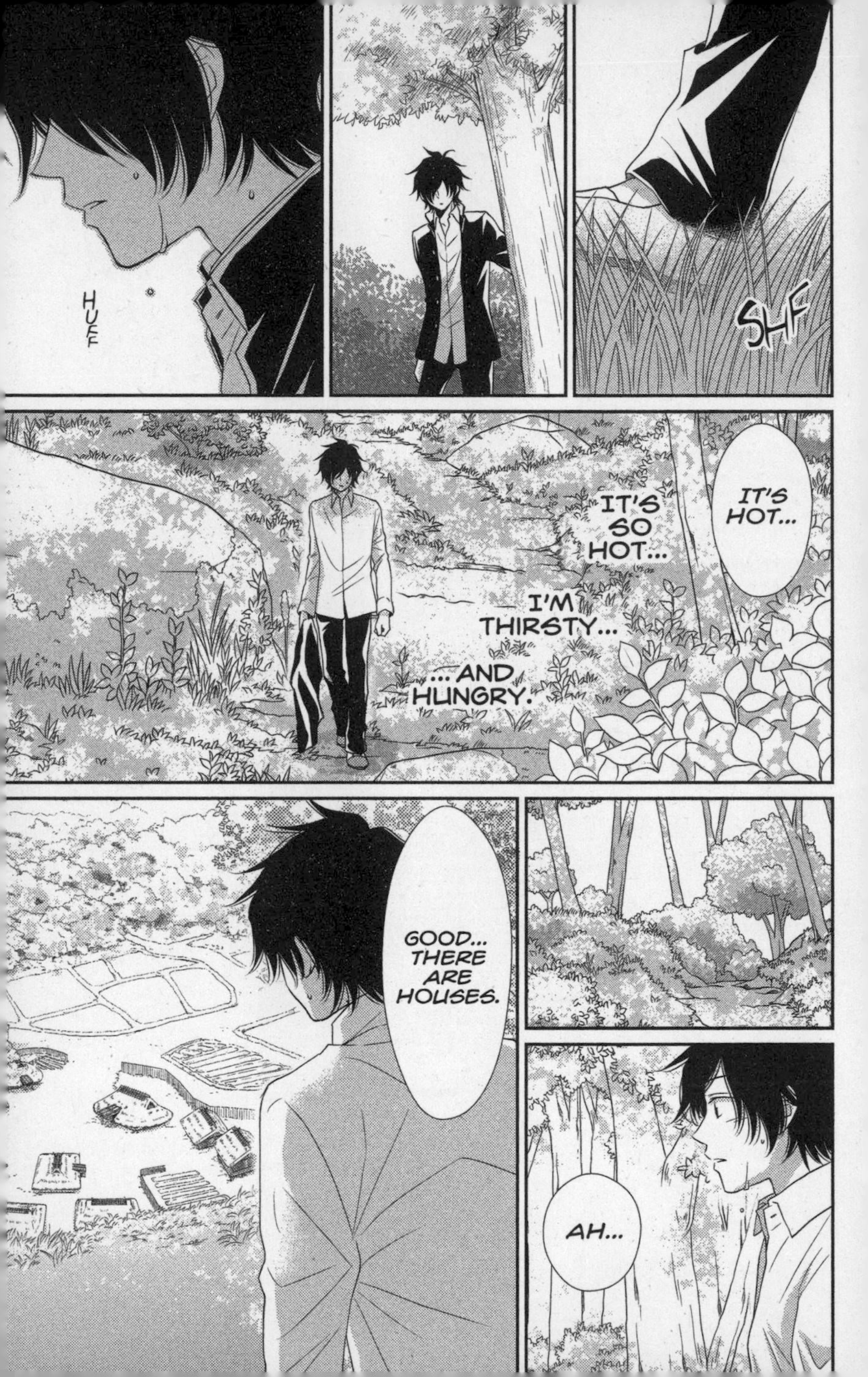
SHF
HUFF
IT'S HOT...
IT'S SO HOT...
I'M THIRSTY...
...AND HUNGRY.
AH...
GOOD... THERE ARE HOUSES.

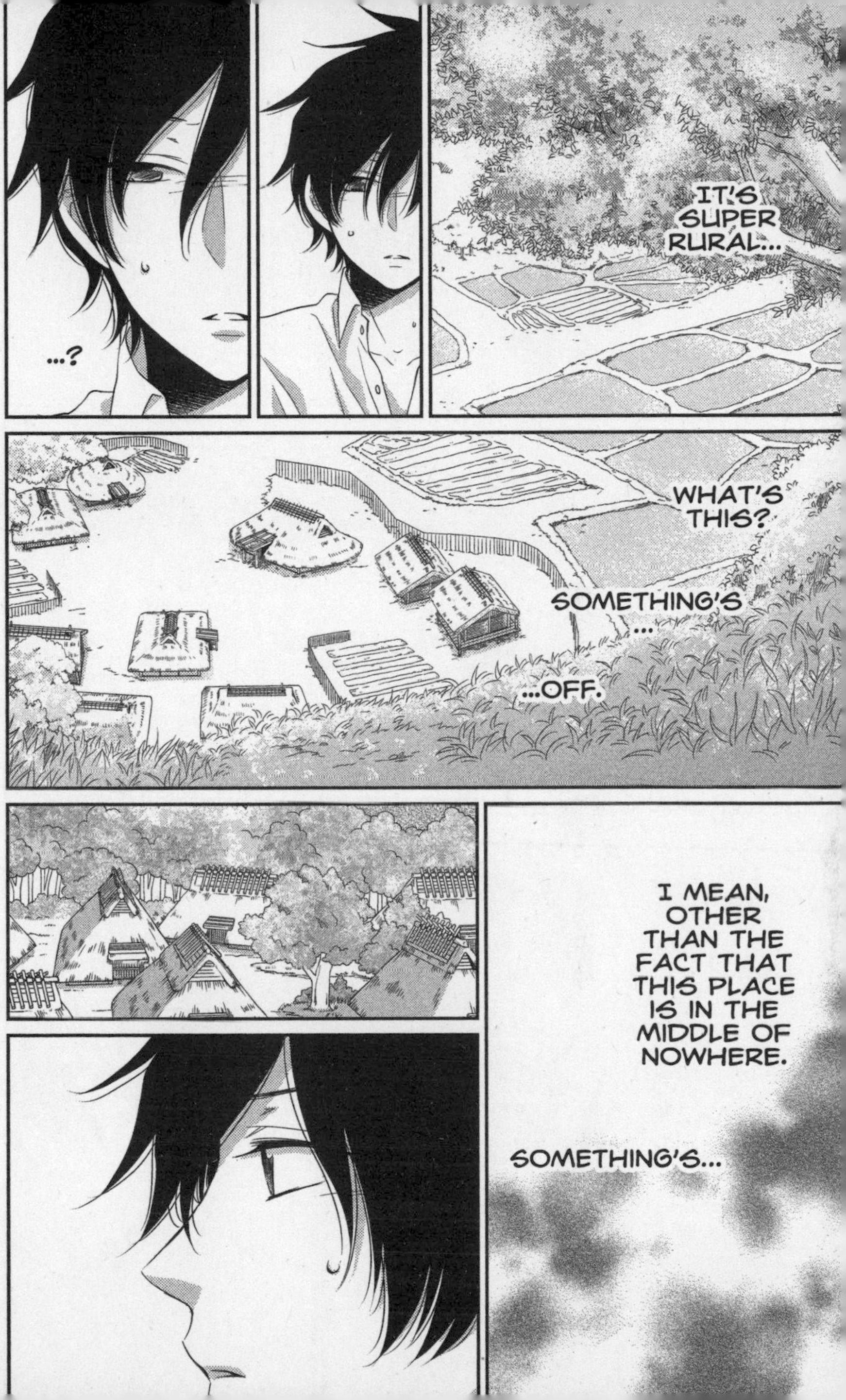
IT'S SUPER RURAL...
...?
WHAT'S THIS?
SOMETHING'S ...
...OFF.
I MEAN, OTHER THAN THE FACT THAT THIS PLACE IS IN THE MIDDLE OF NOWHERE.
SOMETHING'S...

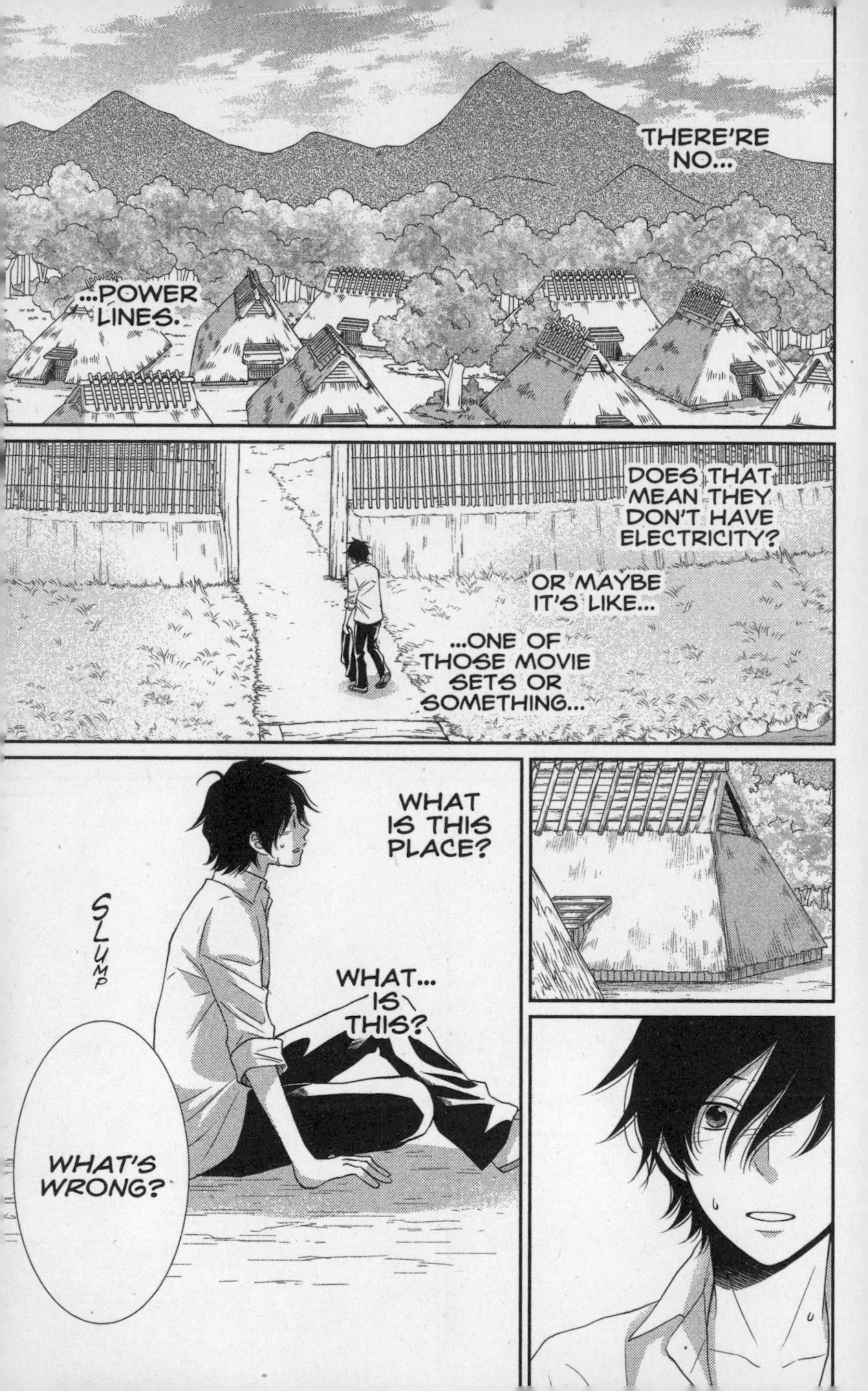
THERE'RE NO...
...POWER LINES.
DOES THAT MEAN THEY DON'T HAVE ELECTRICITY?
OR MAYBE IT'S LIKE...
...ONE OF THOSE MOVIE SETS OR SOMETHING...
WHAT IS THIS PLACE?
SLUMP
WHAT... IS THIS?
WHAT'S WRONG?

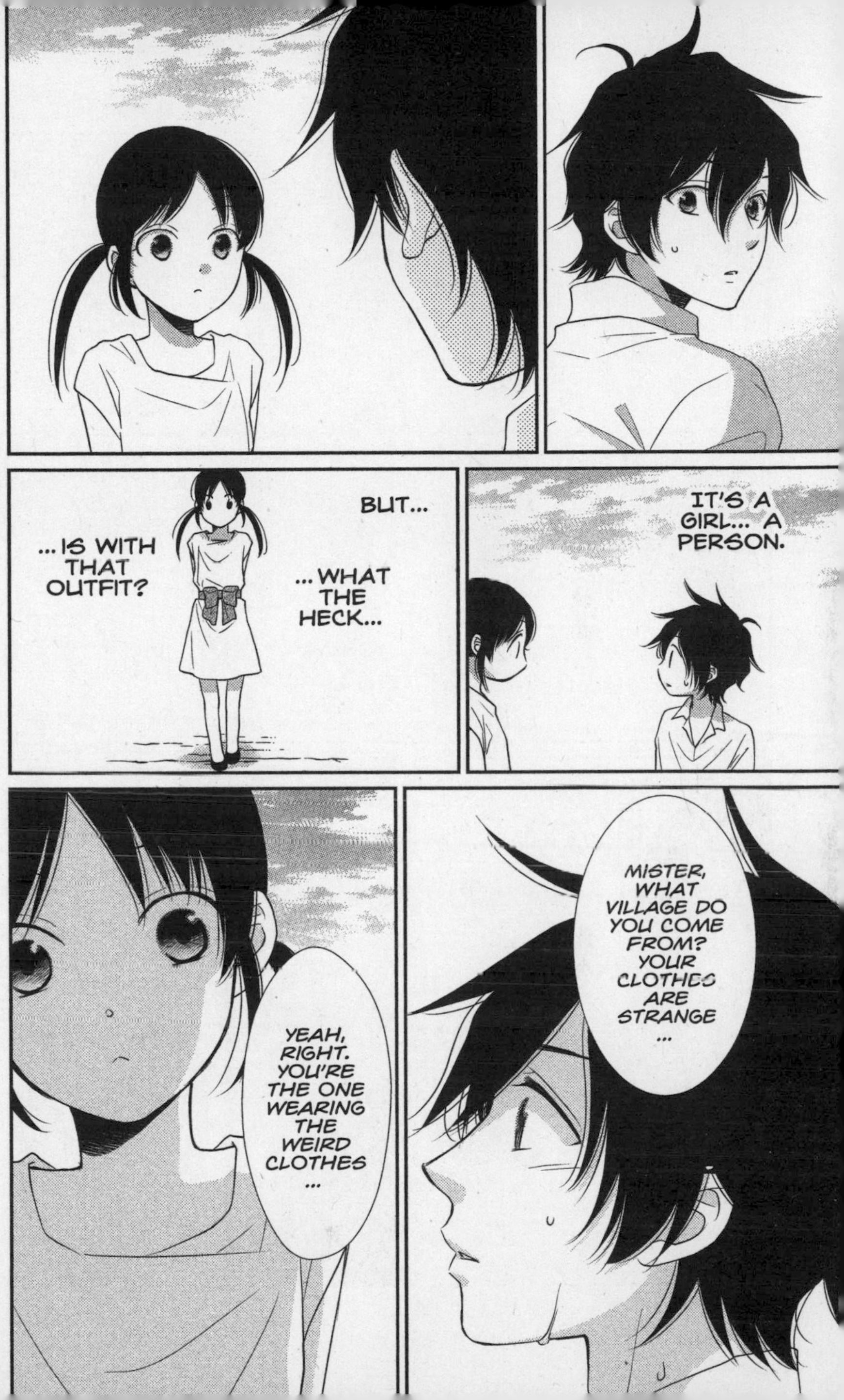
IT'S A GIRL... A PERSON.
BUT...
...WHAT THE HECK...
...IS WITH THAT OUTFIT?
MISTER, WHAT VILLAGE DO YOU COME FROM? YOUR CLOTHES ARE STRANGE...
YEAH, RIGHT. YOU'RE THE ONE WEARING THE WEIRD CLOTHES...

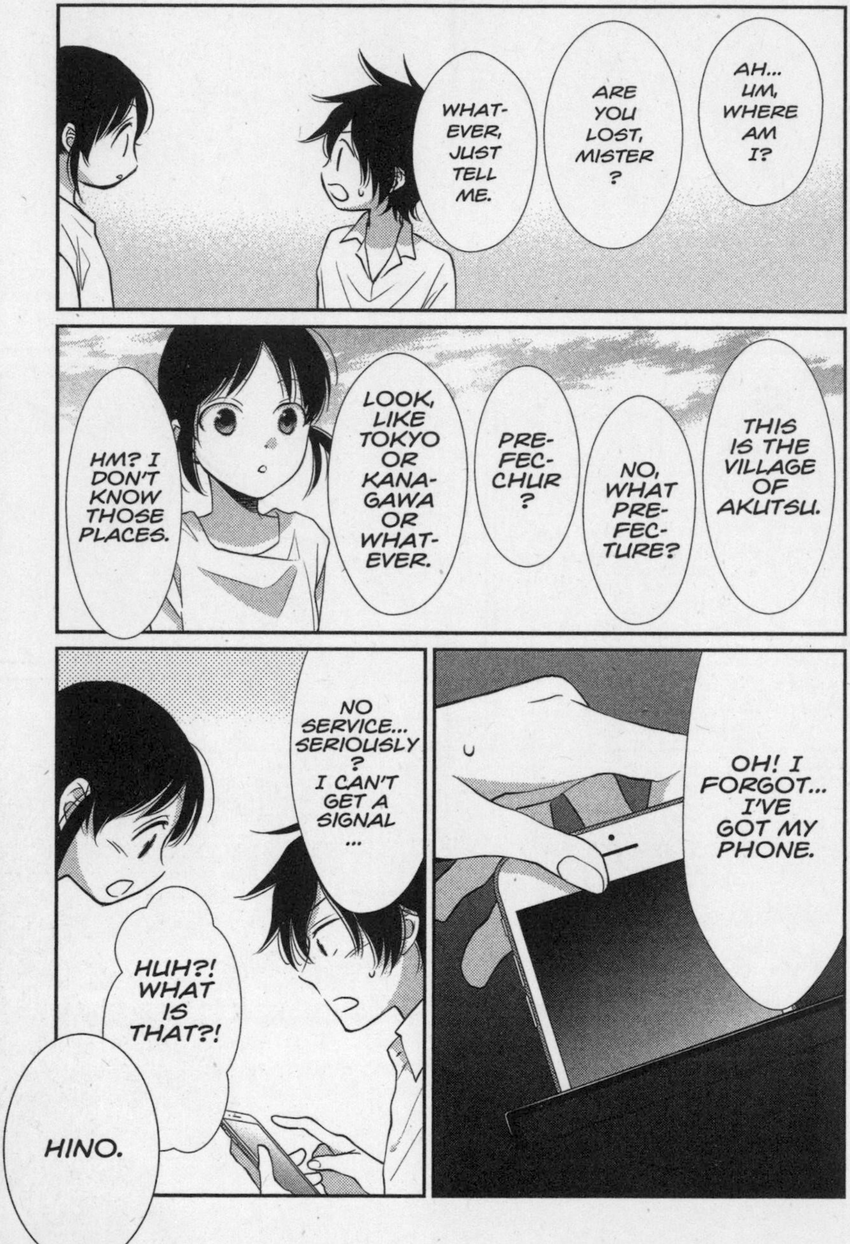
AH... UM, WHERE AM I?
ARE YOU LOST, MISTER?
WHATEVER, JUST TELL ME.
THIS IS THE VILLAGE OF AKUTSU.
NO, WHAT PREFECTURE?
PREFECHUR?
LOOK, LIKE TOKYO OR KANAGAWA OR WHATEVER.
HM? I DON'T KNOW THOSE PLACES.
OH! I FORGOT... I'VE GOT MY PHONE.
NO SERVICE... SERIOUSLY? I CAN'T GET A SIGNAL...
HUH?! WHAT IS THAT?!
HINO.

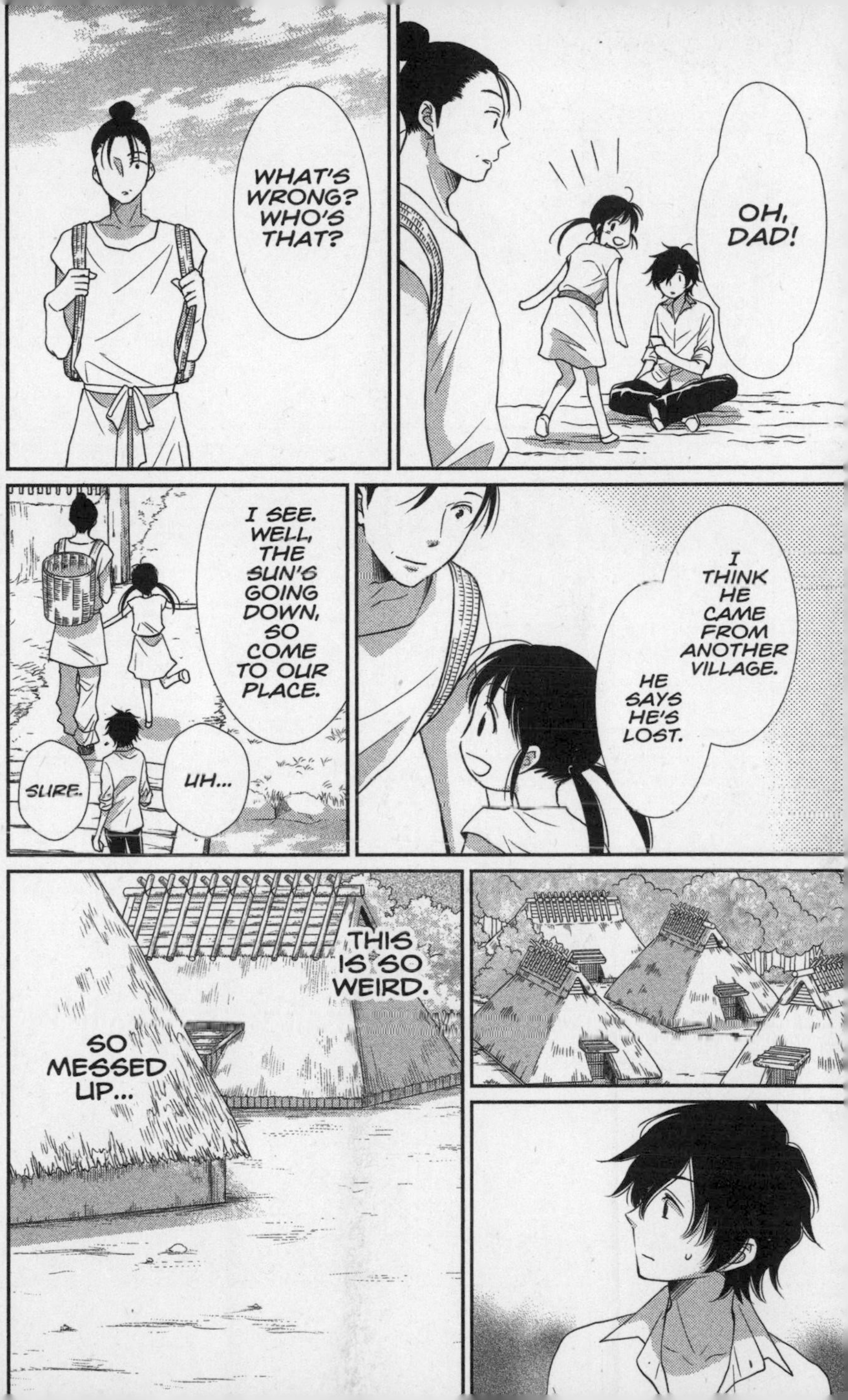
OH, DAD!
WHAT'S WRONG? WHO'S THAT?
I THINK HE CAME FROM ANOTHER VILLAGE.
HE SAYS HE'S LOST.
I SEE. WELL, THE SUN'S GOING DOWN, SO COME TO OUR PLACE.
UH...
SURE.
THIS IS SO WEIRD.
SO MESSED UP...

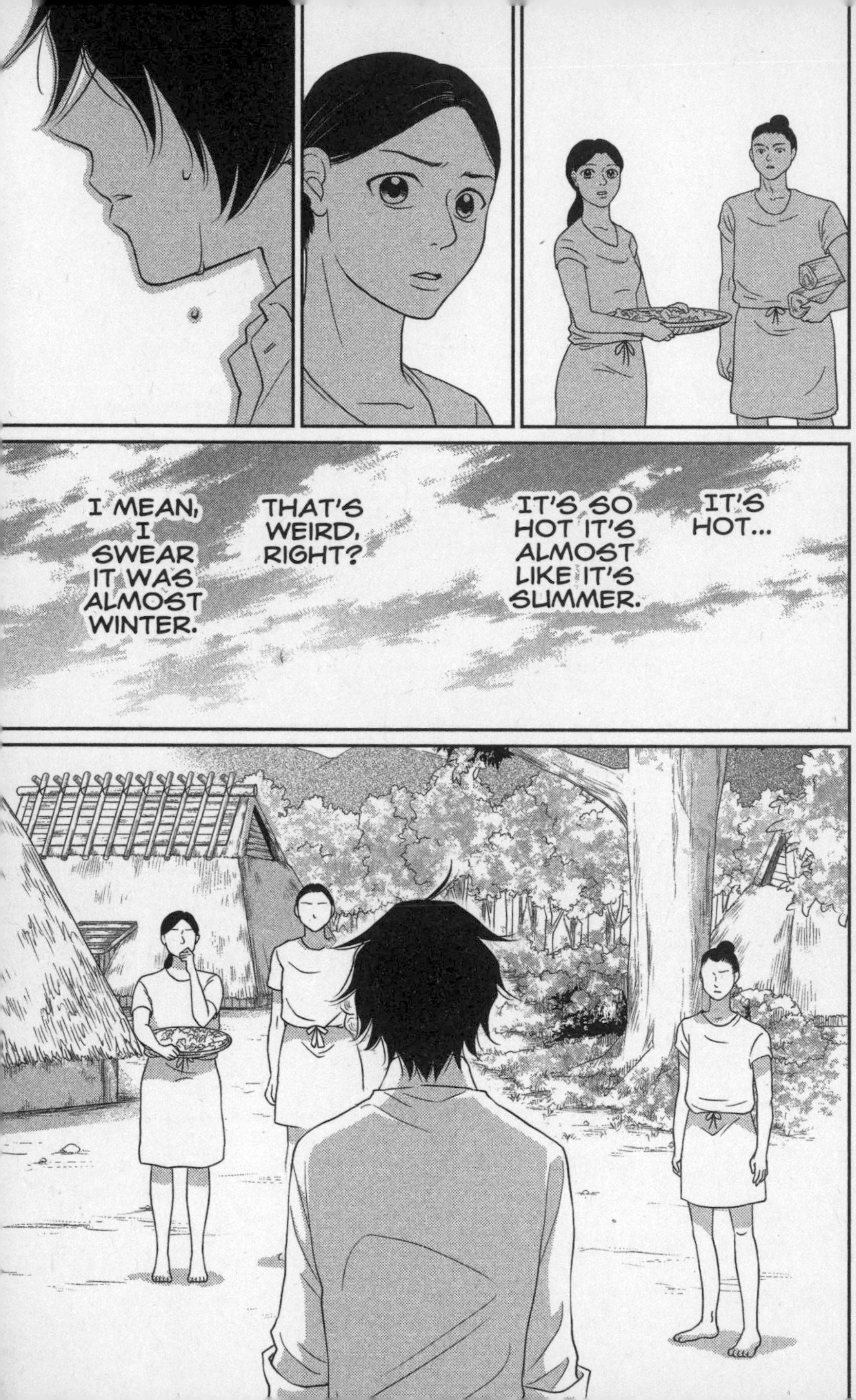
IT'S HOT...
IT'S SO HOT IT'S ALMOST LIKE IT'S SUMMER.
THAT'S WEIRD, RIGHT?
I MEAN, I SWEAR IT WAS ALMOST WINTER.

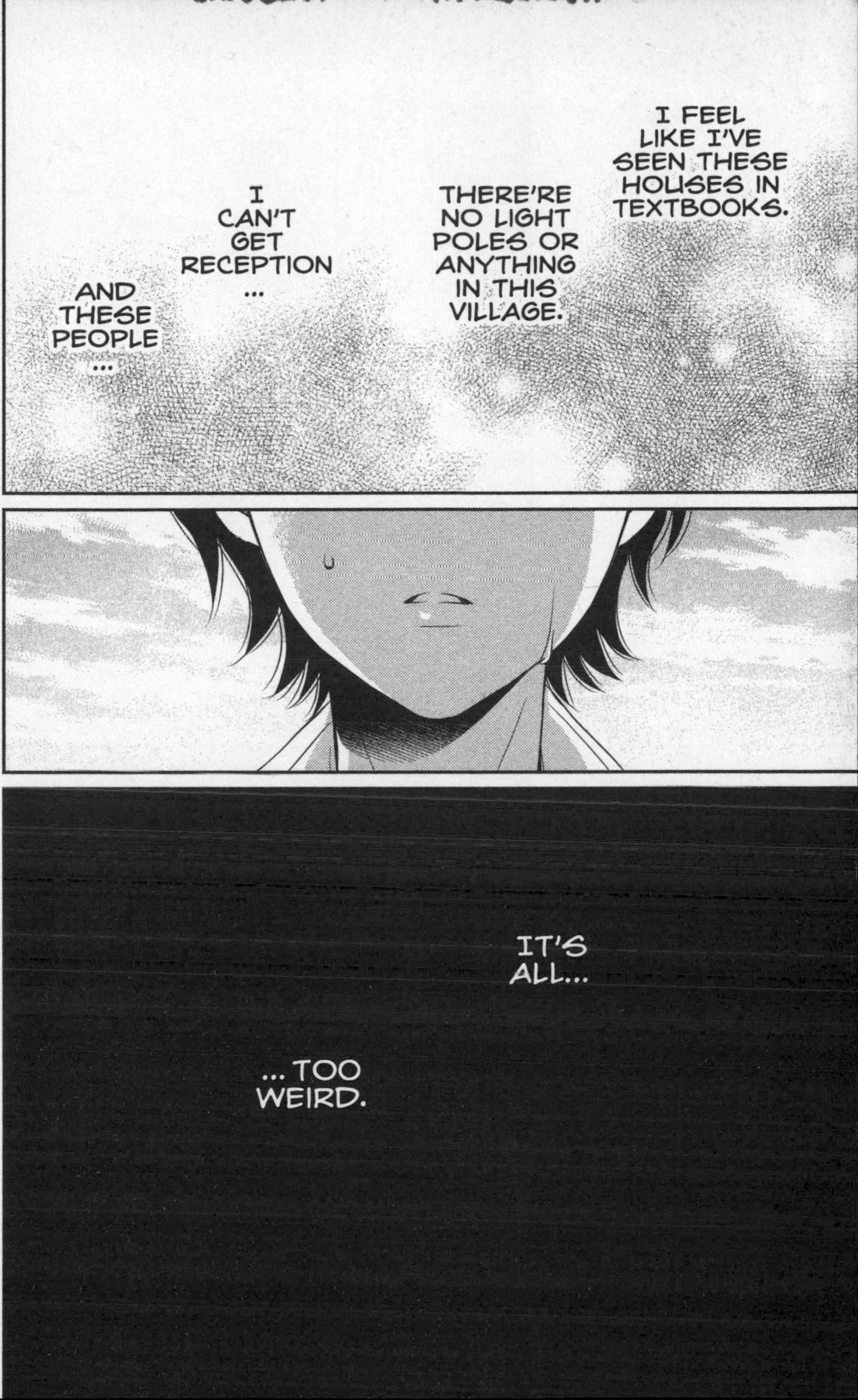
I FEEL LIKE I'VE SEEN THESE HOUSES IN TEXTBOOKS.
THERE'RE NO LIGHT POLES OR ANYTHING IN THIS VILLAGE.
I CAN'T GET RECEPTION ...
AND THESE PEOPLE ...
IT'S ALL...
... TOO WEIRD.

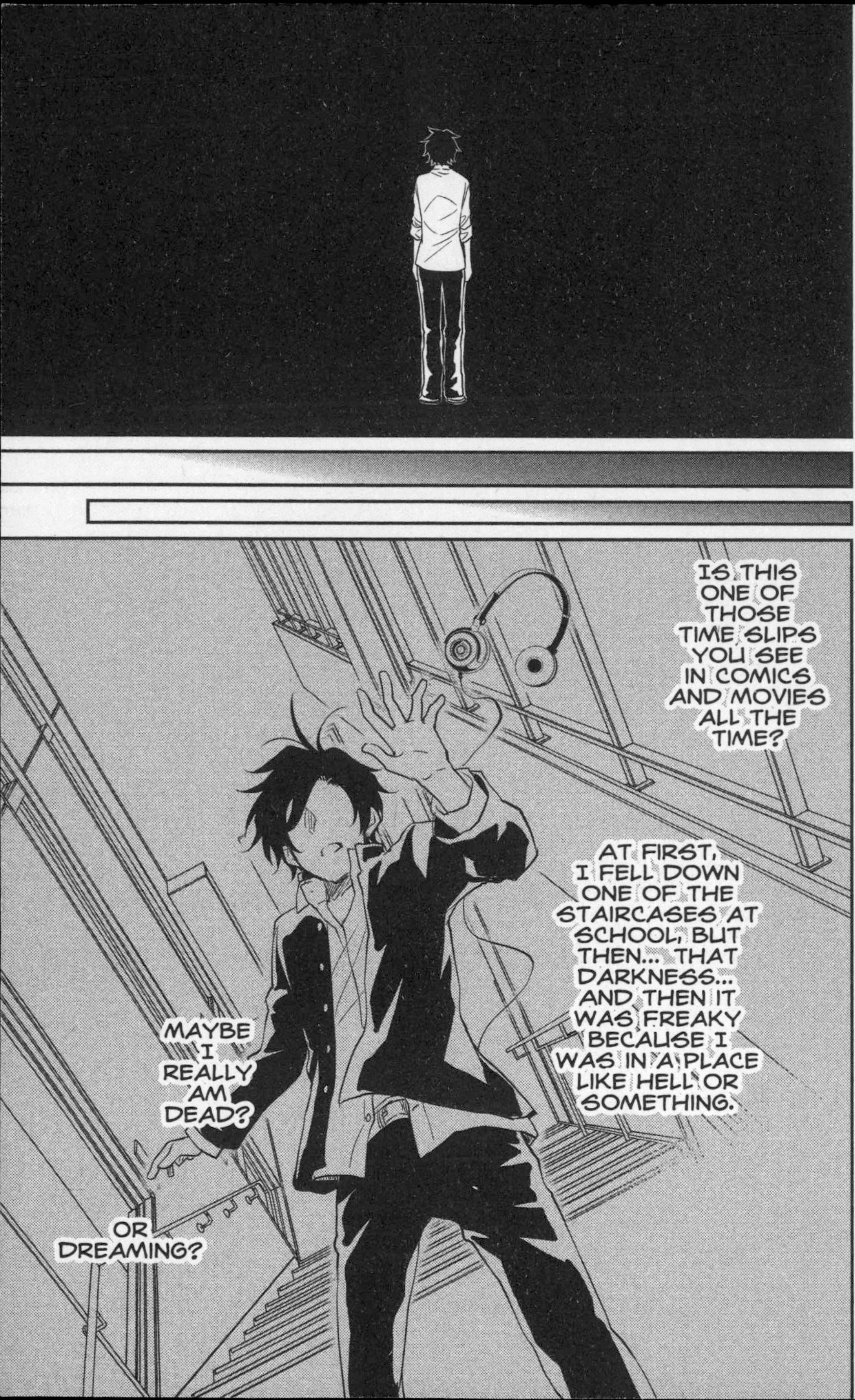
IS THIS ONE OF THOSE TIME SLIPS YOU SEE IN COMICS AND MOVIES ALL THE TIME?
AT FIRST, I FELL DOWN ONE OF THE STAIRCASES AT SCHOOL, BUT THEN... THAT DARKNESS... AND THEN IT WAS FREAKY BECAUSE I WAS IN A PLACE LIKE HELL OR SOMETHING.
MAYBE I REALLY AM DEAD?
OR DREAMING?

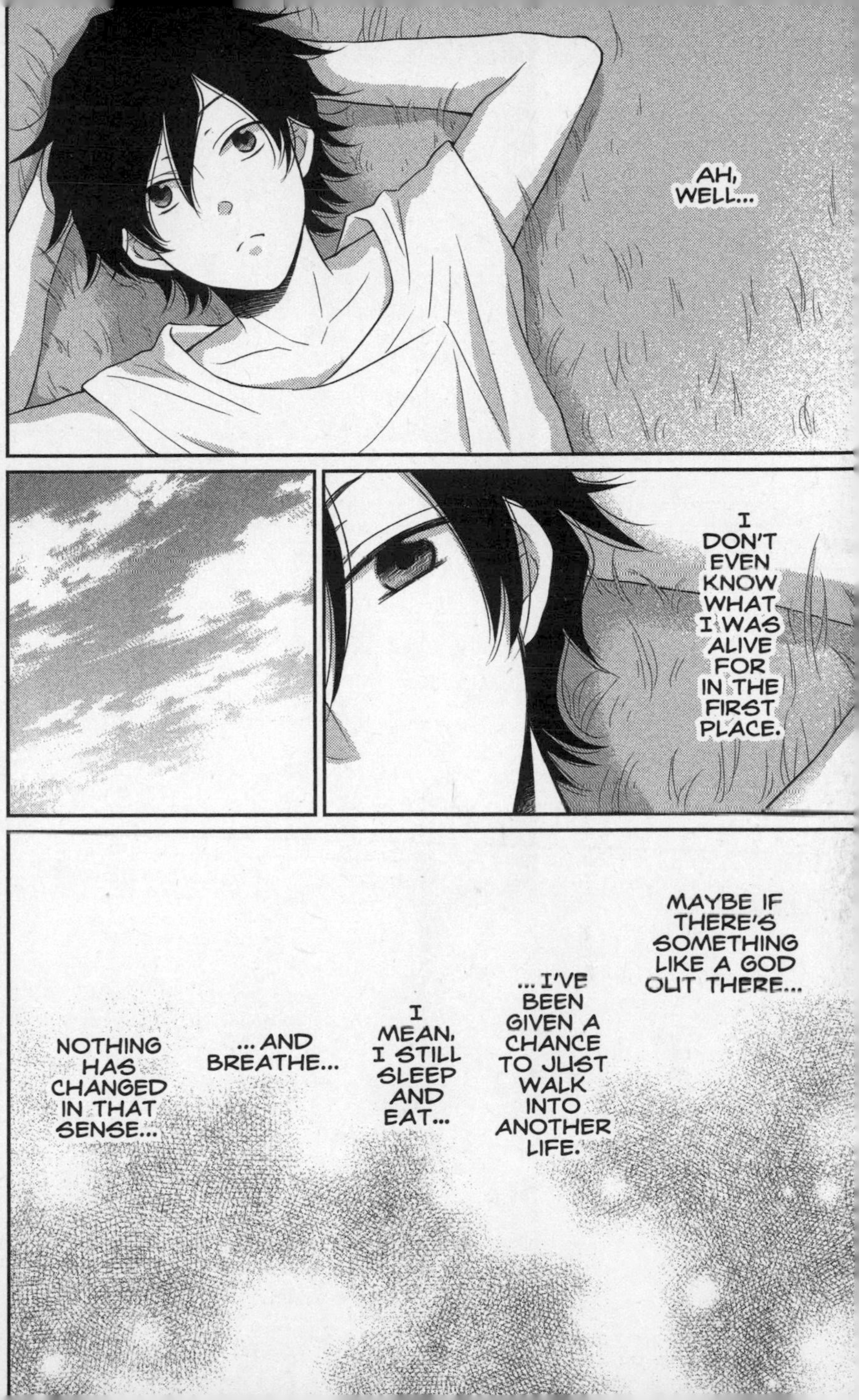
AH, WELL...
I DON'T EVEN KNOW WHAT I WAS ALIVE FOR IN THE FIRST PLACE.
MAYBE IF THERE'S SOMETHING LIKE A GOD OUT THERE...
... I'VE BEEN GIVEN A CHANCE TO JUST WALK INTO ANOTHER LIFE.
I MEAN, I STILL SLEEP AND EAT...
... AND BREATHE...
NOTHING HAS CHANGED IN THAT SENSE...

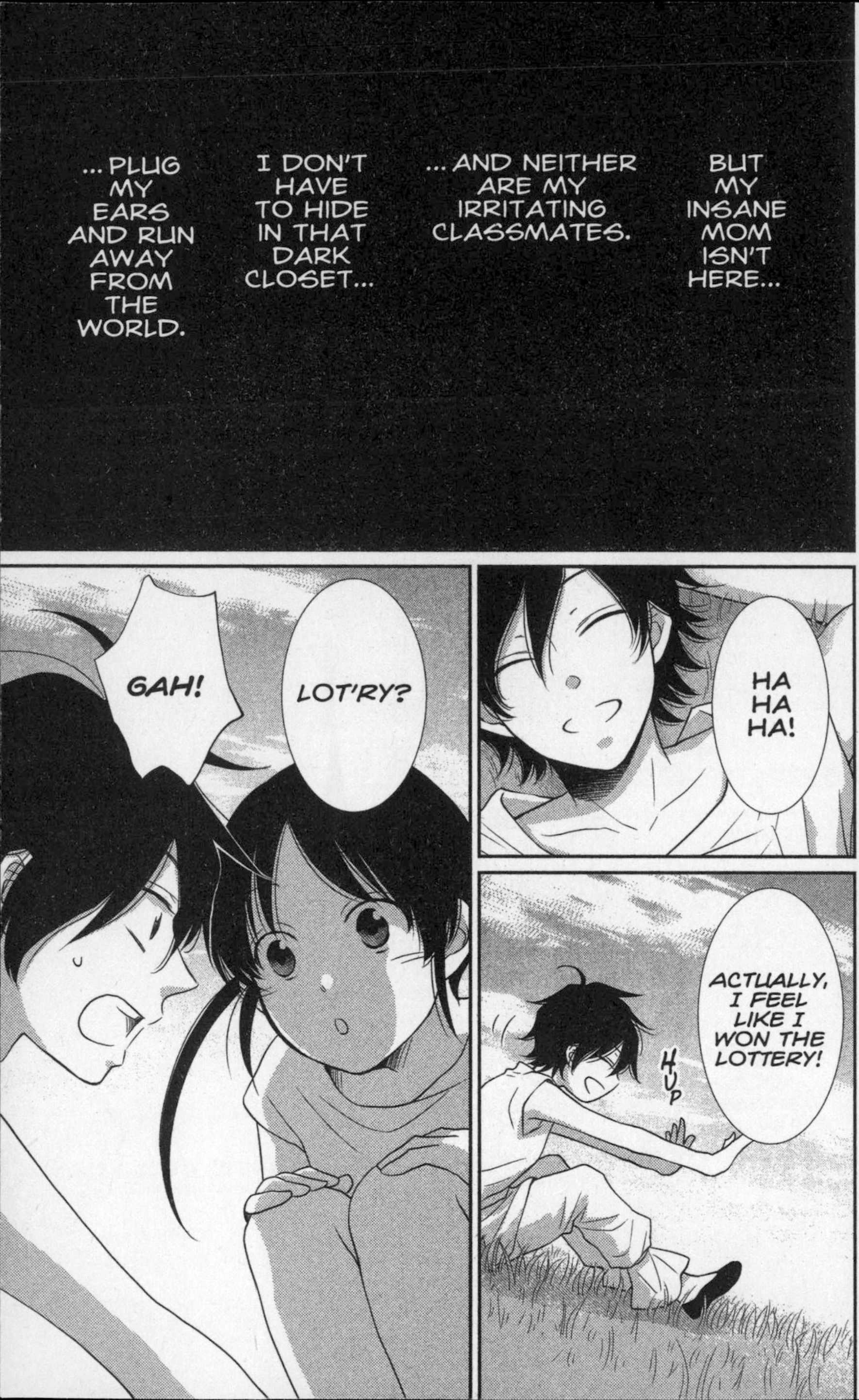
BUT MY INSANE MOM ISN'T HERE...
...AND NEITHER ARE MY IRRITATING CLASSMATES.
I DON'T HAVE TO HIDE IN THAT DARK CLOSET...
...PLUG MY EARS AND RUN AWAY FROM THE WORLD.
HA HA HA!
ACTUALLY, I FEEL LIKE I WON THE LOTTERY!
HUP
LOT'RY?
GAH!

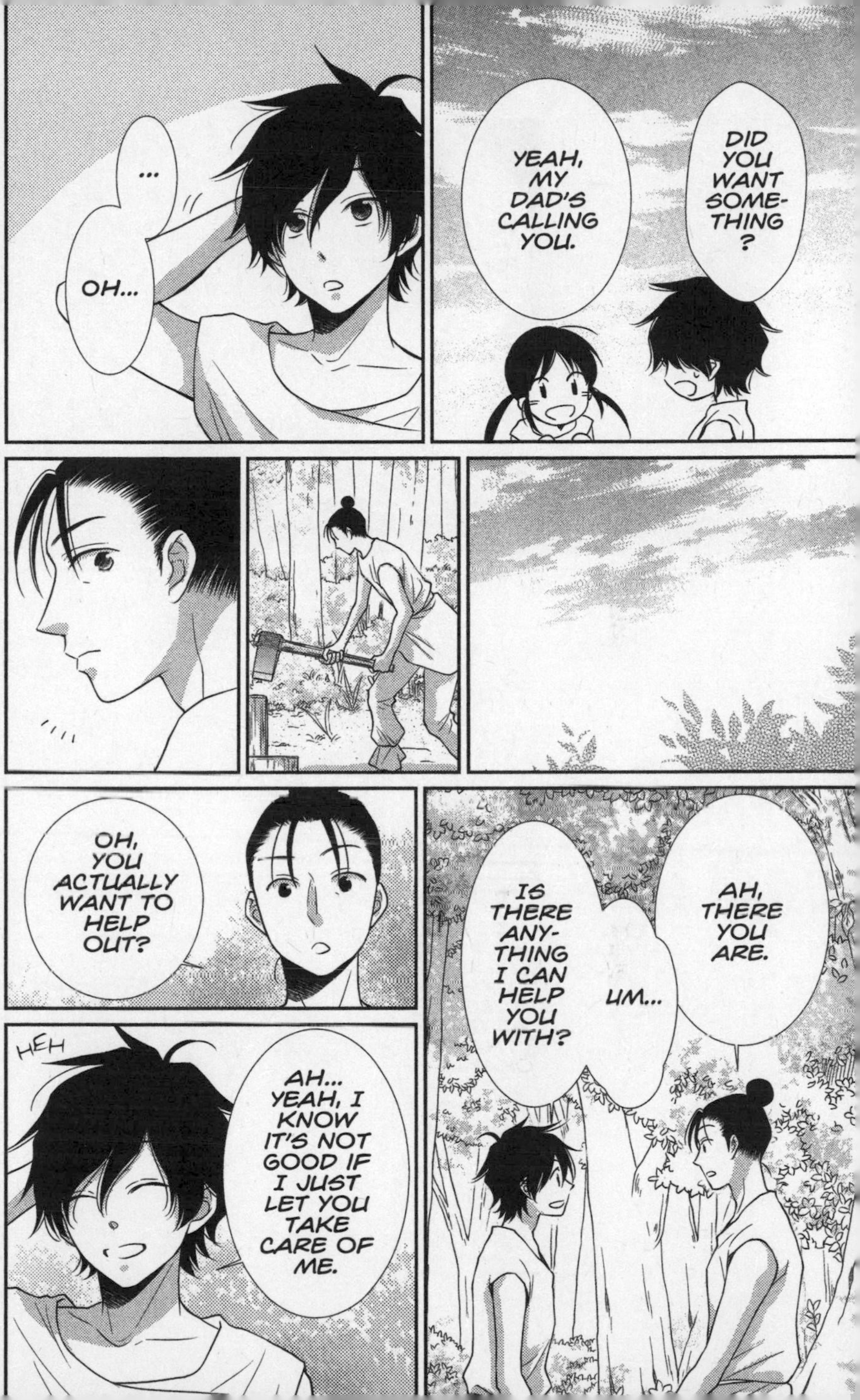
DID YOU WANT SOME-THING?
YEAH, MY DAD'S CALLING YOU.
...
OH...
AH, THERE YOU ARE.
UM...
IS THERE ANY-THING I CAN HELP YOU WITH?
OH, YOU ACTUALLY WANT TO HELP OUT?
HEH
AH... YEAH, I KNOW IT'S NOT GOOD IF I JUST LET YOU TAKE CARE OF ME.

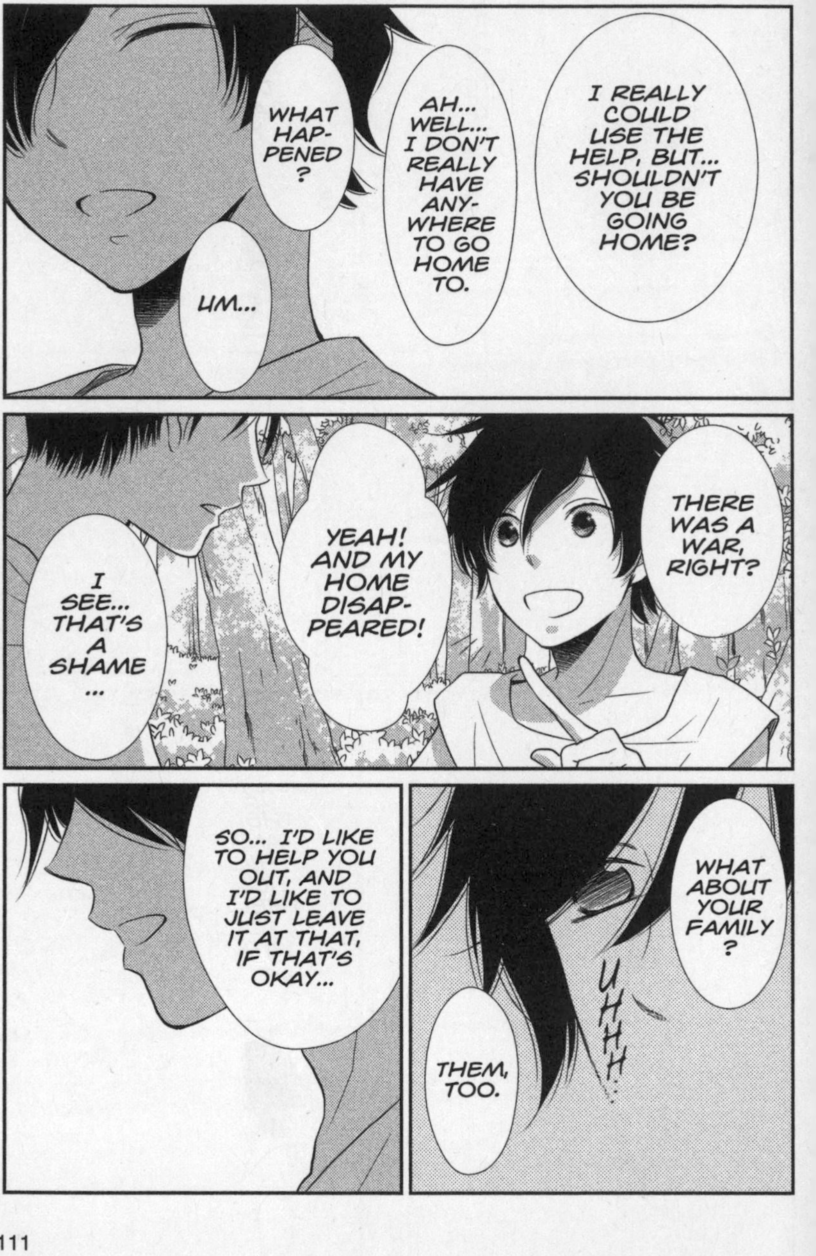
I REALLY COULD USE THE HELP, BUT... SHOULDN'T YOU BE GOING HOME?
AH... WELL... I DON'T REALLY HAVE ANY-WHERE TO GO HOME TO.
WHAT HAP-PENED?
UM...
THERE WAS A WAR, RIGHT?
YEAH! AND MY HOME DISAP-PEARED!
I SEE... THAT'S A SHAME...
WHAT ABOUT YOUR FAMILY?
UHHH...
THEM, TOO.
SO... I'D LIKE TO HELP YOU OUT, AND I'D LIKE TO JUST LEAVE IT AT THAT, IF THAT'S OKAY...

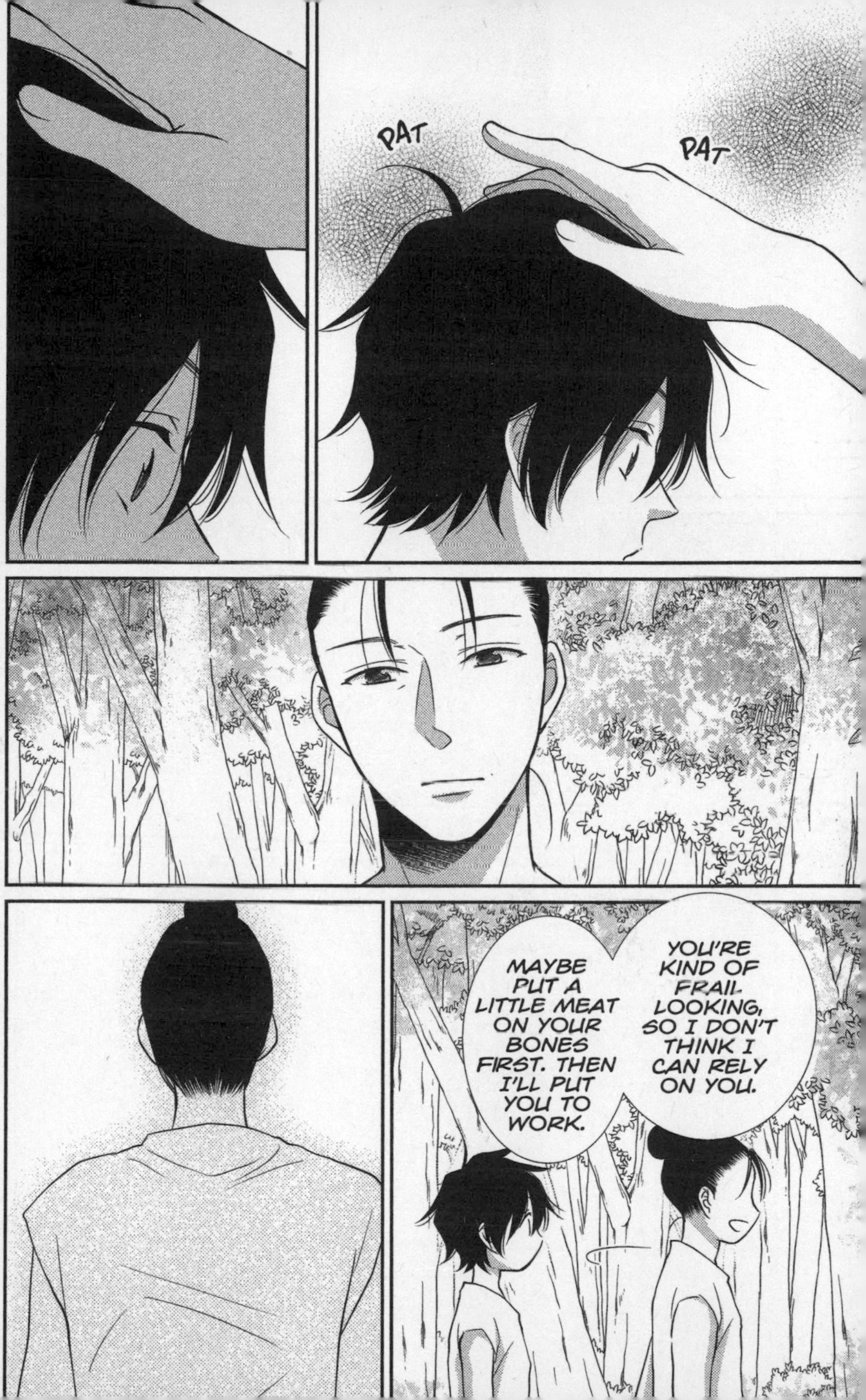
PAT
PAT
YOU'RE KIND OF FRAIL-LOOKING, SO I DON'T THINK I CAN RELY ON YOU.
MAYBE PUT A LITTLE MEAT ON YOUR BONES FIRST. THEN I'LL PUT YOU TO WORK.

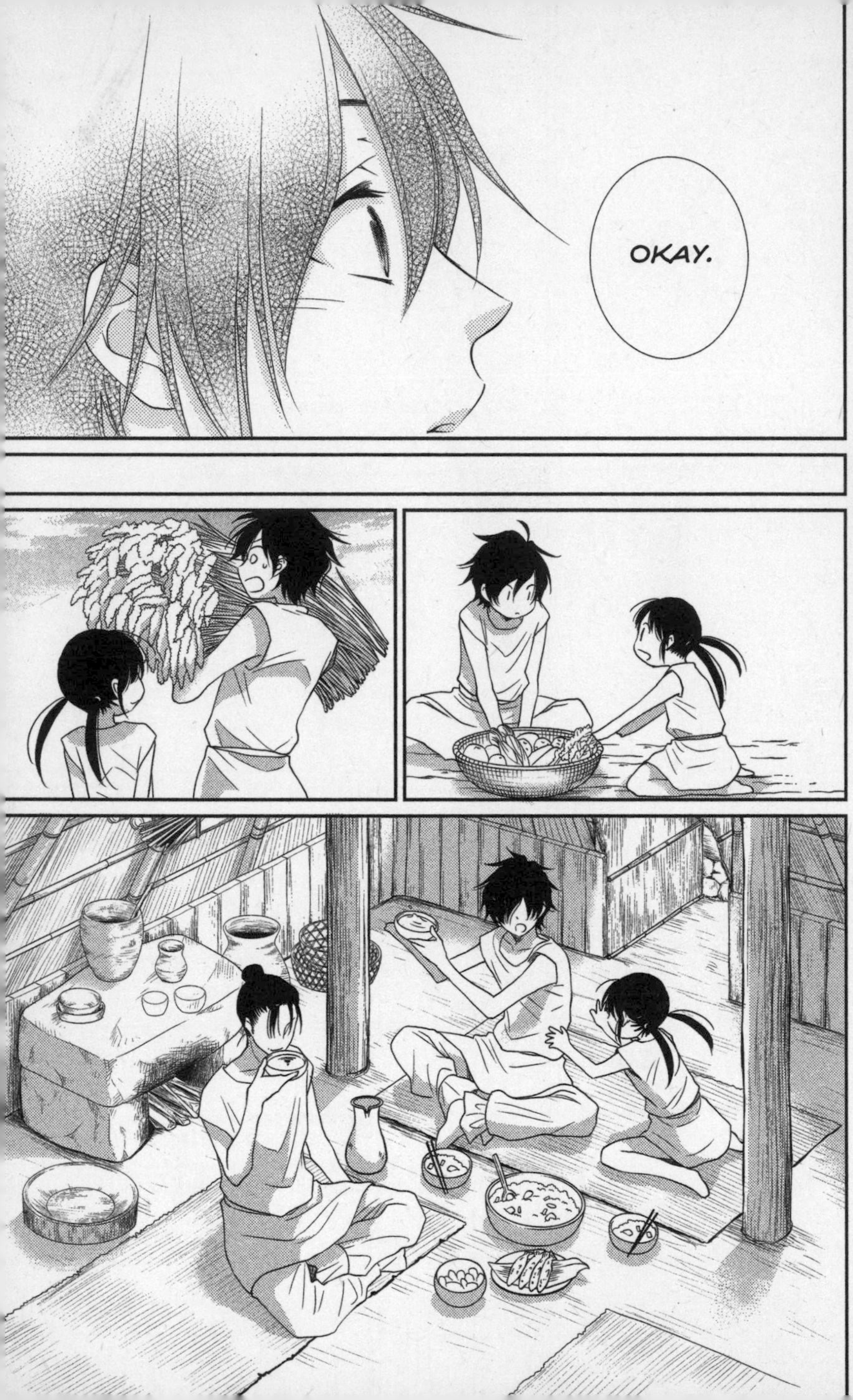
OKAY.

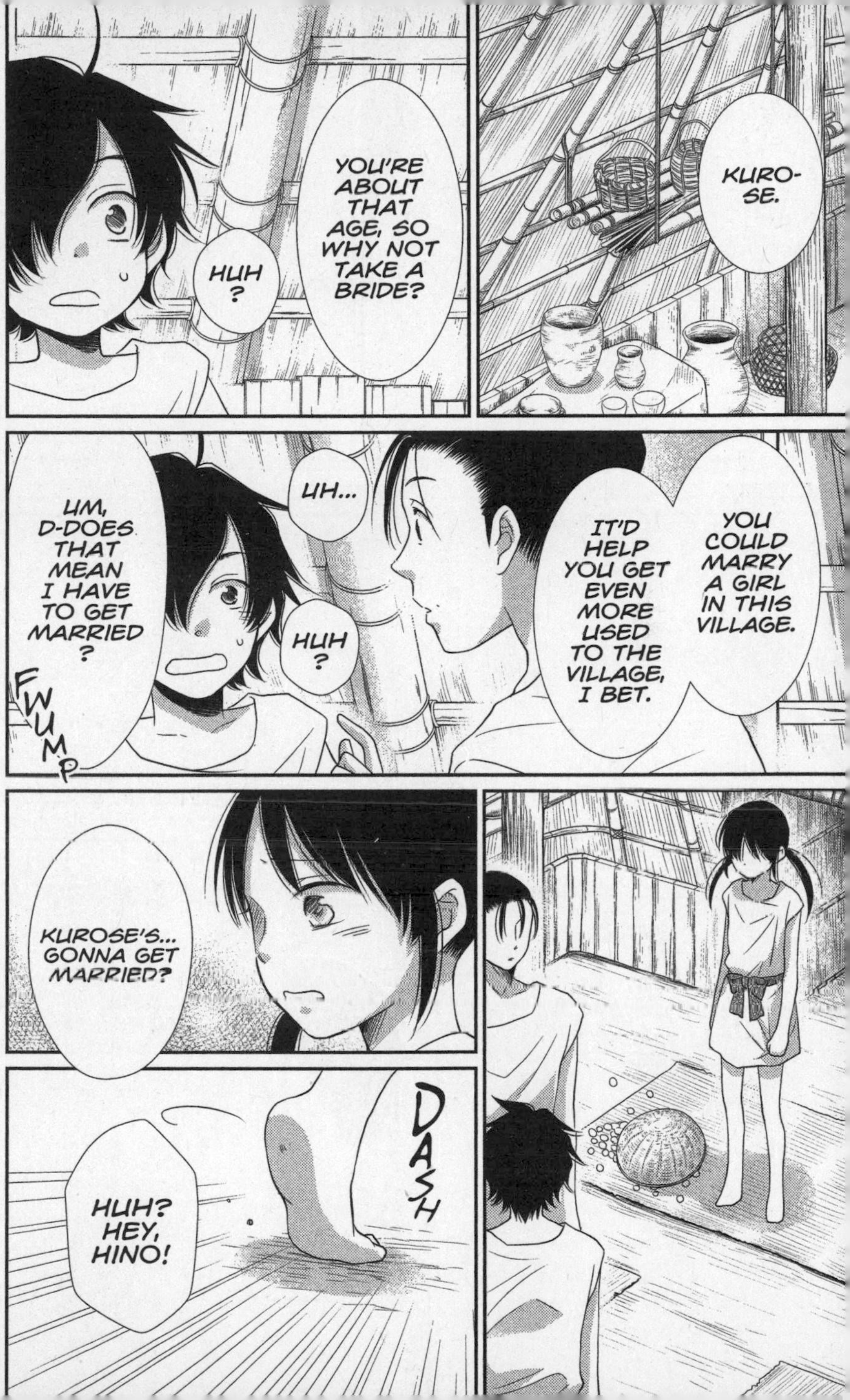
KURO-SE.
YOU'RE ABOUT THAT AGE, SO WHY NOT TAKE A BRIDE?
HUH?
YOU COULD MARRY A GIRL IN THIS VILLAGE.
IT'D HELP YOU GET EVEN MORE USED TO THE VILLAGE, I BET.
UH...
HUH?
UM, D-DOES THAT MEAN I HAVE TO GET MARRIED?
FWUMP
KUROSE'S... GONNA GET MARRIED?
DASH
HUH? HEY, HINO!

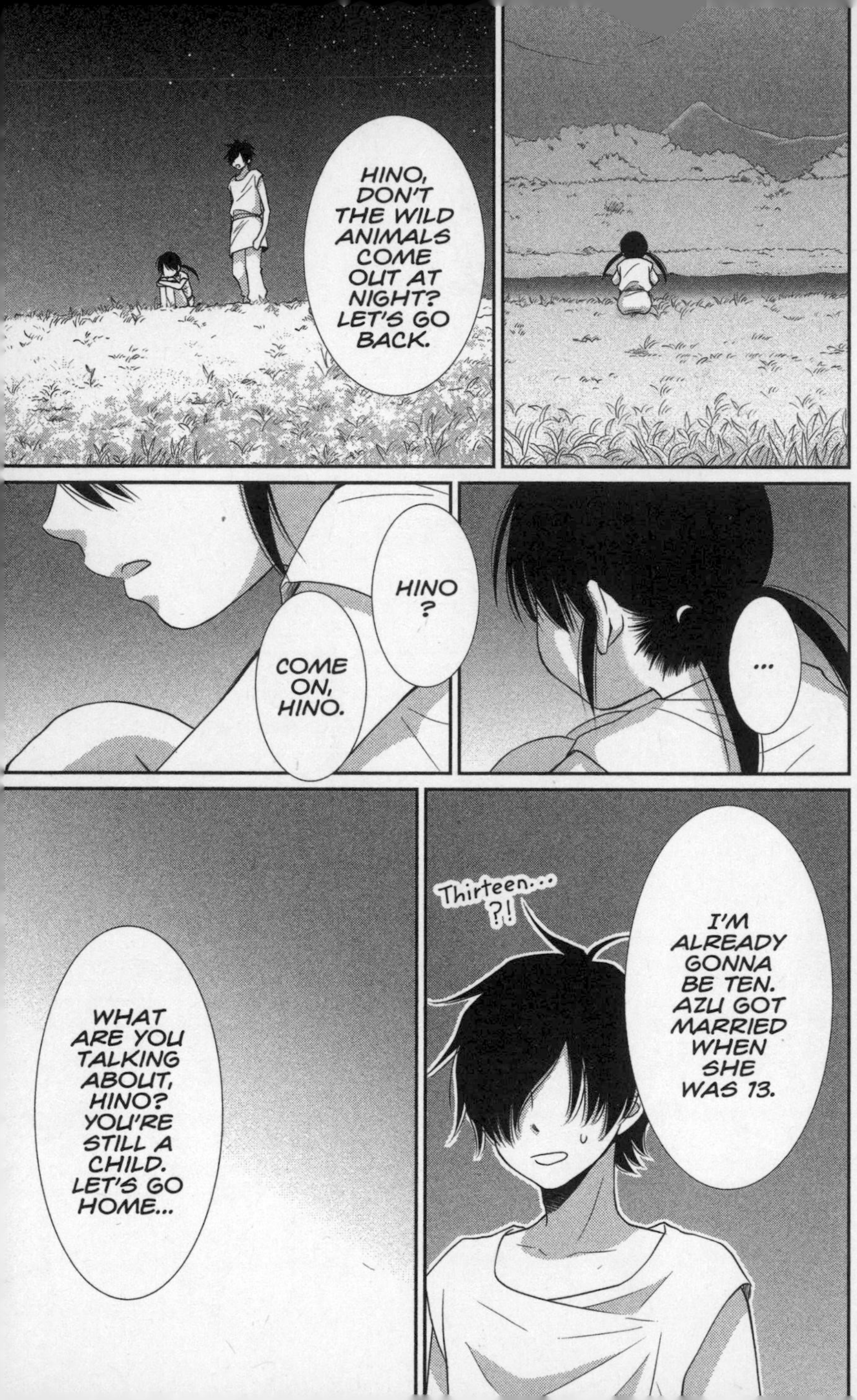
HINO, DON'T THE WILD ANIMALS COME OUT AT NIGHT? LET'S GO BACK.
...
HINO?
COME ON, HINO.
I'M ALREADY GONNA BE TEN. AZU GOT MARRIED WHEN SHE WAS 13.
Thirteen... ?!
WHAT ARE YOU TALKING ABOUT, HINO? YOU'RE STILL A CHILD. LET'S GO HOME...

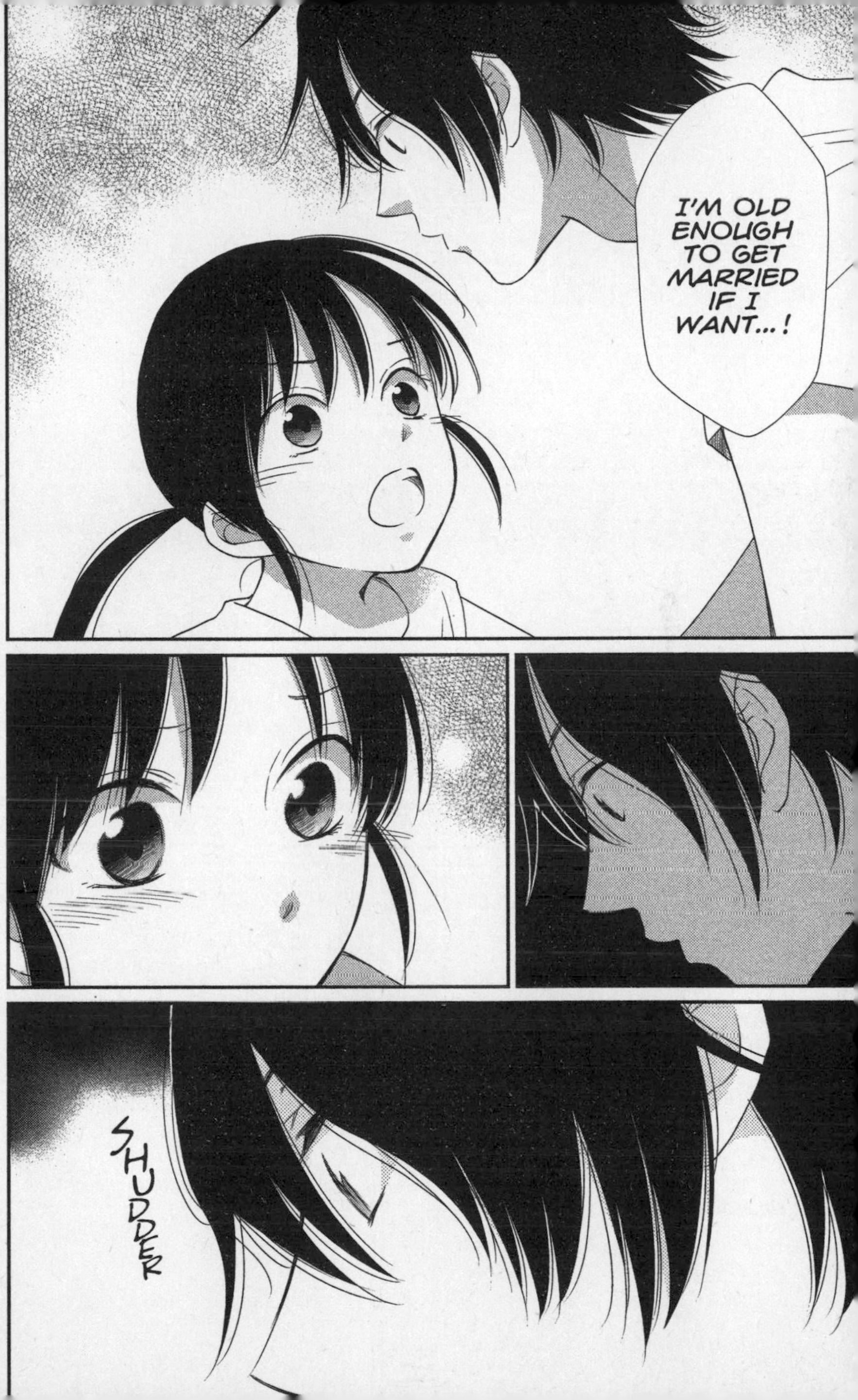
I'M OLD ENOUGH TO GET MARRIED IF I WANT...!
SHUDDER

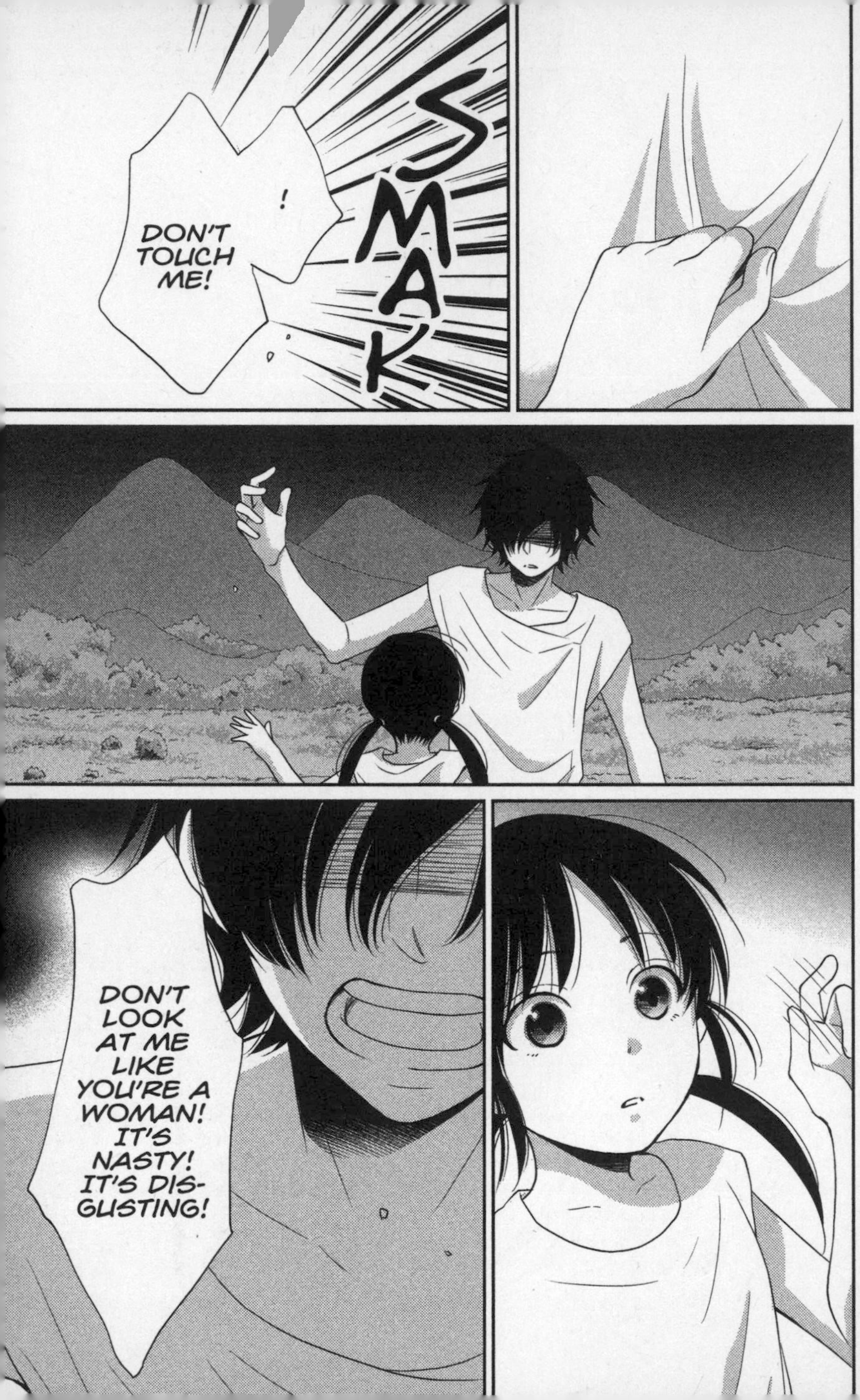
SMAK
!
DON'T TOUCH ME!
DON'T LOOK AT ME LIKE YOU'RE A WOMAN! IT'S NASTY! IT'S DIS-GUSTING!

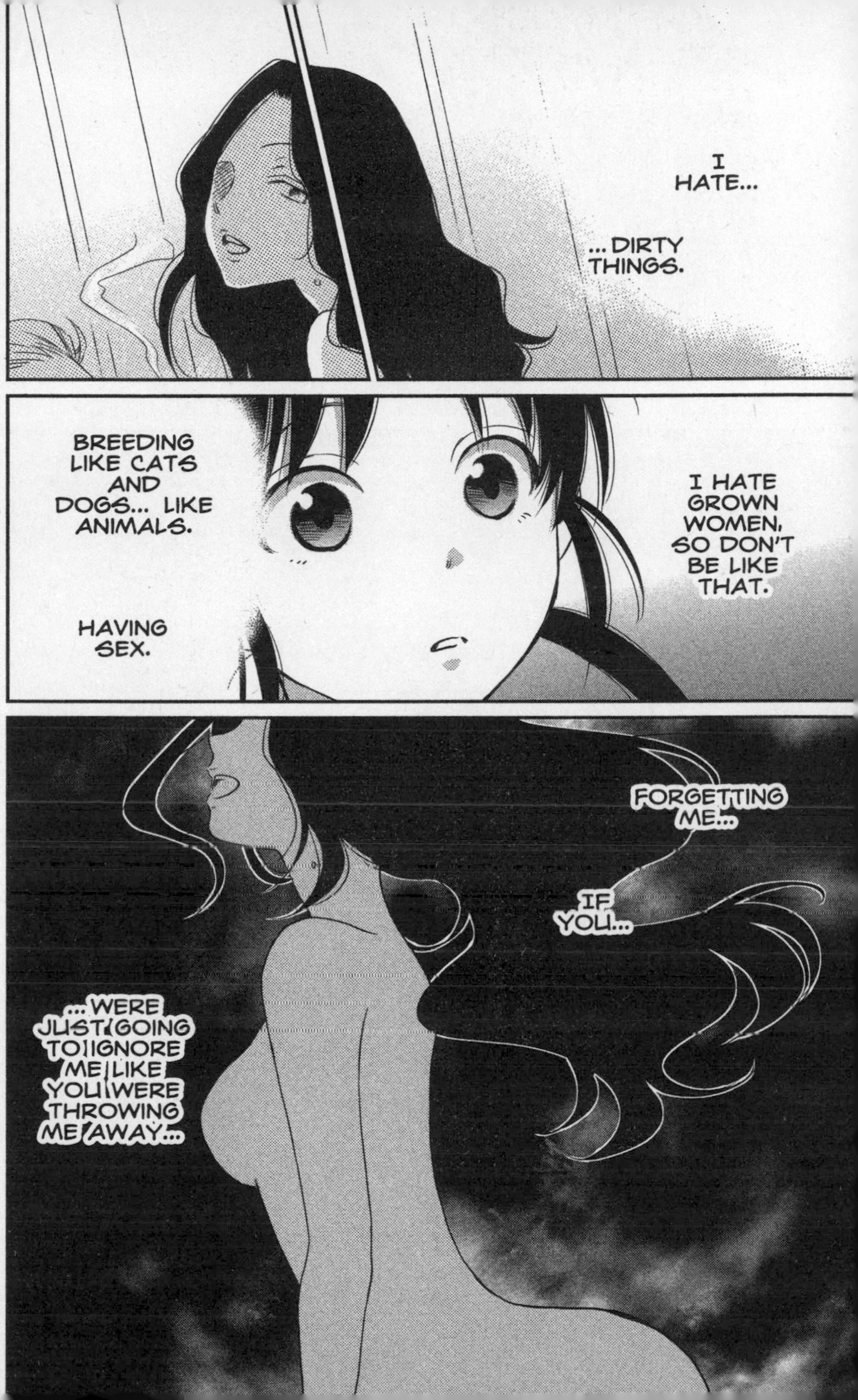
I HATE...
...DIRTY THINGS.
I HATE GROWN WOMEN, SO DON'T BE LIKE THAT.
BREEDING LIKE CATS AND DOGS... LIKE ANIMALS.
HAVING SEX.
FORGETTING ME...
IF YOU...
...WERE JUST GOING TO IGNORE ME LIKE YOU WERE THROWING ME AWAY...

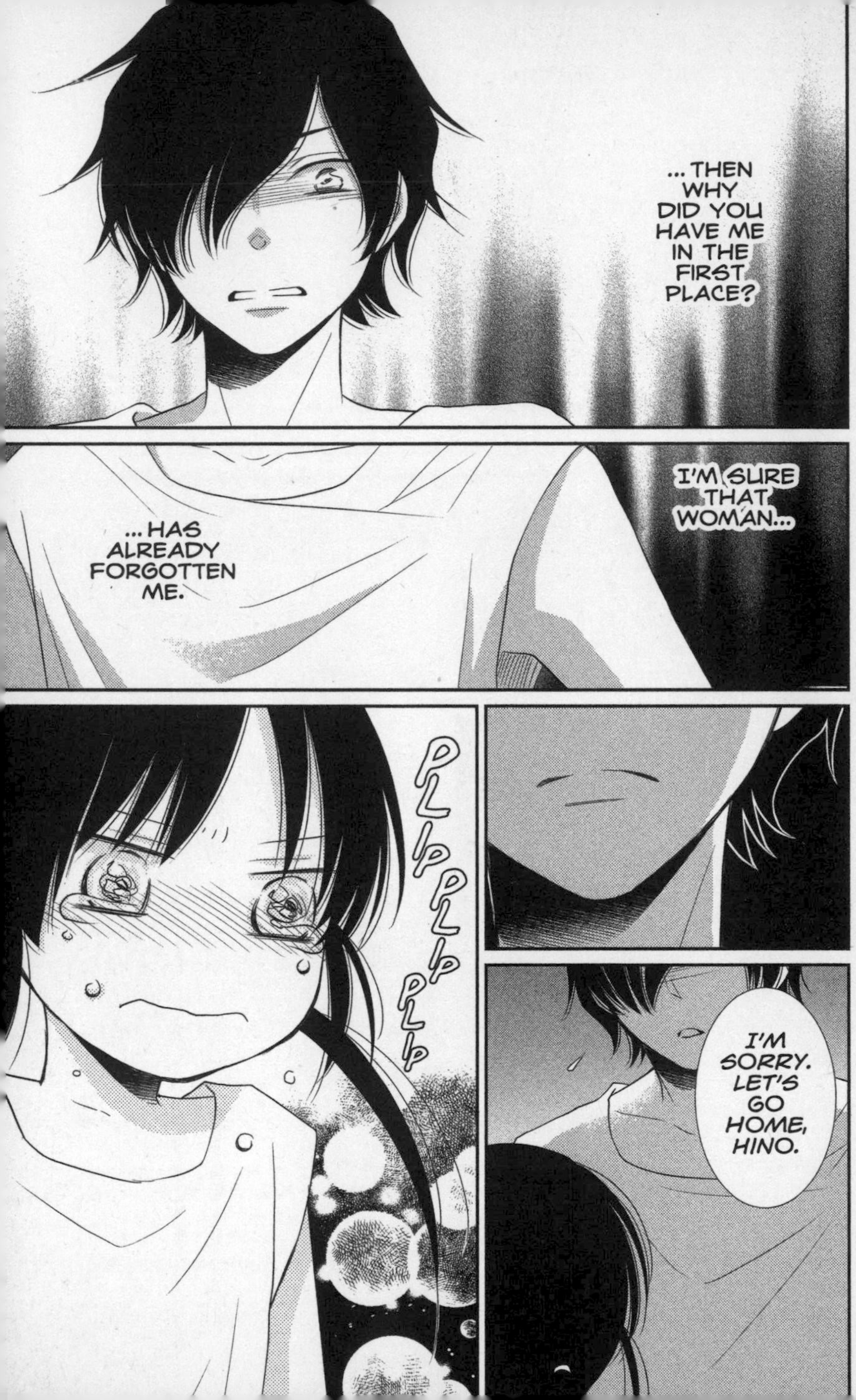
...THEN WHY DID YOU HAVE ME IN THE FIRST PLACE?
I'M SURE THAT WOMAN...
...HAS ALREADY FORGOTTEN ME.
I'M SORRY. LET'S GO HOME, HINO.
PLIP PLIP PLIP

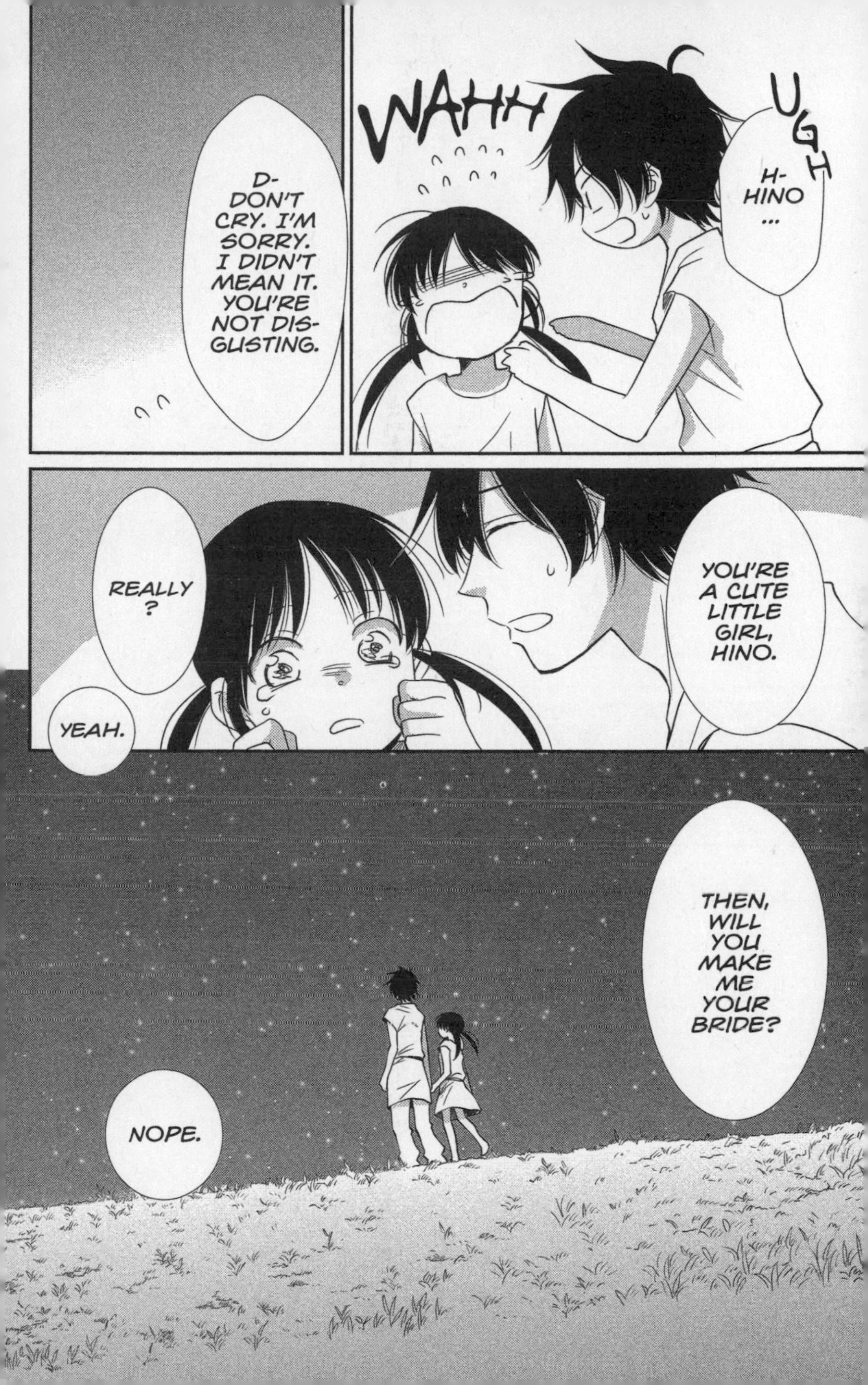
UGH
H-HINO...
WAHH
D-DON'T CRY. I'M SORRY. I DIDN'T MEAN IT. YOU'RE NOT DISGUSTING.
YOU'RE A CUTE LITTLE GIRL, HINO.
REALLY?
YEAH.
THEN, WILL YOU MAKE ME YOUR BRIDE?
NOPE.

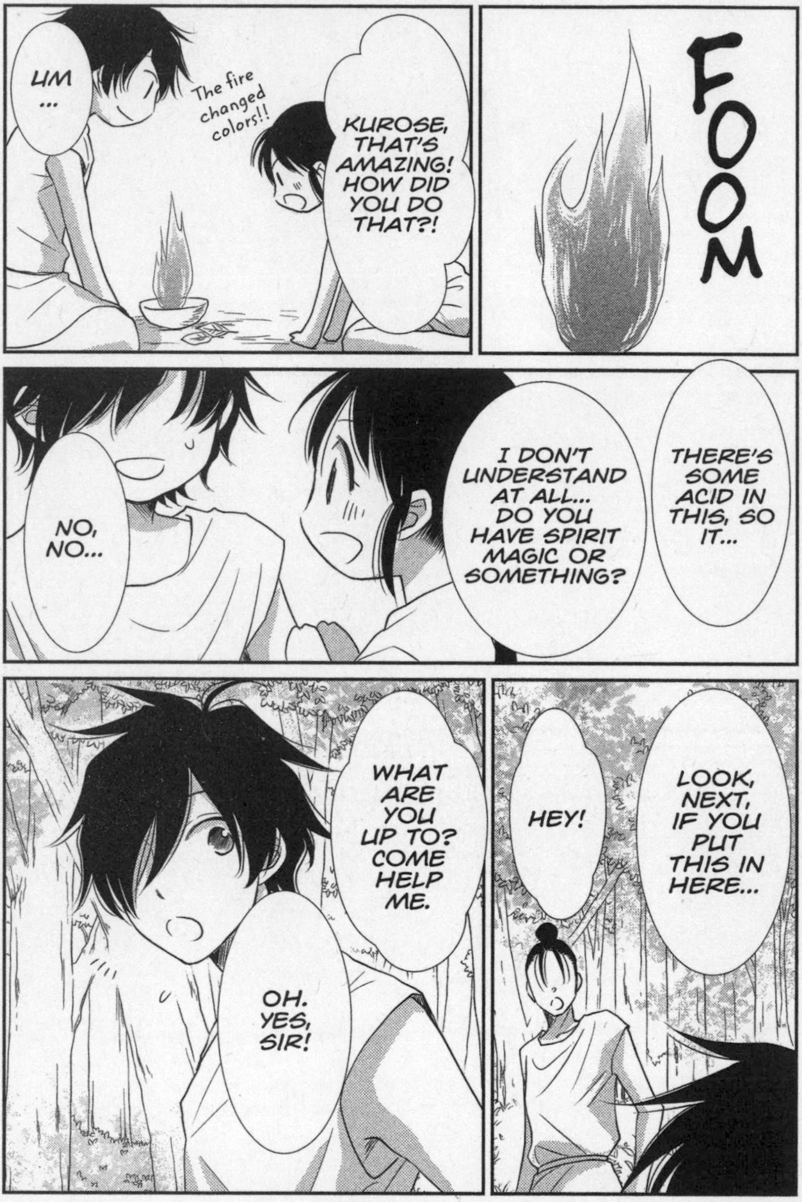
FOOM
KUROSE, THAT'S AMAZING! HOW DID YOU DO THAT?!
The fire changed colors!!
UM ...
THERE'S SOME ACID IN THIS, SO IT...
I DON'T UNDERSTAND AT ALL... DO YOU HAVE SPIRIT MAGIC OR SOMETHING?
NO, NO...
LOOK, NEXT, IF YOU PUT THIS IN HERE...
HEY!
WHAT ARE YOU UP TO? COME HELP ME.
OH. YES, SIR!

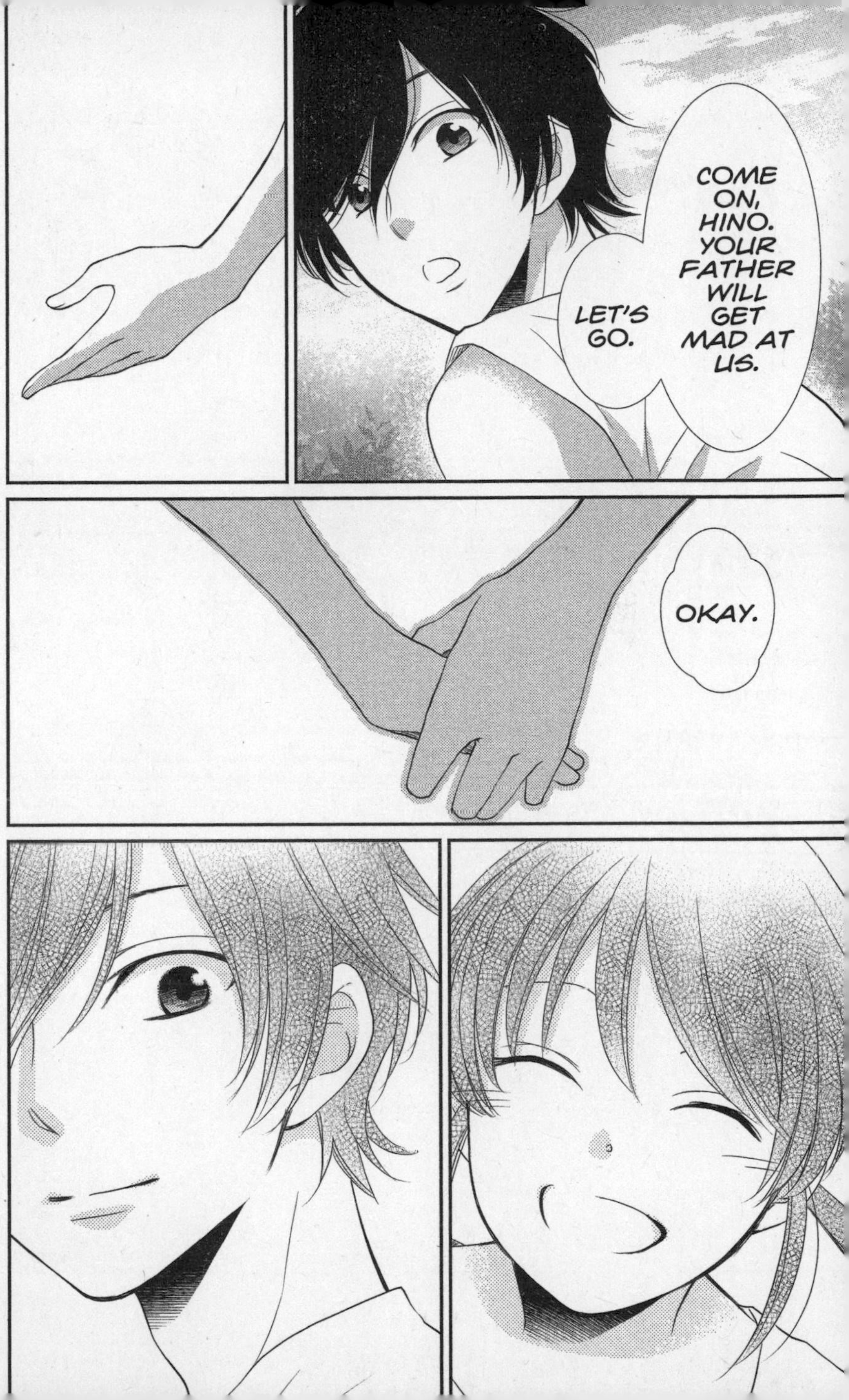
COME ON, HINO. YOUR FATHER WILL GET MAD AT US.
LET'S GO.
OKAY.

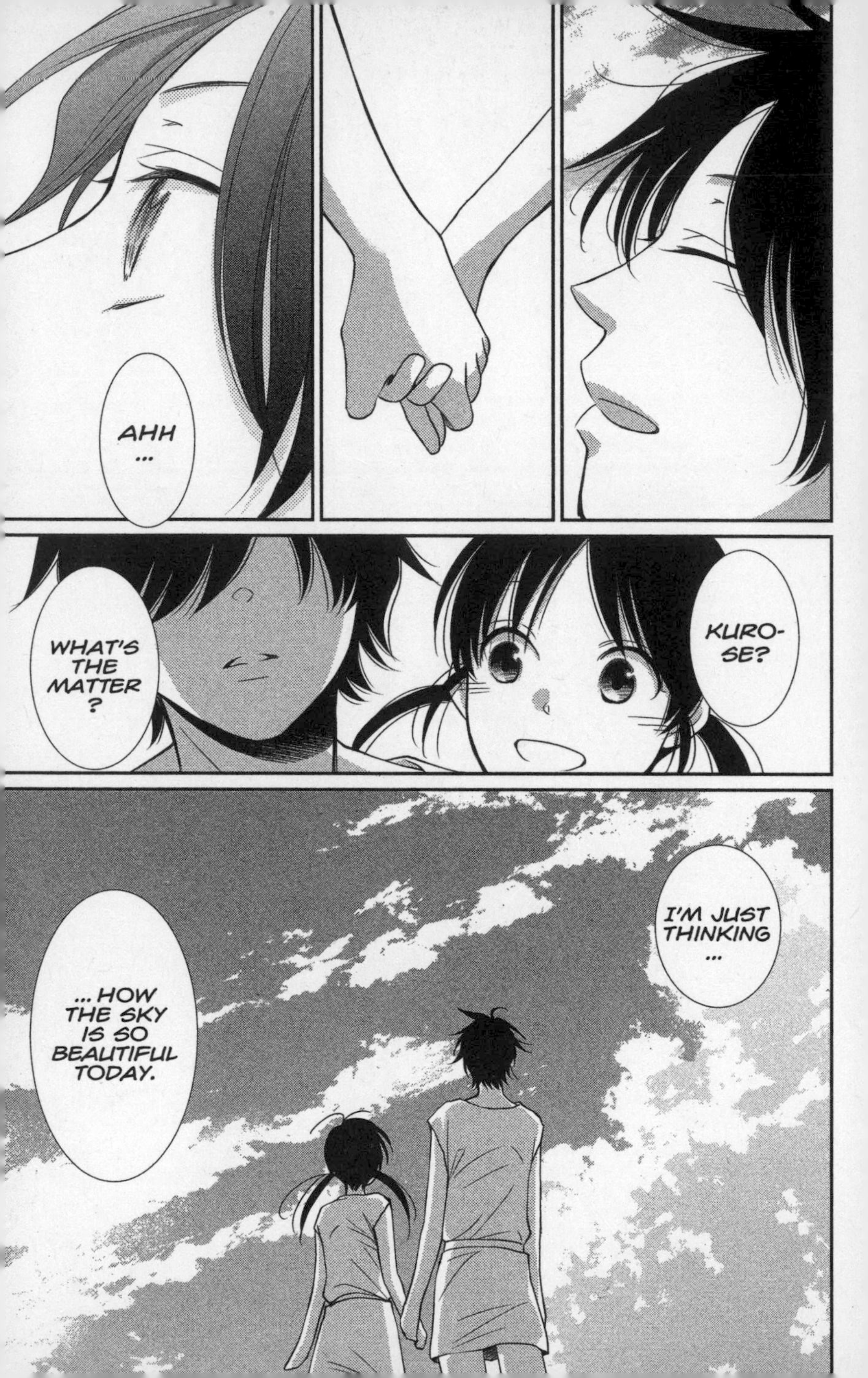
AHH ...
KURO-SE?
WHAT'S THE MATTER?
I'M JUST THINKING ...
... HOW THE SKY IS SO BEAUTIFUL TODAY.

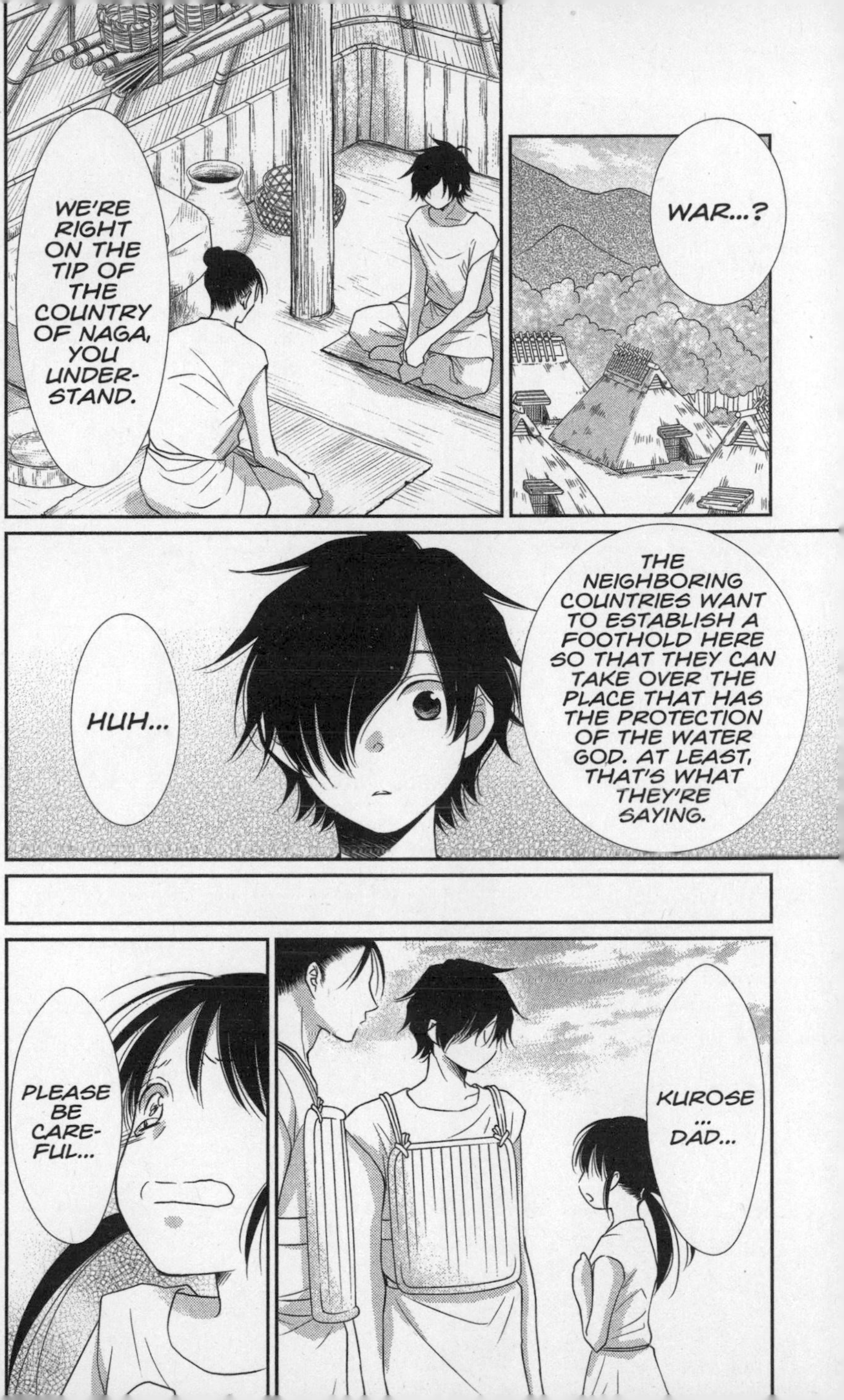
WAR...?
WE'RE RIGHT ON THE TIP OF THE COUNTRY OF NAGA, YOU UNDER-STAND.
THE NEIGHBORING COUNTRIES WANT TO ESTABLISH A FOOTHOLD HERE SO THAT THEY CAN TAKE OVER THE PLACE THAT HAS THE PROTECTION OF THE WATER GOD. AT LEAST, THAT'S WHAT THEY'RE SAYING.
HUH...
KUROSE ... DAD...
PLEASE BE CARE-FUL...

Tokoyami. He's an irregular existence, outside the influence of the five elements of the other gods. I was thinking that since he's the god of darkness, he'd have a really gloomy, dark design, but since everything around him was going to be darkness and spot blacks, I thought it'd be better to make him white... And so, I swapped him over to a white design.

See you again in volume 9!

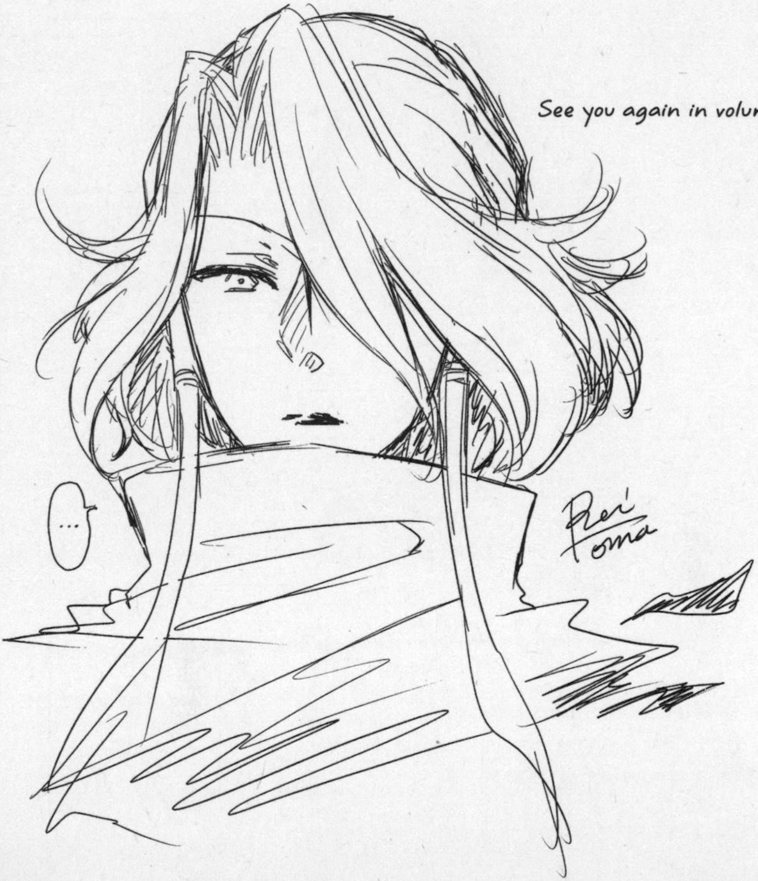
...
Rei Toma

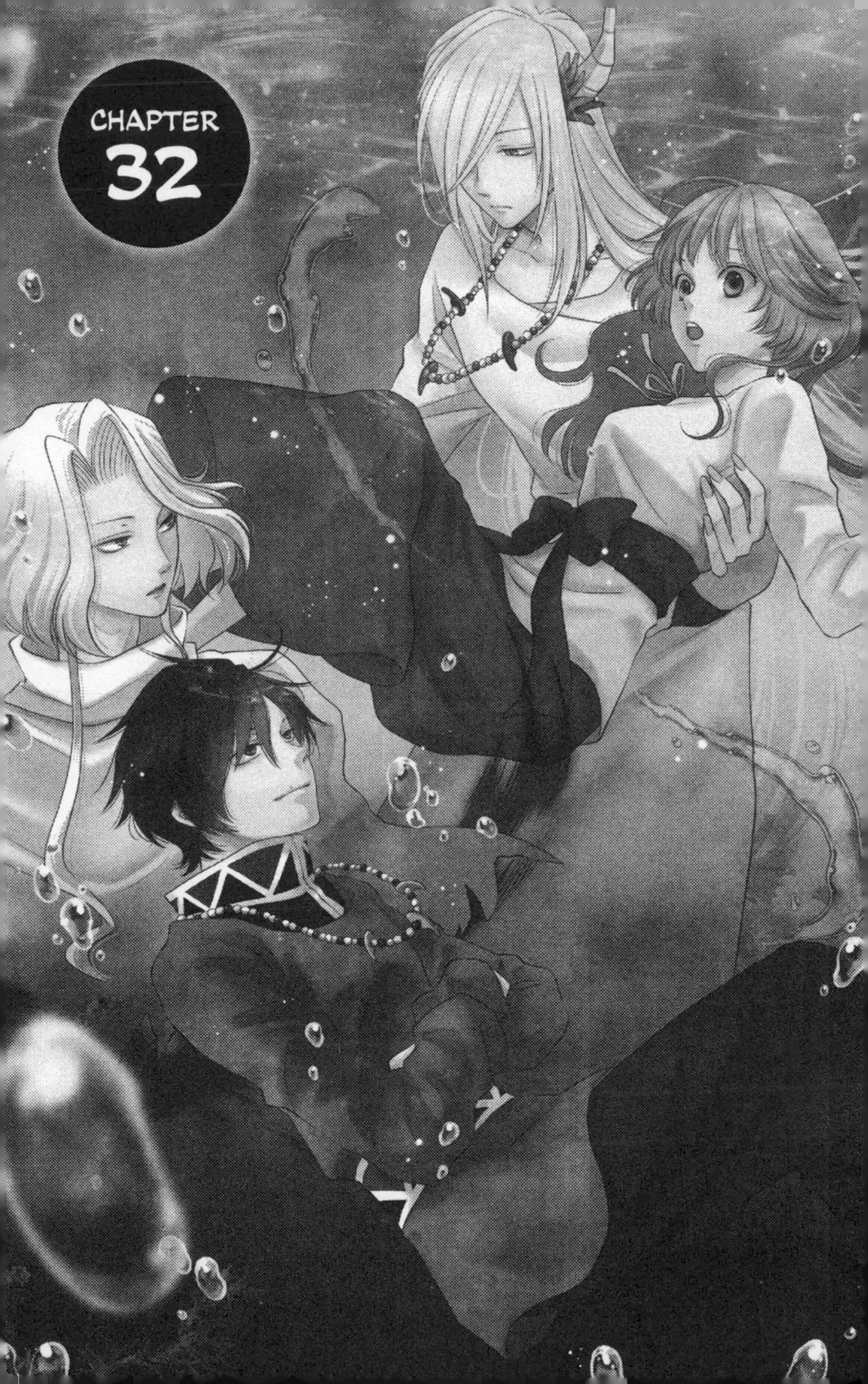
CHAPTER
32

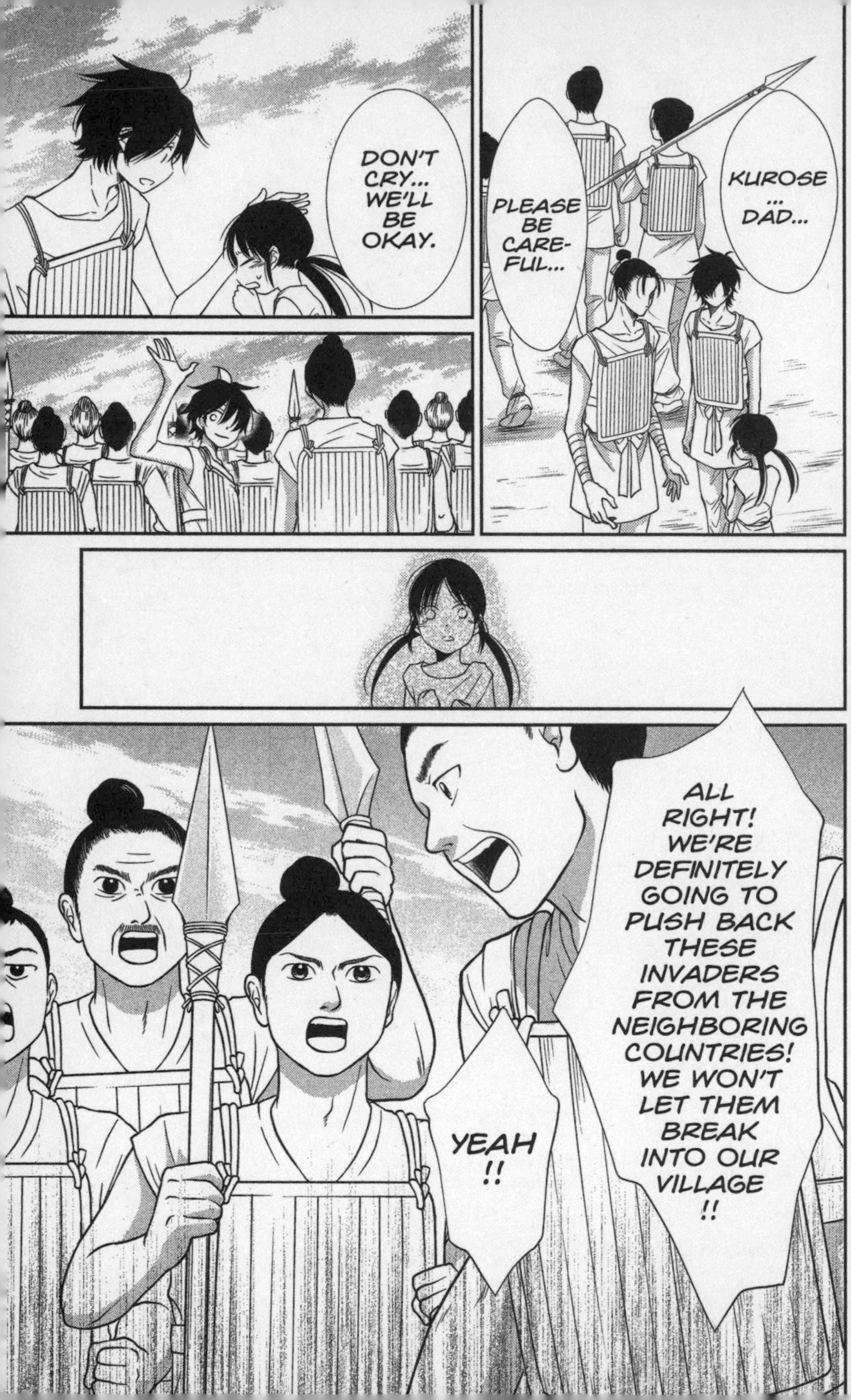
KUROSE... DAD...
PLEASE BE CAREFUL...
DON'T CRY... WE'LL BE OKAY.
ALL RIGHT! WE'RE DEFINITELY GOING TO PUSH BACK THESE INVADERS FROM THE NEIGHBORING COUNTRIES! WE WON'T LET THEM BREAK INTO OUR VILLAGE!!
YEAH!!

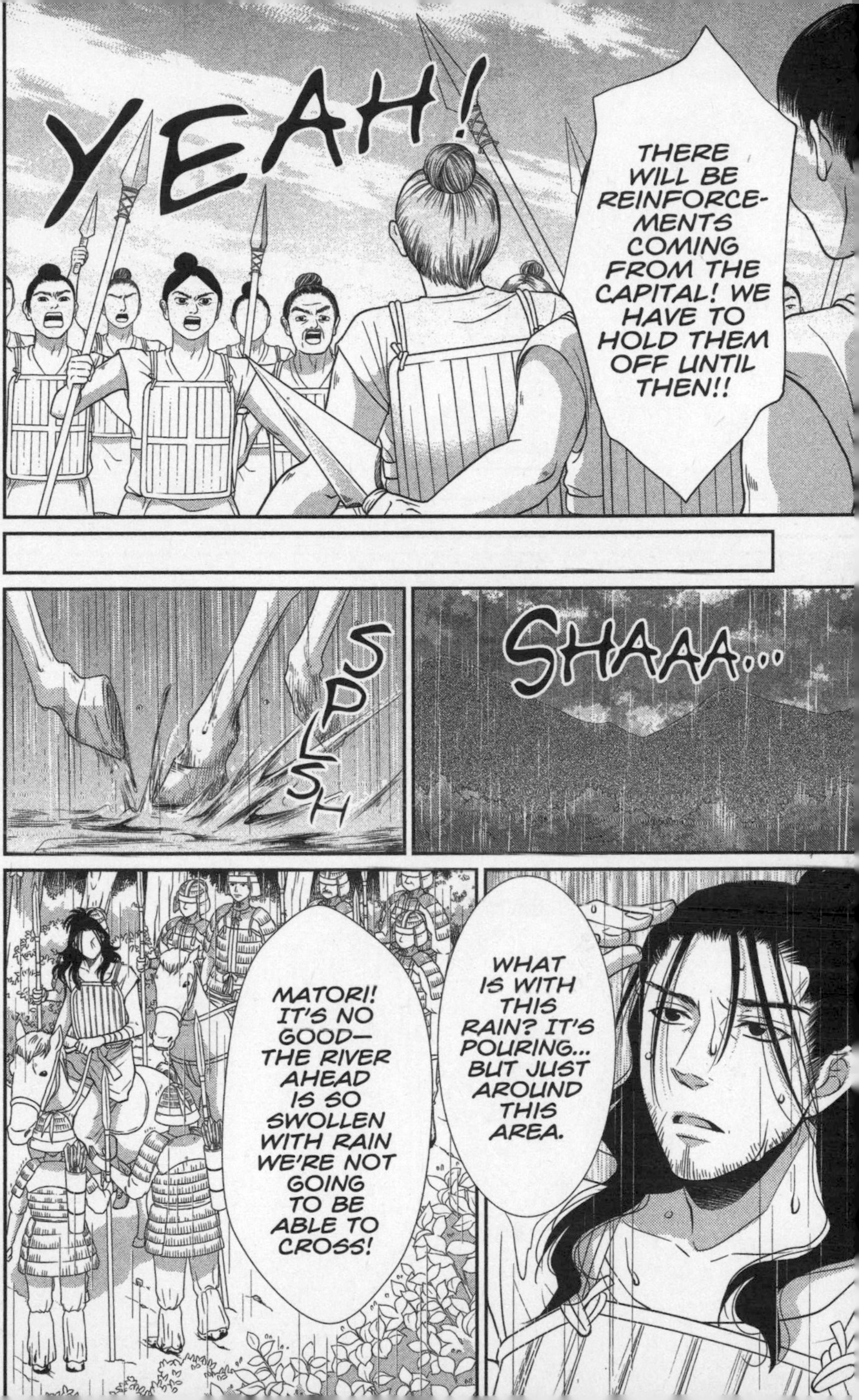
THERE WILL BE REINFORCEMENTS COMING FROM THE CAPITAL! WE HAVE TO HOLD THEM OFF UNTIL THEN!!
YEAH!
SHAAA...
SPLSH
WHAT IS WITH THIS RAIN? IT'S POURING... BUT JUST AROUND THIS AREA.
MATORI! IT'S NO GOOD—THE RIVER AHEAD IS SO SWOLLEN WITH RAIN WE'RE NOT GOING TO BE ABLE TO CROSS!

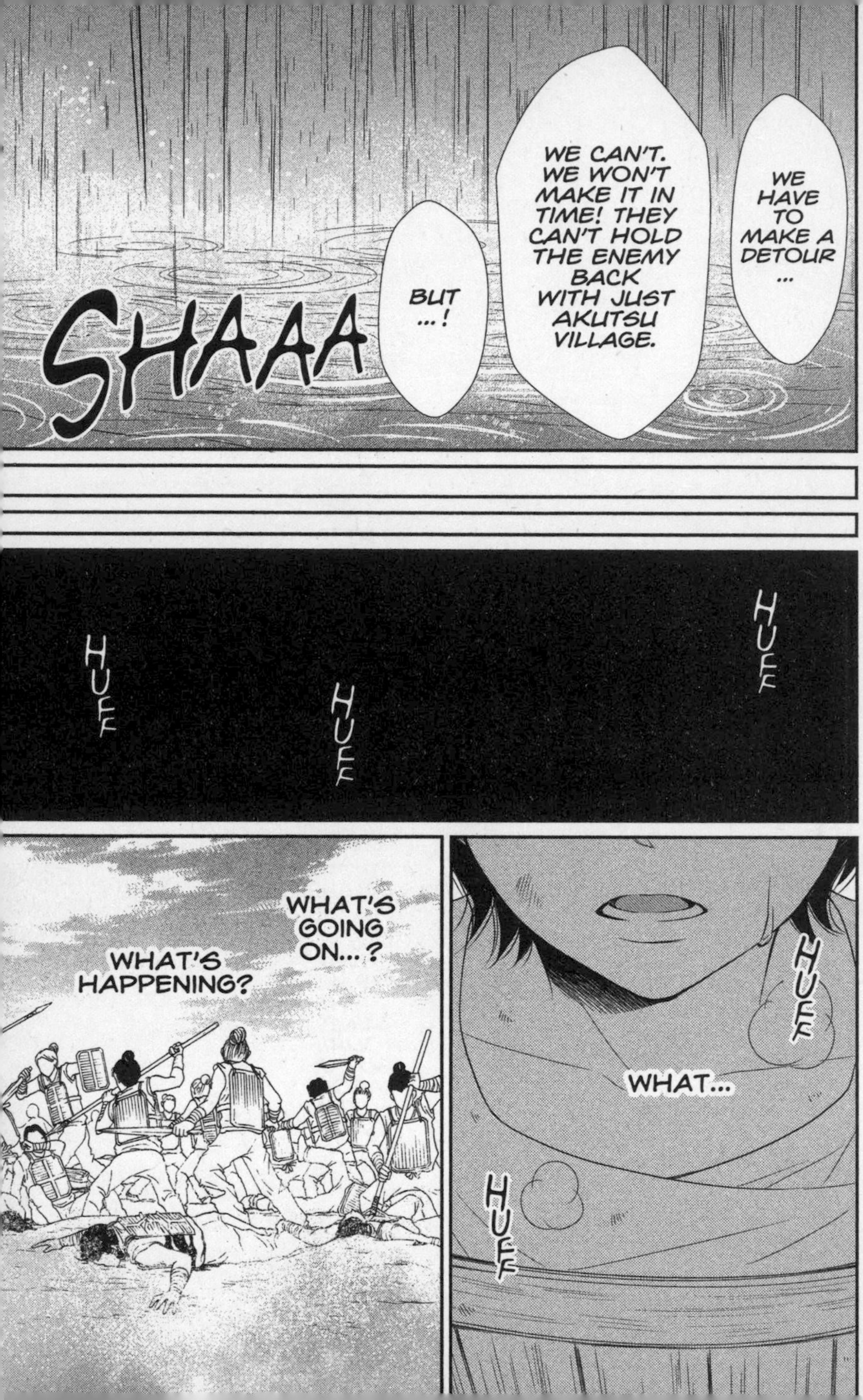
WE HAVE TO MAKE A DETOUR...
WE CAN'T. WE WON'T MAKE IT IN TIME! THEY CAN'T HOLD THE ENEMY BACK WITH JUST AKUTSU VILLAGE.
BUT...!
SHAAA
HUFF
HUFF
HUFF
HUFF
WHAT...
HUFF
WHAT'S GOING ON...?
WHAT'S HAPPENING?

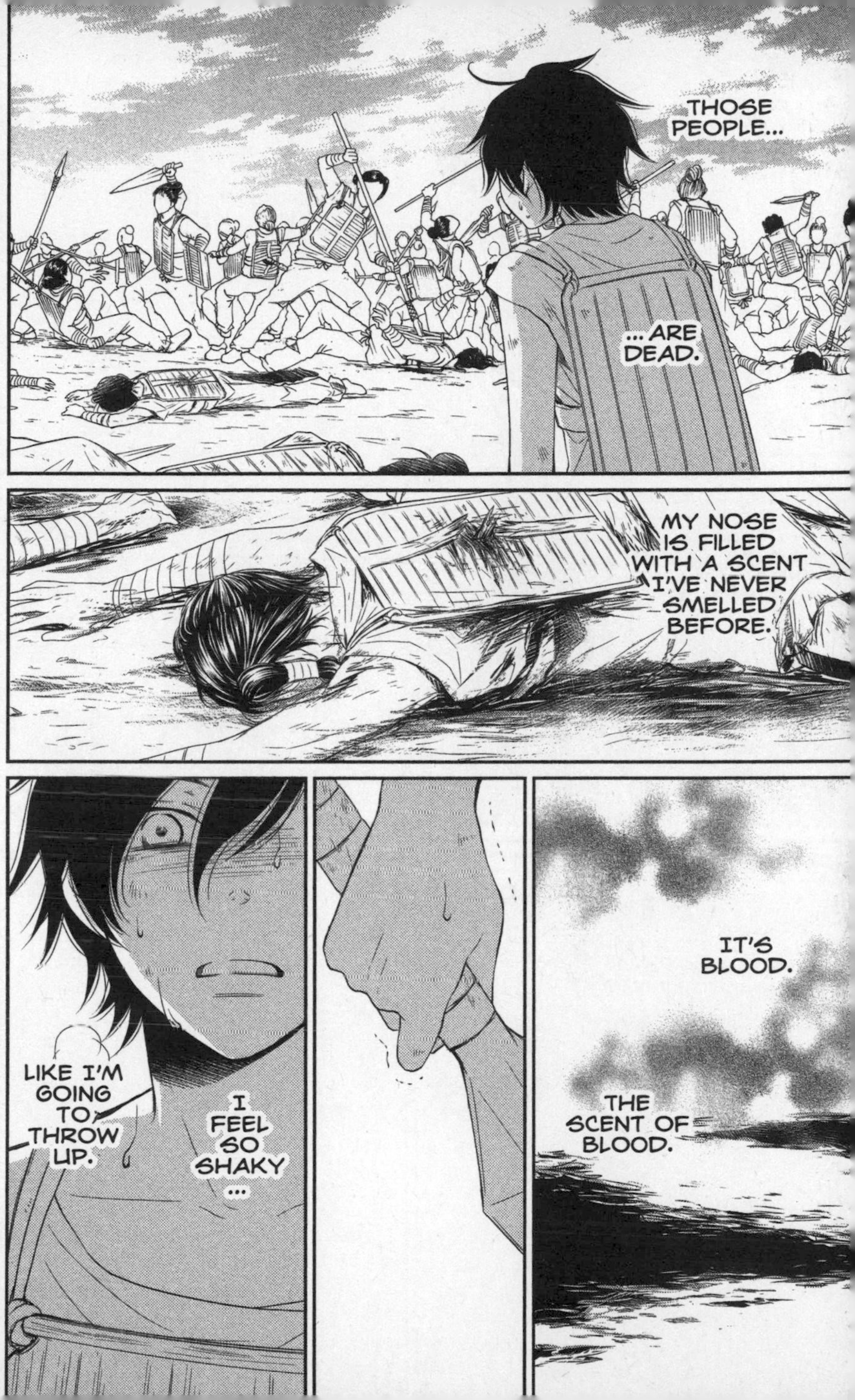
THOSE PEOPLE...
...ARE DEAD.
MY NOSE IS FILLED WITH A SCENT I'VE NEVER SMELLED BEFORE.
IT'S BLOOD.
THE SCENT OF BLOOD.
I FEEL SO SHAKY...
LIKE I'M GOING TO THROW UP.

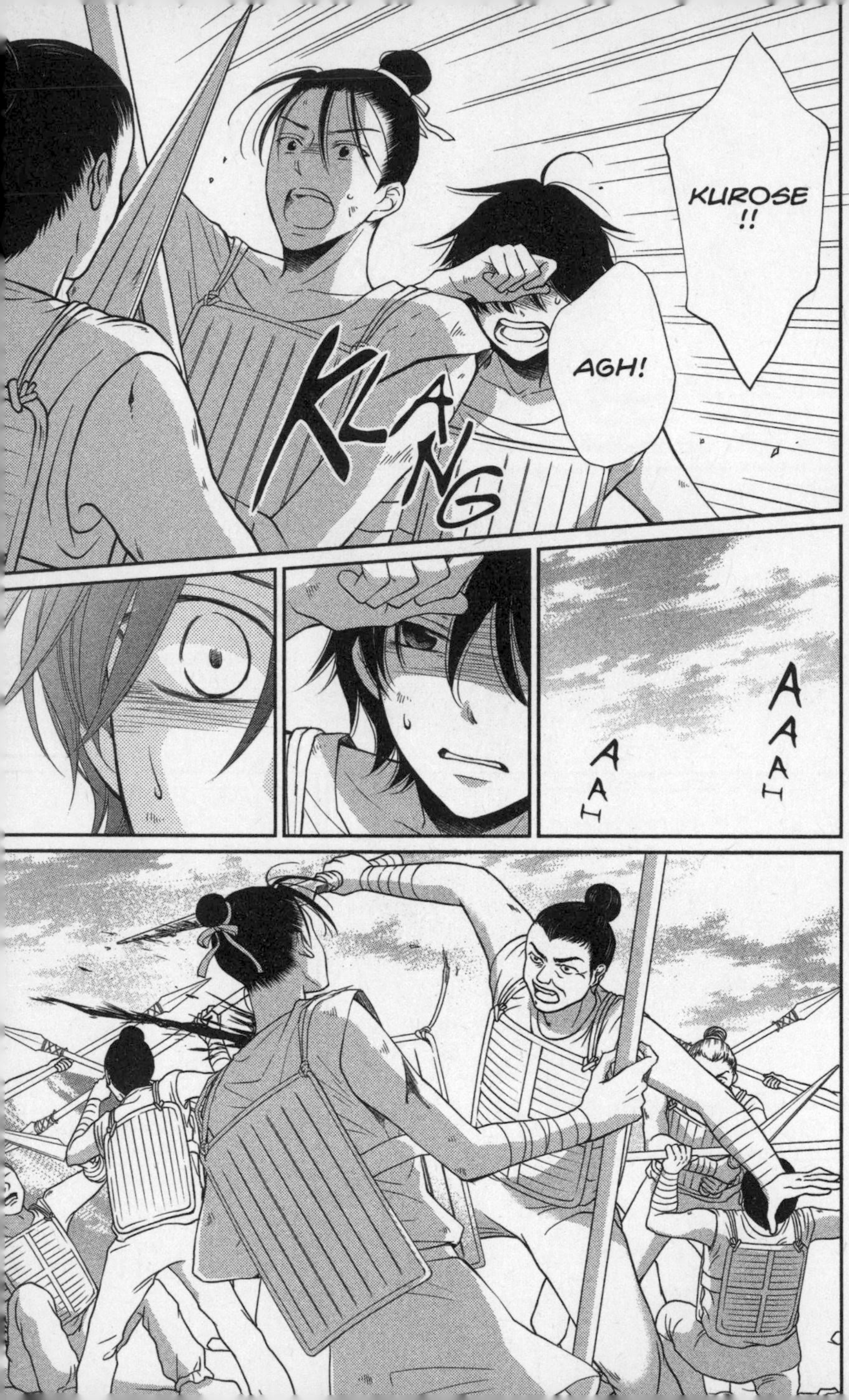
KUROSE !!
AGH!
KLANG
AAAH
AAH

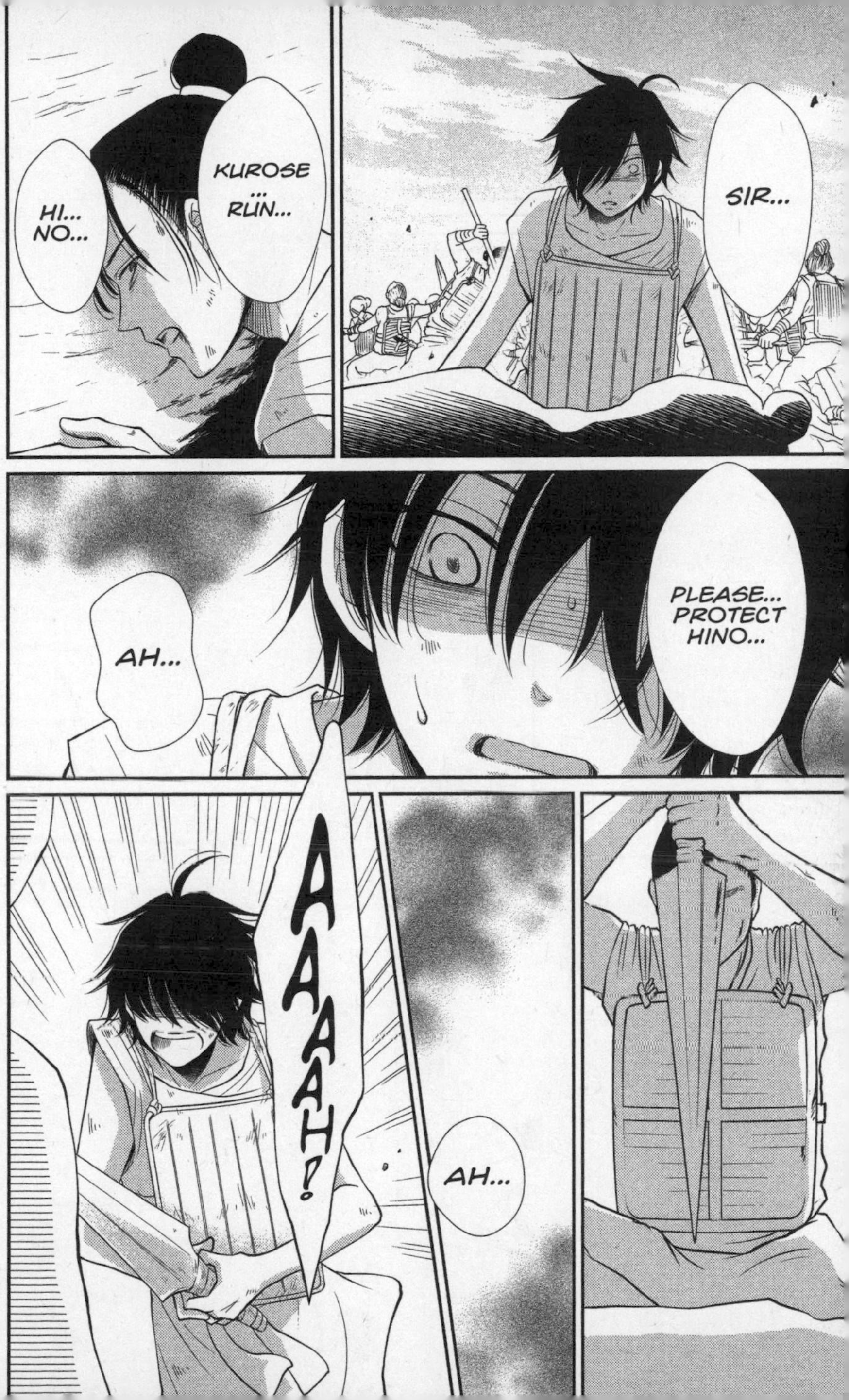
SIR...
KUROSE ... RUN...
HI... NO...
PLEASE... PROTECT HINO...
AH...
AH...
AAAAH!!

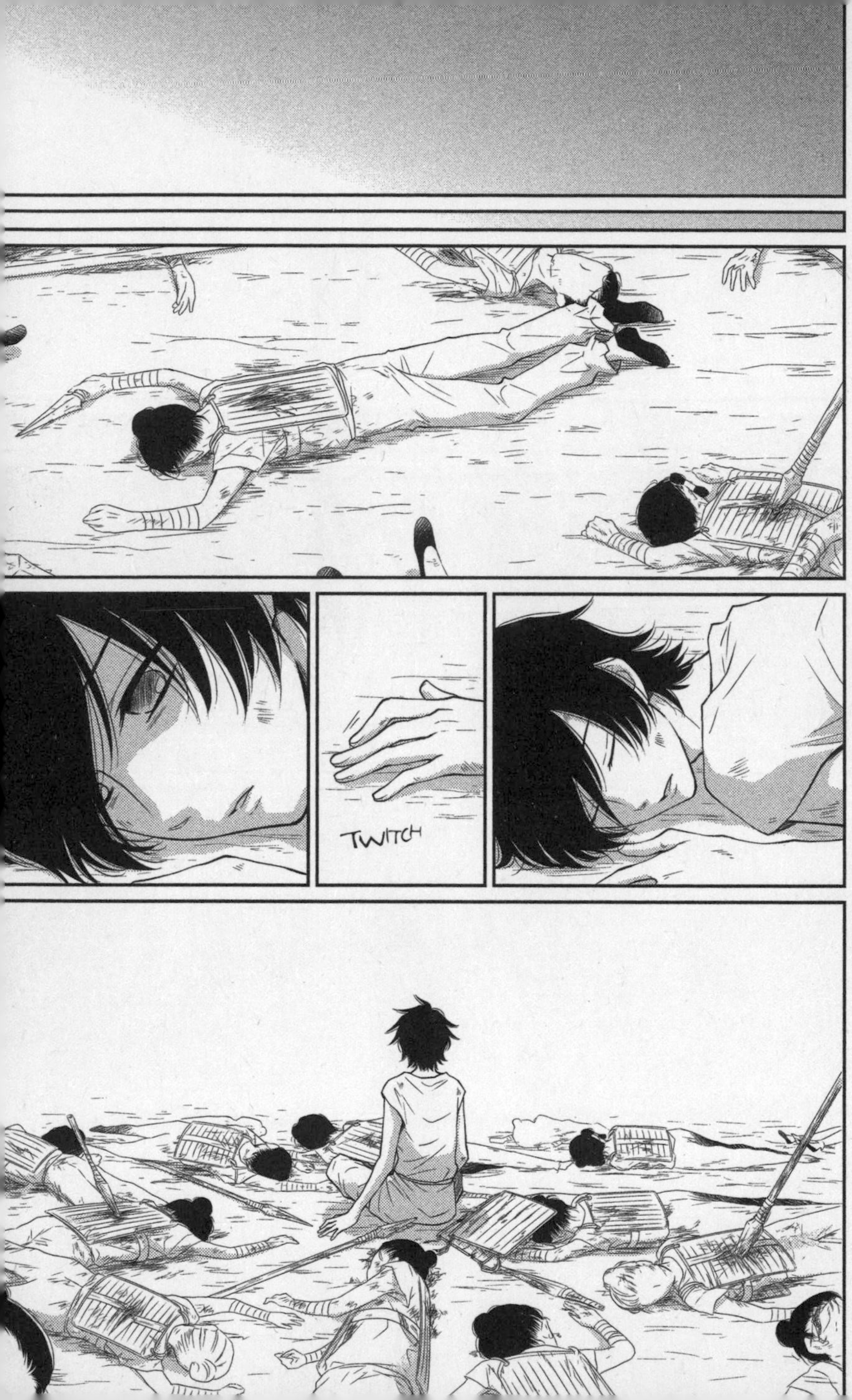
TWITCH

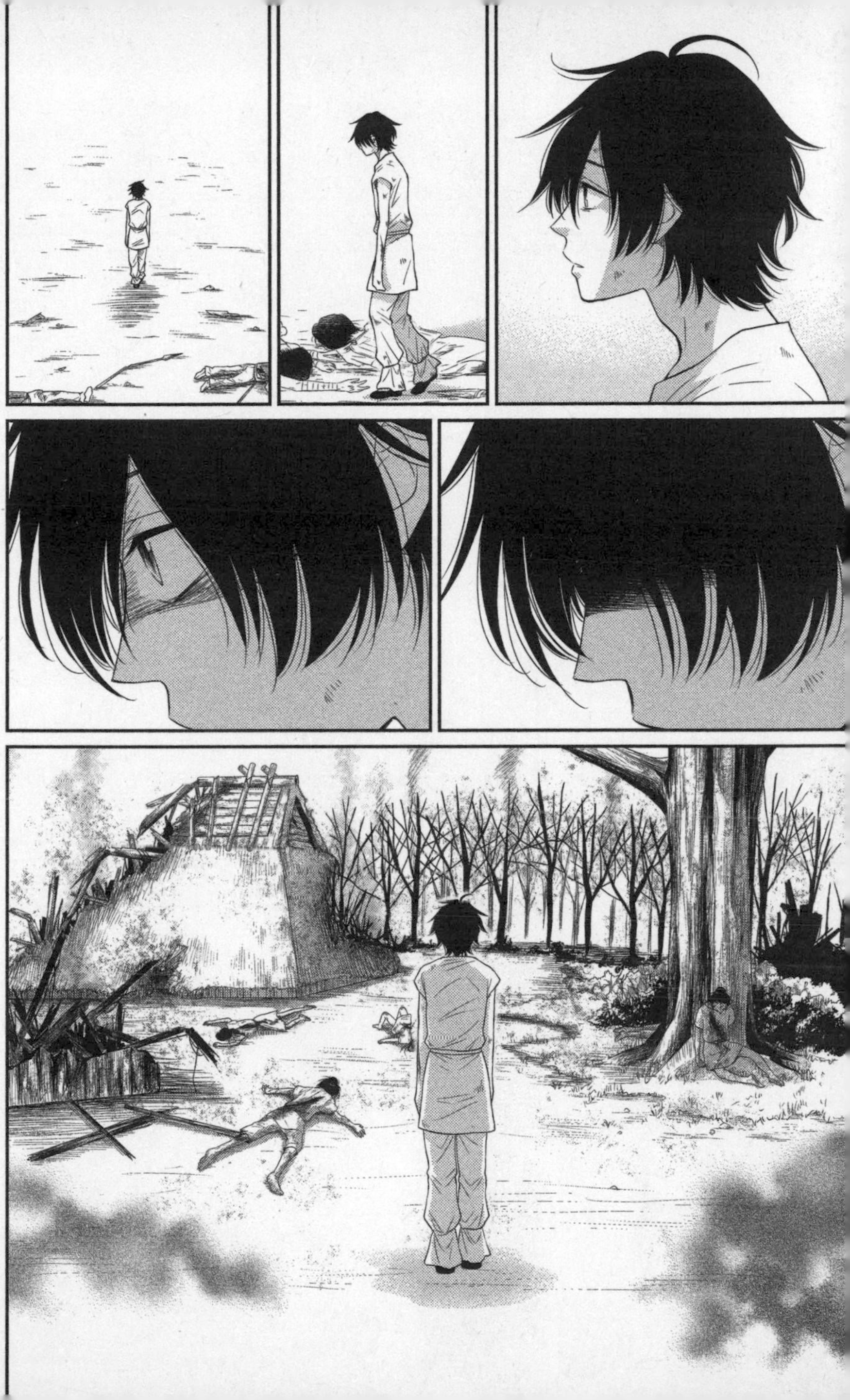

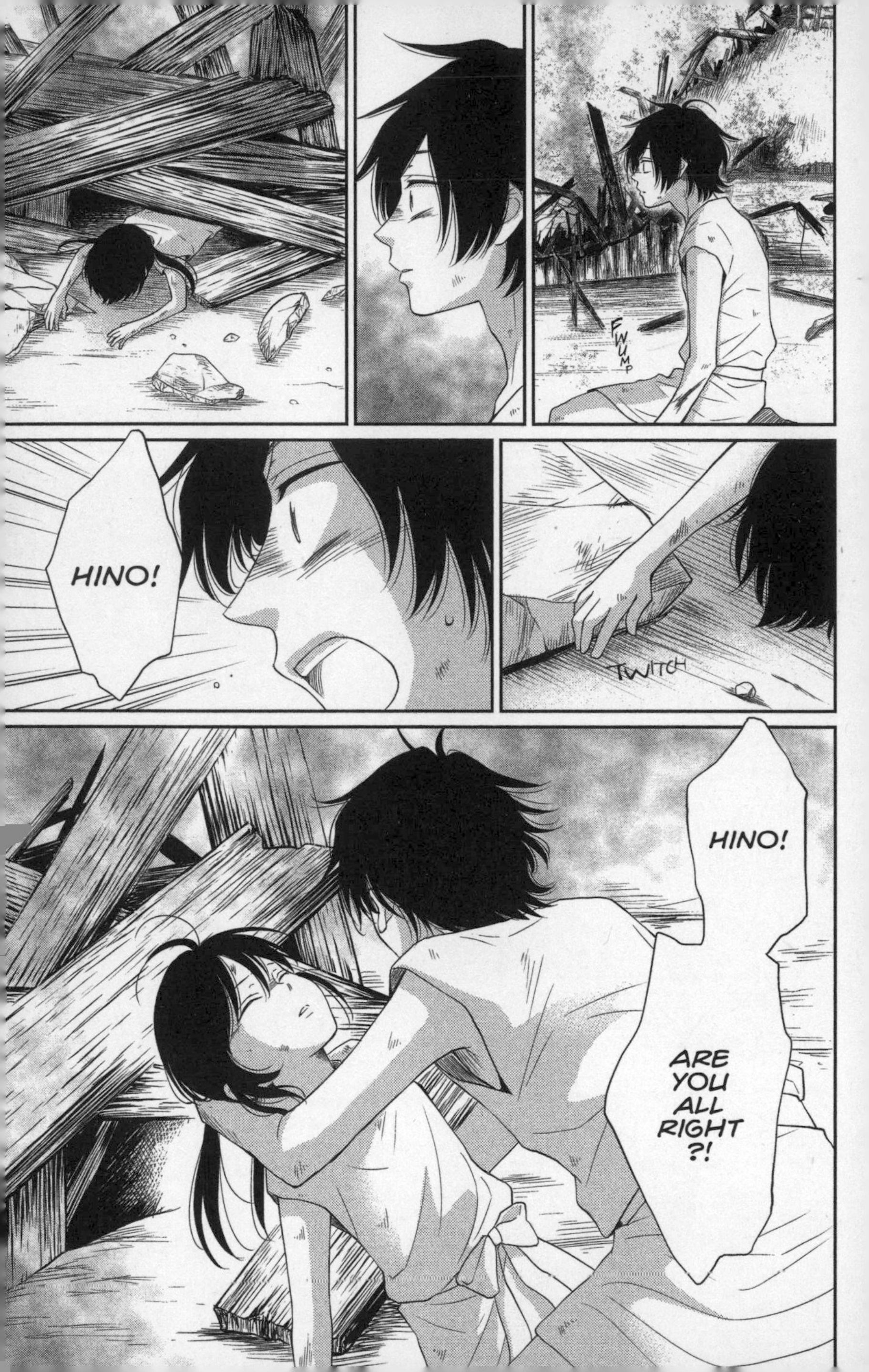
FWUMP
TWITCH
HINO!
HINO!
ARE YOU ALL RIGHT?!

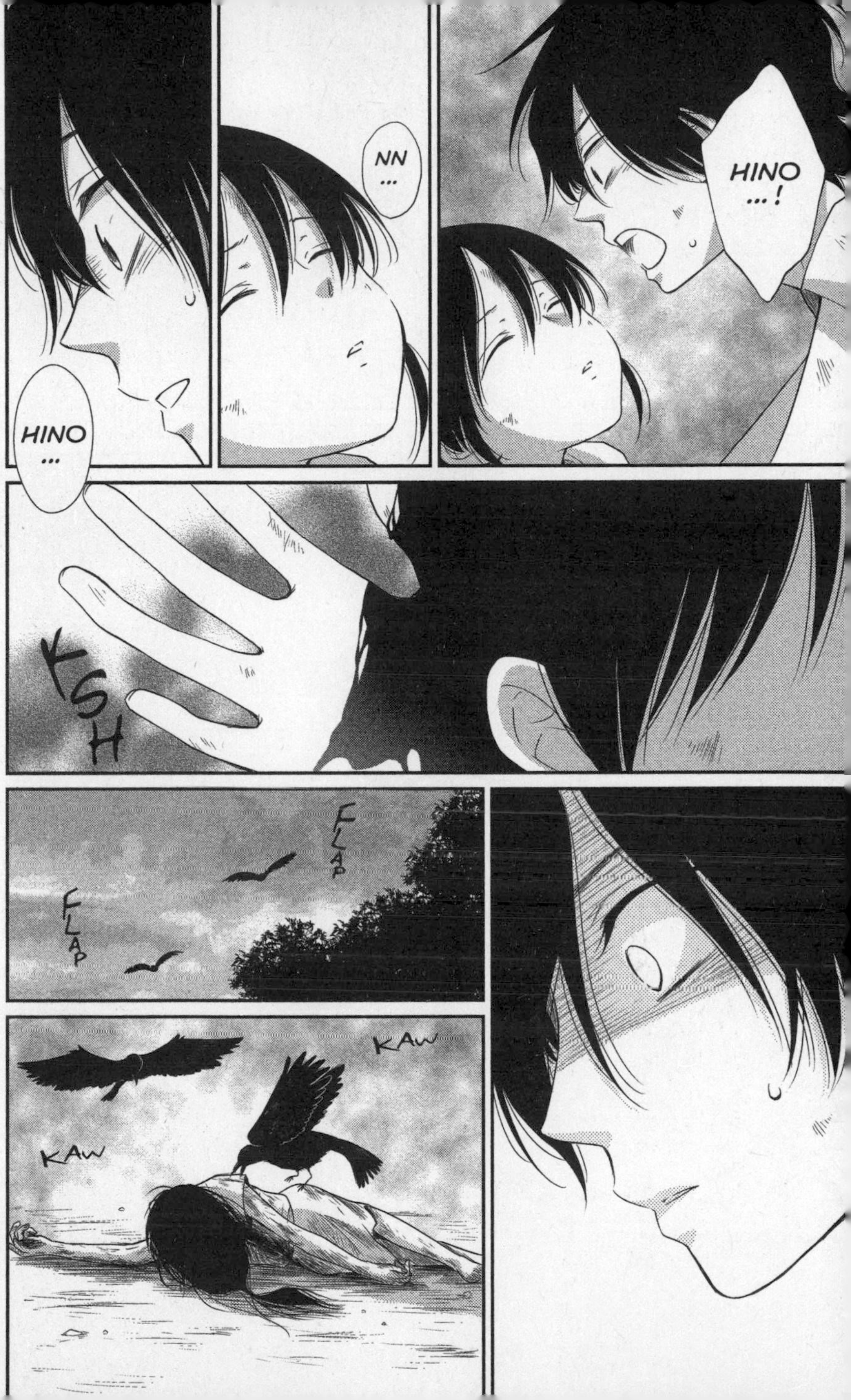
HINO ...!
NN ...
HINO ...
KSH
FLAP
FLAP
KAW
KAW

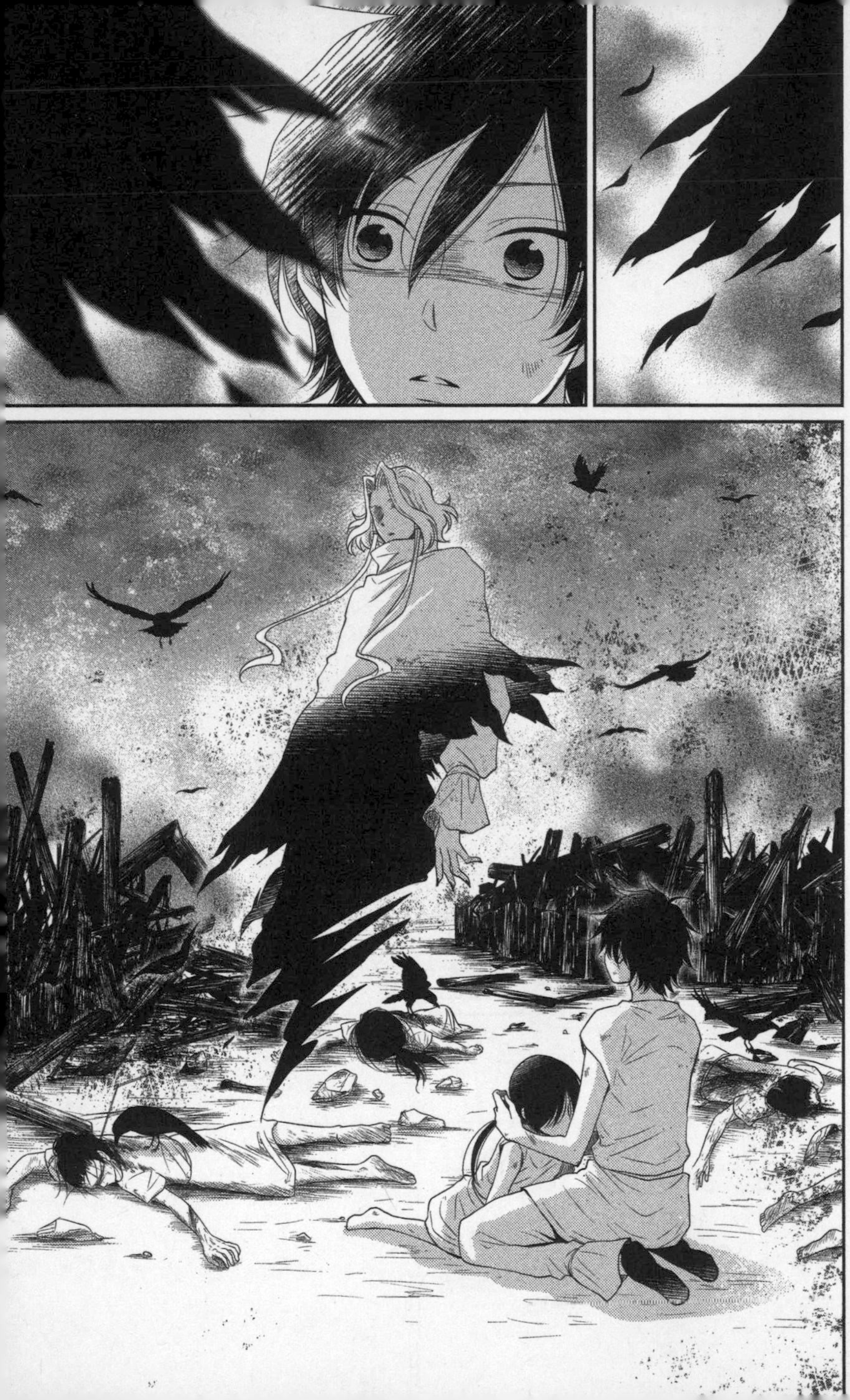

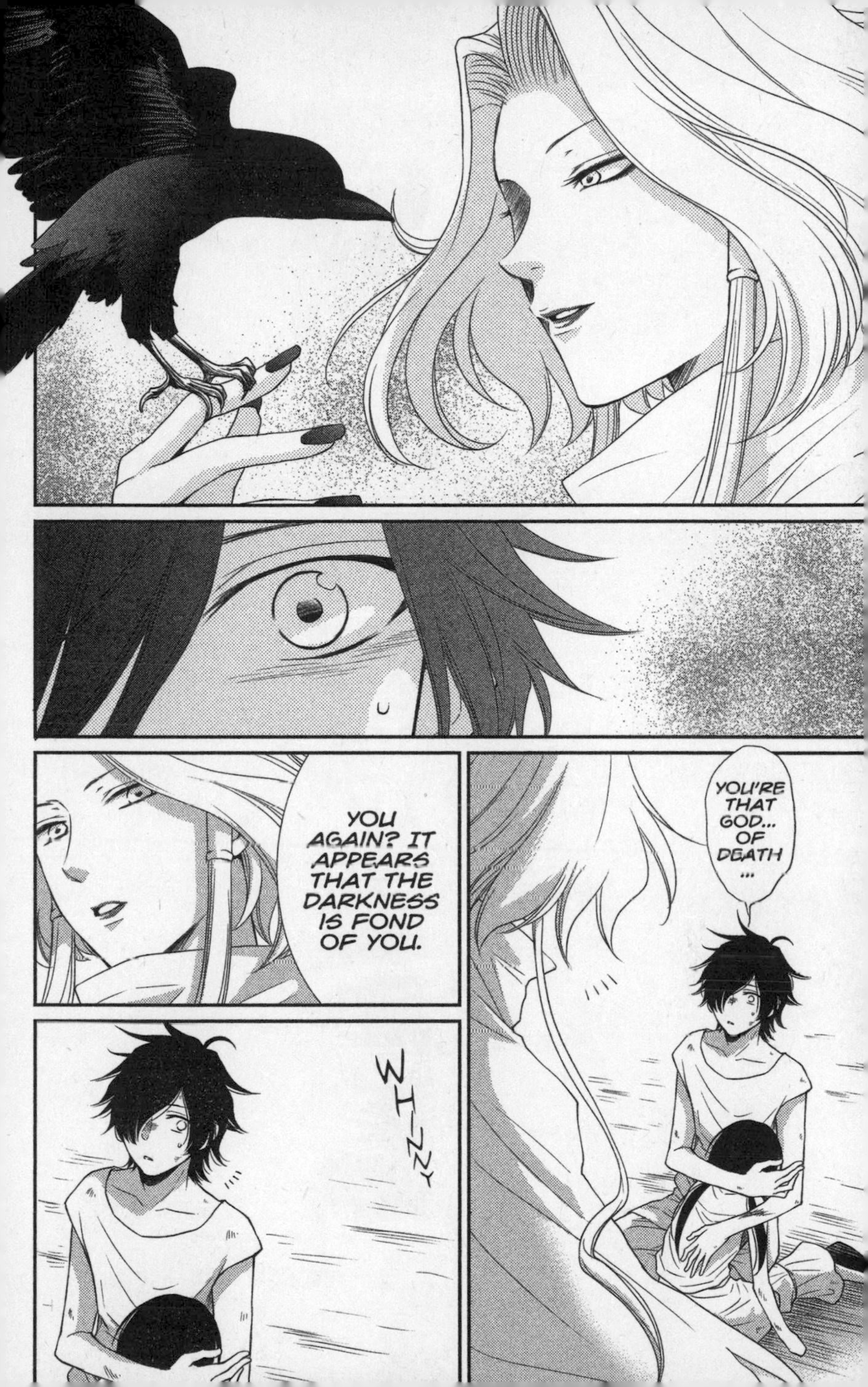
YOU'RE THAT GOD... OF DEATH...
YOU AGAIN? IT APPEARS THAT THE DARKNESS IS FOND OF YOU.
WHINNY

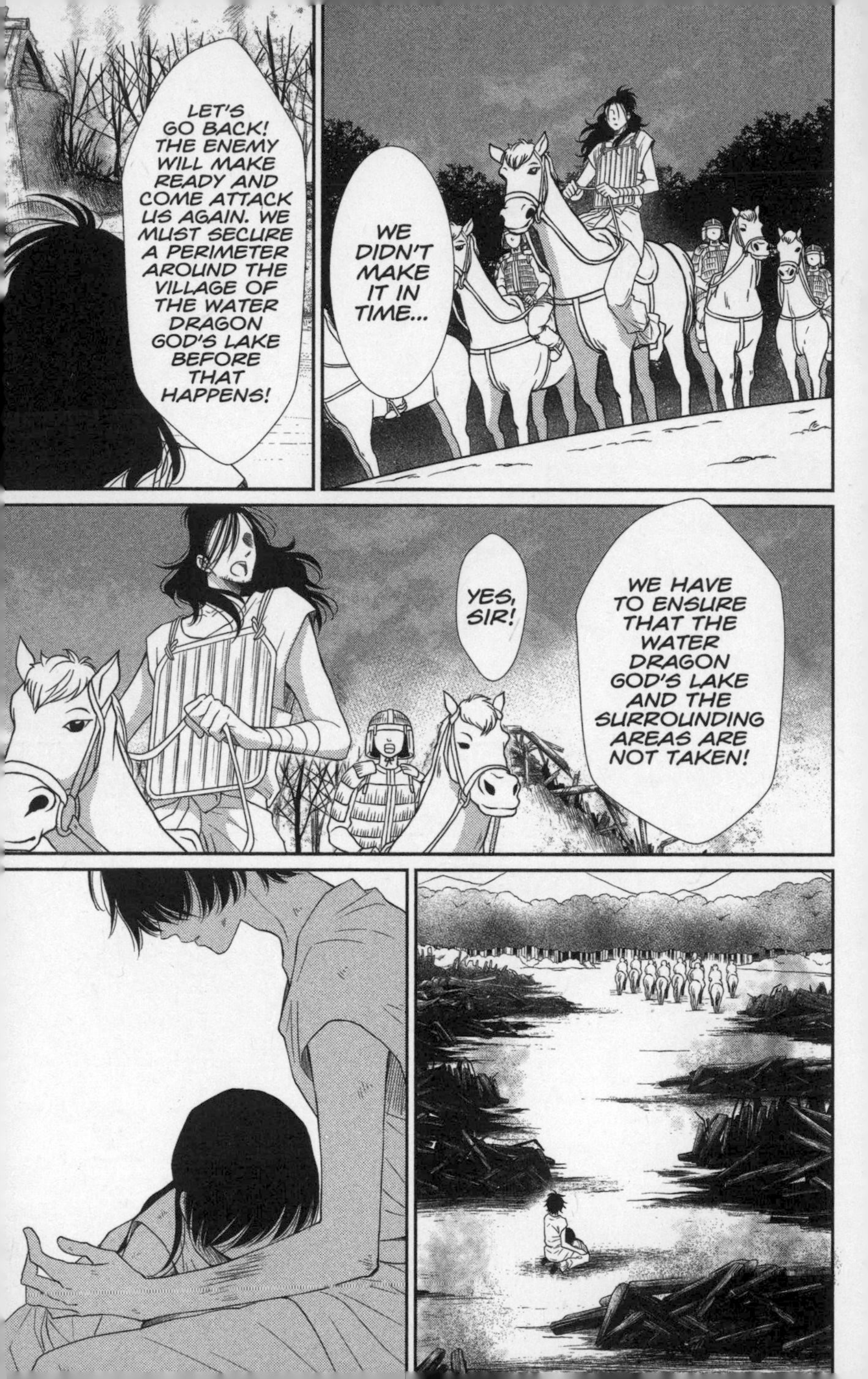
WE DIDN'T MAKE IT IN TIME...
LET'S GO BACK! THE ENEMY WILL MAKE READY AND COME ATTACK US AGAIN. WE MUST SECURE A PERIMETER AROUND THE VILLAGE OF THE WATER DRAGON GOD'S LAKE BEFORE THAT HAPPENS!
WE HAVE TO ENSURE THAT THE WATER DRAGON GOD'S LAKE AND THE SURROUNDING AREAS ARE NOT TAKEN!
YES, SIR!

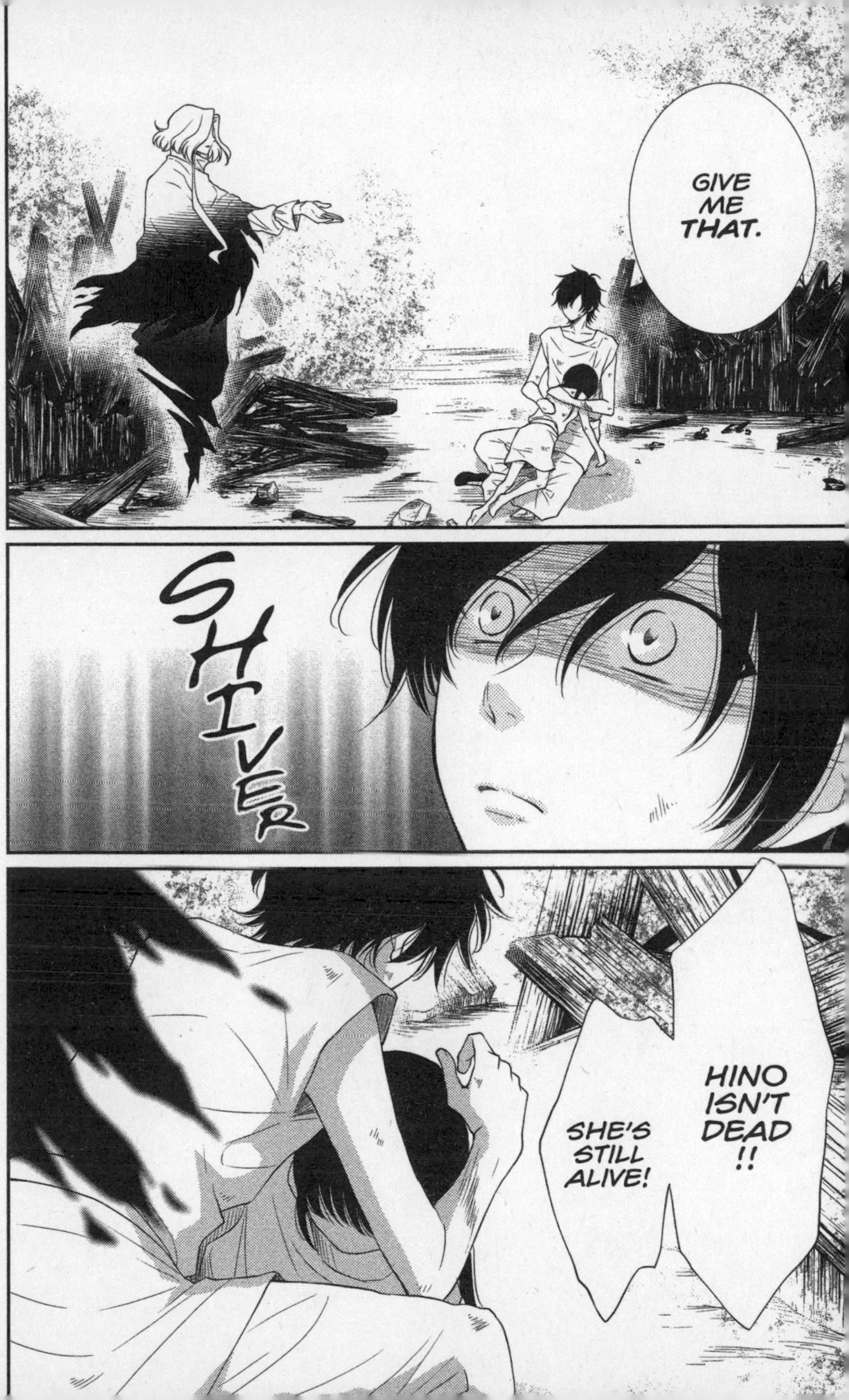
GIVE ME THAT.
SHIVER
HINO ISN'T DEAD!!
SHE'S STILL ALIVE!

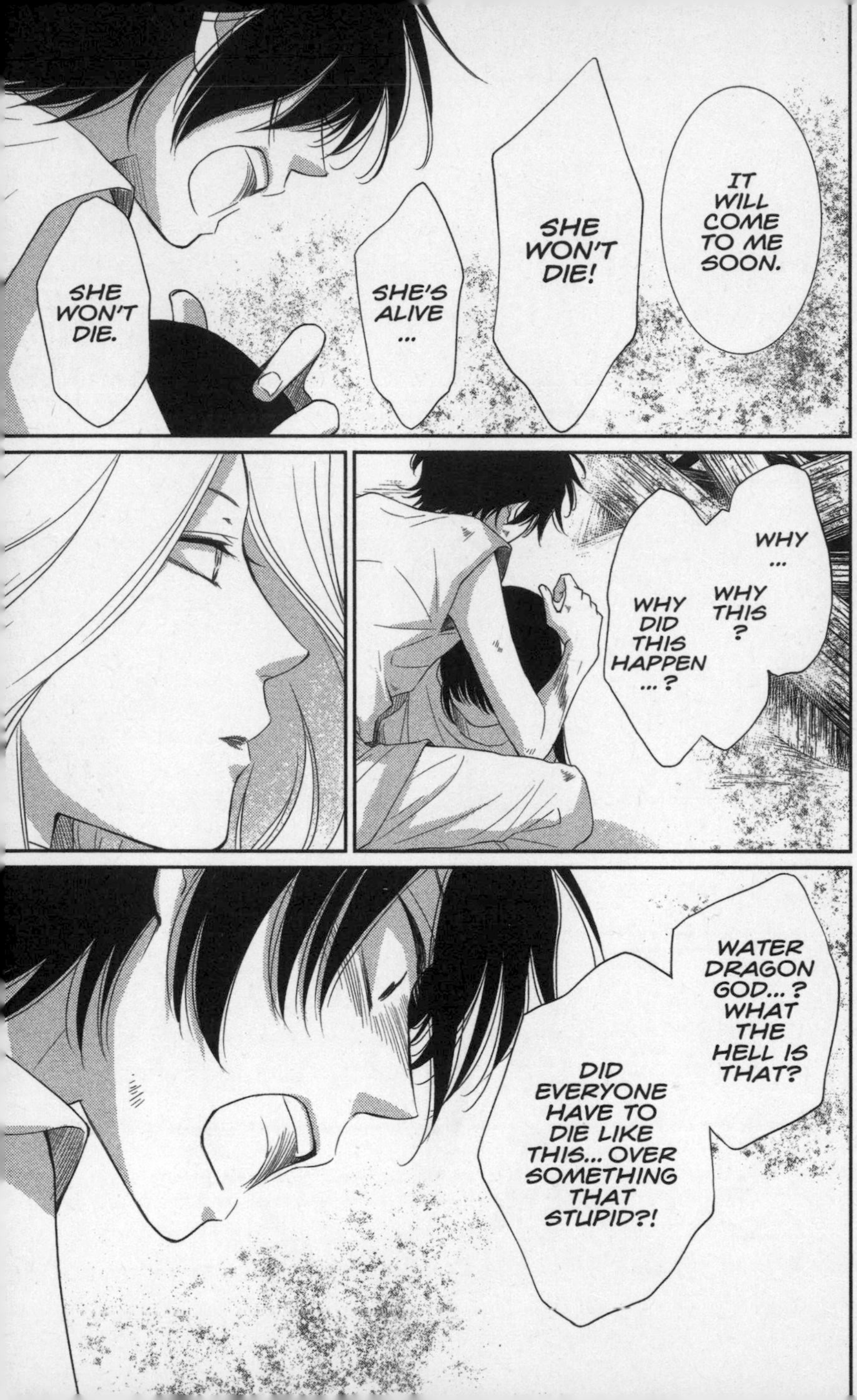
IT WILL COME TO ME SOON.
SHE WON'T DIE!
SHE'S ALIVE...
SHE WON'T DIE.
WHY... WHY THIS?
WHY DID THIS HAPPEN...?
WATER DRAGON GOD...? WHAT THE HELL IS THAT?
DID EVERYONE HAVE TO DIE LIKE THIS... OVER SOMETHING THAT STUPID?!

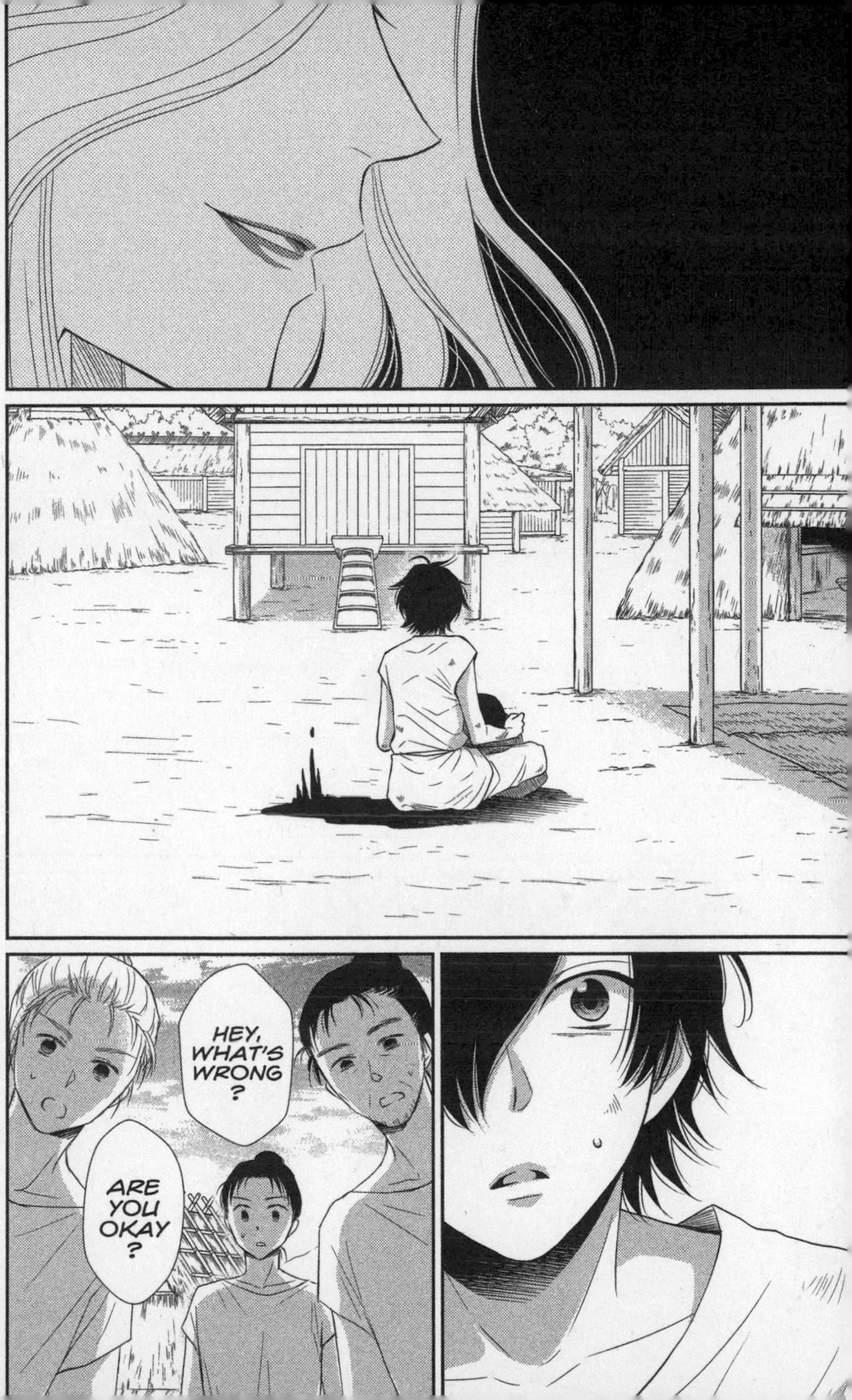
HEY, WHAT'S WRONG?
ARE YOU OKAY?

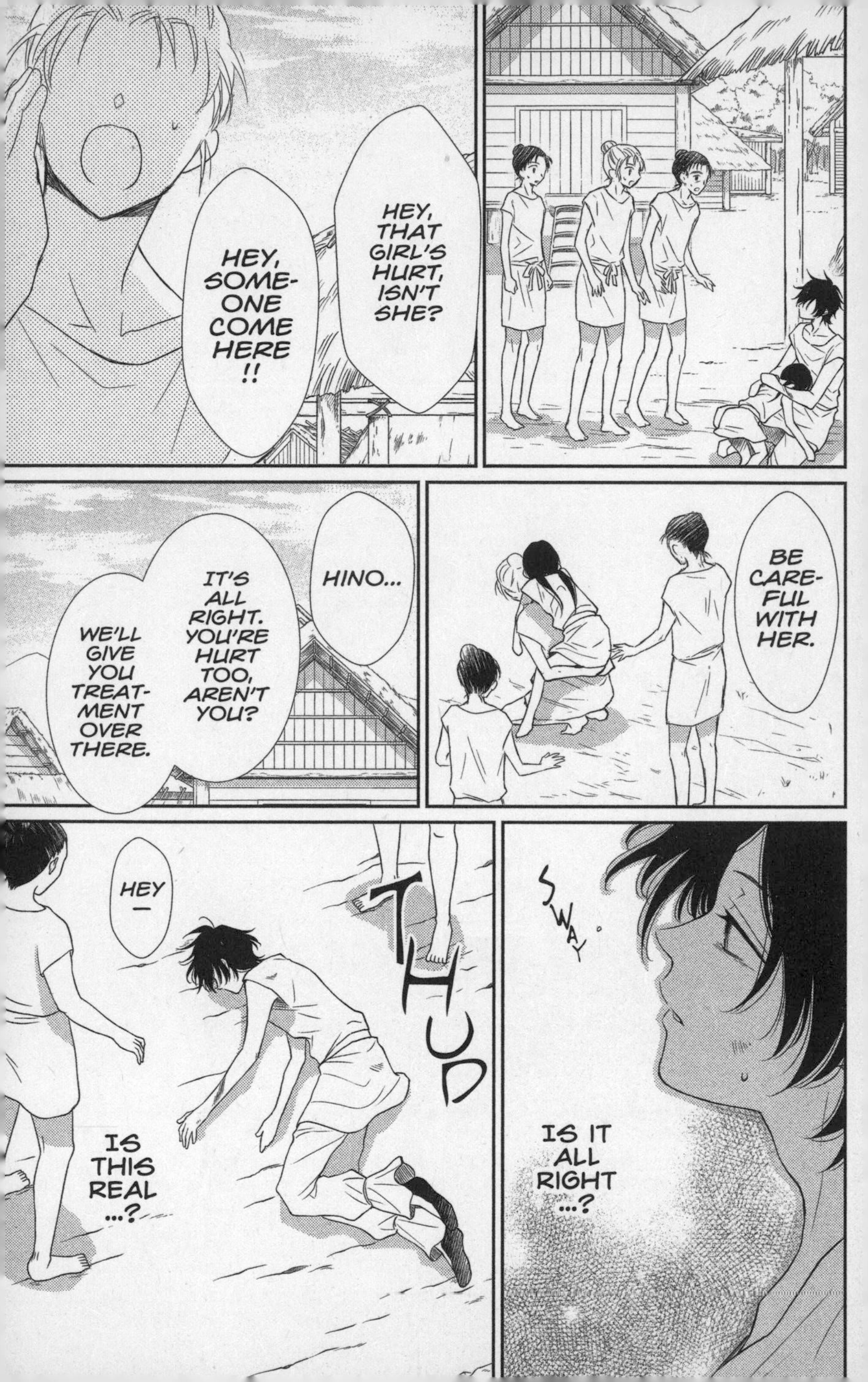
HEY, THAT GIRL'S HURT, ISN'T SHE?
HEY, SOMEONE COME HERE!!
BE CAREFUL WITH HER.
HINO...
IT'S ALL RIGHT. YOU'RE HURT TOO, AREN'T YOU?
WE'LL GIVE YOU TREATMENT OVER THERE.
SWAY
IS IT ALL RIGHT...?
THUD
HEY—
IS THIS REAL...?

THIS IS...

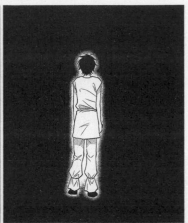

HINO!

KURO-SE...

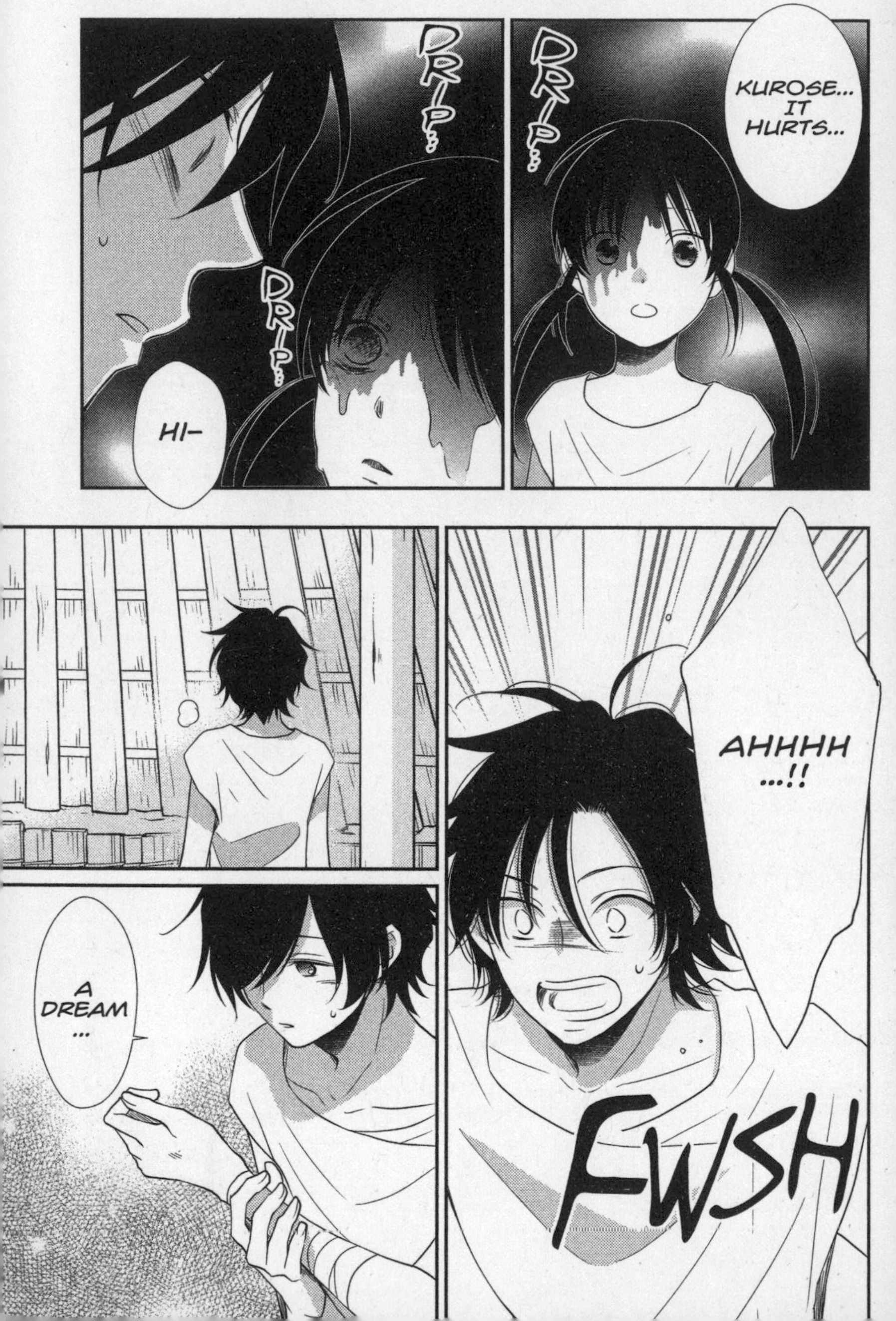
DRIP...
KUROSE... IT HURTS...
DRIP...
DRIP...
HI-
AHHHH ...!!
FWSH
A DREAM ...

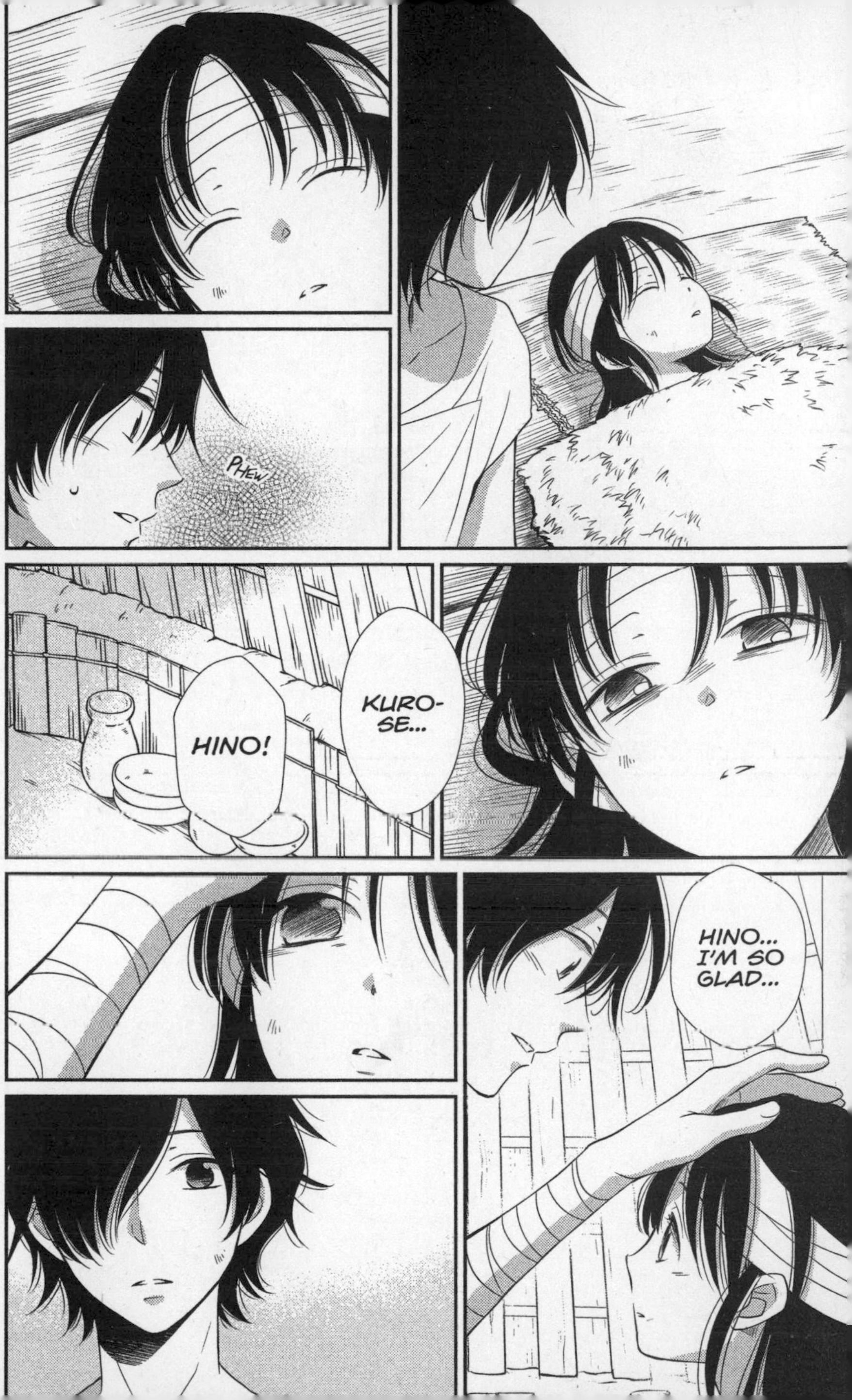
PHEW
KURO-SE...
HINO!
HINO... I'M SO GLAD...

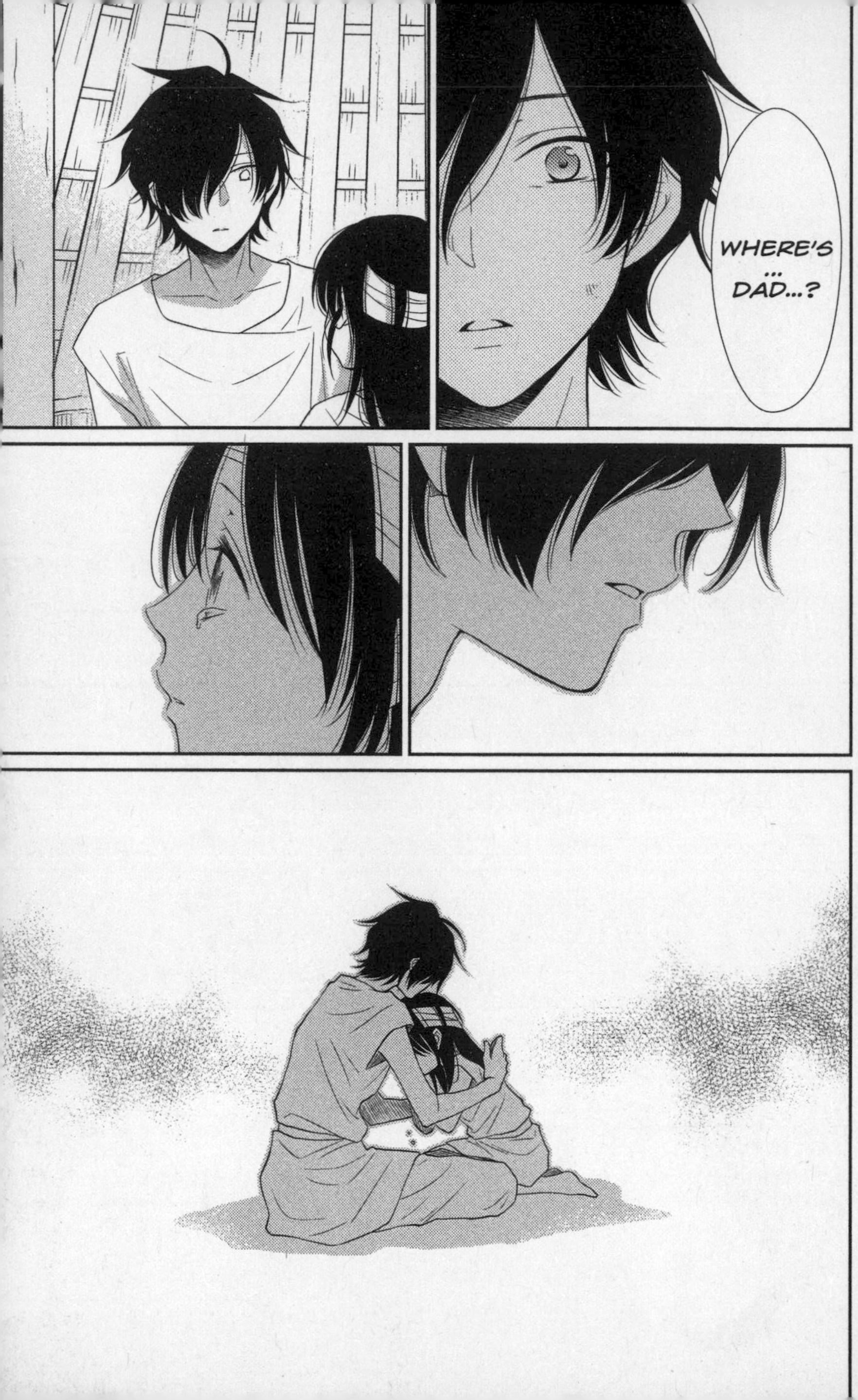
WHERE'S ... DAD...?

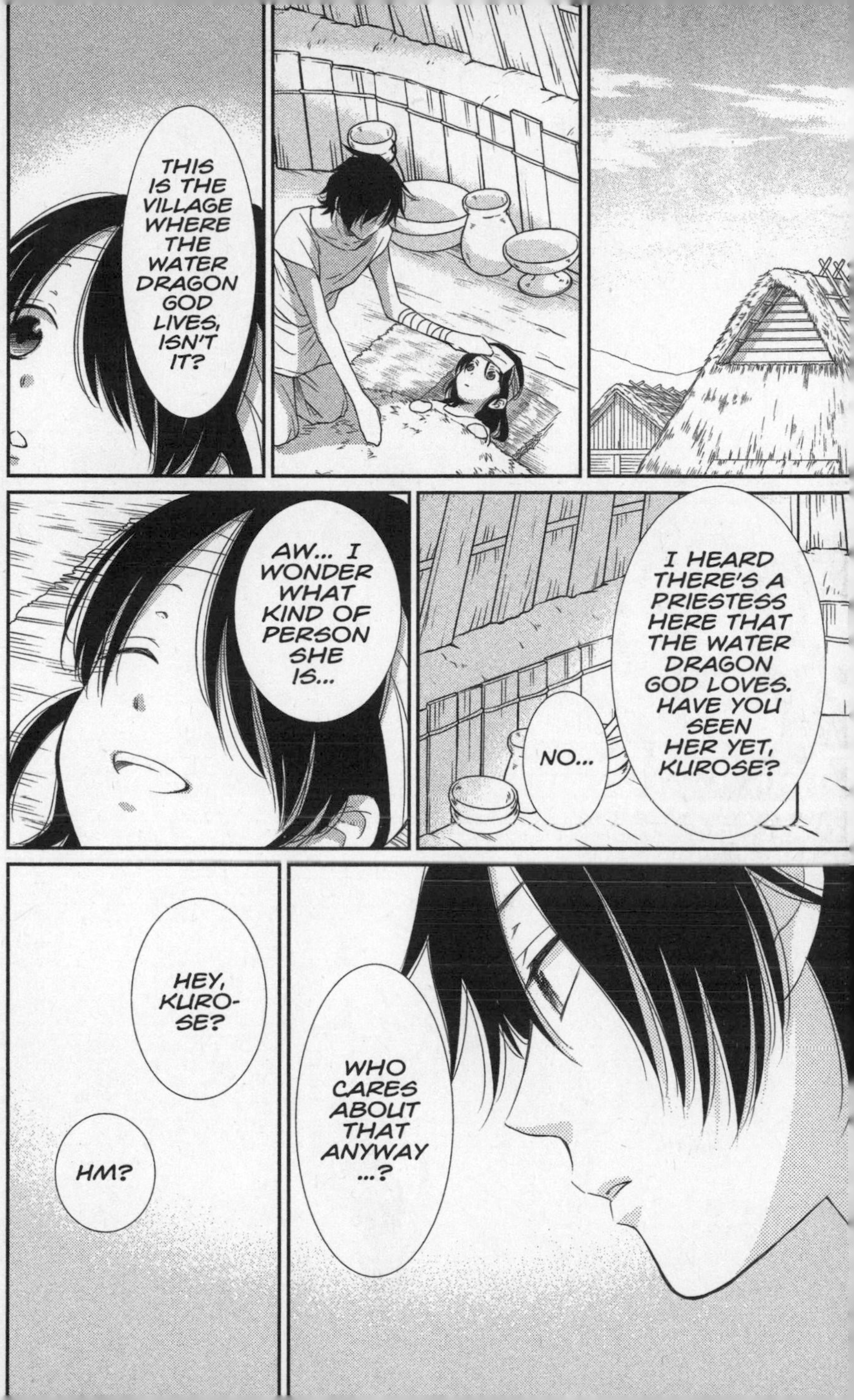
THIS IS THE VILLAGE WHERE THE WATER DRAGON GOD LIVES, ISN'T IT?
I HEARD THERE'S A PRIESTESS HERE THAT THE WATER DRAGON GOD LOVES. HAVE YOU SEEN HER YET, KUROSE?
NO...
AW... I WONDER WHAT KIND OF PERSON SHE IS...
WHO CARES ABOUT THAT ANYWAY ...?
HEY, KURO-SE?
HM?

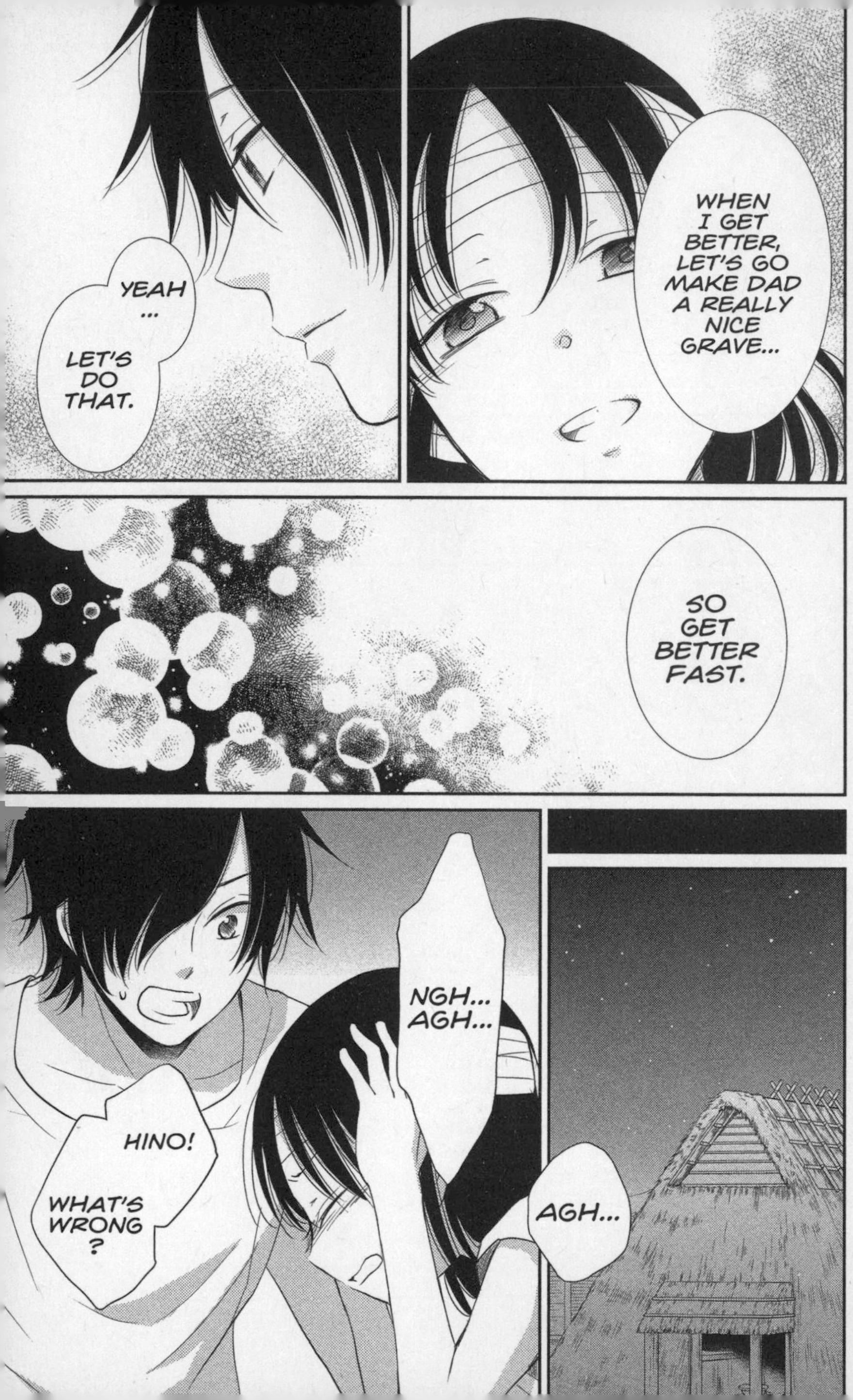
WHEN I GET BETTER, LET'S GO MAKE DAD A REALLY NICE GRAVE...
YEAH ... LET'S DO THAT.
SO GET BETTER FAST.
AGH...
NGH... AGH...
HINO! WHAT'S WRONG ?

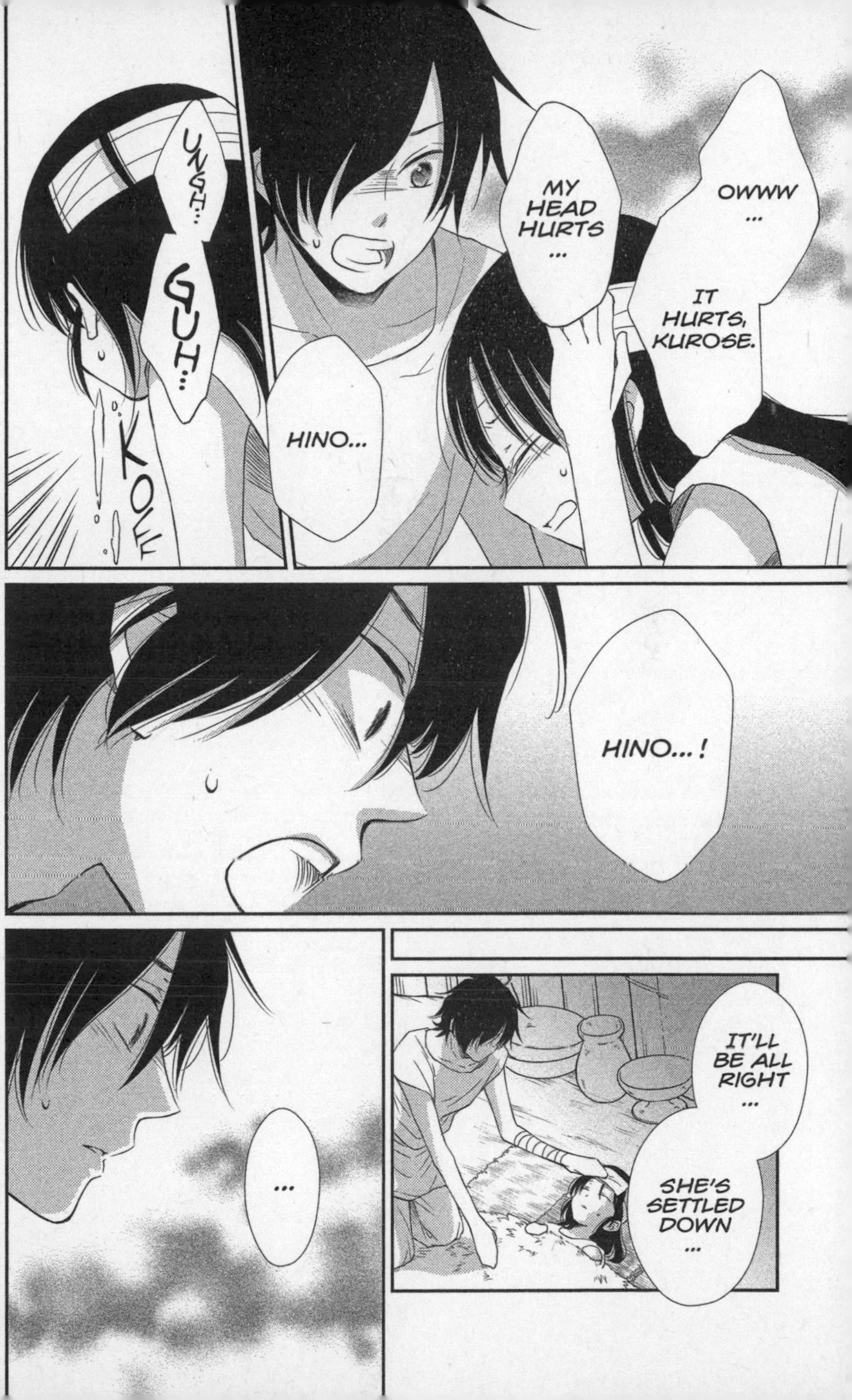
OWWW... IT HURTS, KUROSE.
MY HEAD HURTS...
HINO...
UNGH... GUH...
KOFF
HINO...!
IT'LL BE ALL RIGHT...
SHE'S SETTLED DOWN...
...

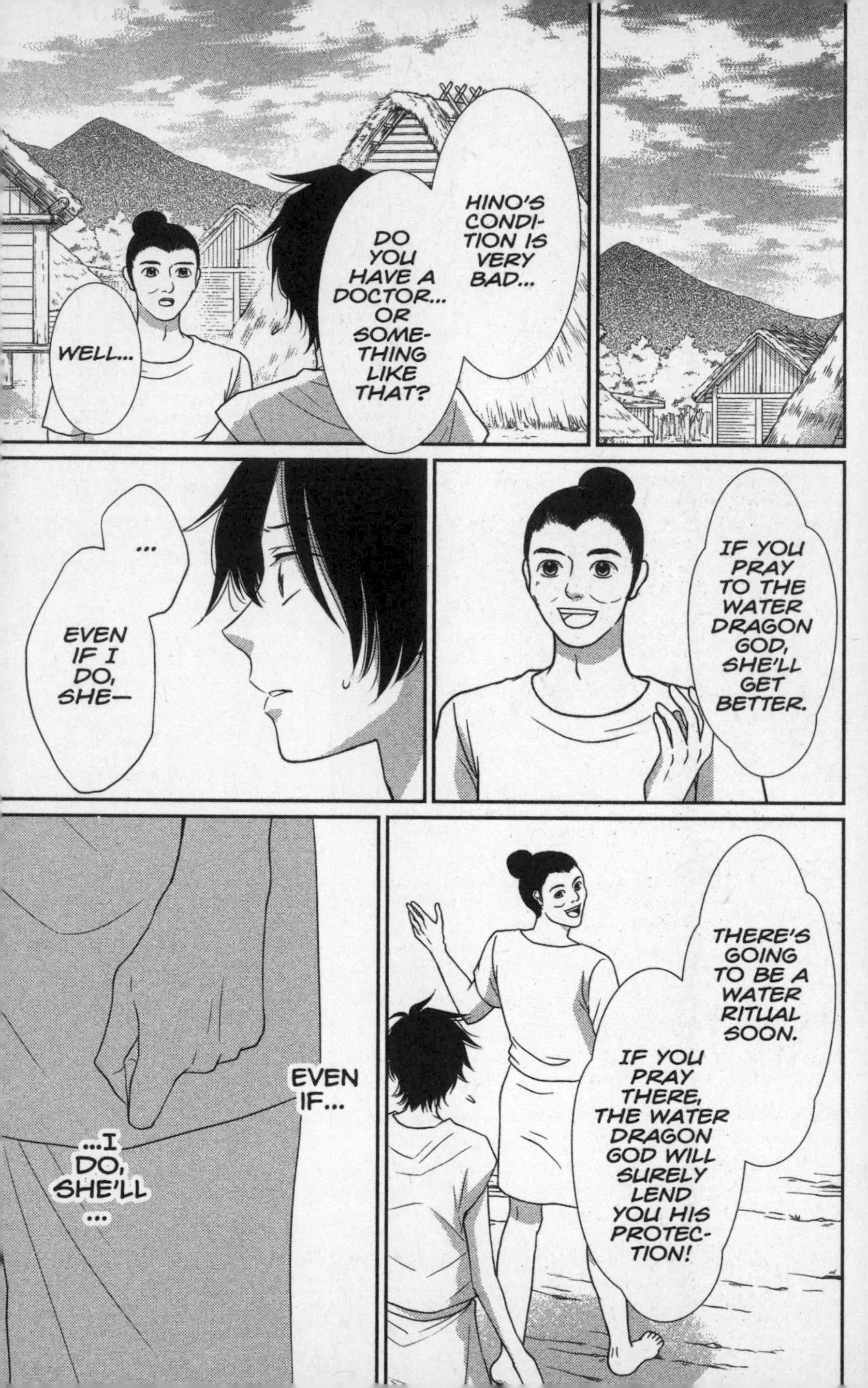
HINO'S CONDITION IS VERY BAD...
DO YOU HAVE A DOCTOR... OR SOMETHING LIKE THAT?
WELL...
IF YOU PRAY TO THE WATER DRAGON GOD, SHE'LL GET BETTER.
...
EVEN IF I DO, SHE—
THERE'S GOING TO BE A WATER RITUAL SOON.
IF YOU PRAY THERE, THE WATER DRAGON GOD WILL SURELY LEND YOU HIS PROTECTION!
EVEN IF...
...I DO, SHE'LL ...

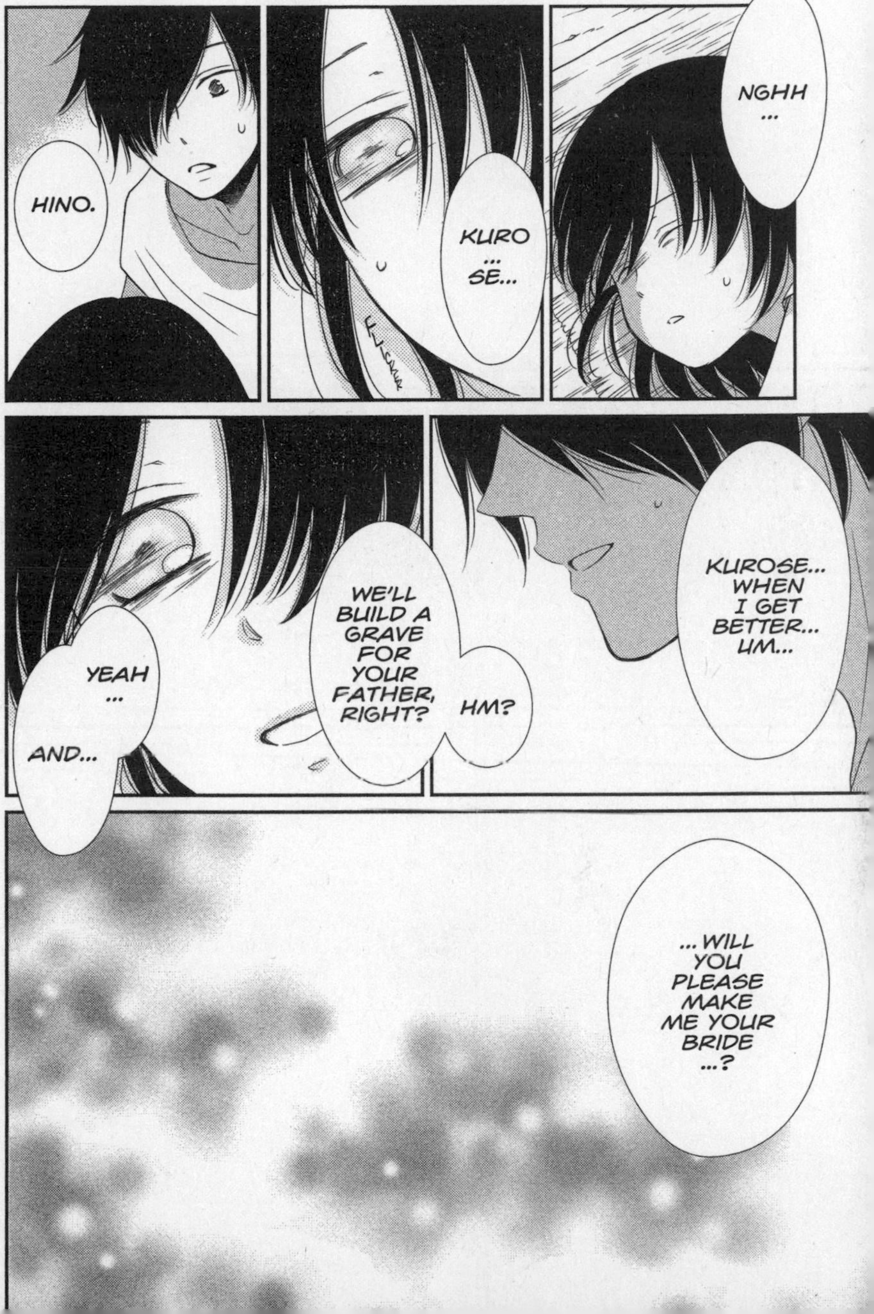
NGHH ...
KURO ... SE...
HINO.
KUROSE... WHEN I GET BETTER... UM...
WE'LL BUILD A GRAVE FOR YOUR FATHER, RIGHT?
HM?
YEAH ... AND...
...WILL YOU PLEASE MAKE ME YOUR BRIDE ...?

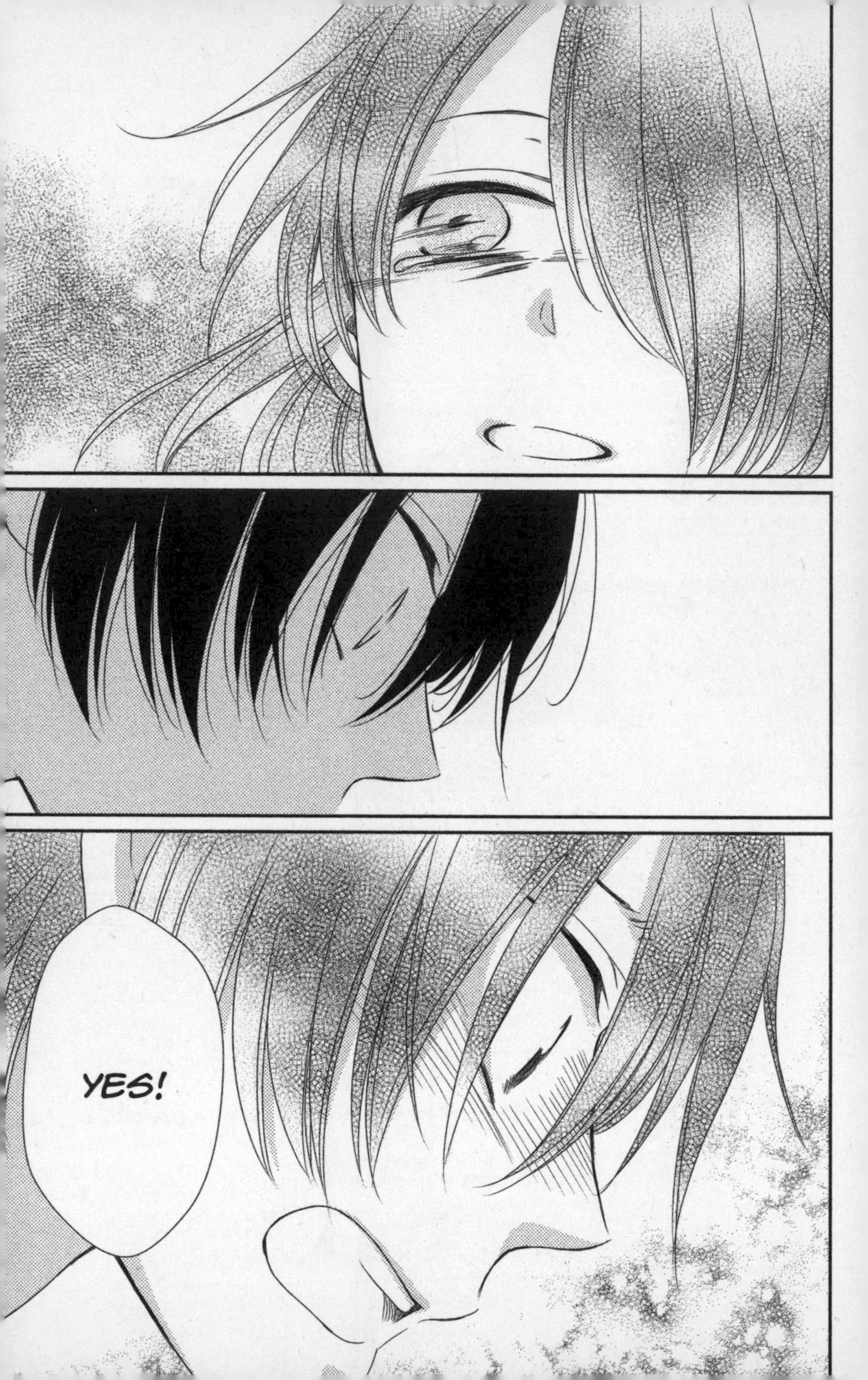
YES!

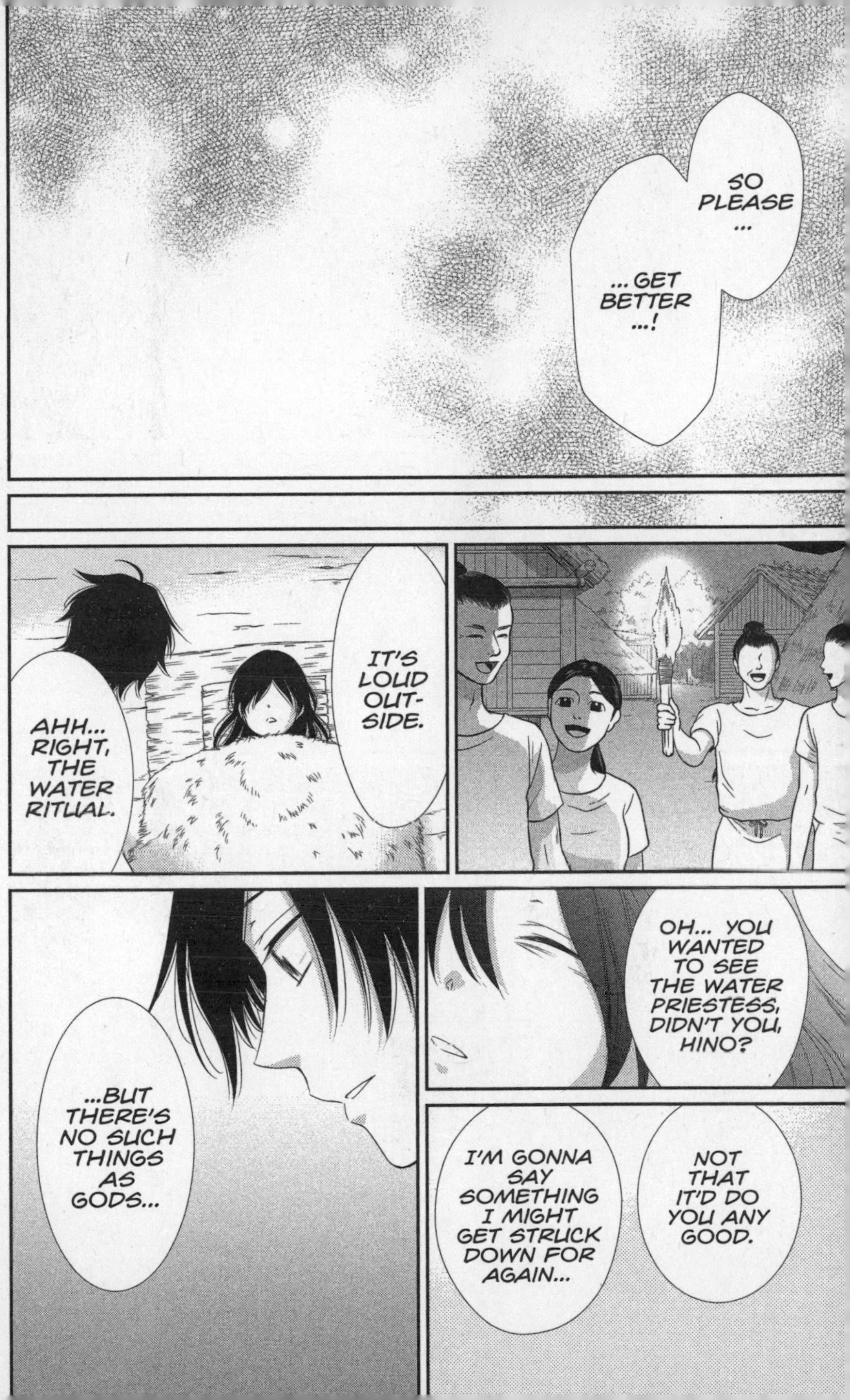
SO PLEASE ...
...GET BETTER ...!
IT'S LOUD OUT-SIDE.
AHH... RIGHT, THE WATER RITUAL.
OH... YOU WANTED TO SEE THE WATER PRIESTESS, DIDN'T YOU, HINO?
...BUT THERE'S NO SUCH THINGS AS GODS...
NOT THAT IT'D DO YOU ANY GOOD.
I'M GONNA SAY SOMETHING I MIGHT GET STRUCK DOWN FOR AGAIN...

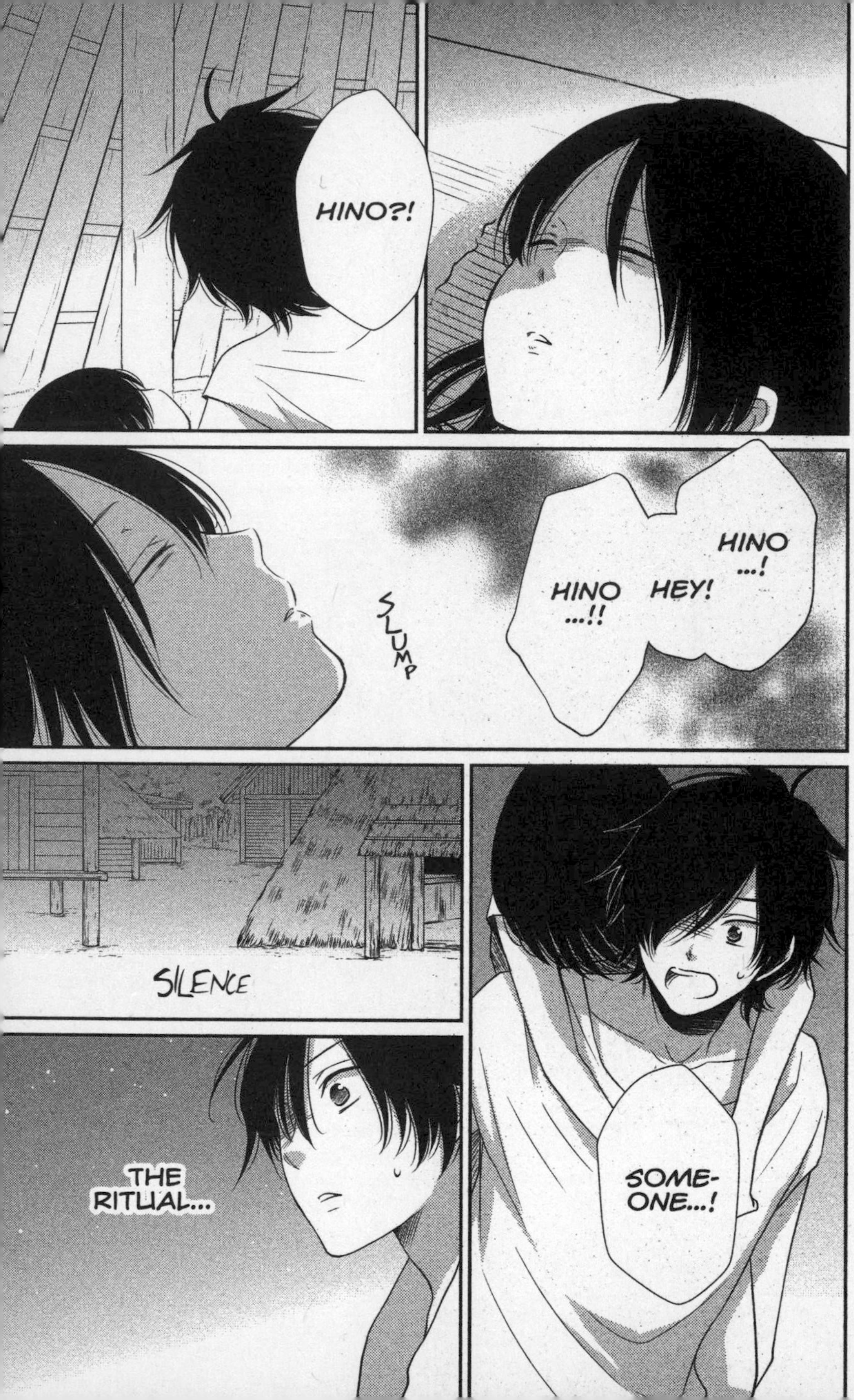
HINO?!
HINO ...!
HEY!
HINO ...!!
SLUMP
SOME-ONE...!
SILENCE
THE RITUAL...

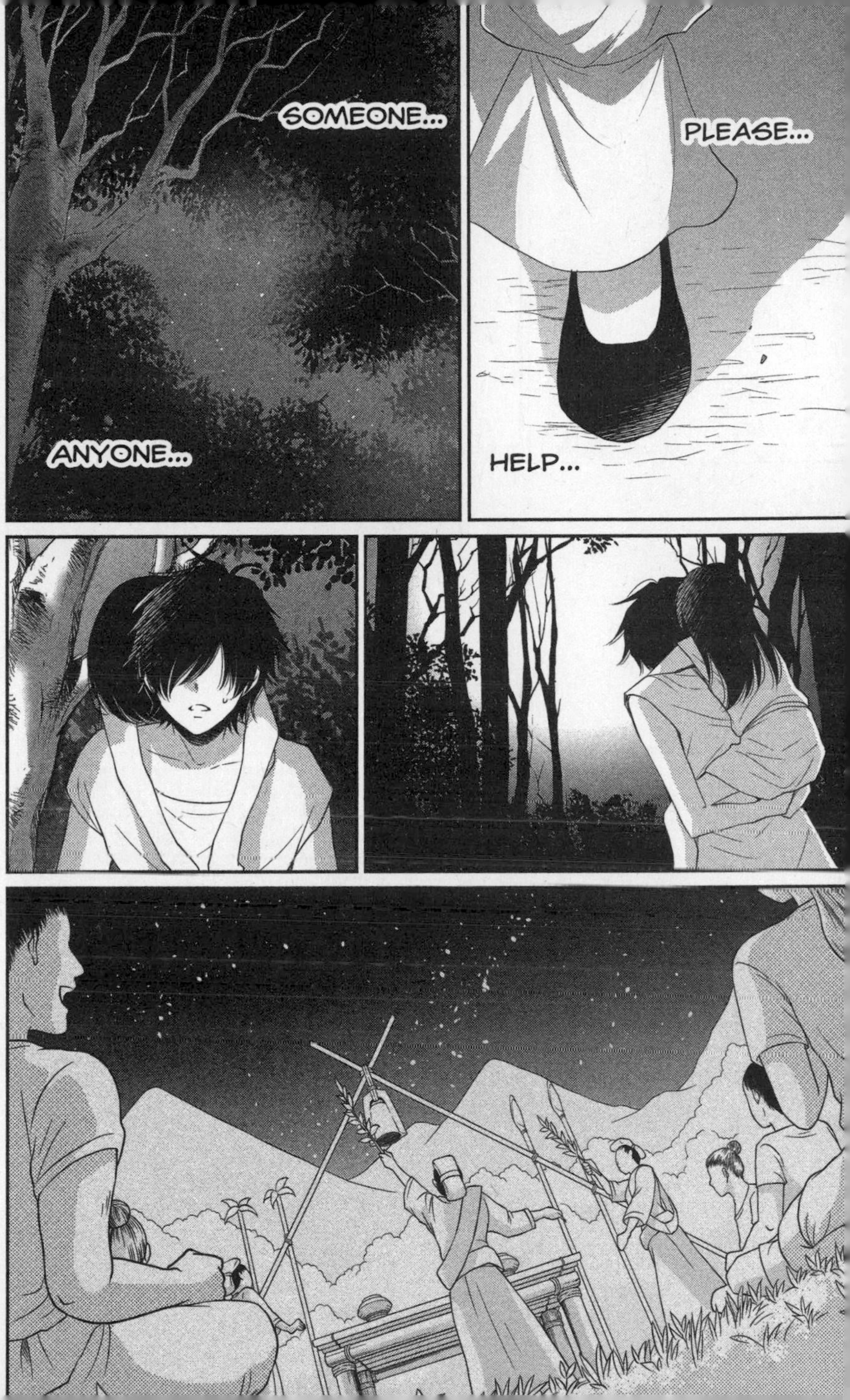
PLEASE...
HELP...
SOMEONE...
ANYONE...

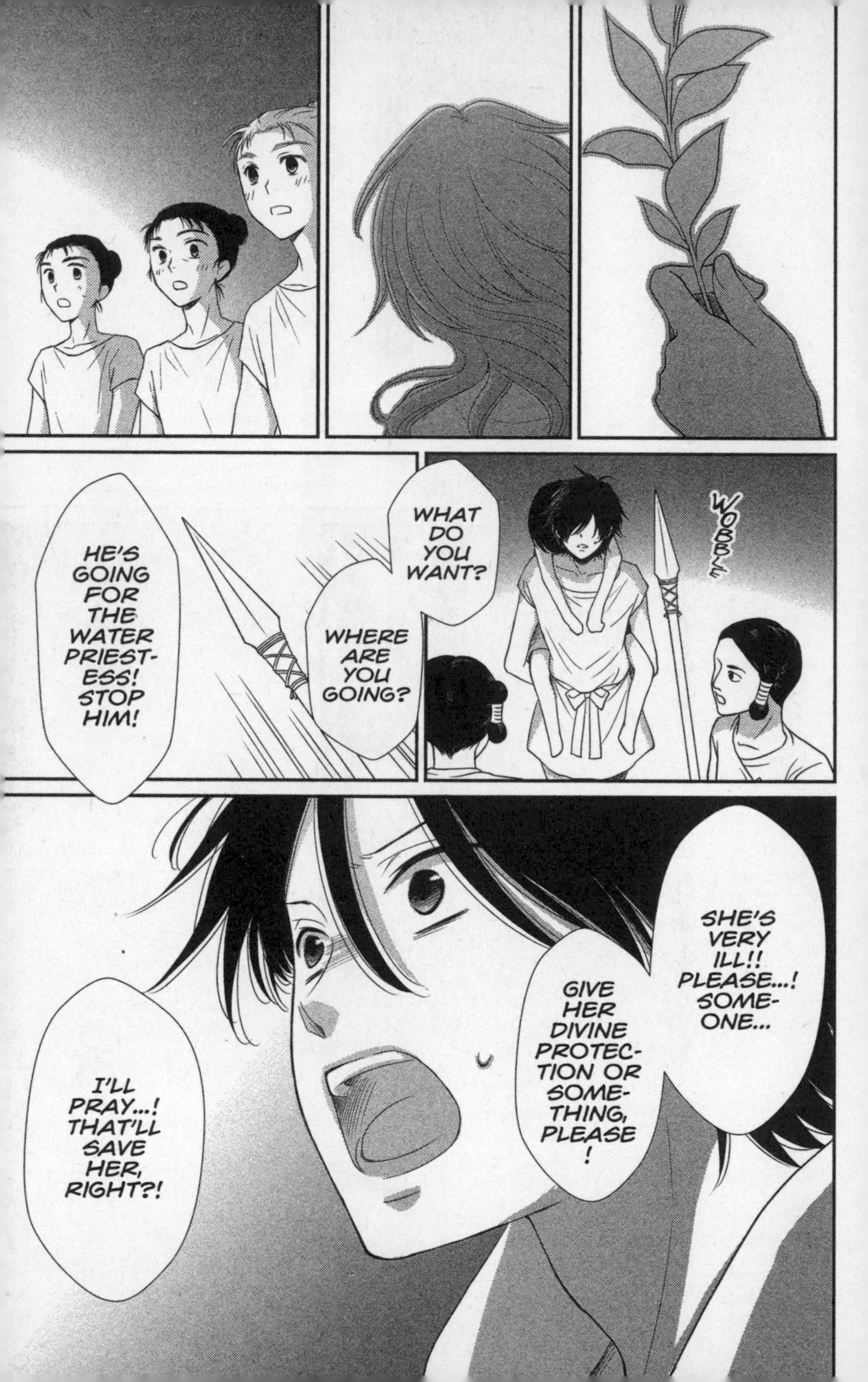
WOBBLE
WHAT DO YOU WANT?
WHERE ARE YOU GOING?
HE'S GOING FOR THE WATER PRIEST-ESS! STOP HIM!
SHE'S VERY ILL!! PLEASE...! SOME-ONE...
GIVE HER DIVINE PROTEC-TION OR SOME-THING, PLEASE!
I'LL PRAY...! THAT'LL SAVE HER, RIGHT?!

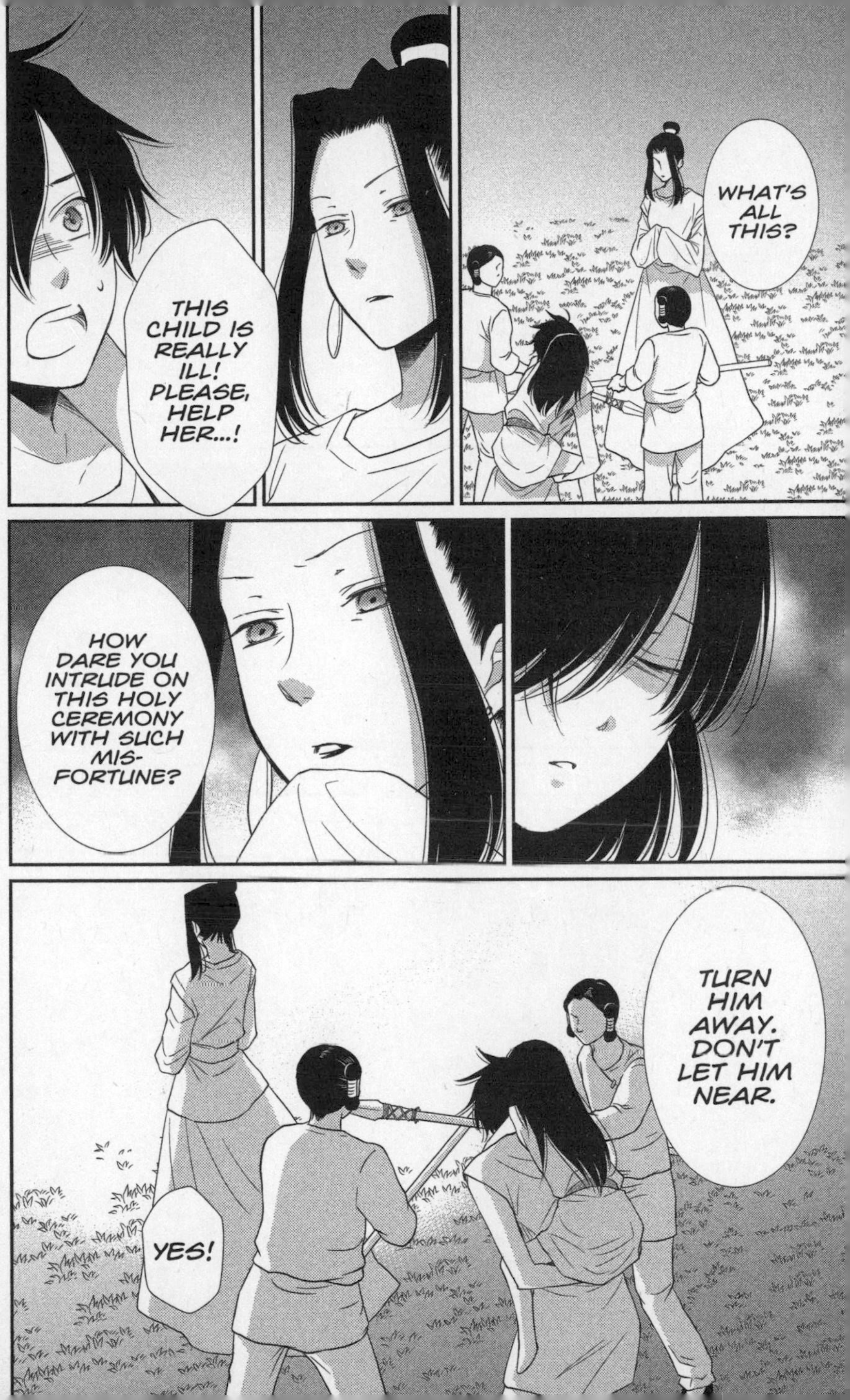
WHAT'S ALL THIS?
THIS CHILD IS REALLY ILL! PLEASE, HELP HER...!
HOW DARE YOU INTRUDE ON THIS HOLY CEREMONY WITH SUCH MIS-FORTUNE?
TURN HIM AWAY. DON'T LET HIM NEAR.
YES!

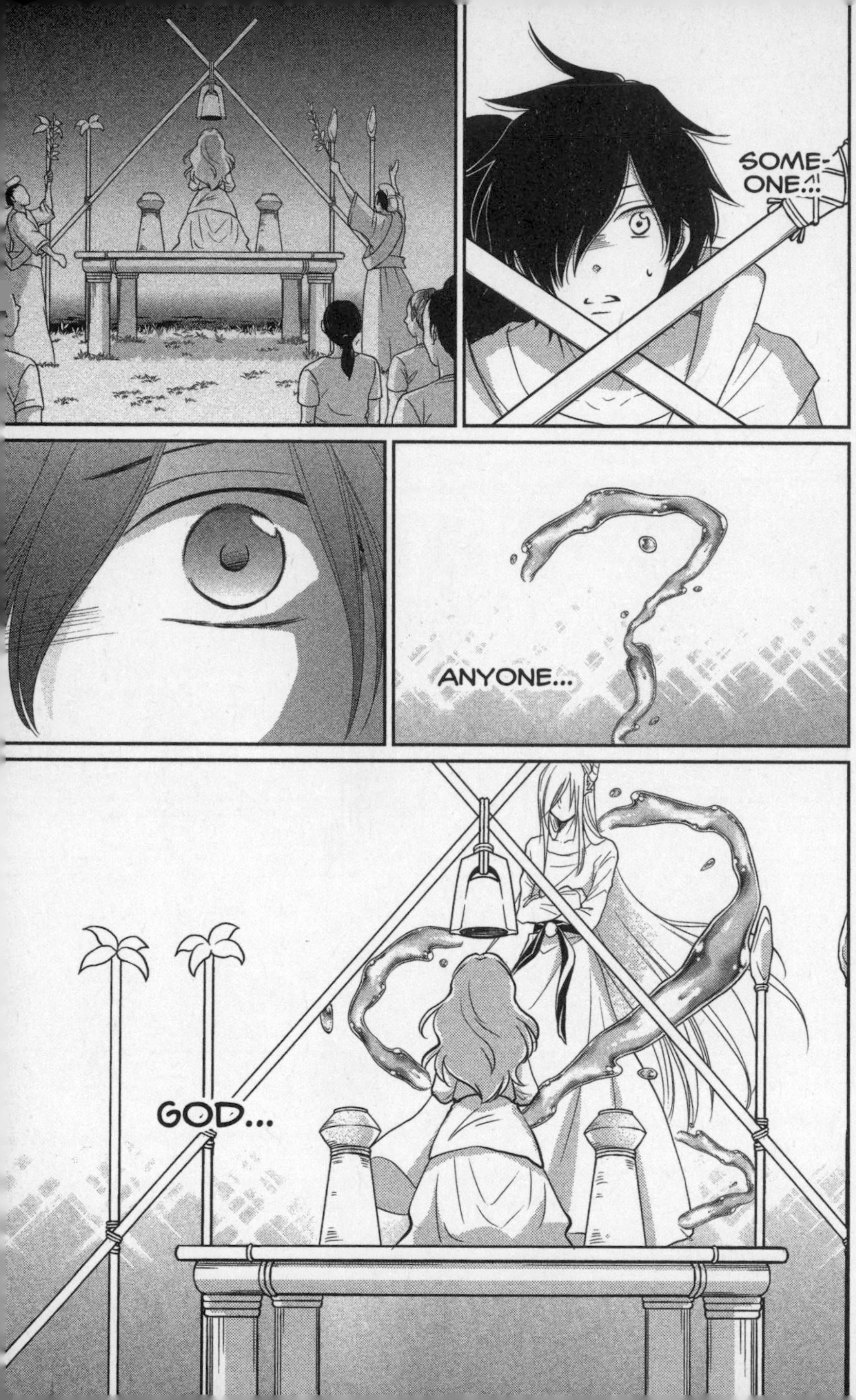
SOME-ONE...!!
ANYONE...
GOD...

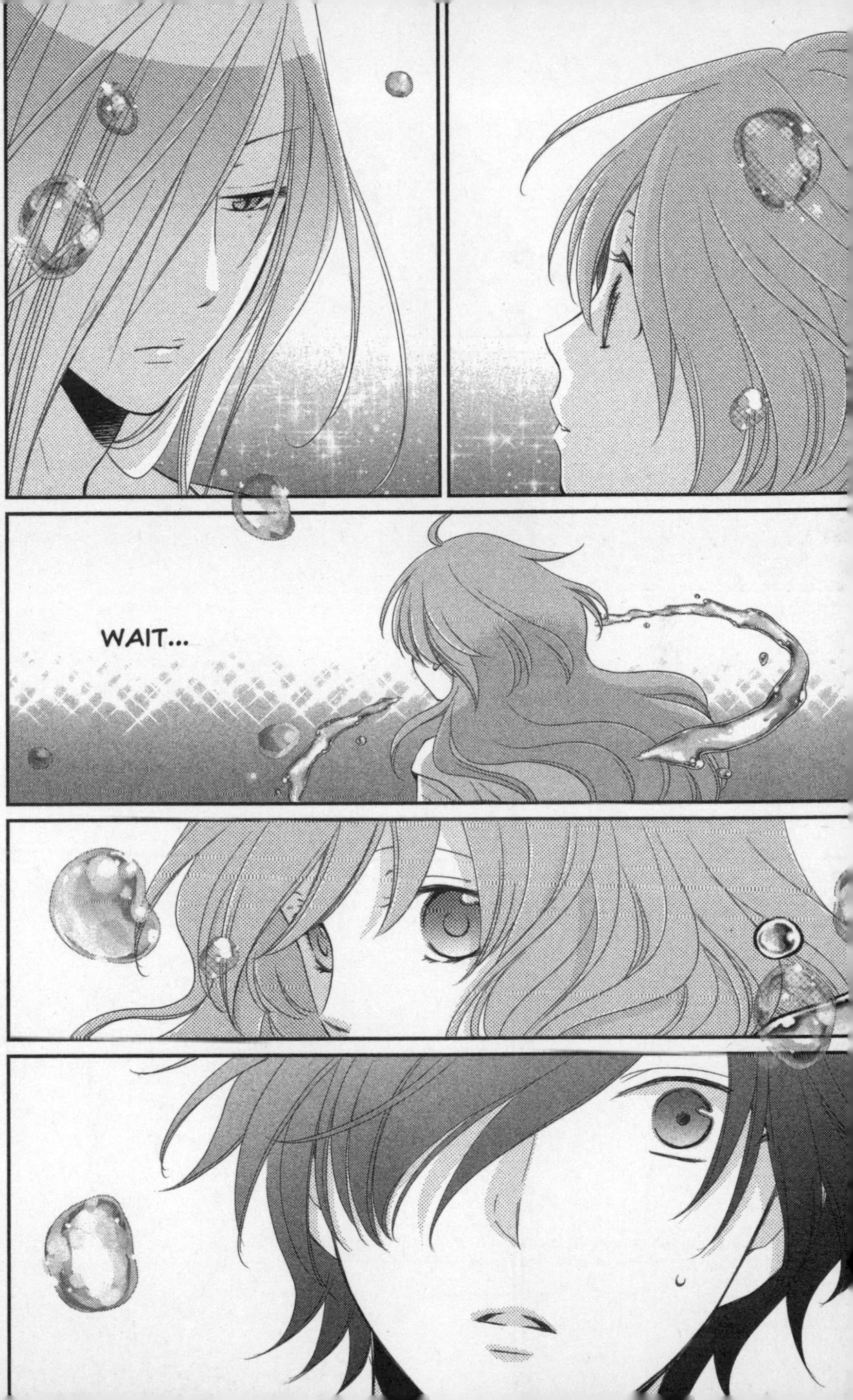
WAIT...

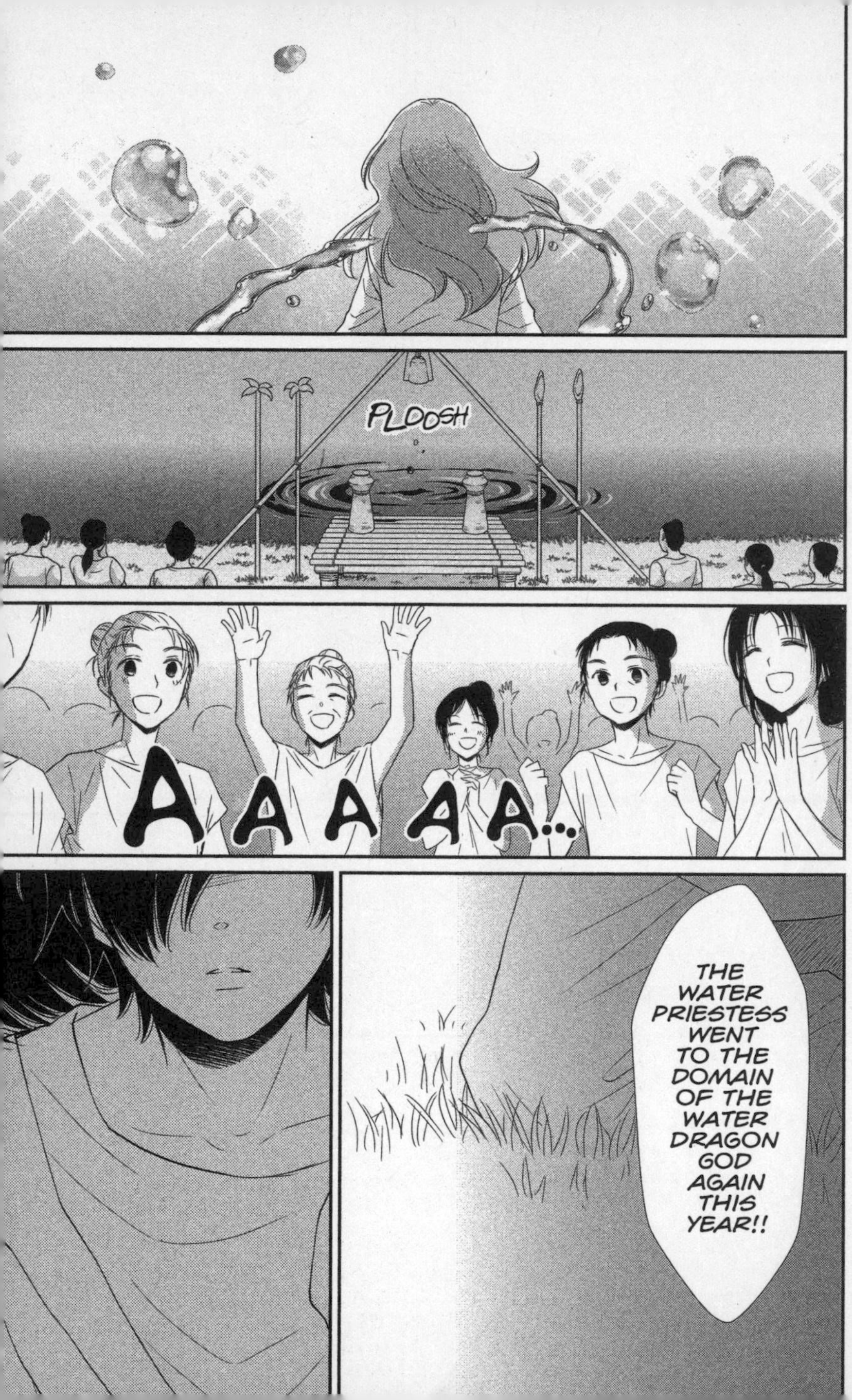
PLOOSH
AAAAA...
THE WATER PRIESTESS WENT TO THE DOMAIN OF THE WATER DRAGON GOD AGAIN THIS YEAR!!

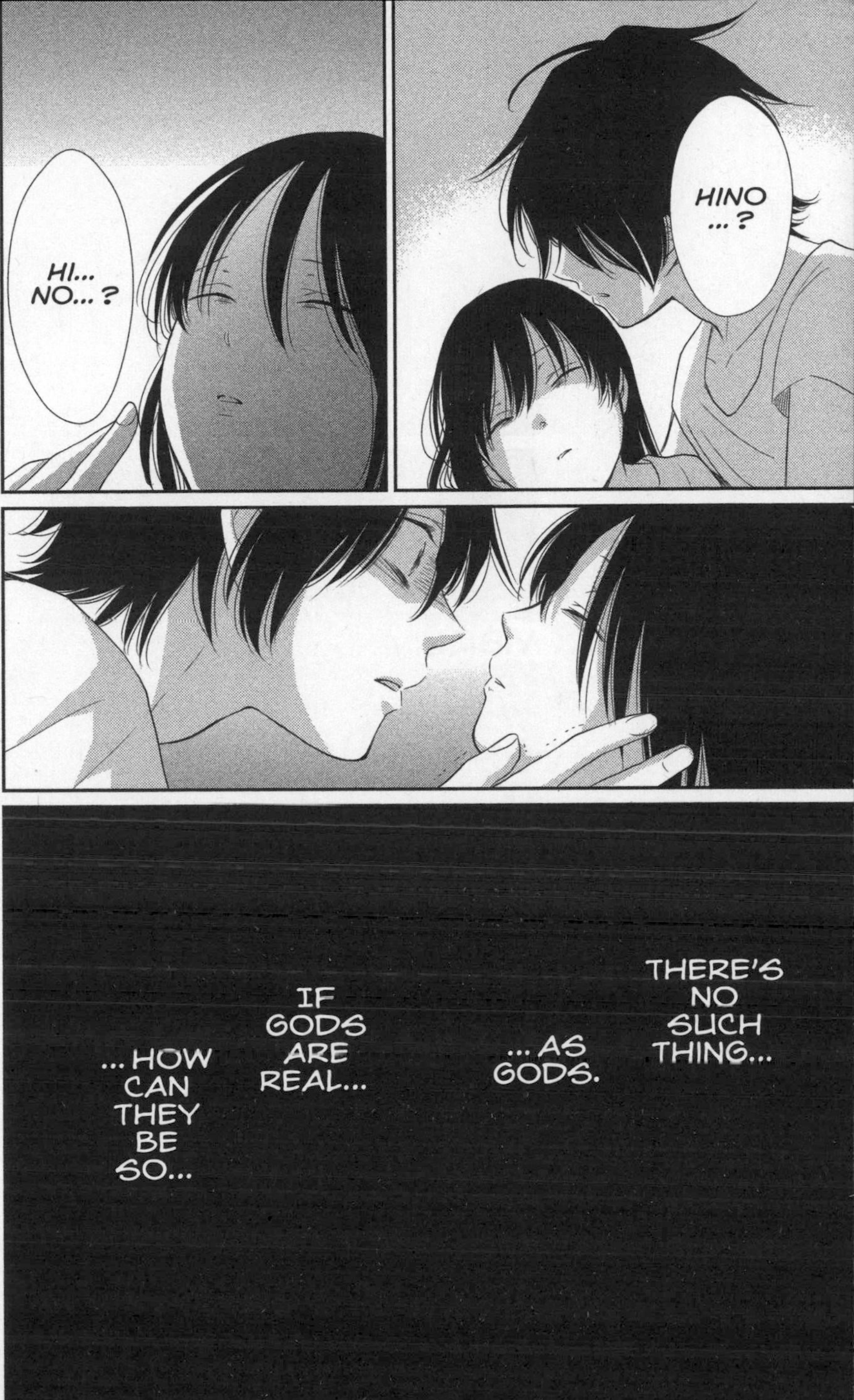
HINO ...?
HI... NO...?
THERE'S NO SUCH THING...
...AS GODS.
IF GODS ARE REAL...
...HOW CAN THEY BE SO...

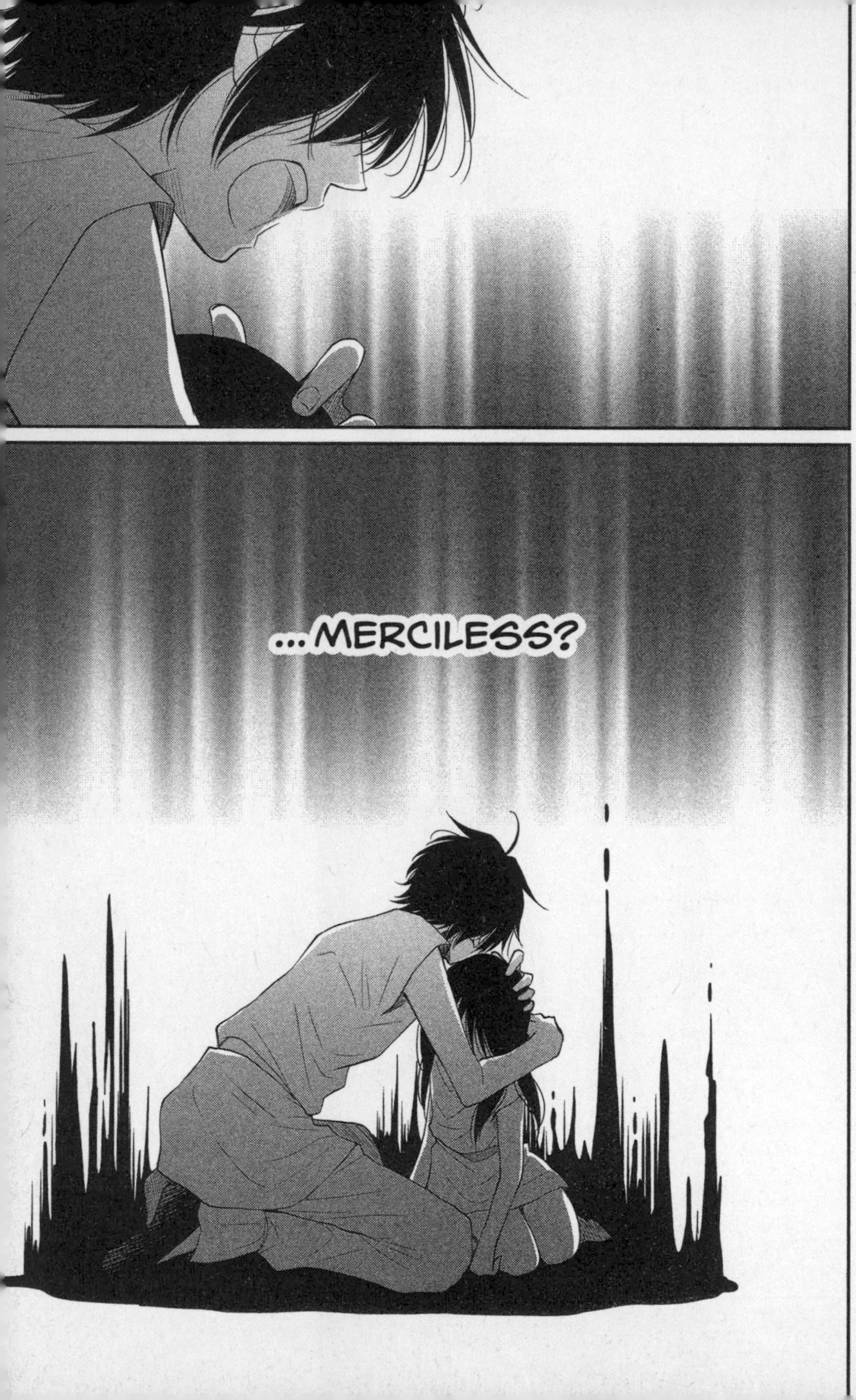
...MERCILESS?

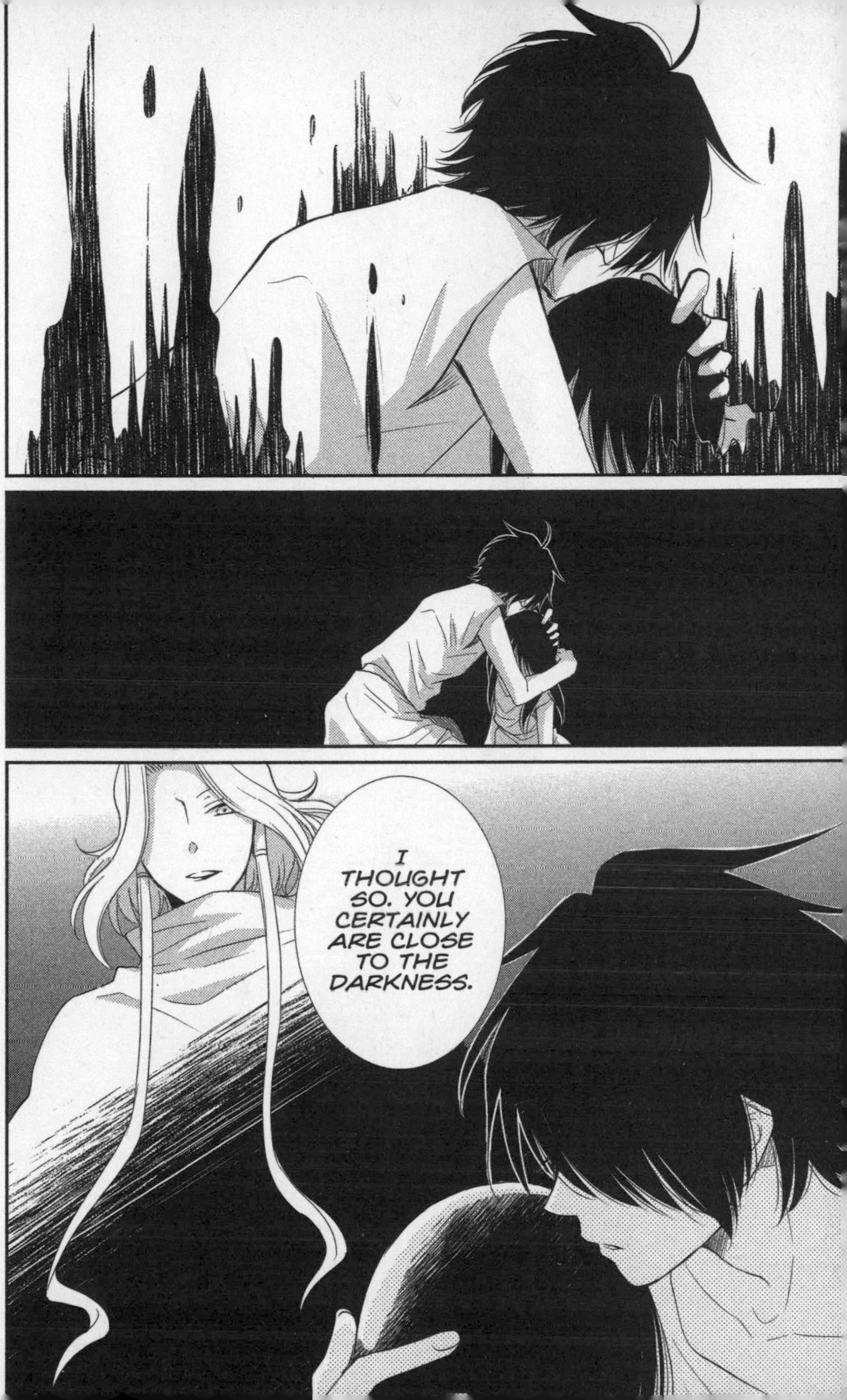
I THOUGHT SO. YOU CERTAINLY ARE CLOSE TO THE DARKNESS.

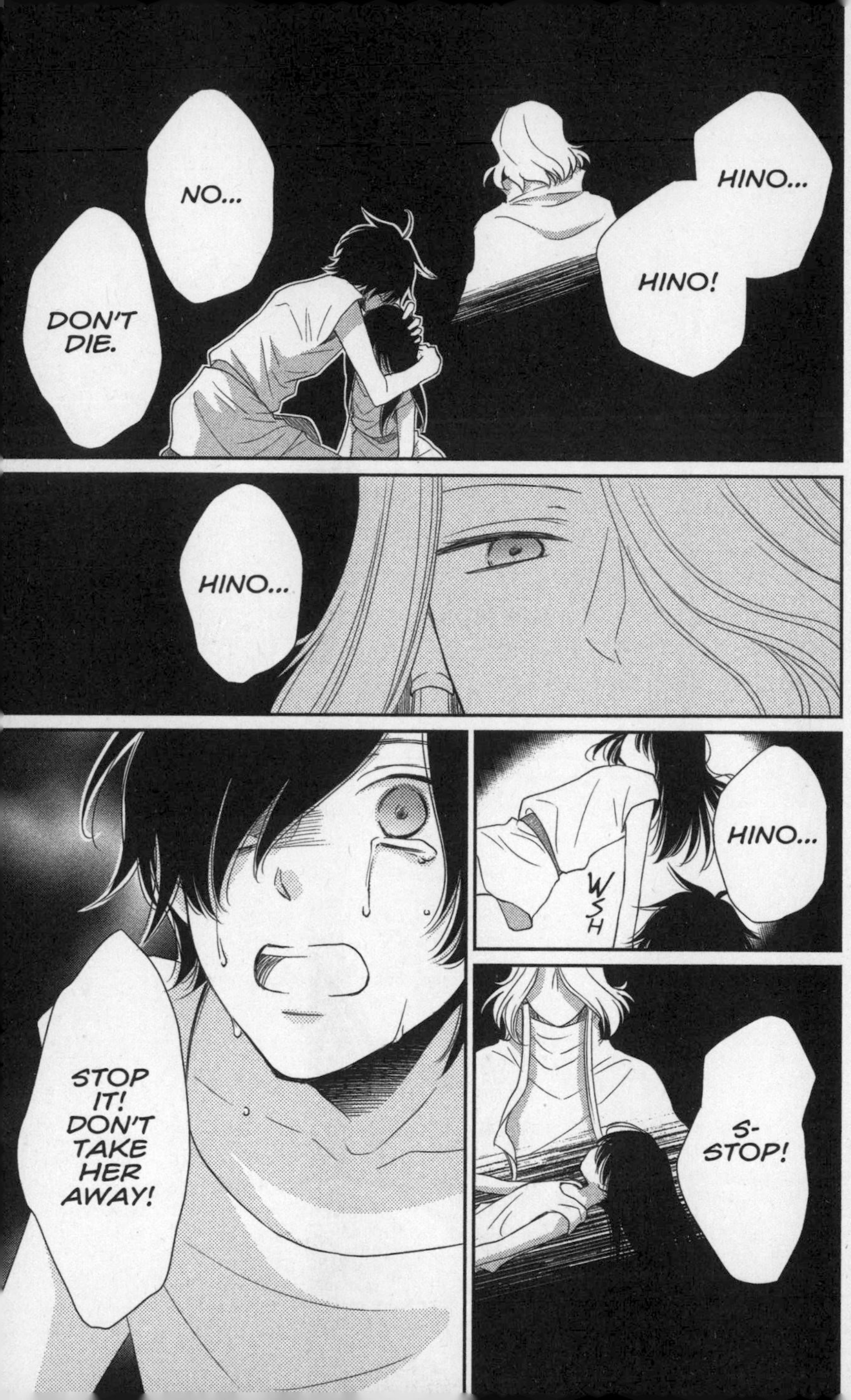
HINO...
HINO!
NO...
DON'T DIE.
HINO...
HINO...
WSH
S-STOP!
STOP IT! DON'T TAKE HER AWAY!

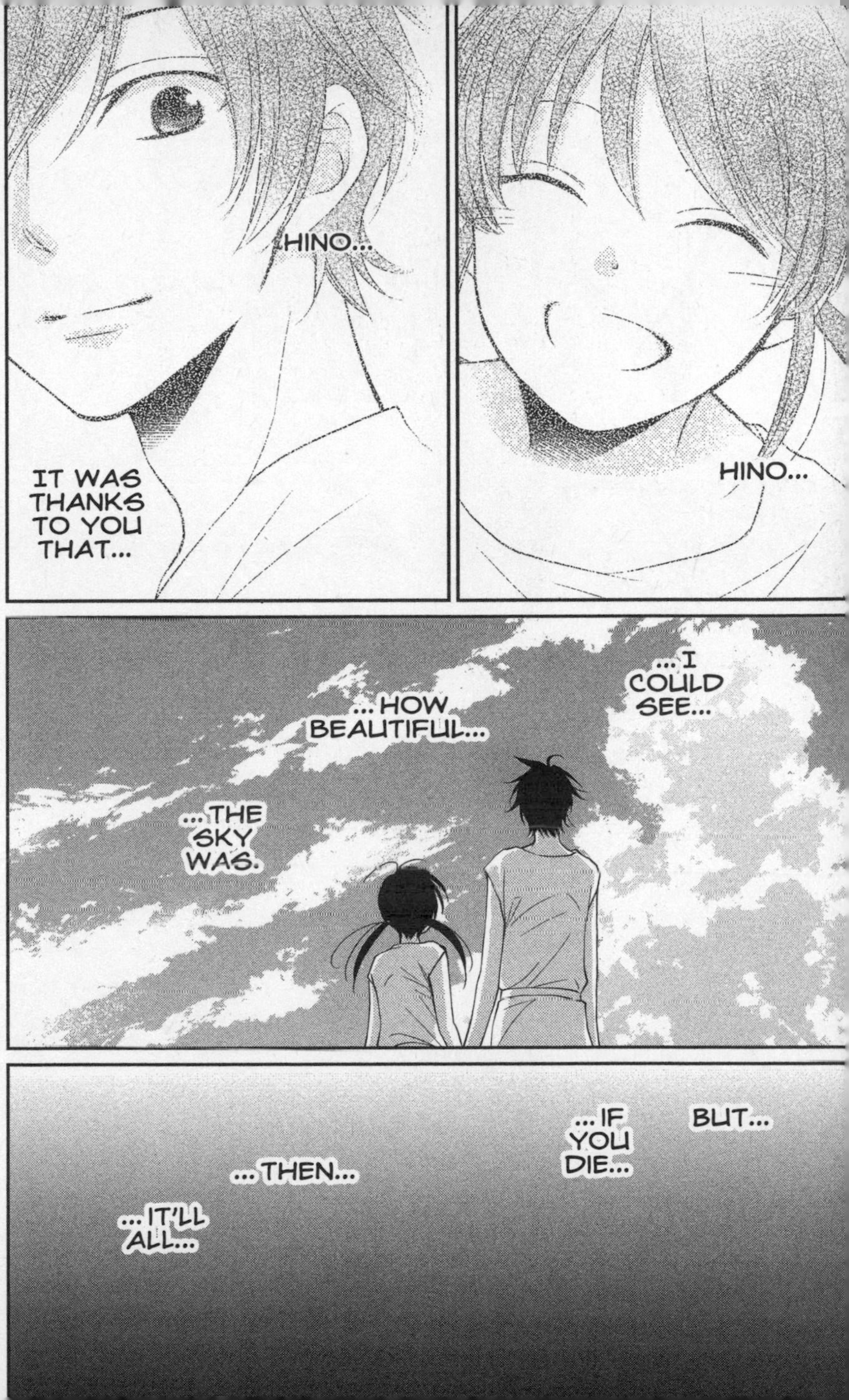
HINO...
HINO...
IT WAS THANKS TO YOU THAT...
...I COULD SEE...
...HOW BEAUTIFUL...
...THE SKY WAS.
BUT...
...IF YOU DIE...
...THEN...
...IT'LL ALL...

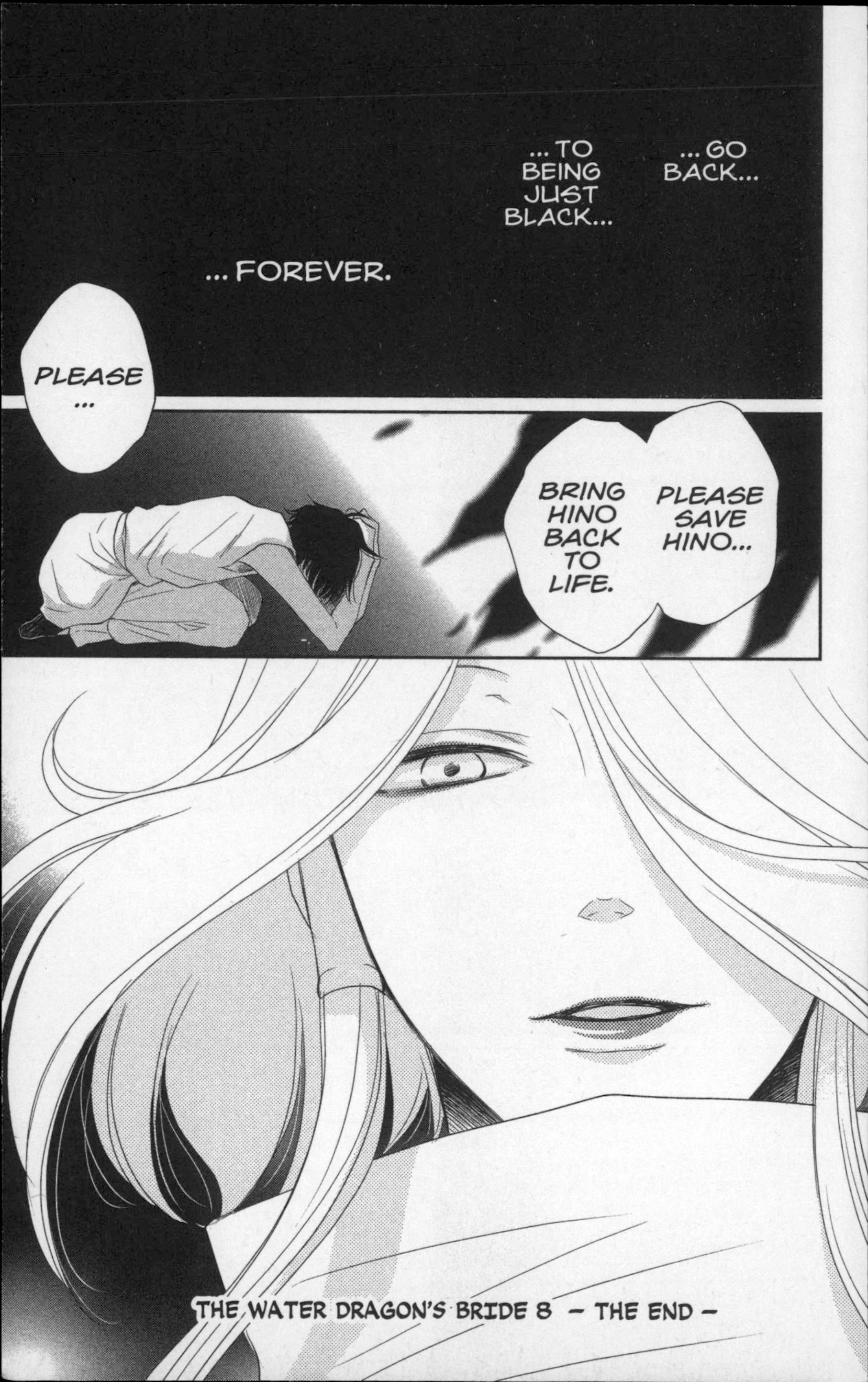
...GO BACK...
...TO BEING JUST BLACK...
...FOREVER.
PLEASE ...
PLEASE SAVE HINO...
BRING HINO BACK TO LIFE.
THE WATER DRAGON'S BRIDE 8 – THE END –

The Water Dragon's Bride

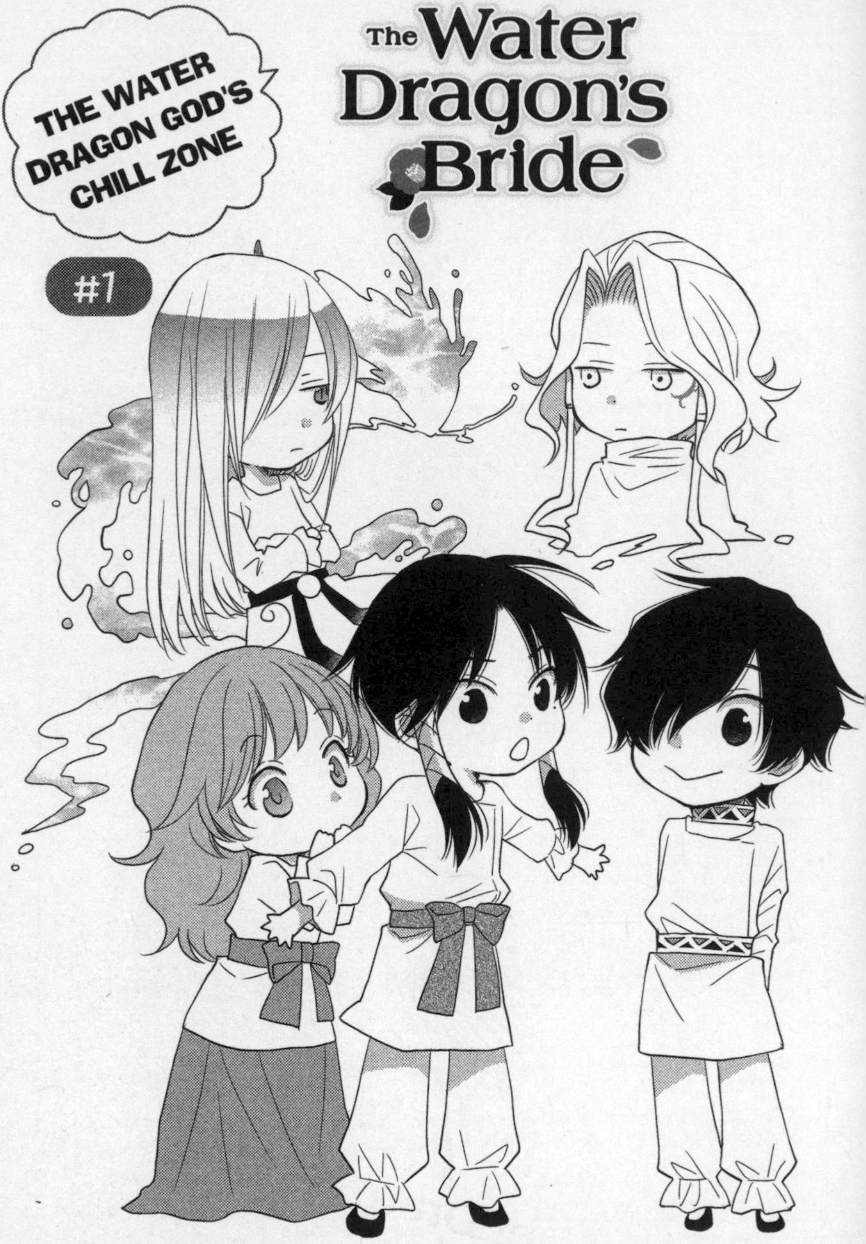
The Water Dragon's Bride
THE WATER DRAGON GOD'S CHILL ZONE
#1

For Reasons

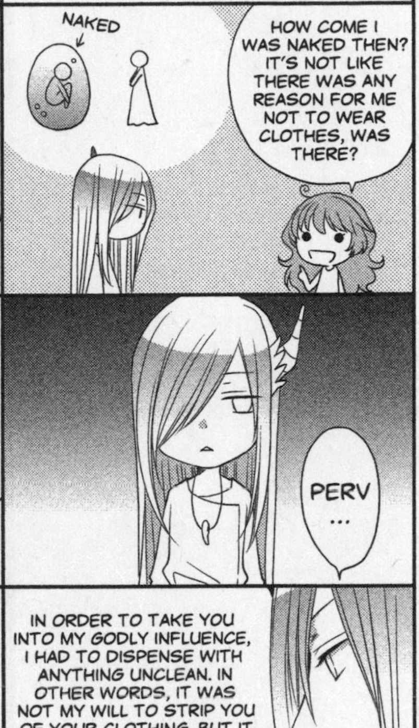
HOW COME I WAS NAKED THEN? IT'S NOT LIKE THERE WAS ANY REASON FOR ME NOT TO WEAR CLOTHES, WAS THERE?
NAKED
PERV ...
IN ORDER TO TAKE YOU INTO MY GODLY INFLUENCE, I HAD TO DISPENSE WITH ANYTHING UNCLEAN. IN OTHER WORDS, IT WAS NOT MY WILL TO STRIP YOU OF YOUR CLOTHING, BUT IT WAS A NATURAL PROCESS THAT RETURNED YOU TO YOUR ORIGINAL AND NATURAL FORM. IT WASN'T AS IF YOU HAD TO BE NAKED BECAUSE I THOUGHT THAT IT WOULD BE COOLER AND THAT IT WOULD PRESERVE THE AESTHETIC. THAT WASN'T MY INTENTION AT ALL.
YAMMER YAMMER YAMMER
GEEZ, SO DESPERATE! HA HA!

Knowledge

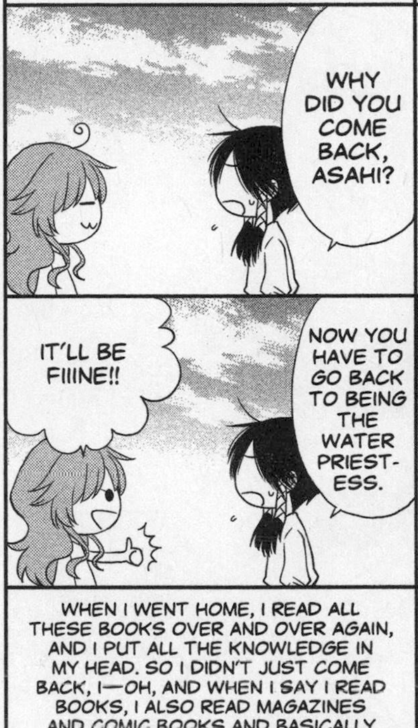
WHY DID YOU COME BACK, ASAHI?
NOW YOU HAVE TO GO BACK TO BEING THE WATER PRIESTESS.
IT'LL BE FIIINE!!
WHEN I WENT HOME, I READ ALL THESE BOOKS OVER AND OVER AGAIN, AND I PUT ALL THE KNOWLEDGE IN MY HEAD. SO I DIDN'T JUST COME BACK, I—OH, AND WHEN I SAY I READ BOOKS, I ALSO READ MAGAZINES AND COMIC BOOKS AND BASICALLY EVERYTHING. I REALLY LIKED THE GIRLS' COMICS THE BEST, BUT I LIKE A LOT OF DIFFERENT GENRES OF COMICS. ALSO, SUBARU, LIKE, THERE'S THIS HORSE-STYLE CHARACTER WHO'S THE MAIN CHARACTER'S CHILDHOOD FRIEND AND HE'S SUPER HANDSOME, BUT HE MIGHT FALL INTO DARKNESS AND DESPAIR BECAUSE THE MAIN CHARACTER DOESN'T REALIZE HIS FEELI—
BABBLE BABBLE BABBLE
WHY DID YOU COME BACK, ASAHI?!

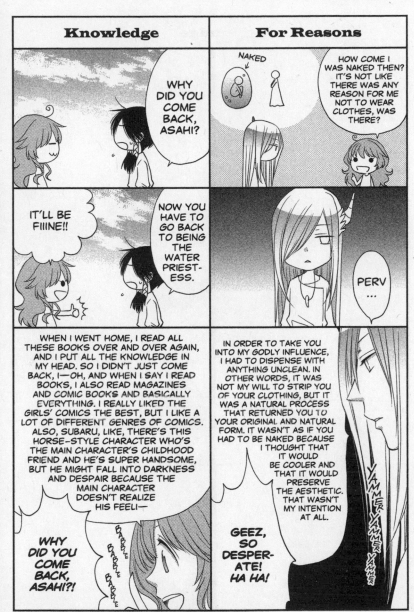

*THIS COMIC HAS NOTHING TO DO WITH THE ACTUAL STORY.

Grudge

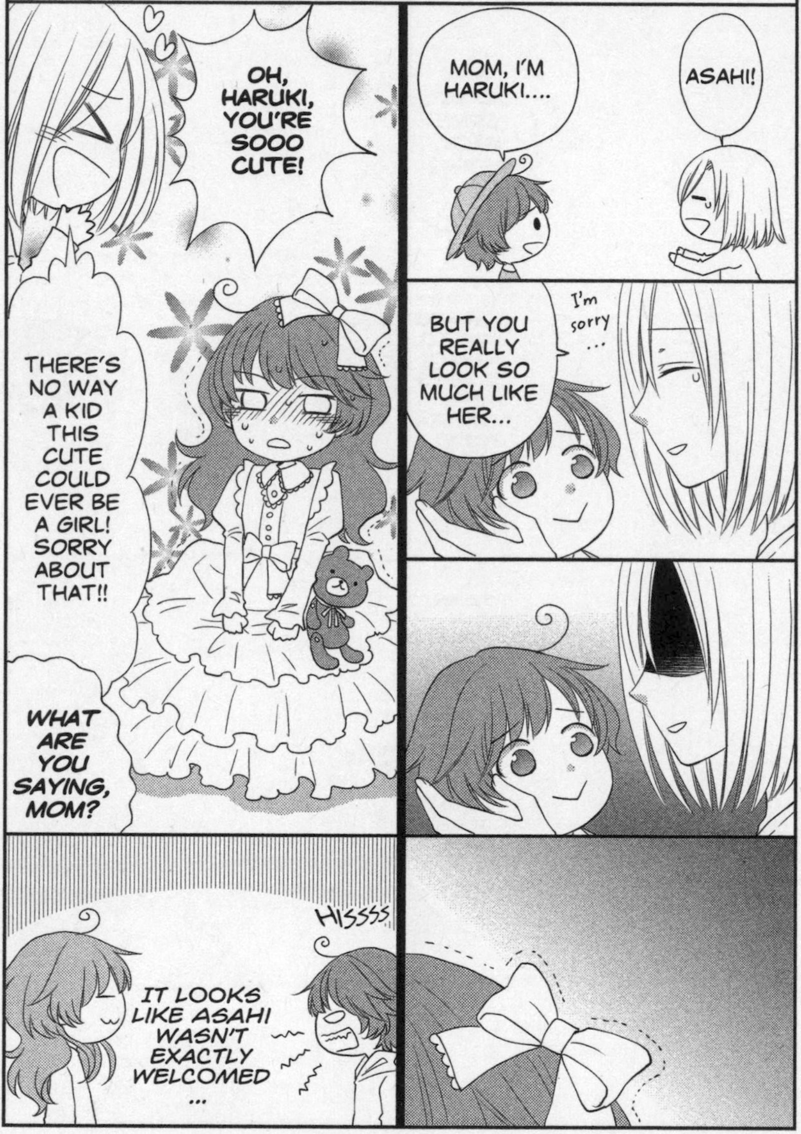
ASAHI!
MOM, I'M HARUKI....
I'm sorry ...
BUT YOU REALLY LOOK SO MUCH LIKE HER...
OH, HARUKI, YOU'RE SOOO CUTE!
THERE'S NO WAY A KID THIS CUTE COULD EVER BE A GIRL! SORRY ABOUT THAT!!
WHAT ARE YOU SAYING, MOM?
HISSSS
IT LOOKS LIKE ASAHI WASN'T EXACTLY WELCOMED ...

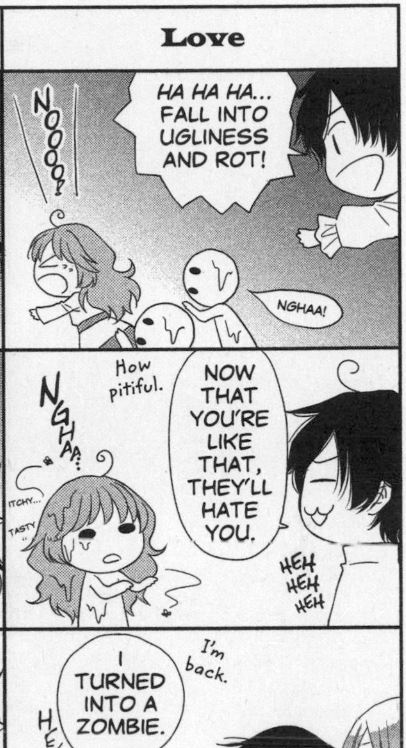
Love
HA HA HA... FALL INTO UGLINESS AND ROT!
NOOOOO!
NGHAA!
NOW THAT YOU'RE LIKE THAT, THEY'LL HATE YOU.
How pitiful.
NGHAA!
ITCHY...
TASTY
HEH HEH HEH
I'm back.
I TURNED INTO A ZOMBIE.
HEY
SUP
WELL... NO MATTER.
I DON'T MIND EITHER.
YOU SHOULD CARE!! I CAN'T BE THE HEROINE LIKE THIS!!

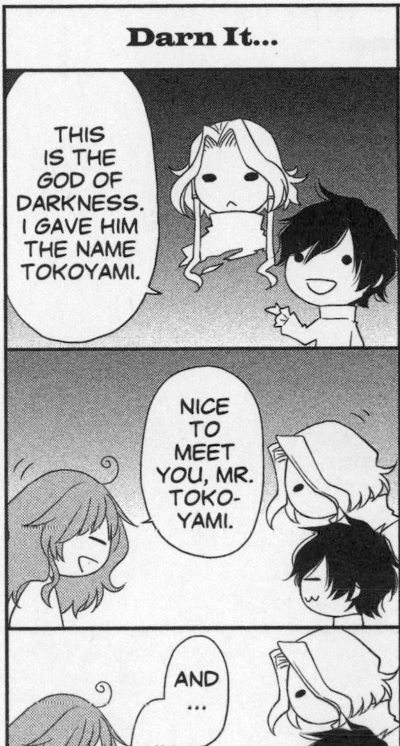
Darn It...
THIS IS THE GOD OF DARKNESS. I GAVE HIM THE NAME TOKOYAMI.
NICE TO MEET YOU, MR. TOKOYAMI.
AND ...
UM ...
TOMA WAS ALL, "OH, A GOD OF DARKNESS... WHAT SHOULD I CALL HIM?
TEE HEE. I KNOW! WHAT ABOUT 'TSUKUYOMI'? NO, THAT'S TOO—I KNOW! TOKOYAMI...!" THEN SHE WAS SO SATISFIED THAT SHE'D GIVEN A NAME TO THE GOD THAT SHE FORGOT TO GIVE ME A NAME...
SHOULD WE ASK THE FANS?

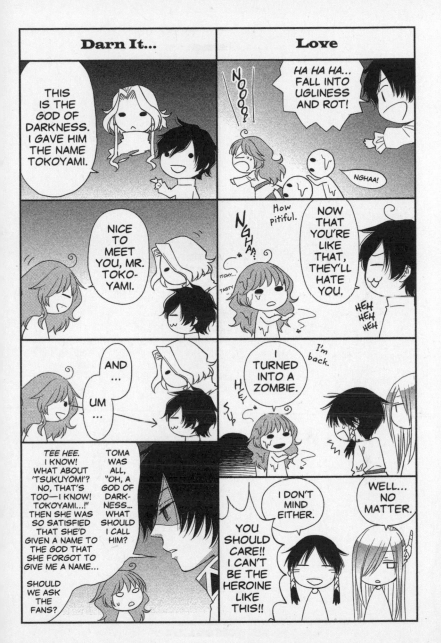

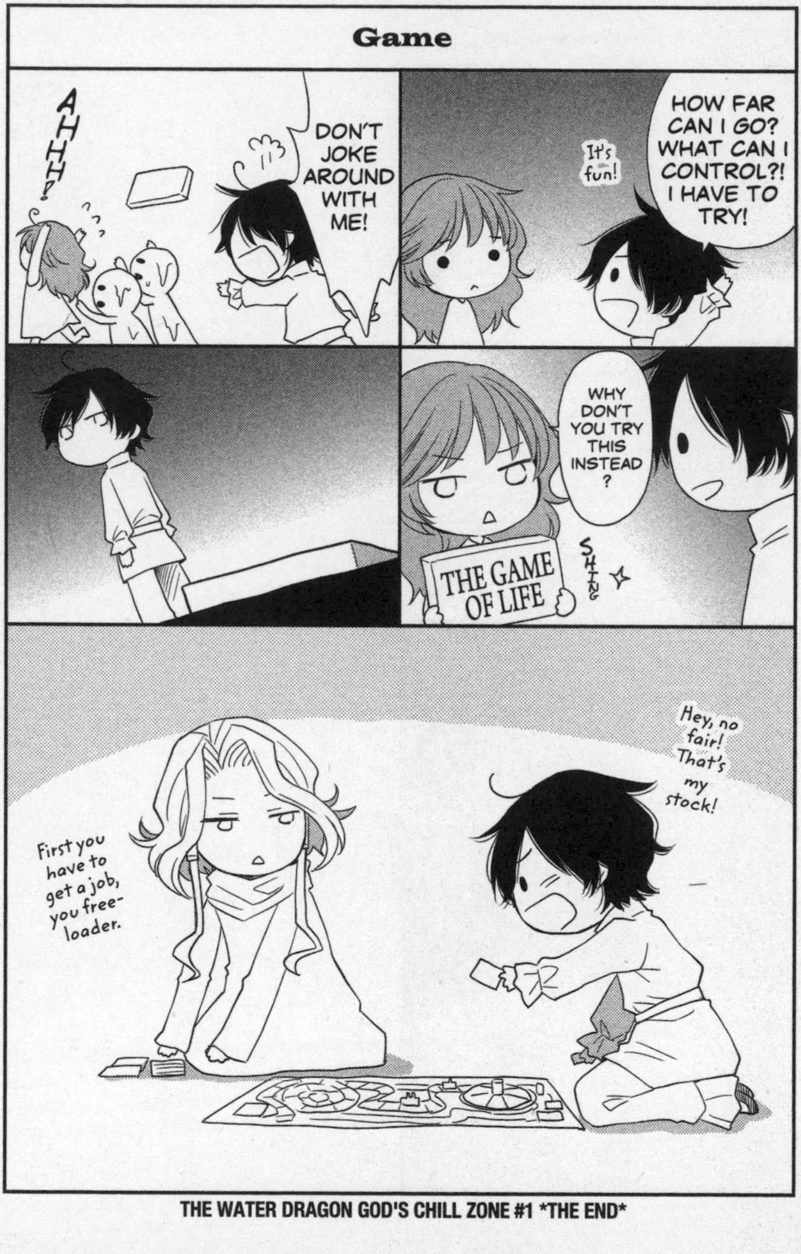
Game
HOW FAR CAN I GO? WHAT CAN I CONTROL?! I HAVE TO TRY!
It's fun!
DON'T JOKE AROUND WITH ME!
AHHHH!
WHY DON'T YOU TRY THIS INSTEAD?
THE GAME OF LIFE
SHING
Hey, no fair! That's my stock!
First you have to get a job, you free-loader.

THE WATER DRAGON GOD'S CHILL ZONE #1 *THE END*

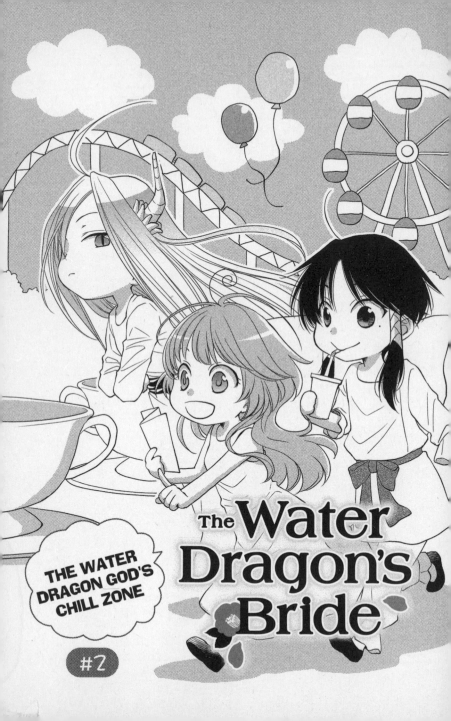

THE WATER
DRAGON GOD'S
CHILL ZONE

#2

The Water
Dragon's
Bride

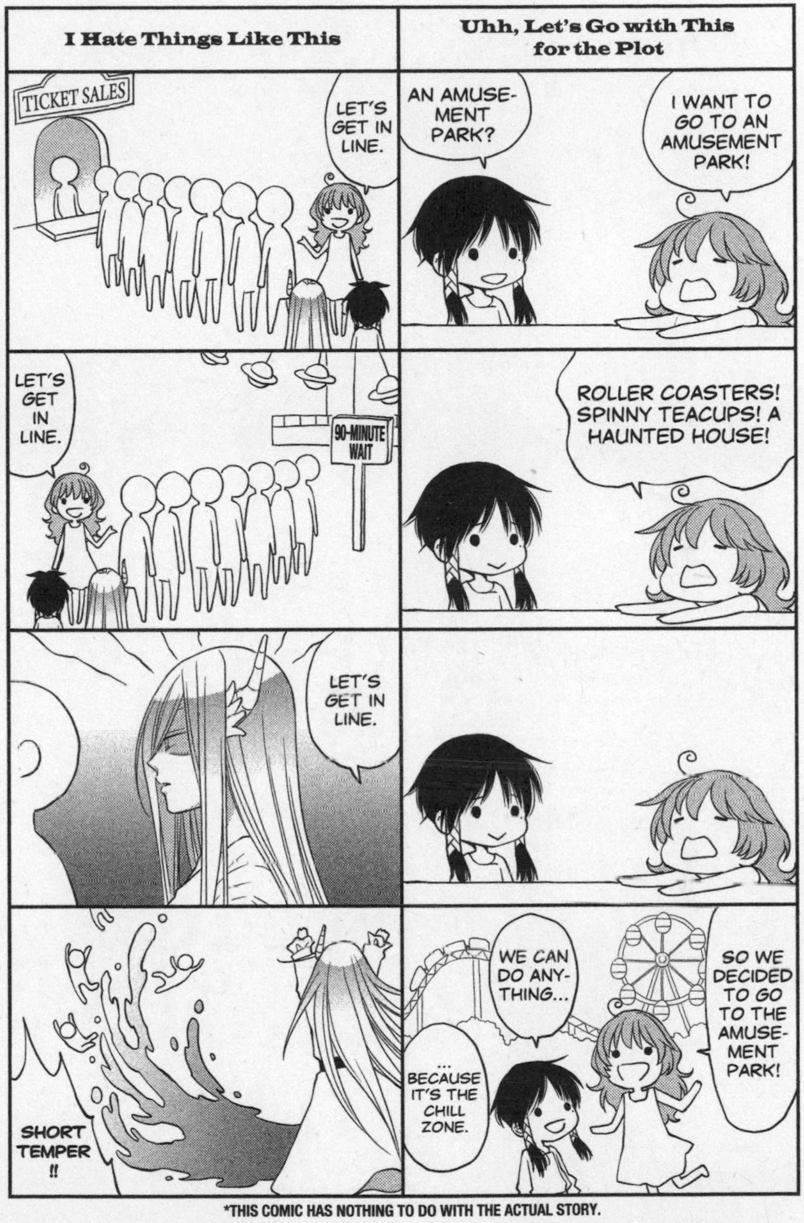
Uhh, Let's Go with This for the Plot
I WANT TO GO TO AN AMUSEMENT PARK!
AN AMUSEMENT PARK?
ROLLER COASTERS! SPINNY TEACUPS! A HAUNTED HOUSE!
SO WE DECIDED TO GO TO THE AMUSEMENT PARK!
WE CAN DO ANYTHING...
...BECAUSE IT'S THE CHILL ZONE.
I Hate Things Like This
LET'S GET IN LINE.
TICKET SALES
90-MINUTE WAIT
LET'S GET IN LINE.
LET'S GET IN LINE.
SHORT TEMPER !!

*THIS COMIC HAS NOTHING TO DO WITH THE ACTUAL STORY.

He's a Little Scary, so It's Understandable

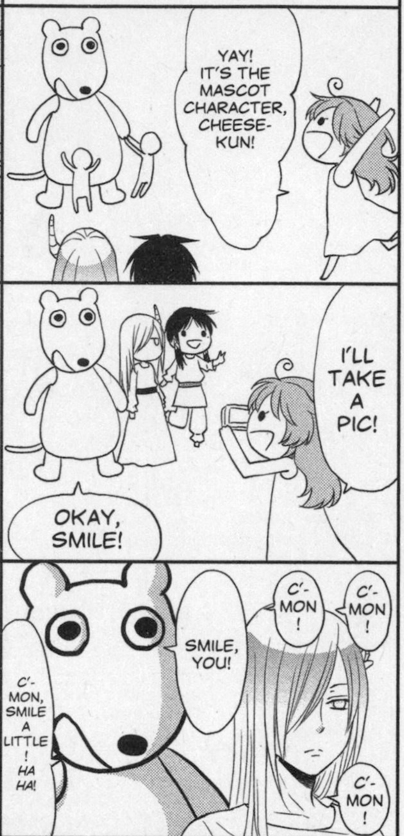
YAY! IT'S THE MASCOT CHARACTER, CHEESE-KUN!
I'LL TAKE A PIC!
OKAY, SMILE!
C'-MON!
C'-MON!
SMILE, YOU!
C'-MON, SMILE A LITTLE! HA HA!
C'-MON!
POW
HE REALLY DID IT!!

It's Really Hard to Draw All That Hair, Huh. Go Ahead, Subaru.

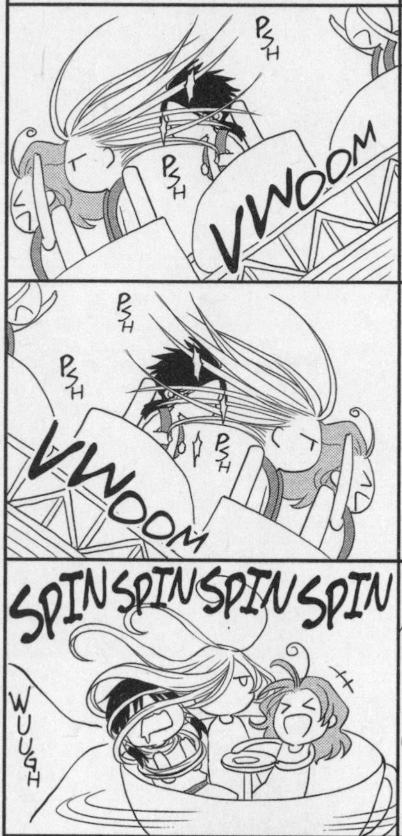
PSH
PSH
VWOOM
PSH
PSH
PSH
VWOOM
SPIN SPIN SPIN SPIN
WUUGH
PANT...
PANT...

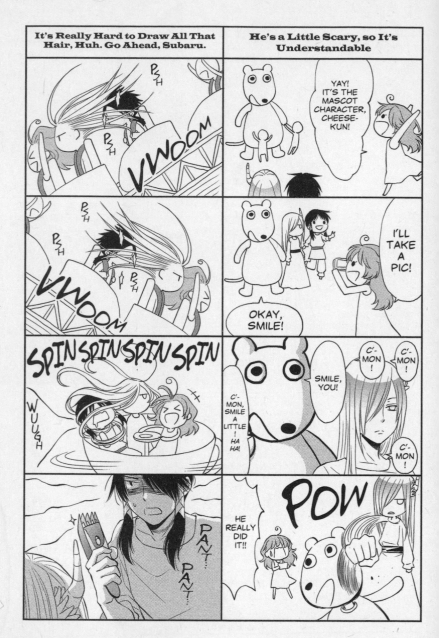

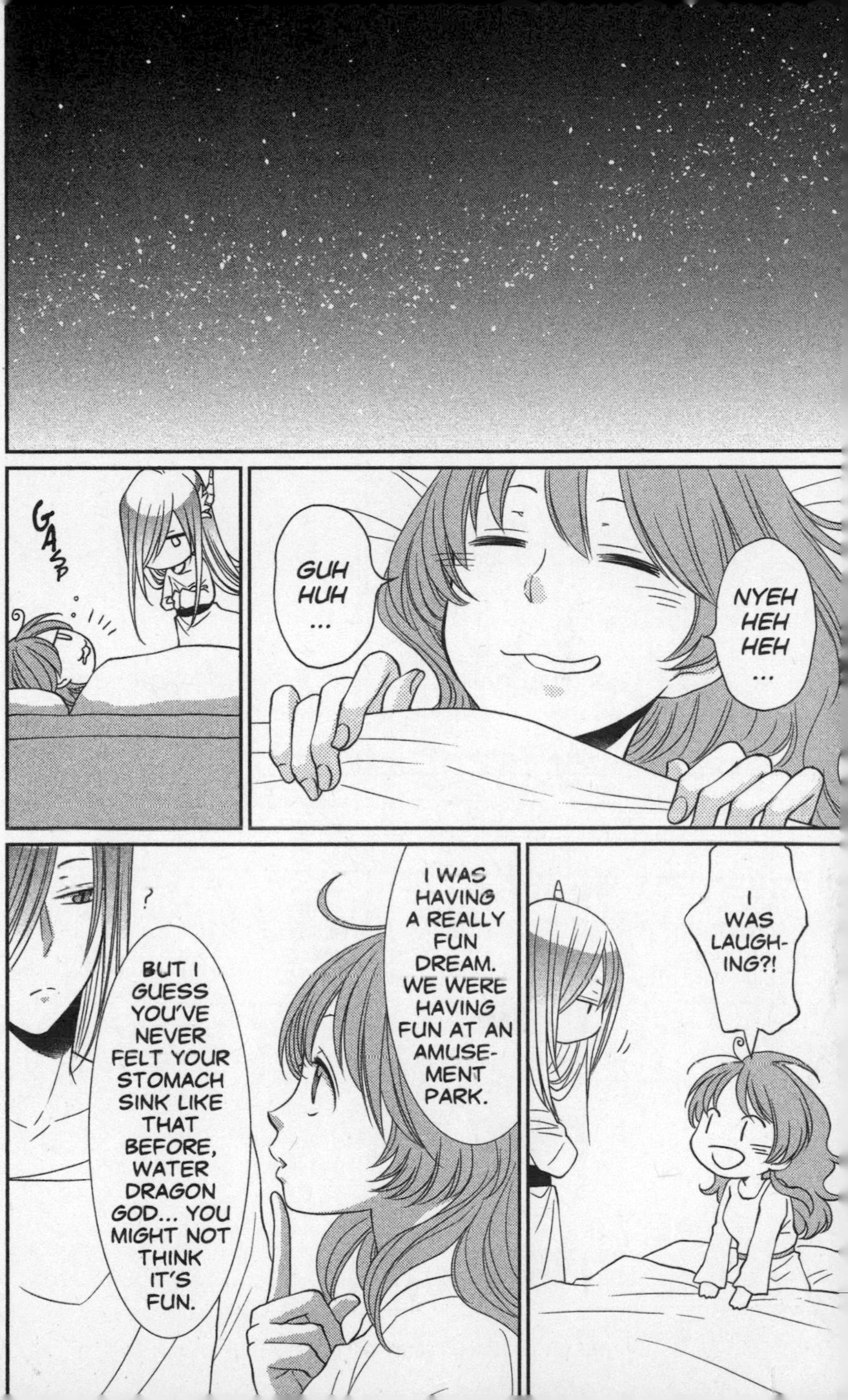
NYEH HEH HEH ...
GUH HUH ...
GASP
I WAS LAUGHING?!
I WAS HAVING A REALLY FUN DREAM. WE WERE HAVING FUN AT AN AMUSEMENT PARK.
?
BUT I GUESS YOU'VE NEVER FELT YOUR STOMACH SINK LIKE THAT BEFORE, WATER DRAGON GOD... YOU MIGHT NOT THINK IT'S FUN.

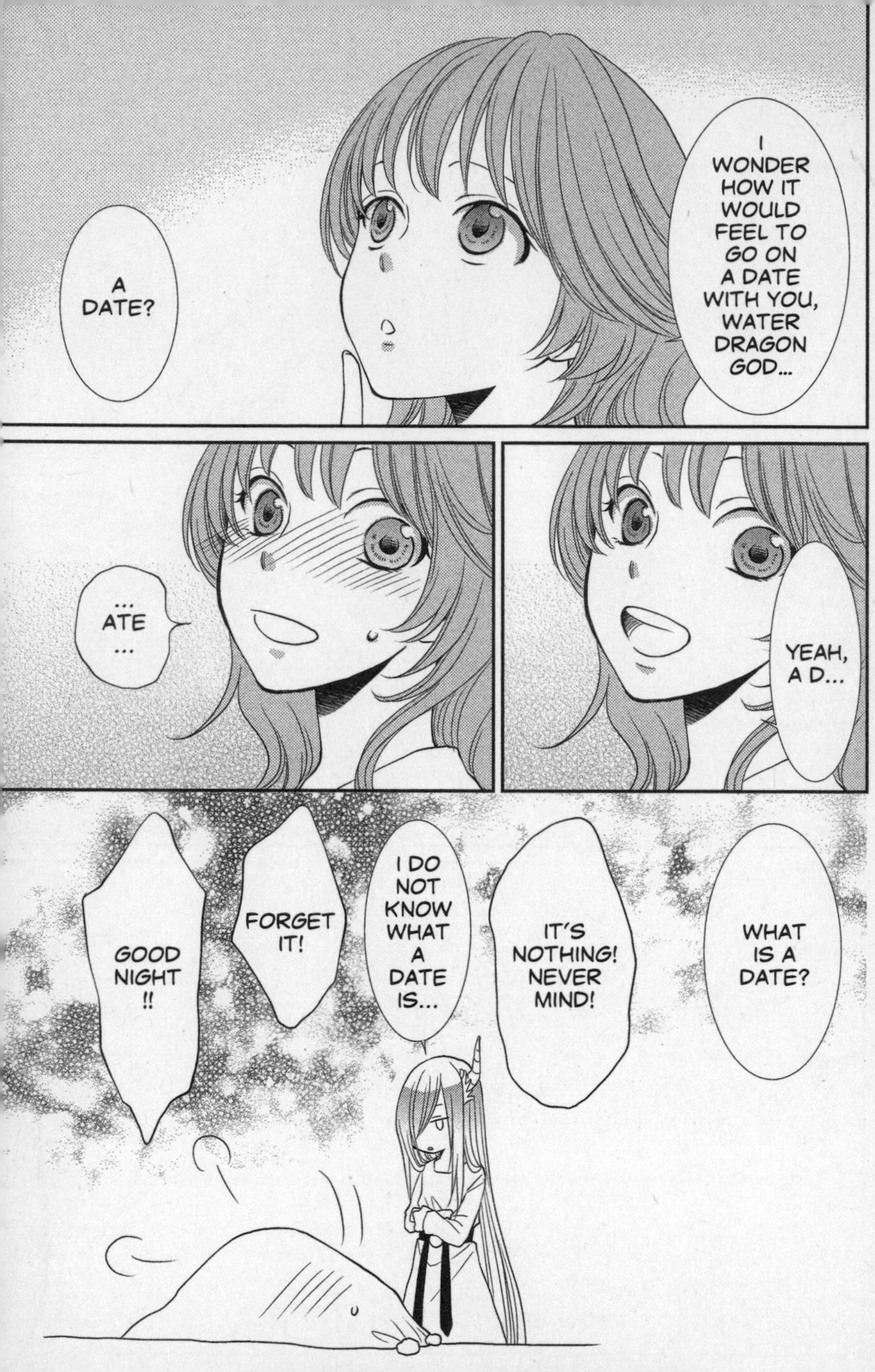
I WONDER HOW IT WOULD FEEL TO GO ON A DATE WITH YOU, WATER DRAGON GOD...
A DATE?
YEAH, A D...
... ATE ...
WHAT IS A DATE?
IT'S NOTHING! NEVER MIND!
I DO NOT KNOW WHAT A DATE IS...
FORGET IT!
GOOD NIGHT !!

THE WATER DRAGON GOD'S CHILL ZONE #2 *THE END*

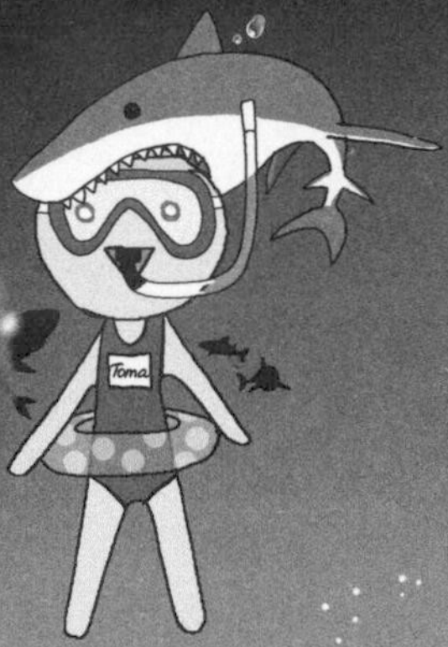
Toma

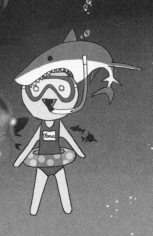

Shark... Cute...

– REI TOMA

Rei Toma has been drawing since childhood, and she created her first complete manga for a graduation project in design school. When she drew the short story manga "Help Me, Dentist," it attracted a publisher's attention and she made her debut right away. After she found success as a manga artist, acclaim in other art fields started to follow as she did illustrations for novels and video game character designs. She is also the creator of *Dawn of the Arcana*, available in North America from VIZ Media.

The Water Dragon's Bride

VOL. 8

Shojo Beat Edition

Story and Art by

Rei Toma

SUIJIN NO HANAYOME Vol.8
by Rei TOMA

Original Japanese edition published by SHOGAKUKAN.
English translation rights in the United States of America, Canada, the United Kingdom, Ireland, Australia and New Zealand arranged with SHOGAKUKAN.

ORIGINAL COVER DESIGN/Hibiki CHIKADA (fireworks.vc)

English Translation & Adaptation **Abby Lehrke**
Touch-Up Art & Lettering **Monaliza de Asis**
Design **Alice Lewis**
Editor **Amy Yu**

Printed in the U.S.A.

Published by VIZ Media, LLC
P.O. Box 77010
San Francisco, CA 94107

10 9 8 7 6 5 4 3 2 1
First printing, January 2019

ratings.viz.com RATED T TEEN

PARENTAL ADVISORY
THE WATER DRAGON'S BRIDE is rated T for Teen and is recommended for ages 13 and up. This volume contains suggestive themes.

VIZ MEDIA
viz.com

Shojo Beat
shojobeat.com

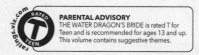

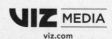

You may be reading the wrong way!

In keeping with the original Japanese comic format, this book reads from right to left—so action, sound effects and word balloons are completely reversed. This preserves the orientation of the original artwork—plus, it's fun!

Check out the diagram shown here to get the hang of things, and then turn to the other side of the book to get started!

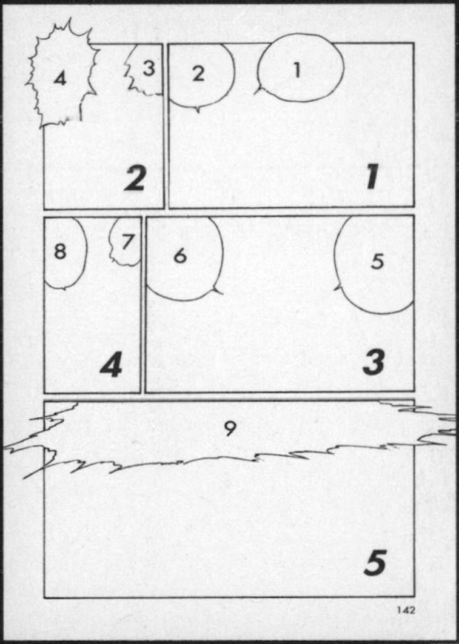

1
2
1
3
4
2
5
6
3
7
8
4
9
5
142

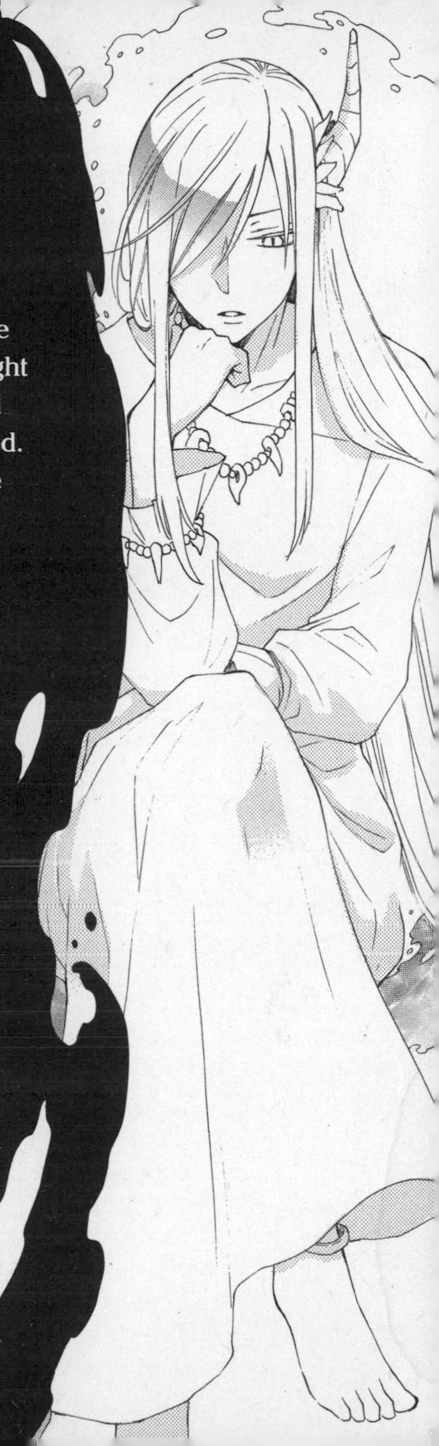

The Water Dragon's Bride

CHARACTER INTRODUCTIONS

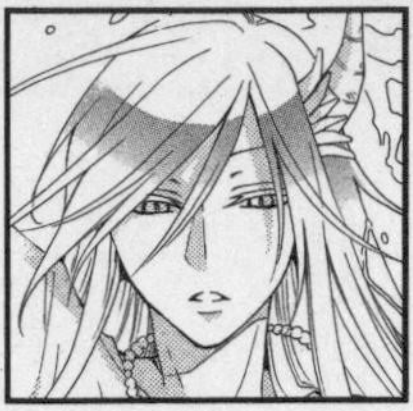

The Water Dragon God

The god who rules over the waters. Though he hates humans, he seems to be intrigued by Asahi and feels compassion for her.

Asahi

She was transported to another world when she was young. Subaru's mother sacrificed her to the water dragon god.

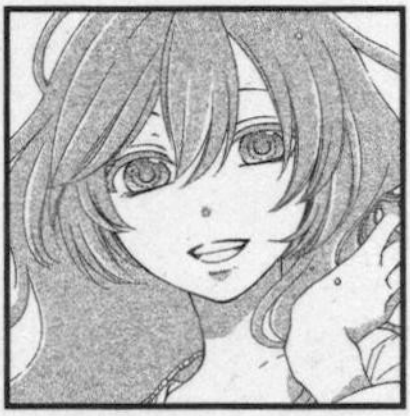

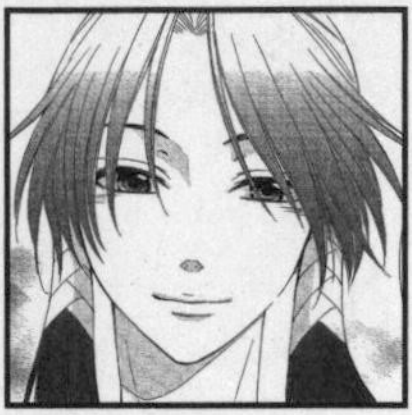

Subaru

He is drawn to Asahi and has resolved to protect her.

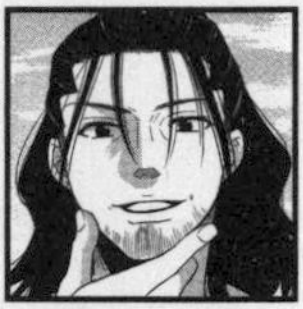

Matori

The captain of the Imperial Defense Force. Subaru's instructor.

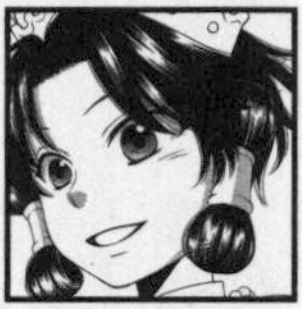

The Emperor

A young boy, the emperor of the country of Naga.

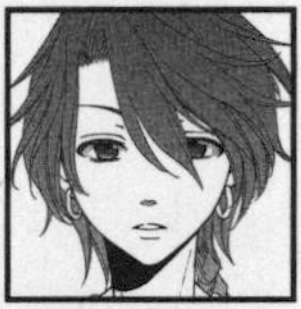

Tsukihiko

Asahi's caretaker. He has the ability to sense people's thoughts and emotions.

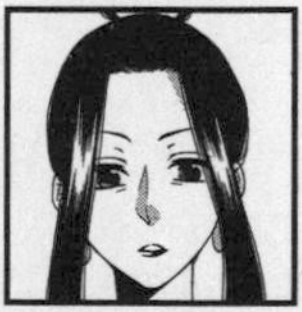

Subaru's Mother

She despises Asahi and has attempted to have her killed before.

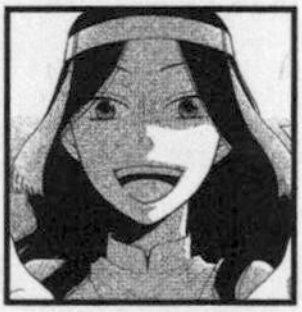

Priestess

A priestess of Naga. She schemes to gain the power of the water dragon god.

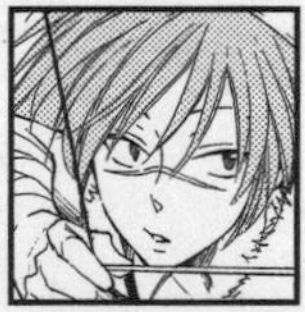

Kogahiko

He's seeking the water dragon god's power by targeting Asahi.

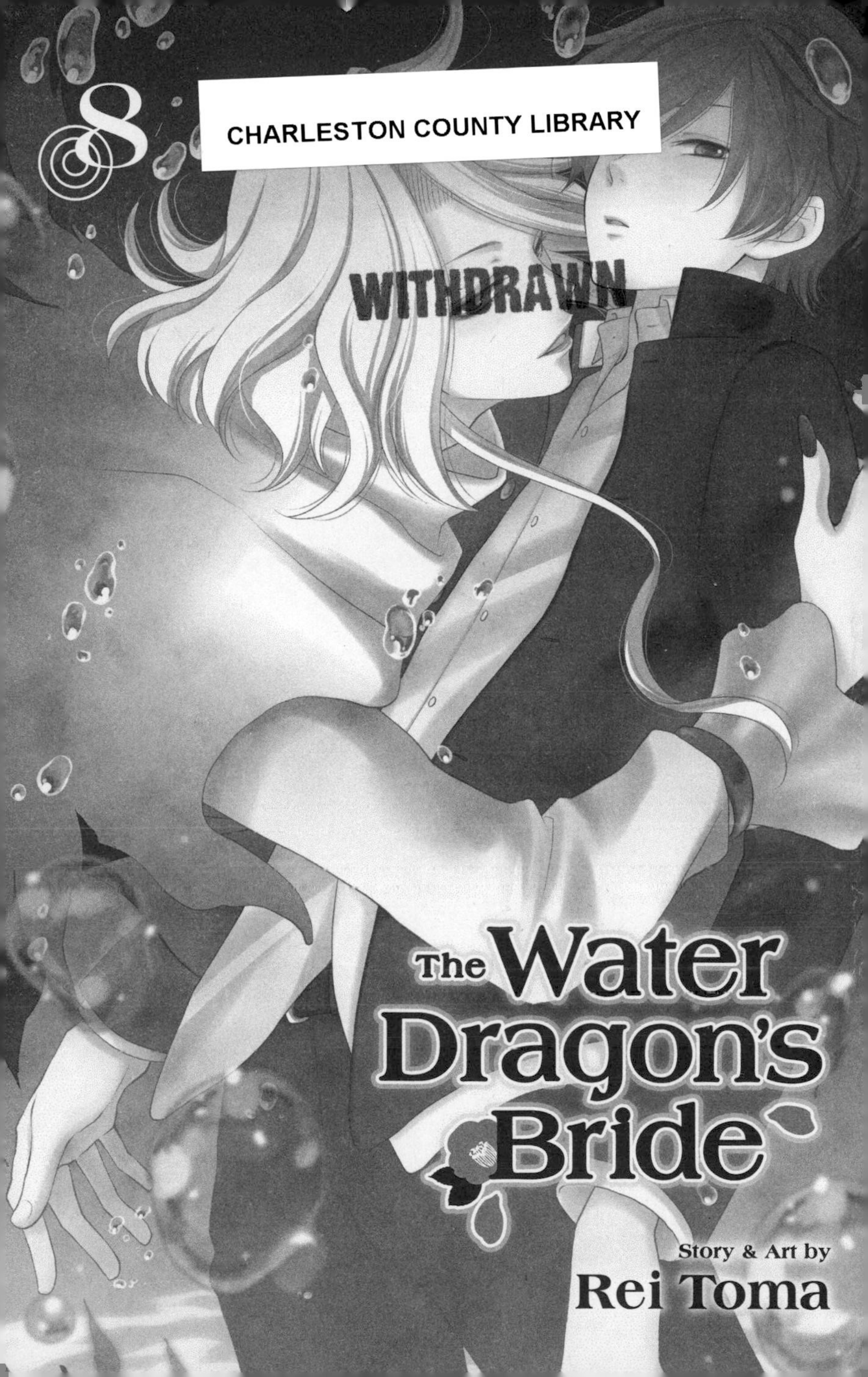
8
CHARLESTON COUNTY LIBRARY
WITHDRAWN
The Water Dragon's Bride
Story & Art by
Rei Toma

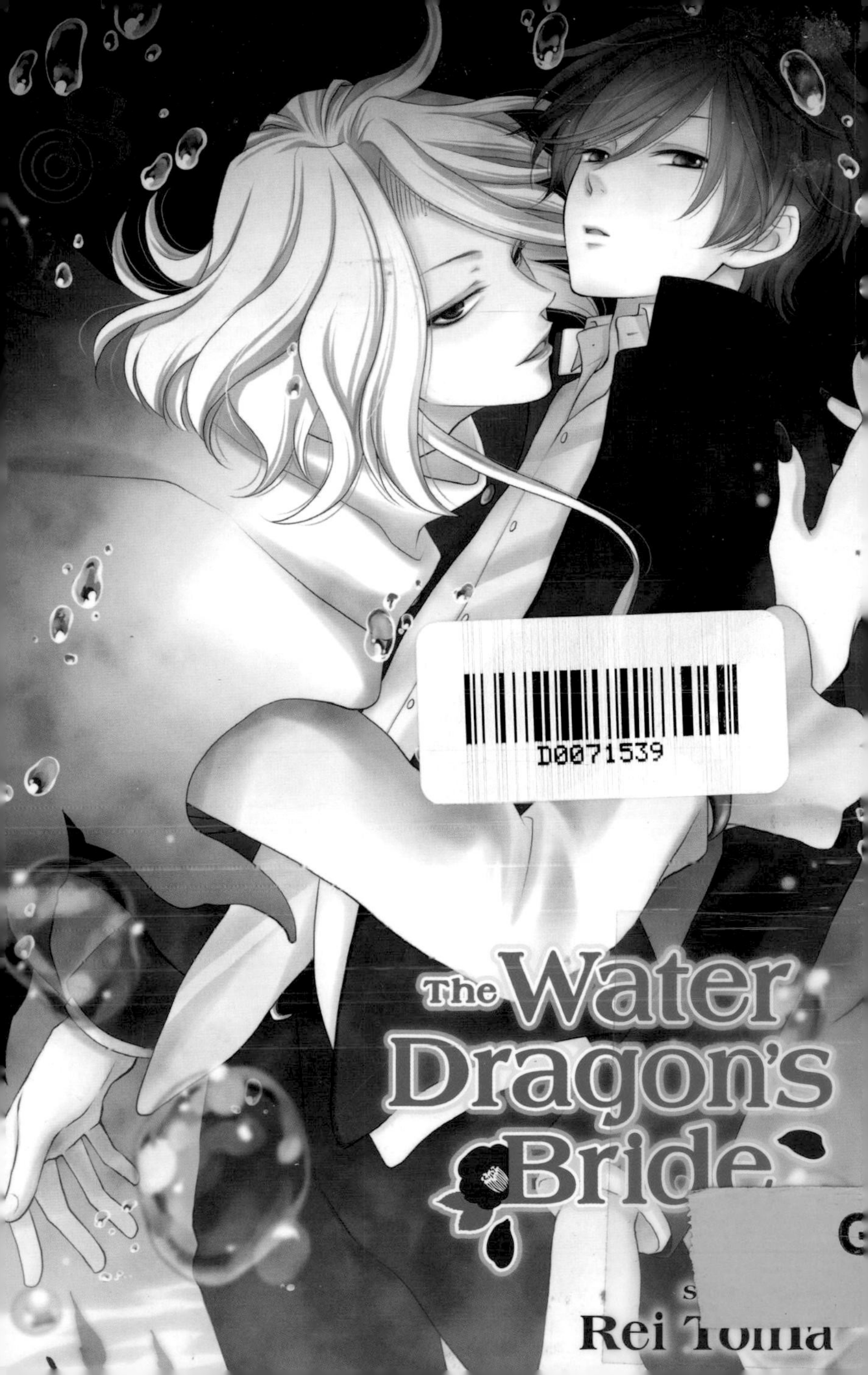
The Water Dragon's Bride
Rei Toma